6/77

D 3.8

D1202349

Sound System Engineering

Sound System Engineering

by

Don and Carolyn Davis

HOWARD W. SAMS & CO., INC.
THE BOBBS-MERRILL CO., INC.
INDIANAPOLIS · KANSAS CITY · NEW YORK

FIRST EDITION

SECOND PRINTING—1976

International Standard Book Number: 0-672-21156-4
Library of Congress Catalog Card Number: 74-33838

Preface

The professional audio engineer daily has occasion to realize that he is "standing on the shoulders" of giants who preceded him. Failure to appreciate the work of these audio pioneers is usually the mark of one who has overlooked the fundamentals of the business. The gifted professional knows and respects the best of the past and skillfully integrates it into the future. The bibliography in Appendix II of this book lists many of these pioneers and their original papers. Because this book deals with audio systems as a whole, it is worthwhile to touch briefly on a few of the most significant persons and events that brought audio systems to the level of technology we now enjoy.

During World War I, two financial groups in the United States came to the realization that the infant motion-picture industry could become as influential in forming public opinion as the daily newspaper. These groups had leaders who understood that they were not in the newspaper business or in the publishing business, but were in the business of influencing communication. Therefore, the motion picture, the radio, and, later, television were natural subjects for their attention.

The initial battleground chosen was "making the motion picture talk," and one of these giant financial firms backed the Bell Telephone Laboratories and Western Electric while the second group backed what was to become RCA. By the beginning of the 1930s, the physicists and engineers hired by these firms developed and brought to commercial production, among many other components:

1. The condenser microphone
2. The compression driver with a properly designed phasing plug
3. The multicellular horn
4. The radial or sectoral horn
5. The feedback amplifier
6. The cardioid microphone
7. Sound on film
8. The folded horn for low frequencies
9. Stereophonic sound
10. The feedback disc cutter

Of equal or greater importance, however, was the generation of the necessary system approaches to standards, techniques, and practices these engineers developed in order to train field engineers to support the literally millions of dollars worth of audio equipment being put into thousands of motion-picture theaters.

Over the years, through consent decrees, mergers, and spin-offs, many new companies in the audio industry were formed by these pioneers and their associates in the business. For almost 40 years, the process then became one of refining designs, lowering the cost of production, and exploring new market outlets for the wealth of basic research done by these pioneers. People like Wente, Thuras, Steinberg, Snow, Fletcher, Munson, Black, Bode, Nyquist, Olson, Volkmann, Wolf, Malter,

Hopkins, Stryker, Molloy, Shannon, Maxfield, Loye, Kellogg, Frayne, Hunt, Hilliard, Hanna, Slepian, Kock, Siven, Dunn, White—to name only a few—became the founders of entire fields of research. Any such list does an injustice to those who belong on it and were not mentioned, but the above list does reveal the central fact that this caliber of researcher today turns his attention to computers, outer-space probes, etc., rather than to audio (except occasionally as a hobby—witness Richard Heyser of JPL).

Parallel to these major coordinated efforts was the growth of the independent audio inventor-entrepreneurs who have helped make the audio field one of the most humanly interesting technological fields. Shure, Kahn, Klipsch, Walsh, Scott, Boner, and others have in their day created complete subcultures within the audio business. The broadcast industry has spawned Bauer, Chinn, Armstrong, Crosby, etc. Preceding, then paralleling, and finally merging into electroacoustic research were the efforts of the architectural acoustic pioneers such as Henry, Rayleigh, Sabine, Knudsen, Norris, Eyring, Watson, Fitzroy, Beranek, etc. All that we have to say about systems has its underpinnings in the work of these and many more men.

It is our feeling that the latter half of the 1970s will see another wave of progress much like the original one, but this time it will be financed by the space race; the digital technology developed for the computers, etc., required to place a man on the moon will seed a veritable revolution in audio technology. Even more important, the wedding of the computer to the synthesizer will once again tie the audio engineer closely to the artist-entertainer, just as they were in the motion-picture days, and the outcome will once again have important sociological as well as technological meaning to us all. It is to those who want to know the best of the past and present, and who sense that they can contribute to this audio revolution, that this book is dedicated.

DON AND CAROLYN DAVIS

Contents

mary—Level Change With Increasing Distance From the Sound Source: Indoors—Critical Distance—Calculating D_c Directly—Sensitivity Versus Efficiency Levels—Room Gain—Q Versus R for Controlling D_c—Q Multipliers and Dividers—Calculating Relative Levels in Semireverberant Spaces—Factors to Watch for in Rooms—Articulation Losses of Consonants in Speech—Calculating the Articulation Loss of Consonants—Usable Percentages—Maxfield's Equation—Using % AL_{cons} Charts—A Sample Exercise—Calculating the Minimum Q—Calculation of the Maximum RT_{60}—Attempting to Equalize for Hearing Loss—Summary

CHAPTER 5

Maximum Physical Distance—Masking Systems—Establishing an EAD—The Needed Acoustic Gain (NAG)—The Number of Open Microphones (NOM)—The Feedback Stability Margin (FSM)—The Needed Acoustic Gain (NAG) Formula—Calculating Potential Acoustic Gain (PAG)—Measuring Acoustic Gain—Limiting Parameters in Sound-Reinforcement System Design—How Much Electrical Power (EPR) Is Required—Finding the Efficiency of a Loudspeaker System—Finding the Efficiency of a Compression Driver Using a Plane-Wave Tube—Finding the Maximum Program Level From the Available Wattage—Summary

CHAPTER 6

The Microphone as the System Input—Microphone Sensitivity—Omnidirectional or Cardioid—Measuring the Frequency Response and Directional Characteristics of a Microphone—Review of Microphone Sensitivity—Division of Electrical Gains and Losses—A Typical Mixer Amplifier—A More Complicated System—Summary of Electrical Gain Adjustments—Converting the Electrical Gain Into Usable Acoustic Power—Loudspeaker Placement—Underwater Sound—Varying the Q of an Array—Summary

CHAPTER 7

Circuit Levels—Grounding and Shielding—Grounding Practices—Serving Cable—Useful Wiring Concepts—Impedance Matching—Fundamentals of Time Delay—Proofing the Installed System

CHAPTER 8

Inserting the Filters in the Sound System—What Is Room-Sound-System Equalization?—Sound Reproduction in Motion-Picture Theaters—Bandwidth of Filters—Characteristics of Successful Filters—Filter Transfer Characteristics—Minimum-Phase Filters—Filter Transient Response—Combining Filter Sections—Increasing Slope Rates—Critical Bandwidths—Adjusting the Equalizers—Using the Real-Time Analyzer in Equalization—Tuning for Playback—Tuning a Reinforcement System—A Real-Time Regenerative-Response Method of Equalizing a Sound System—Summary of RTA Application—The Tuning Environment—Proximity Modes—Checking Microphone Polarity—Loudspeaker Polarity—Charts and Record Keeping—Demonstrating the Equalization—Summary

APPENDIX VI

APPENDIX VII

APPENDIX VIII

APPENDIX IX

APPENDIX X

APPENDIX XI

CHAPTER 1

Audio Systems

The worldwide telephone network is an example of an extremely large and very complex system. A systems approach is employed; therefore, local systems can be integrated into larger and larger combinations. Because each local system is engineered with the whole in mind, it is compatible with other local systems similarly engineered.

Sound systems are normally small local systems. Properly engineered, they can be combined, integrated, or segregated in terms of other local systems or networks.

What types of "sound systems" are we discussing? A partial list would include:

1. *Reinforcement systems*
   Reinforcement systems are normally characterized by supplying "real time" amplification of a talker to a listener, both of whom are usually in the same acoustical environment. Successful reinforcement systems must be loud enough (sufficient acoustic gain), possess clarity (provide a low percentage of articulation loss of consonants in speech), and cover the listeners with uniformity, while avoiding the coverage of areas devoid of listeners.

2. *Reproducing sound systems*
   Reproducing sound systems amplify sound from a time storage system (see below) or from a distant origin (radio transmission, wire transmission, etc.). Careful design practices are necessary in order to provide sufficient electrical input power to the transducers of such a system (within the power-handling capability of the transducer) while controlling coverage and articulation requirements. Freedom from regeneration distinguishes the well designed reproducing system from the reinforcement system.

3. *Synthesizing systems*
   The sound source of a synthesizer is not human. Examples are noise masking systems (speech privacy systems), musical synthesizer systems such as Bell Laboratories' GROOVE (Generated Real-

time Operations On Voltage-controlled Equipment), and even live recordings altered in the recording control room to an essentially synthesized form.

4. *Time storage systems*
   Recording systems of all types—tape recorders, dictaphones, digital time-delay systems, reverberation channels—are time storage systems.

5. *Audio measurement systems*
   Large commercial sound installations have often included in the main control-room rack an audio oscillator, a vtvm, and occasionally an oscilloscope. Today, many professional audio systems incorporate sophisticated real-time analyzing equipment as a normal part of their maintenance subsystems.

6. *Control systems using audio devices*
   A noise-operated automatic level adjuster is a good example of an audio subsystem that never is heard as a system but is used to control another system. Variable-margin disc cutting is another example. Many very creative opportunities open up for the sound engineer who remembers to include this category of system in his overall check list.

7. *Communication systems*
   This is an era in which conference rooms are both locally sound reinforced and interconnected with other conference rooms at remote locations. Therefore, the sound engineer must have an appreciation of basic communication-transmission engineering problems, and specifically he must be familiar with well designed termination equipment such as hybrid transformers, line amplifiers, etc.

Almost every sound-system requirement encountered falls into one of the above categories or into some combination of them. We are going to discuss the accurate scientific engineering approach that makes possible the proper design of all of these types of systems.

SYSTEM ELEMENTS

To construct the simplest of sound systems, we need to use a series of basic elements. These fall into the following broad classifications:

1. *Transducers*

   Transducers are devices that convert acoustical, mechanical, chemical, and other nonelectrical energy into an electrical signal, or electrical energy into acoustical, mechanical, chemical, or other forms of energy. Microphones, loudspeakers, pickups, and sensors are transducers.

2. *Electrical devices*

   Electrical devices include amplifiers, attenuators (the two most basic building blocks), signal conditioners (equalizers, filters, limiters, compressors, companders, expanders, noise controllers, etc.), generators, and analyzers. Storage devices of all types are in this group as well.

3. *The acoustic environment*

   Most textbooks on sound systems fail to recognize that the acoustic environment is an integral part of the sound system. Indeed, as we will show in this book, there are parameters of the room directly intertwined with complementary parameters in the two system-element categories listed above. Few sound engineers would connect a rack full of electronic equipment to an unchecked electrical source hoping it was of the correct voltage, frequency, and type of current (ac or dc); yet the majority of these same engineers will "plug" that same sound system into a strange acoustic environment, often with as disastrous results as if the rack were accidentally connected to 240 volts dc instead of 120 volts ac. The acoustic environment has only a few vital parameters, which can be easily measured. The mathematical manipulations are not complex. Tables and charts, or the new electronic scientific calculators, remove all the difficulties past engineers have experienced with them.

THE FUNCTION OF THE SOUND SYSTEM

First, it is the end user—the man who will pay the bill —who must be consulted. It is vital to remember this is a two-way street. First, there is what he says he wants. Second, there is what it is possible to supply. Only a well-trained, professional audio engineer knows the difference between the two. Rarely will an end user continue to ask for the impossible if the reason why it is impossible is explained to him. Often, his response after such an explanation is, "I will accept the closest approach to what I ask that you can achieve." You then can write a contract meaningful to both parties that allows you to do the best possible, under the circumstances, while accurately describing what the end user will actually get. Crucial factors include the following items:

1. The type or types of systems the end user desires and needs.
2. The determination of the major system elements he requires, especially:
   - (A) The number of microphones and how many will be open (live) at one time.
   - (B) Preliminary tests that reveal if the system has to be distributed or single source.
   - (C) The maximum distance in the acoustic environment at which a listener can easily hear a talker (or other significant sound source) without benefit of a sound system.
   - (D) The loudest expected sound to be produced anywhere in the audience area.

By asking key questions of this type, surveying the environment, making preliminary calculations, and carefully explaining to the end user the viable alternatives and negotiating the data to correlate with his desires, you can arrive at a good idea of the functional requirements of a sound system.

SOUND-SYSTEM ENGINEERING

We now arrive at what this book is about. Having approached the sound-system requirement as a system problem and having gathered data on all the independent variables, we can now use that data to engineer a sound system. This involves the efficient determination of the number and type of elements, their values, adjustment, and reliability, and, at the planning stage, the accurate prediction of the end result that can and will be confirmed by measurements specified in the sound-system specification test clauses—predictions accurate to within ±3 dB at the listener's ears anywhere within a vast auditorium or arena.

BASIC SYSTEM CONFIGURATIONS

Certain obvious mutual exclusions are decided upon by functional requirements. Fig. 1-1 illustrates some of the most obvious of these. The shaded areas indicate methods not normally used to satisfy the functional requirement described.

Fig. 1-2 shows a classic example of a single-source system done with both acoustical and architectural skill.

Fig. 1-3 displays a sophisticated overhead distributed sound system of high coverage density being used in a large conference room.

Fig. 1-4 shows another overhead distributed system used in a lecture hall.

More than 90% of all successful sound systems are either overhead distributed or single source. One immediate legitimate use of divided single sources is for multichannel reproduction. Fig. 1-5 shows this type of

REINFORCEMENT	BACKGROUND – MASKING	BACKGROUND – MUSIC	PAGING – ANNOUNCE	PLAYBACK – THEATRE	PLAYBACK – STUDIO	
	▨					SINGLE SOURCE
		▨	▨			DIVIDED SINGLE SOURCE
					▨	OVERHEAD DISTRIBUTED
					▨	LOCALLY DISTRIBUTED
						MULTIPLE SINGLE SOURCES

Fig. 1-1. System types normally chosen by function.

Fig. 1-2. Example of the blending of function and design.

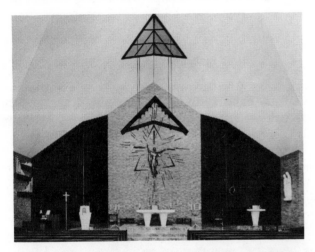

Fig. 1-3. Sophisticated overhead distributed sound system for a large conference hall.

Fig. 1-4. Distributed system in a lecture hall.

Fig. 1-5. Recording-studio playback system.

Fig. 1-6. Home music system.

system using four sources in a major recording studio, and Fig. 1-6 illustrates the normal 2-channel home-type system. This multichannel use can carry over into auditorium work, as shown in Fig. 1-7, but it will be shown that this is a poor choice for speech purposes. In systems similar to that shown in Fig. 1-7, all three channels must cover the entire auditorium by themselves. The middle channel is then used alone for speech, and

Fig. 1-7. Multichannel sound system in auditorium.

the system becomes three channels for music or effects.

Pew-back loudspeakers, when used with modern time-delay devices, become splendid examples of locally distributed systems, and they share with their close relative, the overhead distributed system, the need for high coverage density. Multiple single-source systems are usually encountered in rental situations such as that shown in Fig. 1-8.

In the case of a sound production array, neither reinforcement nor reproduction of sound is the primary goal (Fig. 10-29 in Chapter 10 shows such a system). The original creation of musical sounds from this system makes it, compared to present-day loudspeaker systems, as the pipe organ was to the shepherd's flute in earlier days.

Today, there are a vast number of tools in the sound engineer's kit. Misapplied, they turn into monsters; engineered properly, they can perform seeming miracles. Those of us familiar with the past 25 years in the sound business recognize we are in a "golden age" of sound-system engineering. To those of us privileged to see occasional glimpses of what should logically come to pass in the next 25 years, this present "golden age" is clearly the threshold of really fantastic developments to come. A clear working knowledge of today's most efficient techniques is a prerequisite to any hope of participating in tomorrow's revolution of digital devices—computer-controlled sensing systems and automatic programmable control systems.

SOUND-SYSTEM–ROOM EQUALIZATION

Sound-system–room equalization goes back into the thirties with the work of Volkmann, Hilliard, Harrison, et al. After World War II, investigators such as Rudmose and Boner further developed the theories perti-

Fig. 1-8. Billy Graham Crusade rental system.

Fig. 1-9. Test equipment used in the early narrow-band process by the authors in the late 1960s.

Fig. 1-10. Test equipment used in the early narrow-band process typical of the 1960s. Not necessarily used today.

Fig. 1-11. Remainder of equipment used in early narrow-band process in the late 1960s.

nent to the practical development of such equalization. Dr. C. P. Boner patented the first commercially usable form of these theories. Many people in equalization work can thank Dr. Boner for their early training in the basic concepts of room sound-system equalization.

The early process used by the authors was expensive, laborious, and difficult to learn and practice. It employed a master system of selectable broadband equalizers (lower right-hand case in Fig. 1-9) used together with special tapped toroidal inductors. The special noise test set, audio oscillator, bridges, decades, etc., broadened the backs, as well as the minds, of the early practitioners of the art. A typical job setup required two large tables full of equipment and an inventory of over 90 values of capacitors, plus a supply of resistors, coils, etc. (see Figs. 1-10 and 1-11). Each equalizing system was hand built on the site and was a thorough education in filters and wiring. One chassis of an early equalizing system is shown in Fig. 1-12. Note the capacitors that have been wired in to determine frequency, and the varied taps on the inductors to determine filter depths.

In 1967, a major breakthrough came during an attempt to improve the broadband filters. Don Davis and Arthur C. Davis developed a passive band-rejection filter set with individual filters spaced at ⅓-octave intervals. It turned out to be capable of achieving the same results as the earlier methods—but by combining and shaping, rather than by individual rejections of very narrow segments of the spectrum (see Fig. 1-13).

It is interesting to observe that the shaping method often handles the feedback frequency by changing its slope rate rather than depressing the amplitude at that frequency.

This breakthrough resulted in reducing the tuning time from 3-5 days (for expert practitioners—amateurs

Fig. 1-12. Typical early-period narrow-band filter chassis wired by the authors.

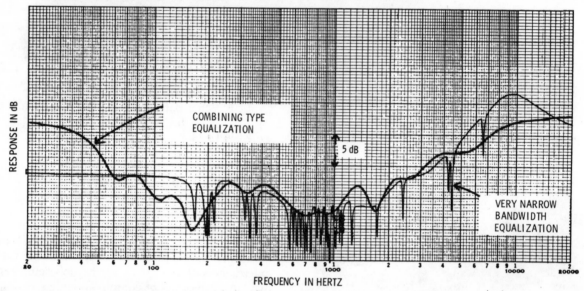

Fig. 1-13. Electrical responses of combining-type equalizer and of a series of discrete filters of very narrow bandwidth.

Fig. 1-15. Early Acousta-Voicing filter set.

Fig. 1-14. Early Acousta-Voicing filter.

Fig. 1-16. Equalization test equipment.

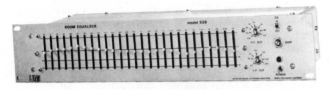

Courtesy United Recording Electronics Industries
Fig. 1-17. Active equalizer.

could spend weeks on the site and often did) to about an hour and a half. Figs. 1-14 and 1-15 show an individual filter and a full set of filters.

In 1968, a further development in instrumentation completed the job of making equalization economically feasible; real-time audio-frequency spectrum analysis was brought to the marketplace. Fig. 1-16 shows a master test set, noise generator, sound-level meter, and real-time analyzer. With this equipment, tuning time was reduced to a matter of ten minutes or less. Fig. 1-17 shows the latest in active equalizers, originally developed by James J. Noble, that include gain makeup, built-in comparator switch, and built-in continuously variable high-pass and low-pass filters.

Concurrent with all these developments was the advent of small, powerful, portable desk-top computers (Fig. 1-18). These instruments allow complete systemization of sound-system design methods into programs that cut design time from several days to several minutes. (The entry of the data is the most time consuming part of the process.)

This book is dedicated to bringing the fruits of this work to you, that you may gain in days what in the past took years to learn. This is normal and right. Knowledge is to be shared; knowledge closely held may temporarily benefit the holder, but eventually he, too, gets left behind. He finds that sharing is a two-way street which returns in proportion to the amount given.

Fig. 1-18. Desk-top computer-calculator.

Courtesy Hewlett-Packard

CHAPTER 2

The Decibel Notation System

The use of the decibel (dB) notation system is frequently encountered in communications work. The decibel is $\frac{1}{10}$ of a bel. (The bel is named in honor of Alexander Graham Bell.) This ubiquitous notation system allows meaningful scale compression or expansion as required and greatly simplifies computations involving large quantities. Since all decibel notation systems are based on logarithms, we can start with a review of basic logarithmic theory.

Our human senses—touch, sight, hearing, sense of weight, etc.—all function logarithmically. That is, in the presence of a stimulus the least perceptible change is proportional to the already existing stimulus (Weber-Fechner law). Humanly perceived equal ratios seem to be equal increments.

The sensitivities of the various senses are not the same. Typical differences are:

Sensitivity to light-intensity changes:
$1\% = 0.087$ dB
Sensitivity to change in the length of a line:
$2\% = 0.176$ dB
Sensitivity to change in a feeling of weight:
$10\% = 0.915$ dB
Sensitivity to change in sound loudness:
$30\% = 3$ dB

HANDLING THE FOUR ARITHMETIC FUNCTIONS

Understanding the basic vector nature of the four basic arithmetic functions can provide insight into many more advanced concepts in audio work such as the j operator in impedance work, etc. Looking at the basic vector diagram (Fig. 2-1), we will concern ourselves initially with the x axis that runs horizontally from negative numbers on the left through zero to positive numbers on the right.

RULE 1: If a number has a $+$ sign, starting at zero, go in a straight line along the x axis toward $0°$.

If a number has a $-$ sign, starting at zero go along the x axis toward $180°$. (You may regard a $-$ sign as an instruction to revolve the sign assignment $180°$.)

The length of the line toward either $0°$ or $180°$ is determined by the *magnitude* of the number. For example, $+4$ goes further along the $0°$ axis line than $+2$. All $+$ signs add in magnitude toward $0°$. All $-$ signs *add* in magnitude toward $180°$. When $-$ signs are added to $+$ signs, the number having the greatest magnitude determines the sign.

RULE 2: Multiplying and dividing magnitudes follow the same rules with the following variations. Every $-$ sign encountered rotates the magnitude sign $180°$. Therefore, $+2 \times (-2) = (2 \times 2) + 180°$, or -4. But $(-2) \times (-2) = 2 \times 2 + 360°$ or $+4$. Remember every $-$ sign rotates the sign assignment $180°$; therefore, $(-2) \times (-2) \times (-2) = (2 \times 2 \times 2) + 540°$, or -8.

Imaginary Numbers

The number $\sqrt{-1}$ is called an *imaginary* number because it is not possible to locate it, even on a graph, though we will use a graph to illustrate what we mean by such a number. However, we know by definition that $\sqrt{-1} \times \sqrt{-1}$ should equal -1; therefore, the $\sqrt{-1}$ should lie at $90°$, between $+1$ and -1 in terms of vector rotation. By the same reasoning, $-(\sqrt{-1})$ would lie at $-90°$ ($270°$) from the $0°$ axis.

ARITHMETIC AND EXPONENTIAL NOTATION COMPARED

A comparison of arithmetic and exponential notation is contained in Table 2-1. Note that positive exponents move the decimal point to the right and that negative exponents move the decimal point to the left of the first numeral by a number equal to the exponent. Also note that roots are indicated by fractional exponents. For example:

$$10^{0.5} \times 10^{0.5} = 10^{(0.5 + 0.5)} = 10 \qquad (2\text{-}1)$$

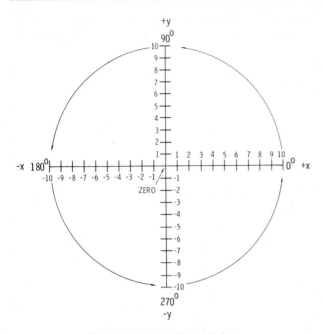

Fig. 2-1. Basic vector notation.

Table 2-1. Arithmetic and Exponential Notation Compared

Arithmetic Notation	Exponential Notation	Result
10×10	10^2	100
$10 \times 10 \times 10$	10^3	1000
$10 \times 10 \times 10 \times 10$	10^4	10,000
$10 \times 10 \times 10 \times 10 \times 10$	10^5	100,000
$\dfrac{100,000}{10}$	10^4	10,000
$\dfrac{10,000}{10}$	10^3	1000
$\dfrac{1000}{10}$	10^2	100
$\dfrac{100}{10}$	10^1	10
$\dfrac{10}{10}$	10^0	1
$\dfrac{1}{10}$	10^{-1}	0.1
$\dfrac{0.1}{10}$	10^{-2}	0.01
$\dfrac{0.01}{10}$	10^{-3}	0.001
$\dfrac{0.001}{10}$	10^{-4}	0.0001
$\dfrac{0.0001}{10}$	10^{-5}	0.00001
100×1000	$10^2 \times 10^3 = 10^{(2+3)}$	100,000
10×100	$10^1 \times 10^2 = 10^{(1+2)}$	1000
$\dfrac{100,000}{1000}$	$\dfrac{10^5}{10^3} = 10^{(5-3)}$	100
$\dfrac{1000}{100}$	$\dfrac{10^3}{10^2} = 10^{(3-2)}$	10
$\sqrt{10}$	$10^{0.5}$ or $10^{1/2}$	3.162
$\sqrt[3]{10}$	$10^{0.33}$ or $10^{1/3}$	2.154
$\sqrt[4]{10}$	$10^{0.25}$ or $10^{1/4}$	1.778
$\sqrt[5]{10}$	$10^{0.2}$ or $10^{1/5}$	1.585

Therefore:

$$10^{0.5} = \sqrt{10} \qquad (2\text{-}2)$$

A GENERAL RULE

Any positive real ratio a/c can be expressed by two numbers, b and n, in exponential form.

$$\frac{a}{c} = b^n \qquad (2\text{-}3)$$

Either b or n can be chosen arbitrarily, with certain obvious restrictions, but the choice of one determines the other. If we thus assigned a value of 10 to b, we could then write the following if a = 10 and c = 1:

$$\frac{10}{1} = 10^1, \text{ and } n = 1 \qquad (2\text{-}4)$$

Another way to express the same quantities is in the logarithmic form:

$$\log_b \frac{a}{c} = n \qquad (2\text{-}5)$$

or

$$\log_{10} \frac{10}{1} = 1 \qquad (2\text{-}6)$$

Fig. 2-2 compares the logarithmic and exponential forms. The arrows indicate how the quantities transpose from one form to the other. The logarithmic form is read, "log to the base b of a over c equals n." The exponential form is read, "A over c equals the base b raised to the power n."

LOGARITHMIC FORM $\qquad \log_b \left(\dfrac{a}{c} \right) = n$

EXPONENTIAL FORM $\qquad \left(\dfrac{a}{c} \right) = b^n$

Fig. 2-2. Logarithmic and exponential forms of a ratio.

ARITHMETIC, EXPONENTIAL, AND LOGARITHMIC FORMS COMPARED

The logarithm of a number is the exponent that the base must be raised to in order to equal that number. Therefore, we can write logarithmic equivalents of arithmetic equations by remembering how exponents are manipulated. See Table 2-2.

Once it is recognized that logarithms are the exponents of some base and that they follow exponential rules of manipulation, then the further extension of that knowledge into the fact that decibel notation is also a logarithmic notation can result in a clearer understand-

Table 2-2. Equivalent Arithmetic, Exponential, and Logarithmic Forms

Arithmetic	Exponential	Logarithmic
$A \cdot B$	$A^1 \cdot B^1$	$10^{(\log A + \log B)}$
$2 \cdot 3$	$2^1 \cdot 3^1$	$10^{(\log 2 + \log 3)}$
$\dfrac{A}{B}$	$\dfrac{A^1}{B^1}$	$10^{(\log A - \log B)}$
$\dfrac{4}{2}$	$\dfrac{4^1}{2^1}$	$10^{(\log 4 - \log 2)}$
A^x	A^x	$10^{(x \log A)}$
2^3	2^3	$10^{(3 \log 2)}$
$\sqrt[x]{A}$	$A^{\frac{1}{x}}$	$10^{\left(\frac{\log A}{x}\right)}$
$\sqrt[2]{3}$	$3^{1/2}$	$10^{\left(\frac{\log 3}{2}\right)}$
$A^x \cdot A^y$	$A^{(x+y)}$	$10^{(x \log A + y \log A)}$
$3^2 \cdot 3^3$	$3^{(2+3)}$	$10^{(2 \log 3 + 3 \log 3)}$
$(A \cdot B)^x$	$A^x \cdot B^x$	$10^{(x \log A + x \log B)}$
$(2 \cdot 3)^4$	$2^4 \cdot 3^4$	$10^{(4 \log 2 + 4 \log 3)}$
$\sqrt[x]{\dfrac{A}{B}}$	$\dfrac{\sqrt[x]{A}}{\sqrt[x]{B}}$	$10^{\left(\frac{\log A}{x} - \frac{\log B}{x}\right)}$
$\sqrt[4]{\dfrac{3}{2}}$	$\dfrac{\sqrt[4]{3}}{\sqrt[4]{2}}$	$10^{\left(\frac{\log 3}{4} - \frac{\log 2}{4}\right)}$
$(A^x)^y$	A^{xy}	$10^{xy \log A}$
$(2^3)^4$	$2^{(3\times4)}$	$10^{3\times4 \log 2}$
$\sqrt[x]{A \cdot B}$	$\sqrt[x]{A} \cdot \sqrt[x]{B}$	$10^{\left(\frac{\log A}{x} + \frac{\log B}{x}\right)}$
$\sqrt[4]{2 \cdot 3}$	$\sqrt[4]{2} \cdot \sqrt[4]{3}$	$10^{\left(\frac{\log 2}{4} + \frac{\log 3}{4}\right)}$
$A^{\frac{1}{x}}$	$\sqrt[x]{A}$	$10^{\left(\frac{\log A}{x}\right)}$
$2^{\frac{1}{3}}$	$\sqrt[3]{2}$	$10^{\left(\frac{\log 2}{3}\right)}$
$\dfrac{A^x}{A^y}$	$A^{(x-y)}$	$10^{(x-y) \log A}$
$\dfrac{2^4}{2^3}$	$2^{(4-3)}$	$10^{(4-3)(\log 2)}$
$\left(\dfrac{A}{B}\right)^x$	$\dfrac{A^x}{B^x}$	$10^{x \log A - x \log B}$
$\left(\dfrac{3}{2}\right)^4$	$\dfrac{3^4}{2^4}$	$10^{4 \log 3 - 4 \log 2}$
A^{-x}	$\dfrac{1}{A^x}$	$10^{-x \log A}$
2^{-4}	$\dfrac{1}{2^4}$	$10^{-4 \log 2}$
$\sqrt[x]{\sqrt[y]{A}}$	$\sqrt[xy]{A}$	$10^{\left(\frac{\log A}{xy}\right)}$
$\sqrt[2]{\sqrt[3]{4}}$	$\sqrt[2\times3]{4}$	$10^{\left(\frac{\log 4}{2\times3}\right)}$
$A^{\frac{x}{y}}$	$\sqrt[y]{A^x}$	$10^{\left(\frac{x \log A}{y}\right)}$
$2^{\frac{3}{4}}$	$\sqrt[4]{2^3}$	$10^{\left(\frac{3 \log 2}{4}\right)}$
A^{x^y}	$A^{(x^y)}$	$10^{10^{(\log \log A + y \log x)}}$
2^{3^4}	$2^{(3^4)}$	$10^{10^{(\log \log 2 + 4 \log 3)}}$
A^0	1	$10^{0 \log A}$

Table 2-3. Terms and Symbols for Logarithmic Scales*

Physical Quantity	Base	Name of One Order	Symbol
Power Attenuation or Gain	10	Bel	B
Stellar Magnitude (Brightness^{-1})	$100^{1/5} = 2.512$	Magnitude	
Musical Pitch and Other Harmonic Analysis (Frequency)	$2\left(\dfrac{f}{f_0} = 2^n\right)$	Octave	OC
Photographic Exposure Settings	$10^{3/10} = 1.995$	Step or Stop	ST
Various Electrical, Acoustical and Mechanical (Proposed for General Use)	$e = 2.718$	Neper	Np or ln
Proposed for General Use	10	Brigg	Br
Proposed for General Use	b	Order to Base b	ORD$_b$

* As proposed by Calvin S. McCamy, N. B. S.

ing of the decibel. Practice with these very basic concepts can serve an audio professional well throughout his career.

Suppose that $a = 2$ and $c = 1$. Then:

$$\frac{2}{1} = 10^n \qquad (2\text{-}7)$$

We already know from Table 2-1 that $10^{0.33} = 2.154$ and that $10^{0.25} = 1.778$. Therefore, we can assume that the value of n must fall between 0.33 and 0.25. It in fact is 0.3010299956 to the first ten places. Therefore, $10^{0.3010299956} = 2$, or $\log_{10} 2 = 0.3010299956$.

The definition of the bel is:

$$\text{Bels} = \log_{10} \frac{P_1}{P_2} \qquad (2\text{-}8)$$

Therefore, if $P_1 = 2$ watts and $P_2 = 1$ watt, the power ratio would equal 0.301 bels. Table 2-3 lists the most common uses of logarithmic scales to various bases.

Suppose now that we need $\sqrt[12]{2}$ (the semitone interval in music). We could write

$$\frac{\log 2}{12} = \log \sqrt[12]{2} \qquad (2\text{-}9)$$

Therefore,

$$10^{\left(\frac{\log 2}{12}\right)} = 10^{\left(\frac{0.301}{12}\right)} \qquad (2\text{-}10)$$

$$= 10^{0.02508} = 1.05946 = \sqrt[12]{2}$$

$10^{0.02508}$ is called the antilog of 0.02508. The antilog is also written as $\log^{-1}$, antilog$_{10}$, or 10 exp of 0.02508. All these terms mean exactly the same thing.

THE DECIBEL

The bel was defined previously so that

$$\log_{10} \frac{P_1}{P_2} = x \text{ bels} \qquad (2\text{-}11)$$

"Deci" means $\frac{1}{10}$, so we can write:

$$\frac{10 \text{ decibels}}{1 \text{ bel}} = 1 \qquad (2\text{-}12)$$

Using a system called the factor-label system as our conversion tool, we can see that if:

$$\frac{12 \text{ in}}{1 \text{ ft}} = 1 \qquad (2\text{-}13)$$

then

$$\frac{2 \text{ ft}}{1} \cdot \frac{12 \text{ in}}{1 \text{ ft}} = 24 \text{ inches} \qquad (2\text{-}14)$$

The labels cancel, leaving the desired label, and the factors are multiplied and divided to obtain the answer. Using this same method, we can write:

$$\frac{1 \text{ bel}}{1} \cdot \frac{10 \text{ decibels}}{1 \text{ bel}} = 10 \text{ decibels} \qquad (2\text{-}15)$$

or

$$1 \text{ bel} = 10 \text{ decibels} \qquad (2\text{-}16)$$

Then $\log_{10} 10 = 1$ bel or 10 decibels.

If we were to write:

$$\log_{10} 10^{10} = ? \qquad (2\text{-}17)$$

we would obtain the number of decibels directly.

$$\log_{10} 10^{10} = 10 \quad \text{or} \quad 10 \log_{10} 10 = 10 \quad (2\text{-}18)$$

Thus we arrive at the formula for finding *power* ratios expressed in decibels:

$$10 \log \frac{P_1}{P_2} = \text{Power ratio in dB} \qquad (2\text{-}19)$$

or $10 \log 2 = 3.01$ dB.

It is important to note that $\frac{20 \text{ watts}}{10 \text{ watts}}$ or $\frac{200 \text{ watts}}{100 \text{ watts}}$ both equal 3.01 dB. This 3.01 dB only means that a 2-to-1 power ratio exists but reveals nothing about the actual powers. The human ear hears the same small difference between 1 watt and 2 watts as it does between 100 watts and 200 watts.

Changing the dB back to a power ratio (exponential form) is the same as for any logarithm with the addition of multiplier (Fig. 2-3). The arrows in Fig. 2-3 indicate the transposition of quantities. Table 2-4 shows the number of decibels corresponding to various power ratios.

Fig. 2-4 shows how to use the Lukasiewicz reverse Polish notation stack to solve basic decibel equations with the Hewlett-Packard Model 21, 45, 55, and 65 calculators. In the following examples, the keyboard operations for solving the given equations are shown below the equations.

1. $$10 \log_{10} 2 = 3.01 \text{ dB}$$

    1 0 enter, 2, blue key, LOG, x (H-P 21)

2. $$10^{3.01/10} = 2$$

    3.01, enter, 1 0, $\div$, 1 0, x^y (H-P 35)
    3.01, enter, 1 0, $\div$, blue key, 10^x (H-P 21)
    or
    1 0, enter, 3.01, enter, 1 0, $\div$, blue key, y^x

The following examples show the use of the Texas Instruments Model SR50 (Fig. 2-5) to solve basic decibel problems.

1. $$10 \log_{10} 2 = 3.01 \text{ dB}$$

    10, X, 2, LOG, = 3.01

2. $$10^{3.01/10} = 2$$

    3.01, $\div$, 10, Y^x, 10, X$\rightleftarrows$Y, = 2

Summary of operations with the SR50:

1. Do highest orders first.
2. Use reciprocal and $+/-$ to exchange positions.
3. Use $=$ to close brackets.
4. Use STO and RCL if disoriented.

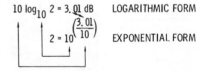

Fig. 2-3. Conversion of decibels from logarithmic form to exponential form.

Table 2-4. Power Ratios in Decibels

Power Ratio	Decibels
2	3.01030
3	4.77121
4	6.02060
5	6.98970
6	7.78151
7	8.45098
8	9.03090
9	9.54243
10	10.00000
100	20.00000
1000	30.00000
10,000	40.00000
100,000	50.00000
1,000,000	60.00000

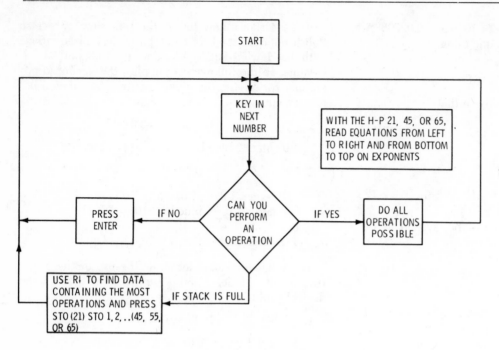

Fig. 2-4. Operation of H-P Model 21, 45, 55, and 65 calculators.

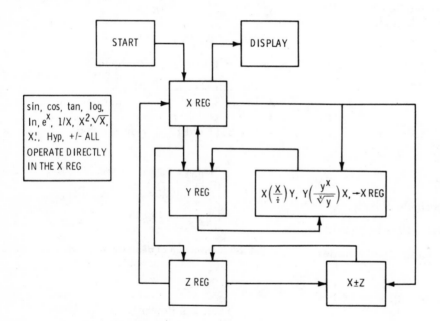

Fig. 2-5. Operation of TI Model SR50 calculator.

Example:

$$1 - e^{-\frac{0.049 \times 500,000}{42,500 \times 2.5}} = 0.206$$

0.049 X, 500,000, ÷, 42,500 ÷ 2.5 =, +/−, e^x, +/−, +, 1, = 0.206

where +/−, +, 1 = (1 − ...)

As an example, suppose that a power of 50 watts is lowered by 8 dB. What is the new power?

Remember that in this case, $10 \log \frac{P_1}{P_2} = -8$ dB.

Therefore, we can write $10 \log \frac{x}{50} = -8$ dB, or

$$10^{\left(\frac{(-8)}{10}\right)} = \frac{x}{50}$$

$$x = 50 \times 10^{\left(\frac{(-8)}{10}\right)} \qquad (2\text{-}20)$$

The new power is 7.924 watts.

To prove this, we calculate

$$10 \log_{10} \frac{7.924 \text{ watts}}{50 \text{ watts}} = -8 \text{ dB} \qquad (2\text{-}21)$$

The use of the term "decibel" always implies a power ratio. Power itself is rarely measured as such. The most common quantity measured is voltage. If in measuring

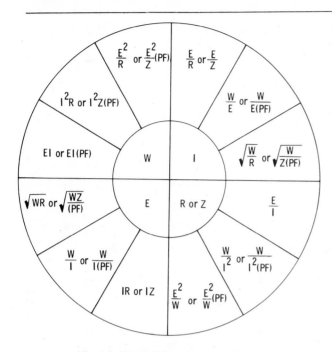

Fig. 2-6. Ohm's law nomograph for ac or dc.

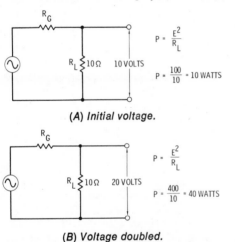

(A) Initial voltage.

(B) Voltage doubled.

Fig. 2-7. Voltage and power relationship in a circuit.

the voltage of a sine-wave signal (oscillators are the most reliable and common of the test-signal sources) we obtain the root-mean-square voltage (rms voltage), we can calculate the *average* power developed by using Ohm's law. It is assumed that you already are familiar with Ohm's law, but Fig. 2-6 can serve as a reminder of its many basic forms.

DECIBELS AS VOLTAGE RATIOS

One confusing factor to many audio technicians is the fact that doubling the voltage results in a 6-dB increase while doubling the power only results in a 3-dB increase. Fig. 2-7 demonstrates what happens if we simultaneously check both the voltage and power in a circuit where we double the voltage. Note that for a doubling of the voltage the power increases four times.

$$10 \log_{10} \frac{4}{1} = 6.02 \text{ dB} \qquad (2\text{-}22)$$

Or we could have written:

$$10 \log_{10} \frac{2^2}{1} = 6.02 \text{ dB} \qquad (2\text{-}23)$$

because the voltage has to be squared in the formula for power. (Remember, the current doubled also.)

Using our knowledge of logarithms we can also write:

$$2 \times 10 \log \frac{2}{1} = 6.02 \text{ dB} \qquad (2\text{-}24)$$

or

$$20 \log \frac{2}{1} = 6.02 \text{ dB} \qquad (2\text{-}25)$$

where $\frac{2}{1}$ is the voltage ratio.

On occasion in acoustics, we may need other multipliers than 10 or 20. Once the ΔdB is known (ΔdB = the number of dB for a 2/1 ratio change), the multiplier may be calculated by:

$$\log \text{ mult} = \frac{\log (\text{Base}) \times \Delta \text{dB}}{\log (\text{Ratio})} \qquad (2\text{-}26)$$

For example, if a 2/1 change is equivalent to 3.01 dB, then:

$$\log \text{ mult} = \frac{\log 10 \times 3.01}{\log 2} = 10 \qquad (2\text{-}27)$$

or:

$$10 \log 2 = 3.01 \qquad (2\text{-}28)$$

If a 2/1 change is equivalent to 6.02 dB, then:

$$\log \text{ mult} = \frac{\log 10 \times 6.01}{\log 2} = 20 \qquad (2\text{-}29)$$

or:

$$20 \log 2 = 6.01 \qquad (2\text{-}30)$$

Finally, if a 2/1 change is equivalent to 8 dB, then:

$$\log \text{ mult} = \frac{\log 10 \times 8}{\log 2} = 26.58 \qquad (2\text{-}31)$$

or:

$$26.58 \log 2 = 8 \qquad (2\text{-}32)$$

This may be reduced to

$$\log \text{ mult} = 3.322 \times \Delta \text{dB} \qquad (2\text{-}33)$$

for any ΔdB corresponding to a 2/1 ratio change involving logarithms to the base 10.

THE DECIBEL AS A POWER QUANTITY

We have seen that a number of decibels by itself is only a ratio. Given any reference (such as the 50 watts used above), you can use decibels to find absolute values. There exists a standard reference for power in audio work. It is 10^{-3} watt (0.001 watt) or 0.775 volt across 600 ohms. Note that when a level is expressed as a wattage, it is not necessary to state an impedance, but when it is stated as a voltage, an impedance is mandatory. This power is called 0 dBm. The small m stands for milliwatt (0.001 watt), or one thousandth of a watt.

For example, the power in watts corresponding to +30 dBm is calculated as follows:

$$10 \log_{10} \frac{x}{0.001} = 30 \qquad (2\text{-}34)$$

$$x = 0.001 \times 10^{\frac{30}{10}} = 1 \text{ watt} \qquad (2\text{-}35)$$

For a power of −12 dBm:

$$0.001 \times 10^{\frac{-12}{10}} = 0.00006309 \text{ watt} \qquad (2\text{-}36)$$

The voltage across 600 ohms is:

$$E = \sqrt{WR} = \sqrt{0.00006309 \times 600} = 0.195 \text{ V} \qquad (2\text{-}37)$$

The power output of Boulder Dam is said to be approximately 3,160,000,000 watts. Expressed in dBm, this would be:

$$10 \log_{10} \frac{3.16 \times 10^9}{10^{-3}} = 125 \text{ dBm} \qquad (2\text{-}38)$$

THE dB IN ACOUSTICS—dB-SPL, dB-PWL

In acoustics, the ratios most commonly encountered are changes in pressure levels. First of all, there exists a reference. The older level was 0.0002 dyne/cm². This has recently been changed to 0.00002 newton/m² (20 micronewtons/m², also written 20 μN/m²). These are identical pressures with different labels. Sound pressure levels are identified as dB-SPL, and sound power levels are identified as dB-PWL.

At sea level, atmospheric pressure is equal to 2116 lbs/ft². Remember the old physics lab stunt of partially filling an oil can with water, boiling the water, and then quickly sealing the can and putting it under the cold-water faucet to condense the steam so that the atmospheric pressure would crush the can as the steam condensed leaving a partial vacuum?

$$1 \text{ atmosphere} = \frac{101,300 \text{ newtons}}{m^2} \qquad (2\text{-}39)$$

Therefore,

$$20 \log \frac{101,300}{0.00002} = 194 \text{ dB-SPL} \qquad (2\text{-}40)$$

This would represent the complete modulation of atmospheric pressure and would be the largest possible sinusoid. Note that SPL is analogous to voltage. A level of 200 dB-SPL is the pressure generated by 50 pounds

Table 2-5. Equivalents of Pressure Levels

Pressure	Equivalent
1 lb/ft²	127.6 dB-SPL
1 lb/in²	170.8 dB-SPL
1 newton/m²	94 dB-SPL
1 microbar	74 dB-SPL
1 microbar	1 dyne/cm²
1 microbar	$\frac{1}{1,000,000}$ atmos

Table 2-6. Common Decibel Notation and References

Quantity	Standard Reference	Symbol	Logarithm Multiplier
Sound Pressure	1 dyne/cm² (water) 0.0002 dyne/cm² (air) or 0.00002 N/m²	SPL or L_p	20
Sound Intensity	10^{-16} watts/cm²		10
Sound Power	10^{-12} watt (new) 10^{-13} watt (old)	PWL or L_p	10
Audio Power	10^{-3} watt	dBm	10
EMF	1 volt	dBV	20
Amperes	1 mA		20
Acceleration	1 gRMS		20
Acceleration Spectral Density	1 g²/Hz		10
Volume Units	10^{-3} watt	VU	10
Distance	1 foot or 1 meter	ΔD_x	20
Noise—Ref	−90 dBm at 1000 Hz	dBrn	10

$$dB = \text{logarithm multiplier} \times \log_{10} \frac{\text{quantity}}{\text{standard reference}}$$

of tnt at 10 feet. Table 2-5 shows the equivalents of some pressure levels.

For additional insights into these basic relationships, the *Handbook of Noise Measurement* is particularly thorough, accurate, and readable. (See the Bibliography, Appendix II.)

A dB IS A dB IS A dB

The decibel is always a power ratio; therefore, when dealing in quantities that are not power ratios, i.e., voltage, use the multiplier 20 in place of 10. As we encounter each reference for the dB, we will indicate the correct multiplier. Table 2-6 lists all the standard references, and Tables 2-7, 2-8, and 2-9 contain additional information regarding reference labels and quantities. The decibel is not a unit of measurement like an inch, a watt, a liter, or a gram. It is the logarithm of a nondimensional ratio of two power-like quantities.

Sound power levels are calculated by

$$\text{dB-PWL} = 10 \log_{10} \frac{\text{acoustic power}}{10^{-12} \text{ watt}} \qquad (2\text{-}41)$$

Table 2-7. Preferred Reference Labels for Acoustical Levels

Name	Definition
Sound pressure level	$L_p = 20 \log (p/p_o)$ dB
Vibratory acceleration level	$L_a = 20 \log (a/a_o)$ dB
Vibratory velocity level	$L_v = 20 \log (v/v_o)$ dB
Vibratory force level	$L_F = 20 \log (F/F_o)$ dB
Power level	$L_P = 10 \log (P/P_o)$ dB
Intensity level	$L_I = 10 \log (I/I_o)$ dB
Energy density level	$L_E = 10 \log (E/E_o)$ dB
Energy level	$L_W = 10 \log (W/W_o)$ dB

or by the old standard

$$\text{dB-PWL} = 10 \log_{10} \frac{\text{acoustic power}}{10^{-13} \text{ watt}} \quad (2\text{-}42)$$

The dB-SPL is approximately equal to the dB-PWL at 0.283 meter from an omnidirectional sound source in a free field. In other words, the power flowing through one square meter of surface area surrounding the sound source will have a dB-PWL approximately equal to the dB-SPL measured anywhere on that surface.

Much earlier, but valuable, literature used 10^{-13} watt as a reference. In that case, the dB-SPL approximately equals the dB-PWL at 0.283 foot from an omnidirectional radiator in a free field. For 1 watt using 10^{-12} watt at 0.283 meter, dB-PWL $\cong$ dB-SPL = 120. For 1 watt using 10^{-13} watt at 0.283 foot, dB-PWL $\cong$ dB-SPL = 130.

$$\text{dB-SPL} = \text{dB-PWL} - 10 \log (4\pi r^2) + 0.5 \quad (2\text{-}43)$$

where,

dB-PWL is 10 log the wattage divided by the reference power, 10^{-12},

r is the distance in meters from the center of the sound source.

As the distance from the sound source doubles, the area surrounding the source quadruples. Therefore, the same power flows through four times the surface area (¼ the power per unit area). This results in a decrease in dB-SPL of 6 dB for every doubling of distance from the sound source. The dB-PWL remains constant, being a function of the total power radiated. Figs. 2-8 and 2-9 show typical sound levels and acoustic powers. The values in Fig. 2-9 do not have a simple relationship to the SPL figures in Fig. 2-8.

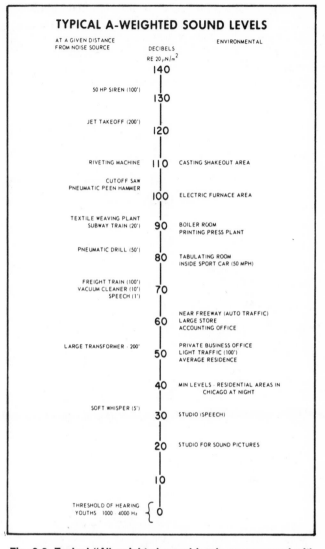

Fig. 2-8. Typical "A"-weighted sound levels as measured with a sound level meter.

COMBINING DECIBELS

If, for example, we have a noisy piece of machinery, say 90 dB-SPL, and we wish to turn on a second machine with an equal level of 90 dB-SPL, we need to know the combined dB-SPL. Since both measured SPLs are the result of the power being applied to the machine, with some percentage being converted into

Table 2-8. Preferred Reference Quantities for Acoustical Levels

SI		cgs	British
$p_o = 20\ \mu N/m^2 =$	$2 \times 10^{-5}\ N/m^2$	2×10^{-4} dyne/cm^2	2.90×10^{-9} lbf/in^2
$a_o = 10\ \mu m/s^2 =$	$10^{-5}\ m/s^2$	10^{-3} cm/s^2	39.4×10^{-5} in/s^2
$v_o = 10\ nm/s =$	$10^{-8}\ m/s$	10^{-6} cm/s	39.4×10^{-8} in/s
$F_o = 1\ \mu N =$	$10^{-6}\ N$	10^{-1} dyne	0.225×10^{-6} lbf
$P_o = 1\ pW =$	$10^{-12}\ W$	10^{-5} erg/s	8.85×10^{-12} in lbf/s
$I_o = 1\ pW/m^2 =$	$10^{-12}\ W/m^2$	10^{-9} erg/s cm^2	5.71×10^{-15} lbf/in s
$E_o = 1\ pJ/m^3 =$	$10^{-12}\ J/m^3$	10^{-11} erg/cm^3	1.45×10^{-16} in lbf/in^3
$W_o = 1\ pJ =$	$10^{-12}\ J$	10^{-5} erg	8.85×10^{-12} in lbf

Table 2-9. Associated Standard Reference Levels

1 Atmosphere = 1.013 bar = 1.033 kp/cm² = 14.70 lbs/in²
= 760 mm Hg = 29.92 inches Hg

Acceleration of Gravity:
g = 980.665 cm/sec² = 32.174 ft/sec² (standard or accepted value)

Sound Level:
The common reference level is the audibility threshold at 1000 Hz, i.e., 0.0002 dyne/cm², 2×10^{-4} μbar, 2×10^{-5} N/m², 10^{-16} watt/cm²

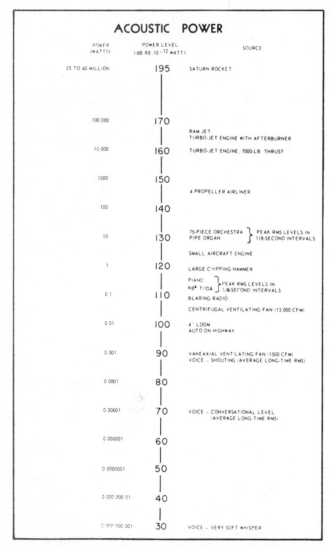

Fig. 2-9. Typical PWL values for various acoustic sources.

acoustic power, we can convert each SPL back to relative power level by using:

$$10^{\frac{90}{10}} + 10^{\frac{90}{10}} = 10^9 + 10^9 = 2 \times 10^9 \quad (2\text{-}44)$$

Therefore,

$$10 \log (2 \times 10^9) = 93 \text{ dB} \quad (2\text{-}45)$$

It is thus seen that doubling the acoustic power results in a 3-dB increase.

SUBTRACTING DECIBELS

When the sound level of a source is measured in the presence of noise, it is necessary to subtract out the effect of the noise on the reading. First, a reading is taken of the source and the noise combined (L_{S+N}). Then another reading is taken of the noise alone (the source having been shut off). The second reading is designated L_N. Then:

$$L_S = 10 \log_{10} \left[10^{\left(\frac{L_{S+N}}{10}\right)} - 10^{\left(\frac{L_N}{10}\right)} \right] \quad (2\text{-}46)$$

COMBINING LEVELS OF UNCORRELATED NOISE SIGNALS

To combine the levels of uncorrelated noise signals use the chart in Fig. 2-10.

To Add Levels

Enter the chart with the numerical difference between the two levels being added (top of chart). Follow the line corresponding to this value to its intersection with the curved line; then move left to read the numerical difference between the total and larger levels. Add this value to the larger level to determine the total.

Example: Combine 75 dB and 80 dB. The difference is 5 dB. The 5-dB line intersects the curved line at 1.2 dB on the vertical scale. Thus the total value is 80 + 1.2, or 81.2 dB.

To Subtract Levels

Enter the chart with the numerical difference between the total and larger levels if this value is less than 3 dB. Enter the chart with the numerical differ-

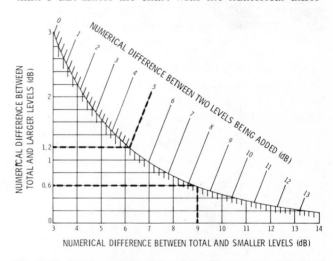

Fig. 2-10. Chart used for determining the combined level of uncorrelated noise signals.

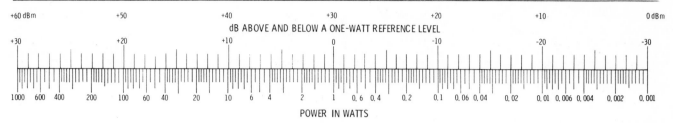

Fig. 2-11. 10 log₁₀ x chart.

ence between the total and smaller levels if this value is between 3 and 14 dB. Follow the line corresponding to this value to its intersection with the curved line, then either left or down to read the numerical difference between total and larger (smaller) levels. Subtract this value from the total level to determine the unknown level.

Example: Subtract 81 dB from 90 dB. The difference is 9 dB. The 9-dB vertical line intersects the curved line at 0.6 dB on the vertical scale. Thus the unknown level is 90 − 0.6, or 89.4 dB.

ADDING AND SUBTRACTING dB LEVELS

The sum of two or more levels expressed in decibels may be found as follows:

$$10 \log \left[10^{\frac{(dB\text{-}SPL_1)}{10}} + 10^{\frac{dB\text{-}SPL_2}{10}} + \dots 10^{\frac{(dB\text{-}SPL_n)}{10}} \right] \quad (2\text{-}47)$$

The difference of two levels expressed in decibels may be found as follows:

$$10 \log \left[10^{\frac{(\text{Total level})}{10}} - 10^{\frac{(\text{Level with one source off})}{10}} \right] \quad (2\text{-}48)$$

Input signals to a mixing network also combine in this same manner, but the insertion loss of the network must be subtracted. Two exactly phase-coherent sine-wave signals of equal amplitude will combine to give a level 6 dB higher than either sine wave.

USING THE 10 LOG X CHART

Note that there are two scales on the top of the 10 log₁₀ x chart (Fig. 2-11). One is in dB above and below a 1-watt reference level, and the other is in dBm (reference 0.001 watt). Power ratios may be read directly from the 1-watt dB scale.

EXAMPLES:

(A) A $\frac{25}{1}$ power ratio is how many dB?
   1. Look up 25 on the watts scale.
   2. Read 14 dB directly above the 25.
(B) I have a 100-watt amplifier but plan to use a 12-dB margin for "head room." How many watts will my program level be?
   1. Above 100 watts find +50 dBm.

   2. Subtract 12 dB from 50 dBm to obtain +38 dBm.
   3. Below +38 dBm read 6.3 watts.
(C) I have a 100-watt amplifier with 64 dB of gain. What input level in dBm will drive it to full power?
   1. Above 100 watts read +50 dBm.
   2. +50 dBm − 64-dB gain = −14 dBm.
(D) My loudspeaker has a sensitivity of 99 dB-SPL at 4 feet with a 1-watt input. How many watts are needed to have 115 dB-SPL at 4 feet.
   1. 115 dB-SPL − 99 dB-SPL = +16 dB.
   2. At +16 on the one-watt scale read 39.8 watts.

USING THE 20 LOG X CHART

Refer to the chart in Fig. 2-12. A 2/1 voltage, distance, or SPL change is found by locating 2 on the ratio or D scale and looking directly above to 6 dB.

(A) My loudspeaker has a sensitivity of 99 dB-SPL at 4 feet with 1 watt of input power. What will the level be at 100 feet?
   1. Find the *relative* dB for 4 feet. Relative dB = 12.
   2. Find the *relative* dB for 100 feet. Relative dB = 40.
   3. Calculate the *absolute* dB. 40 − 12 = 28 dB.
   4. 99 dB-SPL − 28 dB = 71 dB-SPL.
(B) I raise the voltage from 2 volts to 10 volts. How many dB do I increase the power?
   1. Find the *relative* dB for a ratio of 2. Relative dB = 6.
   2. Find the *relative* dB for a ratio of 10. Relative dB = 20.
   3. Absolute dB change = 20 − 6 = 14 dB.
   4. Since a dB is a dB, the power also changed by 14 dB.

FINDING THE LOGARITHM OF A NUMBER TO ANY BASE

In communication theory, the base 2 is used. Occasionally other bases are chosen. To find the logarithm of a number to any possible given base, we can write:

$$x = b^n \quad (2\text{-}49)$$

27

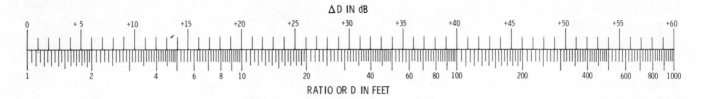

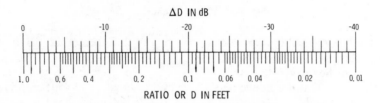

Fig. 2-12. 20 log₁₀ x chart.

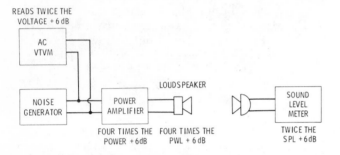

Fig. 2-13. Voltage, electrical power, PWL, and SPL compared.

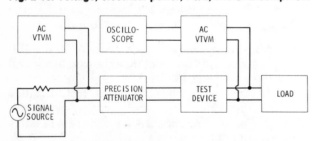

Fig. 2-14. Method of measuring the insertion gain or loss contributed by a device.

where,

x is the number for which a logarithm is to be found,
b is the base,
n is the logarithm.

We then can further write:

$$\log x = n \log b \qquad (2\text{-}50)$$

and

$$\frac{\log x}{\log b} = n \qquad (2\text{-}51)$$

Suppose we want to find the natural logarithm of 2 (written ln 2). The base of natural logarithms is $e = 2.718281828$. Then

$$\frac{\log 2}{\log e} = \frac{0.30103}{0.43425} = 0.69315 \qquad (2\text{-}52)$$

To verify this result:

$$e^{0.69315} = 2 \qquad (2\text{-}53)$$

To find $\log_2$ of 26:

$$\frac{\log 26}{\log 2} = \frac{1.41497}{0.30103} = 4.70044 \qquad (2\text{-}54)$$

The general case is:

$$\frac{\log_{10} \text{ of the number}}{\log_{10} \text{ of the base}} = \log_{\text{BASE}} \text{ of the number} \qquad (2\text{-}55)$$

SYSTEM GAIN CHANGES

Imagine a noise generator driving a power amplifier and a loudspeaker (Fig. 2-13). If the voltage out of the noise generator is raised by 6 dB, what happens?

Voltage	Electrical Power	SPL	PWL
Doubled	Quadrupled	Doubled	Quadrupled
+6 dB	+6 dB	+6 dB	+6 dB

This means that, in a linear system, a level change ahead of any components results in a level change for that same signal in all subsequent components, though it might be measured as quite different voltages or wattages at differing points. *The ratio of change at any point would be the same.* We will work with this concept a little later when we plot the gains and losses through a total system.

MEASURING GAIN OR LOSS USING THE dB

System gains and losses will be covered in detail in Chapter 5, but the basic use of the dB in these measurements is as follows:

Attach a precision attenuator (bridged T) to the 600-ohm output of an audio oscillator (Fig. 2-14). At the input of the attenuator, when it is attached to the input of the device to be tested, read 0.775 volt for zero level. Next set the attenuator to a high value (90 dB) and put a meter and an oscilloscope across the output of the device being tested (both meter and oscilloscope should have very high impedance). Reduce the attenuation until you see signs of clipping just beginning. The voltage read across the output can be used to calculate the power output:

$$\frac{E^2}{Z} = \text{Output power} \qquad (2\text{-}56)$$

The attenuator reading plus this output power in dBm equals the gain of the device:

$$10 \log \frac{\text{Output power}}{0.001} + \text{Atten setting} = \text{Actual gain} \qquad (2\text{-}57)$$

Gain sets were once widely used for this type of work. They are still one of the very best ways of doing it, as they provide the most common input impedances (in a calibrated form) and the most common load impedances, all in one unit, with a 111-dB precision attenuator (in 0.1-dB steps) as well as the two meters required. Fig. 2-15 shows the front panel of a gain set, and Fig. 2-16 is the schematic diagram of a "classic" gain set design.

THE VU AND THE VI METER

Volts, amperes, and watts can be measured by inserting an appropriate meter into the circuit. If all audio signals were sine waves, we could insert a dBm meter into the circuit and get a reading that would correlate with both electrical and acoustical variations. Unfortunately, audio signals are complex waveforms, and their rms amplitude is not 0.707 times peak but can range from as small as 0.04 times peak to as high as 0.99 times peak. (See Fig. 2-17.) To solve this problem,

broadcasting and telephone engineers got together in 1939 and designed a special meter for measuring speech and music in communication circuits. They calibrated this new type of meter in units called *volume units* (VU) because it was used to measure the volume of the sound. The dBm and the VU are almost identical, the only difference being in their usage. The dBm is for sinusoidal measurements only, whereas the VU may be used with any waveform. The meter used to measure dBm is called a dBm meter, and the meter used to measure VU is called the *volume indicator* meter, or VI meter (most users ignore this and call it a VU meter). Both dBm meters and VI meters are specially calibrated voltmeters, and consequently the VU and dBm scales on these meters give correct readings only when the measurement is being made across 600 ohms. Readings taken across 600 ohms are referred to as true levels, whereas readings taken across other impedances are called apparent levels.

Apparent levels can be useful for relative frequency response measurements, for example. When the impedance is not 600 ohms, the correction factor of

$$10 \log \frac{600}{\text{ohms}} \qquad (2\text{-}58)$$

can be added to the formula containing the reference level as in the following equation:

$$VU = 20 \log \frac{E}{0.775} + 10 \log \frac{600}{\text{ohms}} \qquad (2\text{-}59)$$

The result is the true level.

THE VU IMPEDANCE CORRECTION

When a VI meter is connected across 600 ohms and is reading 0 VU on a sine-wave signal, the true level is 4 dB higher, or +4 dBm, instead of 0 dBm or zero level. The reason this is so is shown in Fig. 2-18. The VI

Fig. 2-15. Front panel of a gain set.

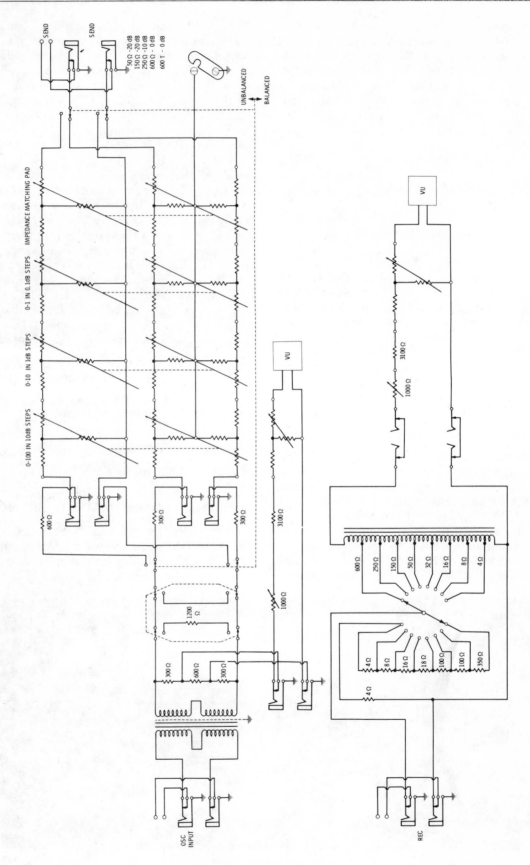

Fig. 2-16. Circuit of a gain set.

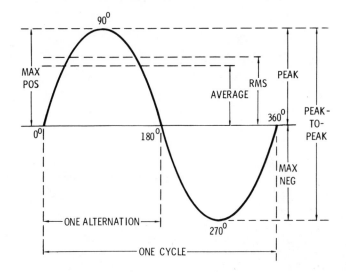

RMS   = 0.707 x PEAK VOLTAGE
RMS   = 1.11 x AVERAGE VOLTAGE
RMS   = 0.3535 x PEAK-TO-PEAK VOLTAGE
PEAK   = 1.414 x RMS VOLTAGE
PEAK   = 1.57 x AVERAGE VOLTAGE
PEAK-TO-PEAK   = 2.828 x RMS VOLTAGE
AVERAGE   = 0.637 x PEAK VOLTAGE
AVERAGE   = 0.9 x RMS VOLTAGE

Fig. 2-17. Sine-wave voltage values.

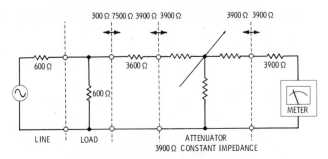

Fig. 2-18. VI meter circuit.

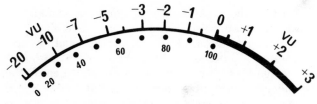

(A) Used in recording studio.

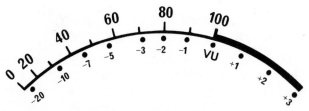

(B) Used in broadcasting.

Fig. 2-19. VI meter scales.

meter uses a 50-μA D'Arsonval movement in conjunction with a copper-oxide bridge-type rectifier. The impedance of the meter and rectifier is 3900 ohms, and to minimize its effect when placed across a 600-ohm line, it is "built-out" an additional 3600 ohms to a total value of 7500 ohms. The addition of this build-out resistance causes a 4-dB loss between the circuit being measured and the meter. Therefore, when a properly installed VI meter is fed with 0 dBm across a 600-ohm line, the meter would actually read −4 VU on its scale. (When the attenuator setting is added, the total reading is indeed 0 VU.)

Two different types of scales are available for VI meters (Fig. 2-19). Scale A is a volume unit scale (recording studio use), and scale B is a modulation scale (broadcast use). On complex waveforms (speech and music), the readings observed and the peak levels present are about 10 dB apart. This means that with a mixer amplifier having a sine-wave output capability of +18 dBm, you are in danger of distortion with any signal indicating more than +8 VU on the VI meter (+18 dBm − 10-dB peaking factor = +8 VU).

Fig. 2-20 shows examples of commercially available VI meter panels that include the VI meter and 3900-ohm attenuator, which also contains the 3600-ohm build-out resistor.

RATING MICROPHONES IN dBm

The effective output level of a microphone can most easily be determined by measuring the open-circuit voltage produced by a sound pressure level of 10 dynes/cm² (94 dB-SPL) at the microphone diaphragm and then using the following equation, inserting the rated (or measured) impedance of the microphone. (See Fig. 2-21.)

Microphone rating in equivalent

$$\text{dBm} = 10 \log \left(\frac{E^2}{0.001Z} \right) - 6 \, \text{dB} \qquad (2\text{-}60)$$

To find the open-circuit voltage of a microphone rated in this manner,

$$E = \sqrt{0.001Z \times 10^{\frac{\text{dBm} + 6}{10}}} \qquad (2\text{-}61)$$

Other methods of microphone rating will be discussed in Chapter 6.

There are several good reasons for measuring the *open-circuit* voltage:

1. If the open-circuit voltage and the microphone impedance are known, the microphone performance can be calculated for any condition of loading.
2. It corresponds to an effective condition of use. A microphone should face a high impedance to yield maximum signal-to-noise ratio.
3. When the microphone faces an impedance high

Fig. 2-20. Examples of commercially available VI meter panels.

Fig. 2-21. Measurement of open-circuit voltage.

compared with its own, variations in microphone impedance do not cause variations in response.

Because the quantity $10 \log \left(\dfrac{E^2}{0.001Z} \right)$ treats the open-circuit voltage as if it appears across a load, it is necessary to subtract 6 dB (the reading is 6 dB higher than it would have been had a load been present).

CALCULATING WITH PHONS AND SONES

1. For two sounds within the same critical bandwidth, add the phon levels as you would dB-SPL levels

Combined level in phons

$$= 10 \log \left(10^{\frac{\text{Phons}}{10}} + 10^{\frac{\text{Phons}}{10}} \right) \qquad (2\text{-}62)$$

Change to sones by:

$$S = 2^{\left(\frac{\text{Phons} - 40}{10} \right)} \qquad (2\text{-}63)$$

Example:

$$10 \log \left(10^{\frac{70}{10}} + 10^{\frac{70}{10}} \right) = 73 \text{ Phons} \qquad (2\text{-}64)$$

$$2^{\left(\frac{73 - 40}{10} \right)} = 9.85 \text{ Sones} \left(\begin{smallmatrix} \text{Subjective judgment} \\ \text{``just barely louder''} \end{smallmatrix} \right) \qquad (2\text{-}65)$$

2. For two sounds separated in frequency by more than a critical bandwidth, change phon levels into sones and then add. For example:

$$2^{\left(\frac{70 - 40}{10} \right)} + 2^{\left(\frac{70 - 40}{10} \right)} = 16 \text{ Sones} \qquad (2\text{-}66)$$

3. To change sones back into phons:

$$10 \left(\frac{\ln \text{ Sones}}{\ln 2} \right) + 40 = \text{Phons} \qquad (2\text{-}67)$$

$$10 \left(\frac{\ln 16}{\ln 2} \right) + 40 = 80 \text{ Phons} \left(\begin{smallmatrix} \text{Subjective judgment} \\ \text{``twice as loud''} \end{smallmatrix} \right)$$

$$(2\text{-}68)$$

This effect explains why distortion (widely spaced frequency components) causes such an apparent increase in loudness in a sound system.

Fig. 2-22 shows free-field equal-loudness contours for pure tones (observer facing source), determined by Robinson and Dadson in 1956 at the National Physical Laboratory, Teddington, England. (ISO/R226-1961.) The piano keyboard below the chart helps identify the frequency scale; only the fundamental frequency of each piano key is indicated. Fig. 2-23 is a graph relating loudness in sones to sound pressure level.

THE ACOUSTICAL MEANING OF HARMONIC DISTORTION

The availability of extremely wide-band amplifiers with distortions approaching the infinitesimal and the gradual engineering of a limited number of loudspeakers with distortions just under 1% at usable levels (90 to 100 dB-SPL at 10 or 12 feet) brings up an interesting question: "How low a distortion is actually needed?"

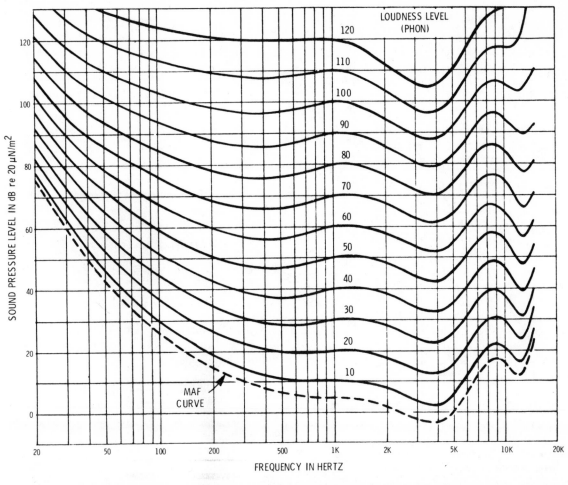

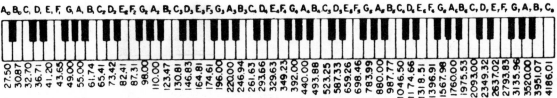

Fig. 2-22. Equal-loudness contours.

Measuring Distortion

Fig. 2-24 illustrates one of the ways of measuring harmonic distortion. Two main methods are employed. One uses a band-rejection filter of narrow bandwidth having a rejection capability of at least 80 dB in the center of the notch. This deep notch "rejects" the fundamental of the test signal (usually a known-quality sine wave from a test audio oscillator) and permits reading the noise voltage of everything remaining in the rest of the bandpass. Unfortunately, this also includes the hum and noise as well as the harmonic content of the equipment being tested. See Fig. 2-25.

The second method is more useful. It uses a tunable wave analyzer. This instrument allows the "tuning" of the amplitudes of the fundamental and each harmonic,

as well as identifying the hum amplitude and the noise spectrum shape (Fig. 2-25).

Such analyzers come in many different bandwidths, with a $1/10$-octave unit allowing readings down to 1% of the fundamental (it is −45 dB at 2f). By looking at Fig. 2-25, it is easy to see that harmonic distortion appears as a spurious signal and could conceivably be masked by ambient noise.

Calculating the Maximum Allowable Total Harmonic Distortion in an Arena Sound System

The most difficult parameter to achieve in the typical arena sound system is sufficient signal-to-noise ratio to ensure acceptable articulation losses for consonants in speech. It must be *at least* 25 dB. In that case, the total harmonic distortion should be at least 10 dB below the

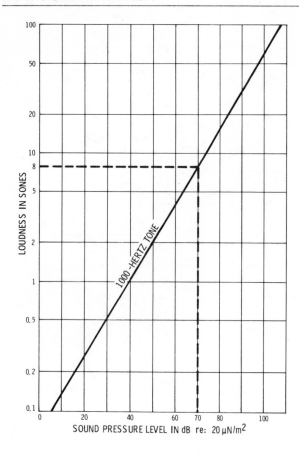

Fig. 2-23. Graph relating loudness in sones to sound pressure level in decibels referred to 20 μN/m².

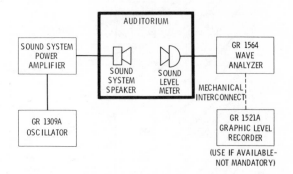

Fig. 2-24. Measurement of harmonic distortion.

$$\text{Percentage} = 100 \times 10^{\frac{\pm dB}{20}} \qquad (2\text{-}69)$$

Therefore, we could calculate:

$$100 \times 10^{\frac{-35}{20}} = 1.78\% \qquad (2\text{-}70)$$

This is, of course, why carefully thought-out designs for use in heavy-duty commercial sound work have a thd of 0.8 to 0.9%.

$$20 \log \left(\frac{100 \pm x\%}{100} \right) = dB \text{ change} \qquad (2\text{-}71)$$

Since the 0.8% already represents $(100 - 99.2)$, we can write

$$20 \log \left(\frac{0.8}{100} \right) = -42 \text{ dB} \qquad (2\text{-}72)$$

Now, suppose an amplifier has 0.001% distortion. What sort of a dynamic range would you need to handle?

$$20 \log \left(\frac{0.001}{100} \right) = -100 \text{ dB} \qquad (2\text{-}73)$$

25 dB s/n ratio to avoid the addition of the two signals. If both signals were at the same level, a 3-dB increase in level would occur. Therefore, $(-25 \text{ dB}) + (-10 \text{ dB})$ means that the thd should not exceed -35 dB.

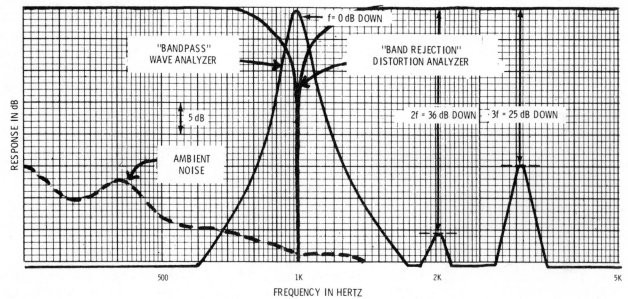

Fig. 2-25. Readout from graphic level recorder.

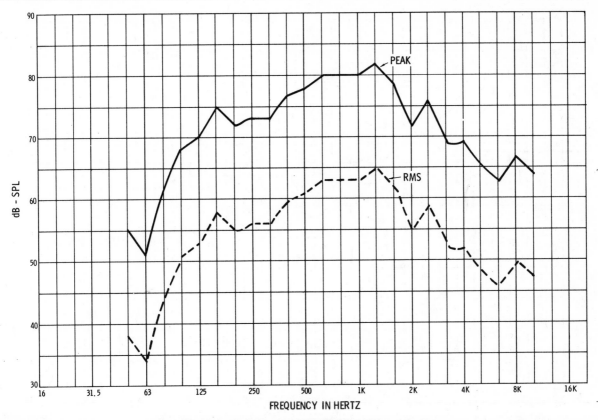

Fig. 2-26. Male speech, normal level 2 feet from microphone.

That is a power ratio of

$$10^{\frac{100}{10}} = 10{,}000{,}000{,}000 \qquad (2\text{-}74)$$

We can conclude that if such a figure were achievable, it would nevertheless not be useful in arena systems.

Playback Systems in Studios

Assume that a monitor loudspeaker can develop 110 dB-SPL at the mixer's ears and that in an exceptionally quiet studio we reach 18 dB-SPL at 2000 Hz (NC-20). We then have 110 dB-SPL − 18 dB-SPL = 92 dB. Adding 10 dB to avoid the inadvertent addition of levels gives 102 dB.

$$100 \times 10^{\frac{-102}{20}} = 0.00079\% \qquad (2\text{-}75)$$

In this case, extraordinary as it is, the previously esoteric figure becomes a useful parameter.

Choosing an Amplifier

As was pointed out earlier, the loudspeaker will establish equilibrium around 1% with its acoustic distortion. To the builder of *systems,* this means that extremely low distortion figures cannot be utilized within the system as a whole. Therefore, a systems-oriented amplifier designer has not attempted to extend his bandpass to extreme limits. He knows that he must balance bandpass, distortion, noise, and hum against stability with all types of loads, extension of mean-time-before-failure characteristics, and versatility of outputs —70 volts, 25 volts, and 0.5 Ω.

EXAMPLE
Let the rms speech value be 65 dB-SPL at 2 feet in the 1000-2000 Hz octave band (Fig. 2-26). Let the ambient noise level be 32 dB-SPL with the air conditioning on and 16 dB-SPL with the air conditioning off in the 1000-2000 Hz octave band (Fig. 2-27).

$$\text{s/n} = 65 - 32 = 33 \text{ dB, A/C on} \qquad (2\text{-}76)$$

and

$$\text{s/n} = 65 - 16 = 49 \text{ dB, A/C off} \qquad (2\text{-}77)$$

For a harmonic to be equal to −33 dB, its percentage would be

$$100 \times 10^{\frac{-33}{20}} = 2.24\% \qquad (2\text{-}78)$$

For a harmonic to be equal to −49 dB, its percentage would be

$$100 \times 10^{\frac{-49}{20}} = 0.355\% \qquad (2\text{-}79)$$

In measuring distortion, two types of analyzers are employed.

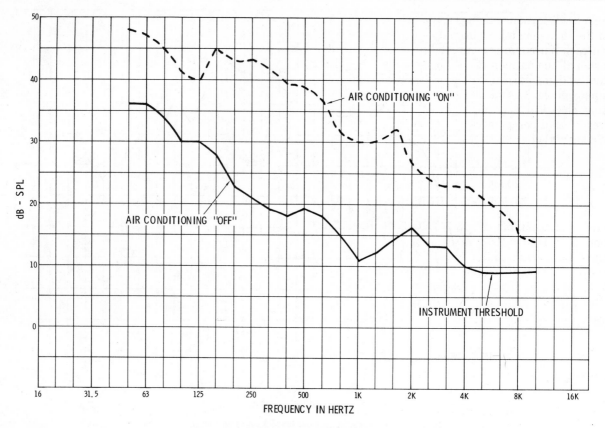

Fig. 2-27. Ambient noise levels (living room).

1. The band-rejection type of filter
   (This rejects the test fundamental and indicates on a wideband voltmeter the sum of everything that is left. This includes—in addition to harmonic distortion—hum, noise, etc.)
2. The bandpass type of filter
   (This is essentially a tunable voltmeter that reads the amplitudes by frequency of the test signal and each component extraneous to the test signal.)

With the second type of analyzer, it is easy to see the signal-to-noise ratio between the desired signal and the harmonic-distortion components and whether or not normal ambient noise provides masking of them.

RATING LOUDSPEAKERS IN dB

The use of the dB in rating loudspeakers is not standardized, but three methods predominate:

1. *W.E. Method*
   x dB-SPL at 4 feet with an electrical input of 1 watt
2. *Jensen Method*
   x dB-SPL at 10 feet with an electrical input of 1 watt
3. *EIA Method*
   x dB-SPL at 30 feet with an electrical input of 1 milliwatt (0.001 watt)

Two factors are required in each of these methods:

1. A reference distance
2. A reference power

The following simple examples should help acquaint you with each method. Using the W.E. system, let us rate a loudspeaker as 99 dB-SPL at 4 feet with 1 watt of electrical input. To convert this rating to the Jensen method:

$$20 \log \frac{4 \text{ ft}}{10 \text{ ft}} = -8 \text{ dB} \qquad (2\text{-}80)$$

$$99 \text{ dB-SPL} - 8 \text{ dB} = 91 \text{ dB-SPL} \qquad (2\text{-}81)$$

Then the equivalent Jensen-method rating is 91 dB-SPL. To convert to the EIA method:

$$10 \log_{10} 0.001 \text{ watt} = -30 \text{ dB, and}$$

$$20 \log \frac{4}{30} = -17 \text{ dB} \qquad (2\text{-}82)$$

$$99 \text{ dB-SPL} - (47 \text{ dB}) = 52 \text{ dB-SPL} \qquad (2\text{-}83)$$

The EIA rating is then 52 dB-SPL.

DECIBELS AND PERCENTAGES

The comparison of data in decibels often needs to be expressed as percentages. The measurement of total harmonic distortion (thd) compares the harmonics with the fundamental. After finding out how many dB down each harmonic is compared to the fundamental, you sum all the harmonics and then compare their sum to the fundamental value. The difference is expressed as a percentage. The efficiency of a loudspeaker in converting electrical energy to acoustical energy is also expressed as a percentage.

We know that

$$20 \log 10 = 20 \text{ dB} \qquad (2\text{-}84)$$
$$20 \log 100 = 40 \text{ dB} \qquad (2\text{-}85)$$
$$20 \log 1000 = 60 \text{ dB} \qquad (2\text{-}86)$$

Therefore, a signal of −20 dB is 1/10 of the fundamental, or $100 \times 1/10 = 10\%$. A signal of −40 dB is 1/100 of the fundamental, or $100 \times 1/100 = 1\%$. A signal of −60 dB is 1/1000 of the fundamental, or $100 \times 1/1000 = 0.1\%$. We can now turn this into a formula for finding the percentage when the level difference in dB is known. For voltage, SPL, distance, etc., ratios:

$$\text{Percentage} = 100 \times 10^{\frac{\pm dB}{20}} \qquad (2\text{-}87)$$

For power ratios:

$$\text{Percentage} = 100 \times 10^{\frac{\pm dB}{10}} \qquad (2\text{-}88)$$

Occasionally you are presented with two percentages and need the decibel difference between them. For example, two loudspeakers of otherwise identical specifications have differing efficiencies; one is 0.1% efficient and the other is 25% efficient. If the same wattage is fed to both speakers, what will be the difference in level between them in decibels?

Since we are now talking about efficiency, we are talking about *power* ratios, not voltage ratios. We know that:

$$10 \log 10 = 10 \qquad (2\text{-}89)$$
$$10 \log 100 = 20 \qquad (2\text{-}90)$$
$$10 \log 1000 = 30 \qquad (2\text{-}91)$$

and so forth. A 0.1% efficiency is a power ratio of 1000 to 1, or −30 dB. We also know that −3 dB is 50% of a signal, so −6 dB would be 25%; $-30 - (-6) = -24$ dB. In other words, there would be a 24-dB difference in level between these two loudspeakers when fed by the same signal. Some home-type hi-fi loudspeakers vary this much in efficiency.

We can now write the formulas for converting percentage differences into decibel equivalents. For voltage, SPL, distance, etc., ratios:

$$dB = 20 \log \left(\frac{x\%}{100} \right) \qquad (2\text{-}92)$$

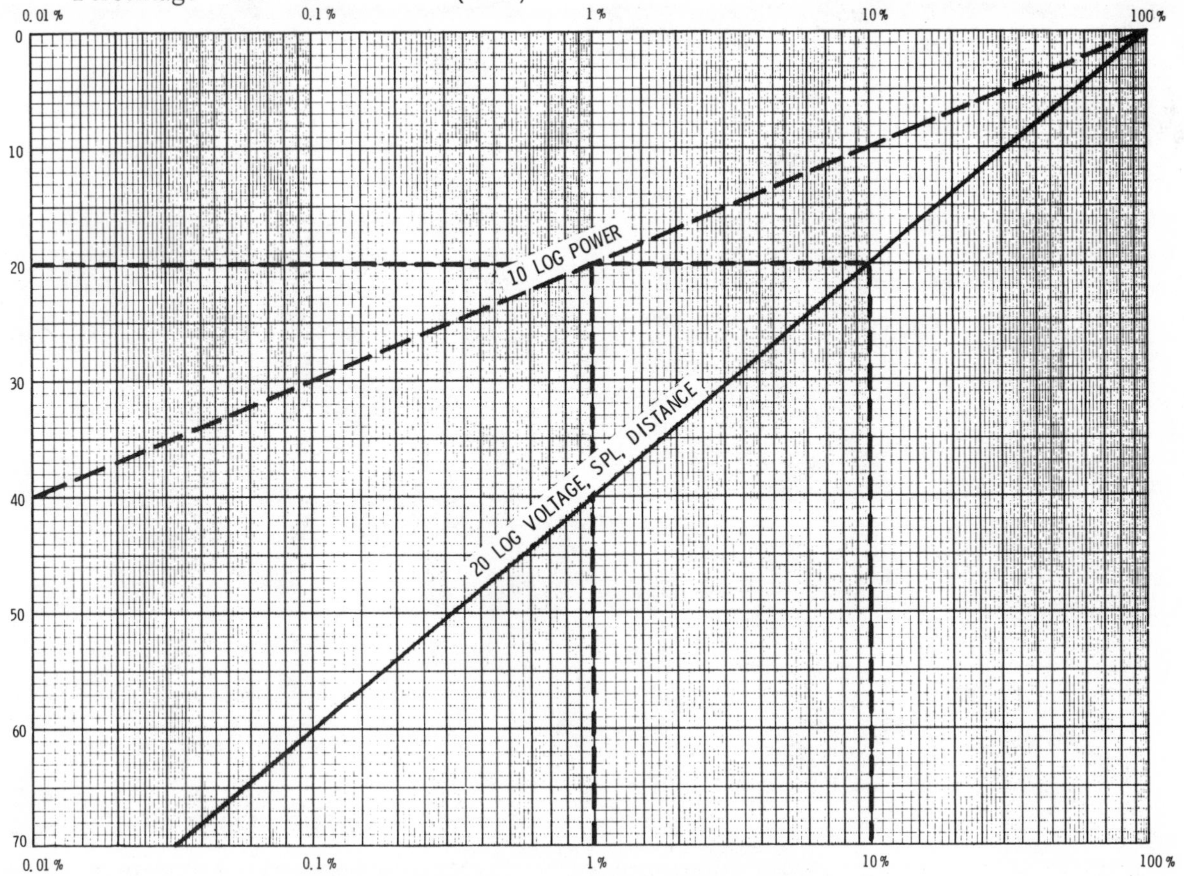

Fig. 2-28. Relationship of decibels and percentages.

For power ratios:

$$dB = 10 \log \left(\frac{x\%}{100} \right) \qquad (2\text{-}93)$$

If you wished to know how many decibels to adjust a circuit to for a voltage change of a given percentage, you would write:

$$dB \text{ change} = 20 \log \left(\frac{100 \pm \% \text{ Change}}{100} \right) \quad (2\text{-}94)$$

For a power change, you would use:

$$dB \text{ change} = 10 \log \left(\frac{100 \pm \% \text{ Change}}{100} \right) \quad (2\text{-}95)$$

For example, a 25% drop in power would equal

$$10 \log \left(\frac{100 - 25}{100} \right) = -1.25 \, dB \qquad (2\text{-}96)$$

Fig. 2-28 shows the relationship between decibels and percentages for power and for voltage, current, SPL, distance, etc. For example, a surface that absorbs 20 dB-SPL of a signal has reduced the power by 99% (1% remains) and the SPL by 90% (10% remains).

This discussion of the basics of the decibel and some typical uses, while not exhaustive, serves as a useful review for the person already expert in its use and as a firm base for the person seeking to develop and expand his capabilities with this most useful tool.

CHAPTER 3

Loudspeaker Directivity and Coverage

Two of the most important parameters of a loudspeaker are its useful *coverage angle*, $C_\angle$, and its *directivity ratio*, Q. The directivity ratio is often called R_θ or *directivity factor*, D_f. These factors are independent of each other to a large degree, and both vary with frequency.

LOUDSPEAKER COVERAGE ($C_\angle$)

Fig. 3-1 illustrates patterns for loudspeakers having the same $C_\angle$ for a given plane but with differing Q. Fig. 3-2 shows patterns for loudspeakers having the same Q but different $C_\angle$. It can be seen that the $C_\angle$ assigned to a given plane of radiation is that angle formed by the −6-dB points (referred to the on-axis reading) and the source center.

The −6-dB point is of interest to the sound engineer inasmuch as that angle should, in the ideal case, intersect the audience area halfway back to the source as compared to where the on-axis beam intersects the audience. We will discuss this aspect of coverage at length in Chapter 6.

The $C_\angle$ should be specified for as many planes as are felt necessary. The usual case is to specify it for the horizontal and vertical planes.

LOUDSPEAKER DIRECTIVITY RATIO (Q)

If it were possible to construct a perfect loudspeaker which radiated sound energy only over its $C_\angle$ and nowhere else, then it would be possible to describe its Q from its $C_\angle$. While this is not the case in real-life loudspeakers, it is useful to *imagine* such a case in order to gain a conceptual view of what Q is and how it affects the results we wish to achieve with the loudspeaker.

Definition of Q

First, let us turn to a rigorous, authoritative definition of Q. In Appendix V of the Seventh Edition of the *Handbook of Noise Measurement* by Arnold P. G. Peterson and Ervin E. Gross Jr., the directivity ratio (called directivity factor, Q, in their text) is defined as follows: "The directivity factor of a transducer used for sound emission is the ratio of sound pressure squared, at some fixed distance and specified direction, to the mean squared sound pressure at the same distance averaged over all directions from the transducer. The distance must be great enough so that the sound appears to diverge spherically from the effective acoustic center of the source. Unless otherwise specified, the *reference direction* is understood to be that of maximum response."[1]

In a note to the above definition, the following additional statement is made: "This definition may be extended to cover the case of finite frequency bands whose spectrum may be specified. The average free field response may be obtained, for example, by integration of *one or two* directional patterns *whenever* the pattern of the transducer is known to possess *adequate symmetry*."

Fortunately, high-quality commercial sound loudspeakers do usually possess adequate symmetry to allow acceptable accuracy with a vertical and horizontal polar response. In cases where the polar response of the loudspeaker is unusually "lobed," diagonal polar plots can be taken in addition to the usual horizontal and vertical plots.

---

[1] Arnold P. G. Peterson has asked the author to point out that while the author uses various forms of Q to explain room effects, it should be kept in mind that *only* axial Q is recognized as a property of the loudspeaker by acoustic authorities.

An Ideal Case—Geometric Q

To begin, imagine a perfect spherical radiation pattern from a loudspeaker—and imagine is all you realistically can do with real-life loudspeakers. Fig. 3-3 illustrates the spherical surface surrounding such a source. In this case, the average SPL expressed in dB-SPL for the entire surface would equal the dB-SPL measured on any specified axis. Therefore, the directivity ratio would be unity. We could then say $Q = 1$.

The next logical question is, "What $C_\angle$ should such a loudspeaker be given?" Nine out of ten people given this question tend to reply intuitively, "$360° \times 360°$," which again proves why the scientific method has outdistanced Aristotelian logic. If a radius is swung $360°$ around a point, a flat two dimensional circle is inscribed. By putting this flat circular surface on gimbals and sweeping it $180°$, the circumference sweeps out the surface area of a sphere. Therefore, a perfect spherically radiating loudspeaker could be specified as having a $C_\angle$ of $360° \times 180°$.

POWER AND SPL OUTPUT OF A SPHERICAL LOUDSPEAKER

Since we have already imagined one impossibility, a perfect spherically radiating loudspeaker, let us imagine it has an additional impossible specification, that of being 100% efficient. If one electrical watt is put into it, one acoustical watt is radiated into the space surrounding it. We now pick a standard measuring distance of four feet from our theoretical sound source so that the general discussion of theory here relates to measured data from real loudspeakers that will be discussed later.

There is an acoustic power reference level, 10^{-12} watt. Therefore, the PWL expressed in dB-PWL is:

$$dB\text{-}PWL = 10 \log \frac{watts}{10^{-12} \, watts} \quad (3\text{-}1)$$

or

$$dB\text{-}PWL = 10 \log watts + 120 \, dB$$

Therefore, a 1-watt acoustic radiator has a PWL rating of

$$10 \log 1 + 120 \, dB = 120 \, dB\text{-}PWL \quad (3\text{-}2)$$

This establishes the reference level in dB-PWL that will approximately equal a level in dB-SPL at a specified measuring distance, in this case, 0.283 meter. We can write:

$$dB\text{-}SPL = dB\text{-}PWL + 10 \log Q - 20 \log r - 0.5 \, dB \quad (3\text{-}3)$$

where,
Q is 1 (the perfect sphere),
r is 4 feet,
0.5 is a correction factor for $0.283 \, m \cong 0.93 \, ft$.

Then,

$$dB\text{-}SPL = 120 \, dB + 10 \log 1 - 20 \log 4 - 0.5 \, dB$$

$$= 107.47 \, dB\text{-}SPL \quad (3\text{-}4)$$

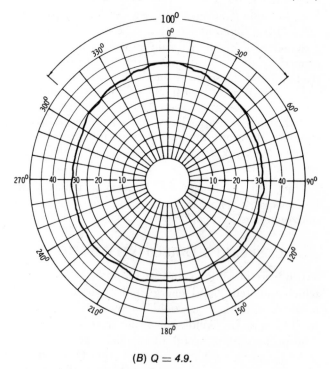

(A) Q = 3.5.

(B) Q = 4.9.

Fig. 3-1. Polar response charts for loudspeakers with useful

This figure, 107.47 dB-SPL, is interesting because it is the level a loudspeaker having a Q of 1 would produce at 4 feet *if* the loudspeaker were 100% efficient. (Note that efficiency is dependent on both Q and sensitivity.) If, for example, we were to apply 1 electrical watt as the input power to a loudspeaker having a Q of 1 and were to measure at 4 feet a dB-SPL of 101.47, we would then know that the loudspeaker was 25% efficient: 107.47 − 101.47 = 6 dB (−3 dB = half power, or 50%; and −6 dB = one quarter power, or 25%).

It is important to note that there are two reference levels commonly used. The newest is 10^{-12} watt, and the earlier is 10^{-13} watt. The difference is the *distance* at which the SPL equals the PWL.

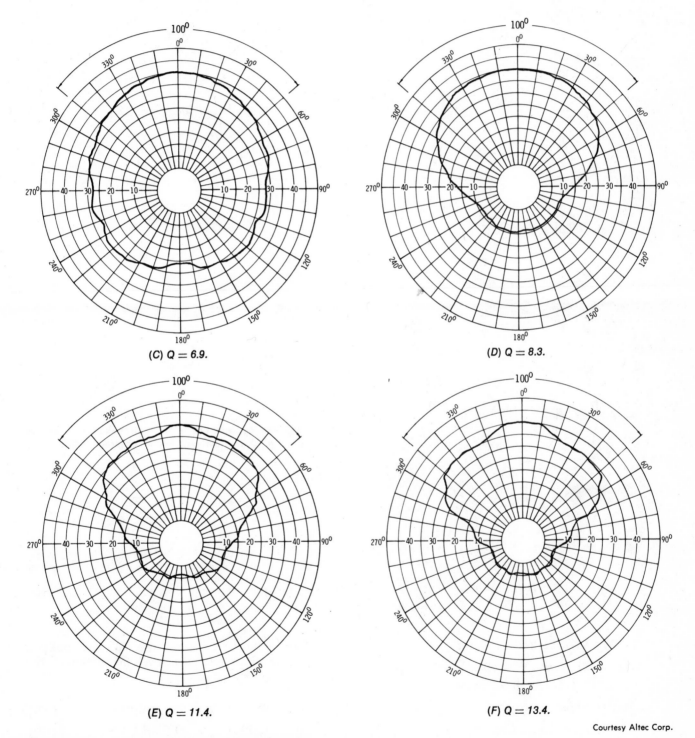

(C) Q = 6.9.

(D) Q = 8.3.

(E) Q = 11.4.

(F) Q = 13.4.

Courtesy Altec Corp.

coverage angle of 100° but different directivity ratios (Q).

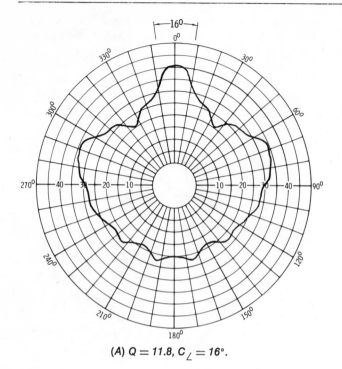

(A) $Q = 11.8$, $C_{\angle} = 16°$.

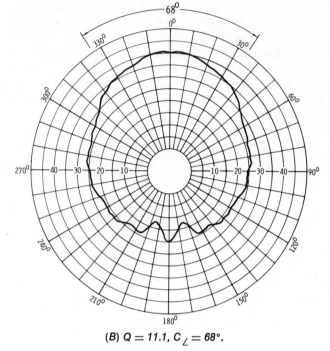

(B) $Q = 11.1$, $C_{\angle} = 68°$.

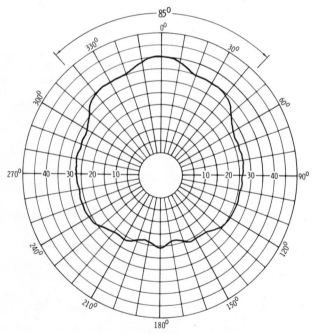

(C) $Q = 11.4$, $C_{\angle} = 85°$.

Courtesy Altec Corp.

Fig. 3-2. Polar response charts for loudspeakers with similar values of Q but different useful coverage angles.

10^{-12}-Watt Reference Level

dB-SPL $\cong$ dB-PWL at 0.282 meter (3-5)

dB-PWL $= 120$ dB at 0.282 meter (3-6)

10^{-13}-Watt Reference Level

dB-SPL $\cong$ dB-PWL at 0.282 feet (3-7)

dB-PWL $= 130$ dB at 0.282 feet (3-8)

When researching articles that use PWL, be sure you understand which reference level the writer of the article used.

dB-PWL$_{-12}$ $+ 10 \cong$ dB-PWL$_{-13}$ (3-9)

dB-PWL$_{-13}$ $- 10 \cong$ dB-PWL$_{-12}$ (3-10)

(When distances are in feet)

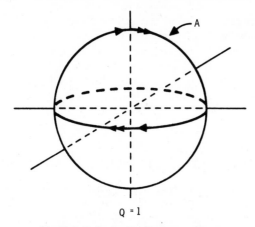

Fig. 3-3. Spherical radiation surface.

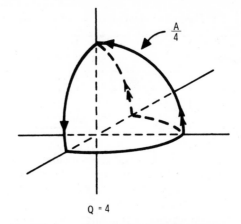

Fig. 3-5. A quarter-spherical radiation surface.

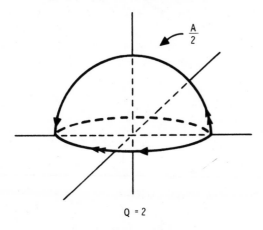

Fig. 3-4. A hemispherical radiation surface.

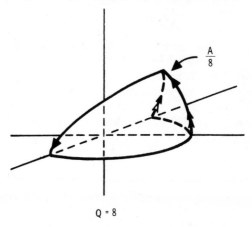

Fig. 3-6. An eighth-spherical radiation surface.

A HEMISPHERICAL RADIATOR

Fig. 3-4 illustrates a common real-life situation: a sound source with a Q of 2. (Ceiling-mounted loudspeakers will radiate hemispherically at low frequencies.) In this case, $C_\angle$ becomes 180° × 180°, and 1 watt of acoustic power now flows through ½ the area it had to flow through in the case of the spherical radiator. If the same power now flows through ½ the area, then *the power per unit area is doubled*. Double the power is +3 dB. Therefore, we would logically expect to see the SPL reading change accordingly:

$$\text{dB-SPL} = 120 \text{ dB} + 10 \log 2 - 20 \log 4 - 0.5 \text{ dB}$$
$$= 110.47 \text{ dB-SPL} \qquad (3\text{-}11)$$

DIRECTIVITY INDEX

It becomes apparent from the above that as the Q is increased, the on-axis SPL of a sound source is increased, so long as the same acoustic power is being developed. This can be written as

$$D_I = 10 \log Q \qquad (3\text{-}12)$$

where D_I is the directivity index in dB.

Then, of course, another way of expressing Q is apparent:

$$Q = 10^{\frac{D_I}{10}} \qquad (3\text{-}13)$$

$C_\angle$, Q, AND D_I FOR SPHERICAL SEGMENTS

Figs. 3-5 and 3-6 depict a quarter of a sphere and an eighth of a sphere. We can now construct a table summarizing these idealized segments and their basic parameters (Table 3-1). Always keep in mind, however, that real-life loudspeakers do not follow these simple relationships.

RELATIONSHIP BETWEEN $C_\angle$ AND Q IN IDEALIZED CASE

Fig. 3-7 is intended to further assist you in developing a conceptual view of Q and D_I in terms of $C_\angle$. Fig. 3-7A shows the angular distribution of a point source defined as the angles formed by the interception of two spherical surface segments. This figure shows what the Q and D_I would be for various combinations of $C_\angle$ if *all* radiation were confined to the angular coverage

Table 3-1. Basic Parameters of Spherical Segments

Segment of Sphere	$C_{\angle}$	Q	dB-SPL	D_I
Sphere	360° × 180°	1	107.47	0 dB
Hemisphere	180° × 180°	2	110.47	3 dB
1/4 sphere	180° × 90°	4	113.47	6 dB
1/8 sphere	180° × 45°	8	116.47	9 dB

shown. So, while looking at these idealized coverages remember that real loudspeakers *with these same coverage angles* also have side, back, top, and bottom lobes that lower the Q, often drastically.

Fig. 3-7B shows that an idealized cone loudspeaker column ($C_{\angle} = 180° \times 40°$ would be limited to a Q of 9. This is because with cones the horizontal coverage would be close to 180°, and, while the vertical beam narrows, it does not become narrower than 40° anywhere in the useful frequency spectrum. Again, keep in mind that this would be for a perfect unit that had *no* back, side, top, or bottom radiation.

As a constrast, if we examine an idealized multicellular horn ($C_{\angle} = 40° \times 40°$), then theoretically Q = 26. This, again, assumes that no back, side, top, or bottom radiation exists.

Of greatest interest to the sound engineer is the fact that raising Q will give useful on-axis increases in SPL. For example, in the case of the ideal column versus the ideal multicell, a D_I of approximately 14 minus a D_I of 9.5 = 4.5 dB of useful on-axis sensitivity improvement. The multicell would allow the necessary power requirement to be almost 1/3 less than that of the sound column.

IDEALIZED LOUDSPEAKER GEOMETRY

Loudspeaker directional geometry is of interest to the audio engineer because it allows the development of relative areas associated with different $C_{\angle}$. The basic formula for finding Q in the idealized case of all energy passing through $C_{\angle}$ is:

$$Q = \frac{180}{\arcsin\left[\left(\sin\frac{\theta}{2}\right) \times \left(\sin\frac{\phi}{2}\right)\right]} \quad (3\text{-}14)$$

Since Q is the inverse of area, we can then write:

$$\text{Area} = \frac{\arcsin\left[\left(\sin\frac{\theta}{2}\right) \times \left(\sin\frac{\phi}{2}\right)\right]}{180} \quad (3\text{-}15)$$

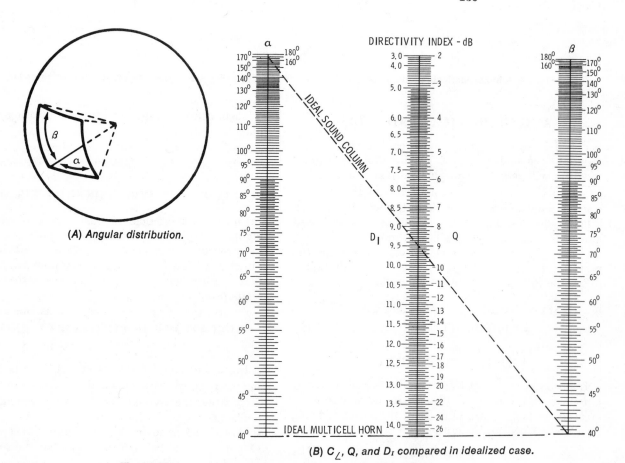

(A) Angular distribution.

(B) $C_{\angle}$, Q, and D_I compared in idealized case.

Fig. 3-7. Coverage angles, directivity ratio, and directivity index.

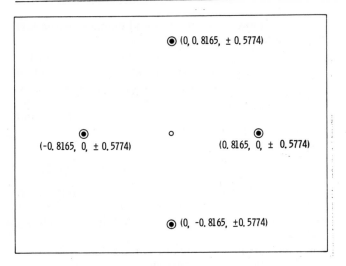

(A) Eight points.

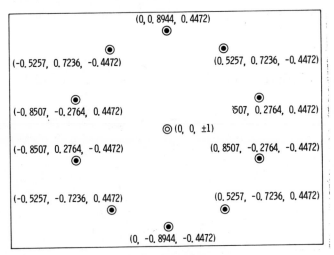

(B) Twelve points.

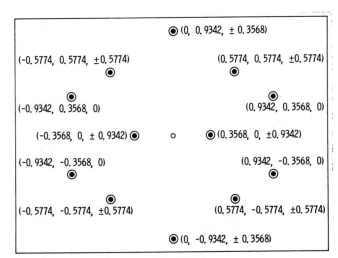

(C) Twenty points.

Fig. 3-8. Plan views of points uniformly distributed on the surface of a sphere of unit radius.

To obtain an idealized square pattern:

$$Q = \frac{180}{\text{arc sin} \left[\sin^2 \frac{\alpha}{2} \right]} \qquad (3\text{-}16)$$

If, on the other hand, you had a desired Q and needed to know the ideal square pattern for that Q, you could write:

$$\alpha = 2 \text{ arc sin} \sqrt{\sin \frac{180}{Q}} \qquad (3\text{-}17)$$

Arbitrary horizontal or vertical coverage angles may be assigned and the missing angle calculated by:

$$\text{Angle} = 2 \text{ arc sin} \frac{\sin^2 \frac{\alpha}{2}}{\sin \frac{\gamma}{2}} \qquad (3\text{-}18)$$

where,

α is the angle for a square pattern having the desired Q,

γ is the arbitrary angle.

When Q is less than 2, one angle becomes 180°, and the other angle is between 180° and 360°:

$$Q = \frac{360°}{\text{angle} > 180°} \qquad (3\text{-}19)$$

These geometrical equations are useful in determining the minimum apparent Q that could theoretically be associated with a given requirement of $C_{\angle}$.

CLASSIC METHOD OF OBTAINING AXIAL Q

In the noise-measurement field, a relatively standard measurement procedure has been in effect since 1953 (first outlined by Gross and Peterson in the 1953 edition of their *Noise Measurement Handbook* and later widely accepted). This method calls for a series of measuring points spaced about the sound source so as to allow each measuring point to represent an *equal area* on the surface of the sphere. Because of the nature of such geometric patterns, only six such sets of uniformly distributed points are possible. These six sets have 2, 4, 6, 8, 12, and 20 uniformly distributed points. Fig. 3-8 illustrates plan views of such points. The coordinates are given in terms of distances from the center along three mutually perpendicular axes (x, y, z). The "±" refers to the existence of two points, one above the x-y reference plane and one below. When measurements are to be made on a hemisphere, only the four points above the plane are used. Fig. 3-9 shows how such coordinates are utilized to find the desired points.

The length of the vector to the point is found by:

$$\text{Vector length} = \sqrt{x^2 + y^2 + z^2} \qquad (3\text{-}20)$$

The angle between the x axis and the vector is found by:

$$\text{Angle} = \text{arc cos}(Z \text{ vector}) \qquad (3\text{-}21)$$

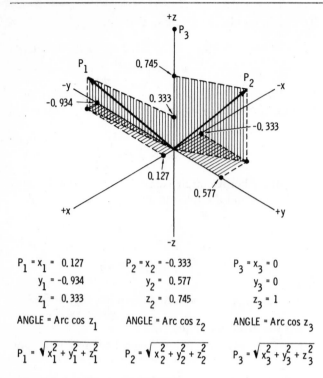

$$P_1 = x_1 = 0.127 \qquad P_2 = x_2 = -0.333 \qquad P_3 = x_3 = 0$$
$$y_1 = -0.934 \qquad y_2 = 0.577 \qquad y_3 = 0$$
$$z_1 = 0.333 \qquad z_2 = 0.745 \qquad z_3 = 1$$

$$\text{ANGLE} = \text{Arc cos } z_1 \qquad \text{ANGLE} = \text{Arc cos } z_2 \qquad \text{ANGLE} = \text{Arc cos } z_3$$

$$P_1 = \sqrt{x_1^2 + y_1^2 + z_1^2} \qquad P_2 = \sqrt{x_2^2 + y_2^2 + z_2^2} \qquad P_3 = \sqrt{x_3^2 + y_3^2 + z_3^2}$$

Fig. 3-9. Locating measuring points on a spherical surface.

The dB-SPL measured at each of the equal-area points is averaged by converting to power ratios, adding them (dividing them by 2 if only hemispherical measurements are taken, as is often the case), taking 10 times the logarithm of the sum of the powers, and subtracting 10 times the logarithm of the number of points sampled. This gives the average dB-SPL around the sound source being measured; this is identified as $\overline{\text{dB-SPL}}$:

$$\overline{\text{dB-SPL}} = 10 \log\left(10^{\frac{\text{dB-SPL}_1}{10}} + 10^{\frac{\text{dB-SPL}_2}{10}} + \ldots 10^{\frac{\text{dB-SPL}_n}{10}}\right)$$
$$- 10 \log (\text{number of points}) \qquad (3\text{-}22)$$

Then Q is found by taking the point of highest level (usually the on-axis point) and subtracting from it the $\overline{\text{dB-SPL}}$. The power antilog of this becomes Q.

$$Q = 10^{\frac{\text{dB-SPL (on-axis)} - \overline{\text{dB-SPL}}}{10}} \qquad (3\text{-}23)$$

This is called the *axial* Q. If some other point instead of the on-axis point is chosen, then the calculation becomes the *relative* Q. This may be further modified into *apparent* Q by multipliers that will be introduced later.

Manufacturers of loudspeakers have not used this method but rather have concentrated over the years on gathering polar response data, usually in the horizontal and vertical planes only. Various methods of utilizing such data in order to obtain Q have been tried over the years. While recognizing that the first attempts were crude, it should also be recognized that at the time the

cruder methods were used the alternative was no Q data at all.

MEASURING THE Q OF REAL LOUDSPEAKERS

Real-life loudspeakers radiate sound over the $C_\angle$ and out of the sides, top, and bottom. In order to find the axial Q, it is necessary to average the SPL over the entire space surrounding the source. The method proposed by the author is one derived out of work done by Ben Bauer, C. T. Molloy, and Bob Beavers. This method requires a horizontal and vertical polar plot for each of seven octave bands—125, 250, 500, 1000, 2000, 4000, and 8000 Hz.

Fortunately, octave intervals offer more than enough detail to allow accurate planning of the effect of Q on gain, articulation loss of consonants, etc. Also, fortunately, most commercial loudspeakers are sufficiently symmetrical in their polar responses to allow the use of

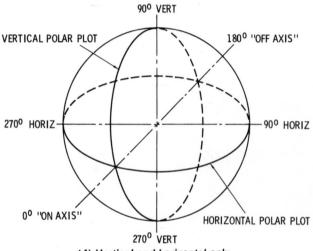

(A) Vertical and horizontal only.

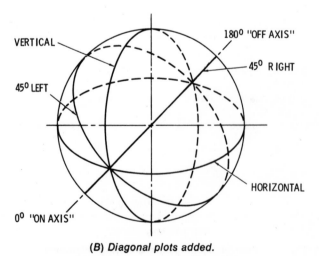

(B) Diagonal plots added.

Fig. 3-10. Polar response alignments.

a horizontal and vertical polar plot at each octave interval. In some rare cases, additional diagonal plots have to be taken. (See Fig. 3-10.)

Since both a vertical and a horizontal polar response are taken at each frequency, the manufacturer must then process fourteen polar plots in order to obtain the desired data for a particular loudspeaker.

PROCESSING THE POLAR PLOTS

The method of processing the polar plots is illustrated in Table 3-2. Starting at the 0° on-axis point of the polar plot, assign an arbitrary value of 100 dB to the 0° point. Tabulate the relative differences in level, referred to this level, for each 10° point all the way around the horizontal plot. Continue on the vertical plot in the same manner but skipping the 0° and 180° points (already recorded). Convert each dB-SPL level to a relative power ratio ("Rel SPL"). Multiply the ratio by a weighting factor proportional to the area surrounding the measuring point in terms of a sphere with a surface of unity. Total all the weighted power ratios ("SPL$_W$"). Then subtract 10 times the logarithm of the sum from the on-axis reading of 100 dB and take the power antilog. This is the axial Q. Fig. 3-11 shows three examples of computer printouts of the calculation of Q.

Figs. 3-12 and 3-13 depict two methods of dividing a sphere into relative areas surrounding each 10° point. Fig. 3-12 shows the zonal method (best for a cone loudspeaker or exactly symmetrical one-cell horns). Fig. 3-13 shows the quadrangle method (best for loudspeaker types other than a single cone or an exactly symmetrical one-cell horn). The dash lines are an extension of the great circles forming the boundaries of the areas under consideration. To avoid an overcrowded diagram, only a few such areas are shown in either view. Table 3-3 shows spherical areas, and Tables 3-4 and 3-5 show weighting factors for zonal and quadrangle areas.

Obviously, the same polar charts used to calculate Q can also be used to obtain C$_\angle$ (the 6-dB-down points from the on-axis reading expressed as an angle). During the calibration of the equipment for the polar responses, the on-axis sensitivity can be measured (the 4-foot, 1-watt rating).

The four primary measurements are:

1. Q in octave bands
2. C$_\angle$ in octave bands
3. Axial sensitivity in octave bands
4. Power handling (program levels)

THE PLANE-WAVE-TUBE METHOD OF MEASURING Q

The plane-wave-tube method of measuring Q allows sine waves, bands of noise, etc., to be used in testing

Table 3-2. Weighting Polar Data Taken at 10° Intervals to Correspond to Measurements Taken From Points Surrounded by Equal Surface Areas

Example Horizontal Polar Data at 1000 Hz

Angles	dB-SPL	Rel SPL	Weighting	SPL$_W$
0° (on axis)	100	1.000000×10^{10}	0.002418	2.418000×10^7
10° & 350°	99	7.943282×10^9	0.004730 (2)	7.514345×10^7
20° & 340°	97	5.011872×10^9	0.008955 (2)	8.976263×10^7
30° & 330°	96	3.981072×10^9	0.012387 (2)	9.862707×10^7
40° & 320°	94	2.511886×10^9	0.014990 (2)	7.530636×10^7
50° & 310°	93	1.995262×10^9	0.016868 (2)	6.731217×10^7
60° & 300°	93	1.995262×10^9	0.018166 (2)	7.249187×10^7
70° & 290°	92	1.584893×10^9	0.019007 (2)	6.024813×10^7
80° & 280°	91	1.258925×10^9	0.019478 (2)	4.904270×10^7
90° & 270°	88	6.309574×10^8	0.019630 (2)	2.477139×10^7
100° & 260°	86	3.981072×10^8	0.019478 (2)	1.550866×10^7
110° & 250°	85	3.162278×10^8	0.019007 (2)	1.202108×10^7
120° & 240°	85	3.162278×10^8	0.018166 (2)	1.148919×10^7
130° & 230°	83	1.995262×10^8	0.016868 (2)	6.731217×10^6
140° & 220°	82	1.584893×10^8	0.014990 (2)	4.751510×10^6
150° & 210°	81	1.258925×10^8	0.012387 (2)	3.118862×10^6
160° & 200°	80	1.000000×10^8	0.008955 (2)	1.791000×10^6
170° & 190°	80	1.000000×10^8	0.004730 (2)	9.460000×10^5
180° (off axis)	80	1.000000×10^8	0.002418	2.418000×10^5
			Total	6.934851×10^8

Example Vertical Polar Data at 1000 Hz

Angles	dB-SPL	Rel SPL	Weighting	SPL$_W$
10° & 350°	100	1.000000×10^{10}	0.004730 (2)	9.460000×10^7
20° & 340°	100	1.000000×10^{10}	0.008955 (2)	1.791000×10^8
30° & 330°	100	1.000000×10^{10}	0.012387 (2)	2.477400×10^8
40° & 320°	99	7.943282×10^9	0.014990 (2)	2.381396×10^8
50° & 310°	96	3.981072×10^9	0.016868 (2)	1.343054×10^8
60° & 300°	94	2.511886×10^9	0.018166 (2)	9.126186×10^7
70° & 290°	93	1.995262×10^9	0.019007 (2)	7.584790×10^7
80° & 280°	92	1.584893×10^9	0.019478 (2)	6.174110×10^7
90° & 270°	91	1.258925×10^9	0.019630 (2)	4.942541×10^7
100° & 260°	89	7.943282×10^8	0.019478 (2)	3.094385×10^7
110° & 250°	87	5.011872×10^8	0.019007 (2)	1.905213×10^7
120° & 240°	85	3.162278×10^8	0.018166 (2)	1.148919×10^7
130° & 230°	79	7.943282×10^7	0.016868 (2)	2.679746×10^6
140° & 220°	75	3.162278×10^7	0.014990 (2)	9.480509×10^5
150° & 210°	72	1.584893×10^7	0.012387 (2)	3.926414×10^5
160° & 200°	74	2.511886×10^7	0.008955 (2)	4.498789×10^5
170° & 190°	72	1.584893×10^7	0.004730 (2)	1.499309×10^5
			Total	1.238267×10^9

$$10 \log [6.934851 \times 10^8 + 1.238267 \times 10^9] = 92.86 \text{ dB-SPL}$$

$$10^{\left(\frac{100 - 92.86}{10}\right)} = 5.18 = Q \text{ at } 1000 \text{ Hz}$$

$$10 \log 5.18 = 7.14 \text{ dB} = D_I \text{ at } 1000 \text{ Hz}$$

transducers and their associated directional control devices (DCDs)—baffles, horns, etc.—to obtain Q. The method to be described can be particularly useful in the case of large low-frequency DCDs.

Description of Method

1. Obtain a free-field response curve at x distance on-axis from the transducer mounted on the DCD.

```
SYN-AUD-CON
DIRECTIVITY
FACTOR (Q)
PROGRAM

0 DEG.DB-SPL=
            100.0
10 DEG.DB-SPL=
            100.0
20 DEG.DB-SPL=
            100.0
30 DEG.DB-SPL=
            100.0
40 DEG.DB-SPL=
            100.0
50 DEG.DB-SPL=
            100.0
60 DEG.DB-SPL=
            100.0
70 DEG.DB-SPL=
            100.0
80 DEG.DB-SPL=
            100.0
90 DEG.DB-SPL=
            100.0
100 DEG.DB-SPL=
            100.0
110 DEG.DB-SPL=
            100.0
120 DEG.DB-SPL=
            100.0
130 DEG.DB-SPL=
            100.0
140 DEG.DB-SPL=
            100.0
150 DEG.DB-SPL=
            100.0
160 DEG.DB-SPL=
            100.0
170 DEG.DB-SPL=
            100.0
180 DEG.DB-SPL=
            100.0
```
HORIZONTAL DATA

```
10 DEG.DB-SPL=
            100.0
20 DEG.DB-SPL=
            100.0
30 DEG.DB-SPL=
            100.0
40 DEG.DB-SPL=
            100.0
50 DEG.DB-SPL=
            100.0
60 DEG.DB-SPL=
            100.0
70 DEG.DB-SPL=
            100.0
80 DEG.DB-SPL=
            100.0
90 DEG.DB-SPL=
            100.0
100 DEG.DB-SPL=
            100.0
110 DEG.DB-SPL=
            100.0
120 DEG.DB-SPL=
            100.0
130 DEG.DB-SPL=
            100.0
140 DEG.DB-SPL=
            100.0
150 DEG.DB-SPL=
            100.0
160 DEG.DB-SPL=
            100.0
170 DEG.DB-SPL=
            100.0
DB-SPL AVER.=
            100.0
DB-SPL DIRECT.=
            100.0
Q=
            1.0
```
VERTICAL DATA

(A) Spherical coverage.

```
SYN-AUD-CON
DIRECTIVITY
FACTOR (Q)
PROGRAM

0 DEG.DB-SPL=
            100.0
10 DEG.DB-SPL=
            100.0
20 DEG.DB-SPL=
            100.0
30 DEG.DB-SPL=
            100.0
40 DEG.DB-SPL=
            100.0
50 DEG.DB-SPL=
            100.0
60 DEG.DB-SPL=
            100.0
70 DEG.DB-SPL=
            100.0
80 DEG.DB-SPL=
            100.0
90 DEG.DB-SPL=
            100.0
100 DEG.DB-SPL=
            0.0
110 DEG.DB-SPL=
            0.0
120 DEG.DB-SPL=
            0.0
130 DEG.DB-SPL=
            0.0
140 DEG.DB-SPL=
            0.0
150 DEG.DB-SPL=
            0.0
160 DEG.DB-SPL=
            0.0
170 DEG.DB-SPL=
            0.0
180 DEG.DB-SPL=
            0.0
```
HORIZONTAL DATA

```
10 DEG.DB-SPL=
            100.0
20 DEG.DB-SPL=
            100.0
30 DEG.DB-SPL=
            100.0
40 DEG.DB-SPL=
            100.0
50 DEG.DB-SPL=
            100.0
60 DEG.DB-SPL=
            100.0
70 DEG.DB-SPL=
            100.0
80 DEG.DB-SPL=
            100.0
90 DEG.DB-SPL=
            100.0
100 DEG.DB-SPL=
            0.0
110 DEG.DB-SPL=
            0.0
120 DEG.DB-SPL=
            0.0
130 DEG.DB-SPL=
            0.0
140 DEG.DB-SPL=
            0.0
150 DEG.DB-SPL=
            0.0
160 DEG.DB-SPL=
            0.0
170 DEG.DB-SPL=
            0.0
DB-SPL AVER.=
            97.0
DB-SPL DIRECT.=
            100.0
Q=
            2.0
```
VERTICAL DATA

(B) Hemispherical coverage.

```
SYN-AUD-CON
DIRECTIVITY
FACTOR (Q)
PROGRAM

0 DEG.DB-SPL=
            100.0
10 DEG.DB-SPL=
            100.0
20 DEG.DB-SPL=
            100.0
30 DEG.DB-SPL=
            100.0
40 DEG.DB-SPL=
            100.0
50 DEG.DB-SPL=
            99.0
60 DEG.DB-SPL=
            98.0
70 DEG.DB-SPL=
            97.0
80 DEG.DB-SPL=
            96.0
90 DEG.DB-SPL=
            95.0
100 DEG.DB-SPL=
            94.0
110 DEG.DB-SPL=
            92.0
120 DEG.DB-SPL=
            90.0
130 DEG.DB-SPL=
            87.0
140 DEG.DB-SPL=
            85.0
150 DEG.DB-SPL=
            82.0
160 DEG.DB-SPL=
            80.0
170 DEG.DB-SPL=
            77.0
180 DEG.DB-SPL=
            75.0
```
HORIZONTAL DATA

```
10 DEG.DB-SPL=
            100.0
20 DEG.DB-SPL=
            100.0
30 DEG.DB-SPL=
            100.0
40 DEG.DB-SPL=
            99.0
50 DEG.DB-SPL=
            98.0
60 DEG.DB-SPL=
            97.0
70 DEG.DB-SPL=
            97.0
80 DEG.DB-SPL=
            96.0
90 DEG.DB-SPL=
            95.0
100 DEG.DB-SPL=
            94.0
110 DEG.DB-SPL=
            93.0
120 DEG.DB-SPL=
            90.0
130 DEG.DB-SPL=
            88.0
140 DEG.DB-SPL=
            85.0
150 DEG.DB-SPL=
            82.0
160 DEG.DB-SPL=
            77.0
170 DEG.DB-SPL=
            76.0
DB-SPL AVER.=
            95.9
DB-SPL DIRECT.=
            100.0
Q=
            2.6
```
VERTICAL DATA

(C) Unidirectional microphone.

Fig. 3-11. Computer printouts of Q calculations.

This measurement should be taken at 1 watt of electrical input power.

$$W = EI(PF) \qquad (3-24)$$

where,

W is the average power in watts,
E is the rms voltage,
I is the rms current in amperes,

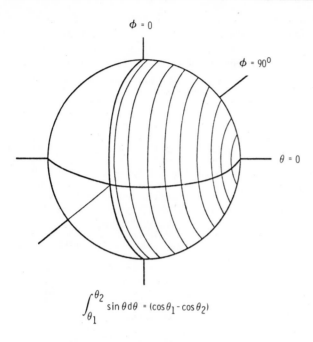

$$\int_{\theta_1}^{\theta_2} \sin\theta\, d\theta = (\cos\theta_1 - \cos\theta_2)$$

Fig. 3-12. Sphere divided into zones.

PF is the power factor (cosine of the phase angle).

2. Obtain a plane-wave-tube response curve (Fig. 3-14) of the test loudspeaker, and calculate the efficiency of the transducer in percent by:

$$\% \text{ eff} = \frac{10^{\frac{\text{dB-SPL} - 20\log\frac{28.2}{0.25D}}{10}} \times 10^{-12}}{\text{EI(PF)}} \times 100 \quad (3\text{-}25)$$

Table 3-3. 10° Spherical Areas for Zones and Quadrangles

10° Intervals	Area of Spherical Zone	Area of Spherical Quadrangle
0° (On axis)	0.003805302	0.004835888
10°	0.030268872	0.037841512
20°	0.059618039	0.071640216
30°	0.087155743	0.099098832
40°	0.112045263	0.119916888
50°	0.133530345	0.134945232
60°	0.150958174	0.145327696
70°	0.163799217	0.152053952
80°	0.171663302	0.155822296
90°*	0.087155744	0.078517492
	Total = 1.000000001	Total = 1.000000004

* The 90° area is to the hemisphere dividing point only.

For horizontal and vertical plots there are:
  2 "on-axis" areas, 8 areas for angles between 0° and 90°, and 4 areas at 90°.

When right and left diagonal polar plots are added, then there are:
  2 "on-axis" areas, 16 areas for angles between 0° and 90°, and 8 areas at 90°.

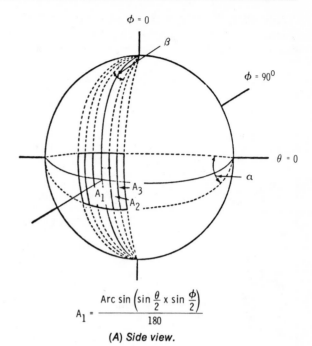

$$A_1 = \frac{\text{Arc}\sin\left(\sin\frac{\theta}{2} \times \sin\frac{\phi}{2}\right)}{180}$$

(A) Side view.

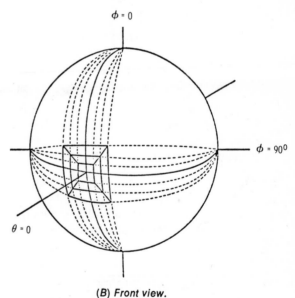

(B) Front view.

Fig. 3-13. Sphere divided by polar lunes.

where,
  dB-SPL is the level at the precision microphone in the plane-wave tube,
  D is the diameter of the tube in centimeters,
  E is the rms voltage,
  I is the rms current,
  PF is the power factor (cosine of the phase angle).

3. Convert the free-field response levels to 4-foot levels by:
4-ft dB-SPL level =

$$\text{x-distance dB-SPL} + 20\log\frac{\text{x distance}}{4\,\text{ft}} \quad (3\text{-}26)$$

Table 3-4. Areas of Spherical Zones Surrounding Each Increment of 10° on a Set of Horizontal, Vertical, and Right and Left Diagonal Polar Plots Around a Sphere With a Unity Surface Area

Angles	Number of Areas	Area Weighting
0° (On Axis)	1 (On Axis)	1×0.001902651
10° & 350°	2 Horiz, 2 Vert, 4 Diagonal	8×0.001891805
20° & 340°	2 Horiz, 2 Vert, 4 Diagonal	8×0.003726127
30° & 330°	2 Horiz, 2 Vert, 4 Diagonal	8×0.005447234
40° & 320°	2 Horiz, 2 Vert, 4 Diagonal	8×0.007002829
50° & 310°	2 Horiz, 2 Vert, 4 Diagonal	8×0.008345647
60° & 300°	2 Horiz, 2 Vert, 4 Diagonal	8×0.009434886
70° & 290°	2 Horiz, 2 Vert, 4 Diagonal	8×0.010237451
80° & 280°	2 Horiz, 2 Vert, 4 Diagonal	8×0.010728956
90° & 270°	2 Horiz, 2 Vert, 4 Diagonal	8×0.010894468
100° & 260°	2 Horiz, 2 Vert, 4 Diagonal	8×0.010728956
110° & 250°	2 Horiz, 2 Vert, 4 Diagonal	8×0.010237451
120° & 240°	2 Horiz, 2 Vert, 4 Diagonal	8×0.009434886
130° & 230°	2 Horiz, 2 Vert, 4 Diagonal	8×0.008345647
140° & 220°	2 Horiz, 2 Vert, 4 Diagonal	8×0.007002829
150° & 210°	2 Horiz, 2 Vert, 4 Diagonal	8×0.005447234
160° & 200°	2 Horiz, 2 Vert, 4 Diagonal	8×0.003726127
170° & 190°	2 Horiz, 2 Vert, 4 Diagonal	8×0.001891805
180° (Off Axis)	1 (Off Axis)	1×0.001902651
		Total = 1.000000006

Table 3-5. Areas of Spherical Quadrangles Surrounding Each Increment of 10° on a Set of Horizontal, Vertical, and Right and Left Diagonal Polar Plots Around a Sphere With a Unity Surface Area

Angles	Number of Areas	Area Weighting
0° (On Axis)	1 (On Axis)	1×0.002417944
10° & 350°	2 Horiz, 2 Vert, 4 Diagonal	8×0.002365095
20° & 340°	2 Horiz, 2 Vert, 4 Diagonal	8×0.004477514
30° & 330°	2 Horiz, 2 Vert, 4 Diagonal	8×0.006193677
40° & 320°	2 Horiz, 2 Vert, 4 Diagonal	8×0.007494806
50° & 310°	2 Horiz, 2 Vert, 4 Diagonal	8×0.008434077
60° & 300°	2 Horiz, 2 Vert, 4 Diagonal	8×0.009082981
70° & 290°	2 Horiz, 2 Vert, 4 Diagonal	8×0.009503372
80° & 280°	2 Horiz, 2 Vert, 4 Diagonal	8×0.009738894
90° & 270°	2 Horiz, 2 Vert, 4 Diagonal	8×0.009814687
100° & 260°	2 Horiz, 2 Vert, 4 Diagonal	8×0.009738894
110° & 250°	2 Horiz, 2 Vert, 4 Diagonal	8×0.009503372
120° & 240°	2 Horiz, 2 Vert, 4 Diagonal	8×0.009082981
130° & 230°	2 Horiz, 2 Vert, 4 Diagonal	8×0.008434077
140° & 220°	2 Horiz, 2 Vert, 4 Diagonal	8×0.007494806
150° & 210°	2 Horiz, 2 Vert, 4 Diagonal	8×0.006193677
160° & 200°	2 Horiz, 2 Vert, 4 Diagonal	8×0.004477514
170° & 190°	2 Horiz, 2 Vert, 4 Diagonal	8×0.002365095
180° (Off Axis)	1 (Off Axis)	1×0.002417944
		Total = 1.000000040

4. Calculate Q at the desired frequency by:

$$Q = 10^{\frac{(\text{4-ft, 1-watt dB-SPL}) - 10 \log\left(\frac{\%\text{effic}}{100}\right) - 107.47}{10}} \qquad (3\text{-}27)$$

Obviously, this may be done for any frequency or band of frequencies by taking the levels from each curve in the same manner (free-field curve and plane-wave-tube curve.)

Example

A well-known commercially available transducer when mounted on a sectoral horn has a 4-foot, 1-watt sensitivity rating of 109 dB-SPL at 1000 Hz. A plane-wave-tube measurement of this same driver yields an efficiency of 14.22% at 1000 Hz. Therefore, we can calculate the Q of this transducer on the DCD by:

$$Q = 10^{\frac{109 - 10 \log\left(\frac{14.22}{100}\right) - 107.47}{10}} = 10 \qquad (3\text{-}28)$$

It is interesting to note that the manufacturer of this transducer and DCD quotes a Q of 10 at 1000 Hz for this combination.

Summary

This method frees the Q measurement from the academic quandary of which weighting method "strains

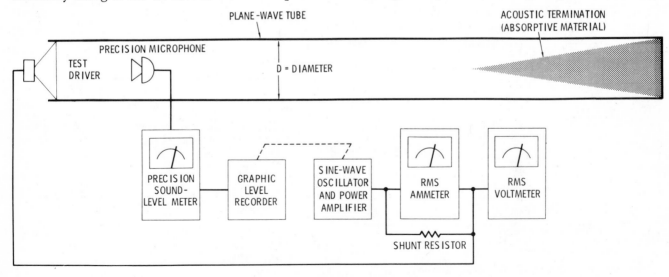

Fig. 3-14. Plane-wave-tube measurement.

out the smallest gnat" and gives a direct value from data normally already available in the manufacturers' files. This method would appear to ease greatly the measurement of the Q of low-frequency DCDs too large to be rotated conveniently in existing anechoic chambers.

Philosophically, the accuracy of this method exceeds any foreseeable requirements for such transducers and DCDs in field applications. By reducing the parameter to the difference between the power response and the free-field response, the user of the devices can gain a better conceptual view of the interactions between the acoustic environments, DCDs, and transducers as the frequency varies.

After we discuss the effect of the major room parameters, we will take up the "field methods" of obtaining Q when you have a calibrated loudspeaker on hand as a reference. There are both a relative Q (Q referred to some point other than on axis) and the apparent Q (where Q multipliers and dividers are present). An accurate Q for the test loudspeaker is necessary in order to calibrate the room to measure the multipliers and dividers. These are actually critical-distance modifiers but appear *as if* Q were multiplied or divided.

CHAPTER 4

The Acoustic Environment

We are concerned about the effect the acoustic environment has on sound. We need to know the effect of a particular acoustic environment on the unaided talker or musician, on the sound system, if installed, and on unwanted sounds (noise) that may be present in the same environment.

THE ACOUSTIC ENVIRONMENT OUTDOORS

If you are standing in a flat, open field, common experience tells you that a sound generally gets weaker as you move away from it. A careful observer has noted in his experience that distant thunder rumbles, whereas lightning that strikes close by results in a sharp crack. A marching band, heard at a distance, sounds like it is all bass drums, but as it nears the listener, the music brightens; finally, right at hand, the music sounds brilliant. On some days and in some weather conditions, high-pitched sounds can be heard at greater distances than is normally the case.

These are all manifestations of the characteristics of sound transmission through the air. If we assume a point source of sound without wind or temperature gradients, we would discover that each time we doubled the distance from the sound source we would measure a 6-dB decrease in SPL on a sound level meter (SLM). For example, if we measured 75 dB-SPL at 4 feet from the sound source, we would find the following to be true:

Distance	SPL on SLM
8 ft	69 dB-SPL
16 ft	63 dB-SPL
32 ft	57 dB-SPL
64 ft	51 dB-SPL
128 ft	45 dB-SPL

Remembering the basic decibel formulas from Chapter 2, we see that the formula for attenuation with increasing distance would be:

dB-SPL at Measured Distance =

$$\text{Ref Dist SPL} + 20 \log \frac{D_r}{D_m} \qquad (4\text{-}1)$$

where,

D_r is the reference distance (in this case, 4 feet),
D_m is the measured distance.

Using the formula, we can find all the distances between those above, e.g.:

Distance	SPL on SLM
12 ft	65.5 dB-SPL
24 ft	59.5 dB-SPL
48 ft	53.5 dB-SPL
96 ft	47.5 dB-SPL

It is important to realize that it is the energy per unit area, not the total energy in a sound wave, that decreases. In other words, a pin drop has only so much acoustic energy. Spread evenly over a 1000-seat auditorium, no one would hear it, but if all the energy created by the pin drop were to be focused into one area, then the pin drop would be clearly heard in that area.

In a spherical wave, each doubling of the distance increases by 4 times the area intercepted by the spherical wave. That is, the unit area intercepted increases by the square of the distance. This is known as the inverse square law of level change. Many natural forces follow this law.

The formula for the surface area of a sphere is $4\pi r^2$. If r = 4 ft, then the total surface area would be 201 ft². If we made r = 8, then the total surface area would be 804 ft², just four times greater than for a sphere with 1/2 the radius. The total power radiated at the center would be the same, but the power per square foot would drop with increasing distance from the center.

If inverse-square-law level change were the only factor, then distant sounds would sound the same as close sounds, except they would be weaker. All that is happening is that the available sound power is spreading out with increasing distance from the source. Unfortu-

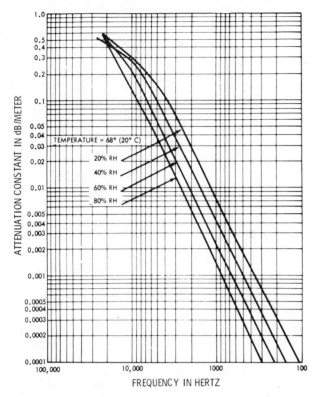

Fig. 4-1. Absorption of sound for different frequencies and values of relative humidity.

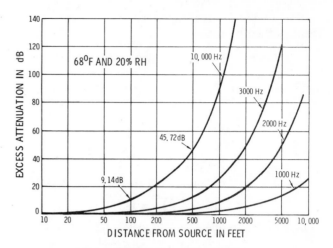

Fig. 4-2. Excess attenuation for different frequencies and distances from the source.

4. Refraction and shadow formation by wind and temperature gradients
5. Scattering of sound by small-scale temperature and wind variations
6. Reflection and absorption by the ground surface itself

VELOCITY, FREQUENCY, AND WAVELENGTH

The relationship among velocity, wavelength, and frequency is expressed by:

$$V = WF \qquad (4\text{-}2)$$

where,
V is the velocity in feet per second or meters per second,
W is the wavelength in feet or meters,
F is the frequency in hertz.

Therefore:

$$W = \frac{V}{F} \quad \text{and} \quad F = \frac{V}{W} \qquad (4\text{-}3)$$

TEMPERATURE AND VELOCITY

The velocity of sound is temperature dependent. The formula for calculating velocity is:

$$V = 49 \sqrt{459.4 + {}^{\circ}F} \qquad (4\text{-}4)$$

where,
V is the velocity in feet per second,
°F is the temperature in degrees Fahrenheit.

For Celsius temperatures:

$$V = 20.06 \sqrt{273 + {}^{\circ}C} \qquad (4\text{-}5)$$

where,
V is the velocity in meters per second,
°C is the temperature in degrees Celsius.

Therefore, at a normal room temperature of 72.5°F, we can calculate:

$$49 \sqrt{459.4 + 72.5} = 1130 \text{ ft/sec} \qquad (4\text{-}6)$$

nately, other processes also are going on. These other processes represent actual dissipation of sound energy. Energy is lost due to the combined action of the viscosity and heat conduction of the air and a relaxation of behavior in the rotational energy states of the molecules of the air. These losses are independent of the humidity of the air. Additional losses are due to a relaxation of behavior in the vibrational states of the oxygen molecules in the air, because this behavior is strongly dependent on the presence of water molecules in the air (absolute humidity). Both of these energy-loss effects cause increased attenuation with increased frequency (see Fig. 4-1).

This frequency-discriminative attenuation is referred to as *excess attenuation* and must be added to the level change due to divergence of the sound wave. Total level change is the sum of inverse-square-law level change and excess attenuation. Fig. 4-2 shows the excess attenuation difference between 1000 Hz and 10,000 Hz at various distances.

Up to this point, we have accounted for

1. Inverse-square-law level change
2. Excess attenuation by frequency due to humidity and related factors

Other factors that can materially affect sound outdoors include:

3. Reflection by and diffraction around solid objects

Some typical wavelengths for midfrequency octave centers then become:

Frequency (Hz)	Wavelength (ft)
250	4.52
500	2.26
1000	1.13
2000	0.57
4000	0.28
8000	0.14
16,000	0.07

Now suppose the temperature increases 20° to 92.5°F.

$$49 \sqrt{459.4 + 92.5} = 1151 \text{ ft/sec} \qquad (4\text{-}7)$$

The table of frequencies and wavelengths becomes:

Frequency (Hz)	Wavelength (ft)
250	4.60
500	2.30
1000	1.15
2000	0.58
4000	0.29
8000	0.14
16,000	0.07

Suppose we had "tuned" to the peak of a 1000-Hz standing wave in a room first at 72.5°F and then later at 92.5°F. The apparent frequency shift would be:

$$\left(\frac{1151}{1.13} \right) - 1000 = 18.58 \text{ Hz} \qquad (4\text{-}8)$$

where,

1151 is the velocity (feet per second) at the temperature of measurement,

1.13 is the wavelength at the original temperature.

This is one of the reasons very narrow-band filters cannot be used successfully in sound-system–room equalization work. (A more important reason is the degradation of the system transient response.)

DOPPLER EFFECT

We all have experienced the effect of hearing a sound change pitch as the source passed us at high speed. Car horns, train whistles, etc., are typical examples. The frequency that we hear is found by:

$$F = \left(\frac{V \pm V_L}{V \pm V_S} \right) F_0 \qquad (4\text{-}9)$$

where,

F is the frequency heard,

F_0 is the frequency of the sound source,

V is the velocity of sound,

V_L is the velocity of the listener,

V_S is the velocity of the source.

Use − if V_L or V_S is in the direction the sound travels; use + if V_L or V_S is in the opposite direction.

For example, assume V = 1130 ft/sec, V_L = 0, V_S = 60 mph (approaching listener), and F_0 = 1000 Hz.

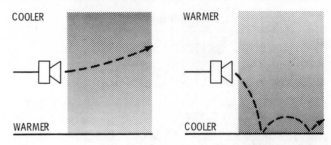

Fig. 4-3. Effect of temperature differences between the ground and the air on the propagation of sound.

Then:

$$\frac{60 \text{ mi}}{1 \text{ hr}} \times \frac{1 \text{ hr}}{3600 \text{ sec}} \times \frac{5280 \text{ ft}}{1 \text{ mi}} = 88 \text{ ft/sec} \qquad (4\text{-}10)$$

$$F = \left(\frac{1130 - 0}{1130 - 88} \right) 1000 = 1084 \text{ Hz} \qquad (4\text{-}11)$$

As the source passes the listener, the pitch swings from 1084 Hz to:

$$F = \left(\frac{1130}{1130 + 88} \right) 1000 = 928 \text{ Hz} \qquad (4\text{-}12)$$

This rapid "sweep" of 157 Hz is what is called the Doppler effect. This effect can also be caused by the excursion of a loudspeaker diaphragm responding to a low-frequency signal while simultaneously producing a higher-frequency signal. So-called "long throw" low-frequency drivers in infinite baffles are prone to this type of distortion.

REFLECTION AND REFRACTION

Sound can be reflected by hitting an object larger than ¼ wavelength of the sound. When the object is ¼ wavelength or slightly smaller, it also causes *diffraction* of the sound (bending around the object). *Refraction* occurs when the sound passes from one medium to another (from air to glass to air, for example, or when it passes through layers of air having different temperatures). The velocity of sound increases with increasing temperature. Therefore, sound emitted from a source located on the frozen surface of a large lake on a sunny day will encounter warmer temperatures as the wave diverges upward, causing the upper part of the wave to travel faster than the part of the wave near the surface. This causes a lens-like action to occur which bends the sound back down toward the surface of the lake (Fig. 4-3).

Sound will travel great distances over frozen surfaces on a quiet day. Wind blowing against a sound course causes temperature gradients near the ground surface that result in the sound being refracted upward. Wind blowing in the same direction as the sound causes temperature gradients along the ground surface that tend to refract the sound downward. We hear it said, "The wind blew the sound away." That is not so;

it refracted it away. There is no way for even a 50-mph wind (and that's a strong wind) to blow away something traveling 1130 feet per second:

$$\frac{1130\,\text{ft}}{1\,\text{sec}} \times \frac{3600\,\text{sec}}{1\,\text{hr}} \times \frac{1\,\text{mile}}{5280\,\text{ft}} = 770.45\,\text{mph} \tag{4-13}$$

770.45 mph is the velocity of sound at sea level at 72.5°F.

ABSORPTION

Absorption is the inverse of reflection. When sound strikes a large surface, part of it is reflected and part of it is absorbed. For a given material, the absorption coefficient, a, is:

$$a = \frac{I_A}{I_R} \tag{4-14}$$

where,

I_A is the absorbed sound,
I_R is the incident sound.

This makes the absorption coefficient, a, some value between 0 and 1. For a = 0, no sound is absorbed; it is all reflected. If we say a material has an a of 0.25, we are saying that it will absorb 25% of all sound energy having the same frequency as the absorption coefficient rating, and it will reflect 75% of the sound energy having that frequency.

For example, an anechoic room absorbs 99% of the energy received from the sound source. What percentage of the SPL from the source is reflected? Assume 10 watts of total energy output from the source. Then the chamber absorbs 9.9 watts of it.

$$10 \log \frac{10\,\text{watts}}{0.1\,\text{watt}} = 20\,\text{dB} \tag{4-15}$$

Therefore, the SPL drops by 20 dB also:

$$100 \times 10^{\left(\frac{-\text{dB}}{20}\right)} = 10\%\ \text{Reflected SPL} \tag{4-16}$$

Or 10% of the SPL returns as a reflection. If the sound source had directed a 100 dB-SPL signal at the wall of the chamber, a signal of 80 dB would be reflected back. Remembering how dB are combined, we can see that this reflection will not change the 100-dB reading of the direct sound by a discernible amount on any normal SLM.

The desirability of a reflective surface can be seen when it is realized that the direct sound and the reflected sound from a single surface can combine to be as much as 3 dB higher than the direct sound alone. At the Indianapolis and Ontario Motor Speedways, the loudspeakers are directed to reflect off the ground during the cool early morning hours; then when the refraction effect of the sun on the hard surfaces causes the sound to bend upward during the hot part of the day, the sound bends up into the grandstand area. In the case of the Ontario Motor Speedway, most of the time the reflected sound is assisting the direct sound, thereby saving another 30,000 watts of audio power (+3 dB).

THE EFFECT OF AMBIENT NOISE

If, for example, the ambient noise level measured 70 dBA (a not unreasonable reading outdoors) and the most SPL you could generate at 4 feet was 110 dB-SPL, how far could you reach before your signal was submerged in noise?

$$110\,\text{dB-SPL} - 70\,\text{dB-SPL} = 40\,\text{dB} \tag{4-17}$$

$$20 \log \frac{x}{4} = 40\,\text{dB} \tag{4-18}$$

$$x = 4 \times 10^{\frac{40}{20}} = 400\,\text{ft} \tag{4-19}$$

The problem actually is more complicated than this outdoors, but this serves as an illustration of how to begin.

We have now touched on the most important basics of the acoustic environment outdoors. Before going indoors, let us apply some of this knowledge to a series of ancient outdoor problems. A simple rule of thumb dictates that when a change of +10 dB occurs, the higher level will be subjectively judged as approximately twice as loud as the level 10 dB below it. While the computation of loudness is more complex than this, the rule is useful for midrange sounds. Using such a rule, we could examine a sound source radiating hemispherically due to the presence of the surface of the earth. Fig. 4-4 shows sound in an open field with no wind. The sound at 100 feet is one-half as loud as that at 30 feet, although the amplitude of the vibration of the air particles is roughly one third. Similarly, the sound at 30 feet is one-half as loud as the sound at 10 feet. Because the sound is outdoors, atmospheric effects, ambient noise, etc., cause difficulty for the talker and listener. The ancients learned to place a back wall behind the talker, and many Indian council sites were at the foot of a stone cliff so the talker could address more of the tribe at one time. Fig. 4-5 illustrates how such a reflecting structure can double the loudness as compared to the totally open space. The weather and some noise still interfere with listening.

Fig. 4-6 illustrates the absorptive effect of an audience on the sound traveling to the farthest listener. Fig. 4-7 shows the right way and the wrong way to arrange a sound source on a hill. In Fig. 4-7A, the loudness of the sound at the rear of the audience is enhanced by sloping the seating upward. In addition, the noise from sources on the ground is reduced. Fig. 4-7B is a poor way to listen outdoors. The sound at the rear is one-half as loud as it is at the rear in Fig. 4-7A.

While the Bible doesn't say which way Jesus addressed the multitudes, we can deduce from the acous-

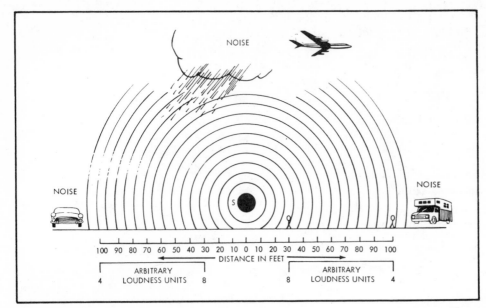

Fig. 4-4. Sound in an open field with no wind.

tical clues present in the Bible text that the multitude arranged themselves above him because:

1. He addressed groups as large as 5000. This required a very favorable position relative to the audience and a very low ambient noise level.
2. Upon departing from such sessions, He could often step into a boat in the lake, suggesting He was at the bottom of a hill or mountain.

We can further surmise that the reason Jesus led these multitudes into the countryside was to avoid the higher noise levels present even in small country villages.

The Greeks built their amphitheaters to take advantage of these acoustical facts:

1. They provided a back reflector for the performer.
2. They increased the talker's acoustic output by building megaphones into the special face masks they held in front of their faces to portray various emotions.
3. They sloped the audiences upward and around the talker at an included angle of approximately 120°, realizing, as many modern designers do not seem to, that man does not talk out of the back of his head.
4. They defocused the reflective "slapback" by changing the radius at the edges of the seating area.

Because there were no aircraft, cars, motorcycles, air conditioners, etc., the ambient noise levels were relatively low, and large audiences were able to enjoy the performances. They had discovered absorption and used jars partially filled with ashes (as tuned Helm-

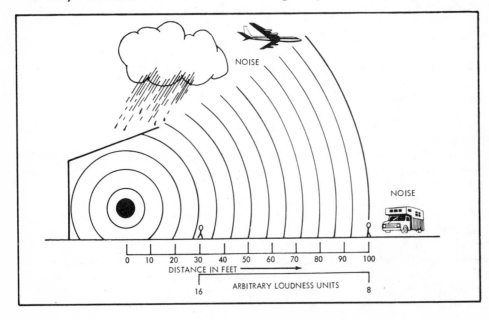

Fig. 4-5. Sound from an orchestra enclosure in an open field with no wind present.

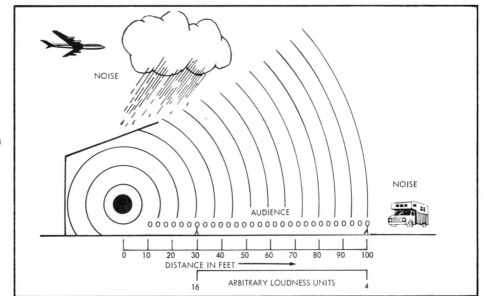

Fig. 4-6. Sound from an orchestra enclosure with an audience.

holtz resonators) to reduce the return echo of the curved stepped seats back to the performers. It remained only for some unnamed innovative genius to provide walls and a roof to have the first auditorium, "a place to hear" (Fig. 4-8). No enhancement of sound is provided in Fig. 4-8 because there is no reverberation in a room whose walls are highly sound absorbent.

Sometimes acoustic progress was backward. For example, the Romans, when adopting Christianity, took over the ancient echo-ridden pagan temples and had to convert the spoken service into a chanted or sung service pitched to the predominant room modes of these large, hard structures. Today, churches still often have serious acoustical shortcomings and require a very carefully designed sound system in order to allow the normally spoken word to be heard.

It is also of real interest to note that in large halls and arenas the correct place for the loudspeaker system is most often where the roof should have gone if the building had been designed specifically for hearing. A loudspeaker is therefore usually an electroacoustic replacement for a natural reflecting surface that has not been provided.

THE ACOUSTIC ENVIRONMENT INDOORS

The moment we enclose the sound source, we greatly complicate the transmission of its output. We have considered one extreme when we put the sound source in a well-elevated position and observed the sound being totally absorbed by the "space" around it. Now, let us go to the opposite extreme and imagine an enclosed space that is completely reflective. The sound source would put out sound energy, and none of it would be absorbed. If we continued to put energy into the enclosure long enough, we could theoretically arrive at a pressure that would be explosive. Human speech power

is quite small. It has been stated by Harvey Fletcher in his book *Speech and Hearing in Communication* that it would take ". . . 500 people talking continuously for one year to produce enough energy to heat a cup of tea." Measured at 39.37 inches (3.28 feet), a typical male talker generates 67.2 dB-SPL, or 34 microwatts of power, and a typical female talker generates 64.2 dB-SPL, or 18 microwatts. From a shout at this distance (3.28 feet) to a whisper, the dB-SPL ranges from 86 dB to 26 dB, or a dynamic range of about 60 dB.

Not only does the produced sound energy tend to remain in the enclosure (dying out slowly), but it tends to travel about in the process.

Let us now examine the essential parameters of a typical room to see what does happen. First, an enclosed space has an internal volume (V), usually measured in cubic feet. Second, it has a total *boundary* surface area (S), measured in square feet (floor, ceiling, two side walls, and two end walls). Next, each of the many individual surface areas has an absorption coefficient. The average absorption coefficient ($\bar{a}$) for all the surfaces together is found by:

$$\bar{a} = \frac{s_1 a_1 + s_2 a_2 + \ldots s_n a_n}{S} \qquad (4\text{-}20)$$

where,

$s_{1, 2 \ldots n}$ are the individual boundary surface areas in square feet,

$a_{1, 2 \ldots n}$ are the individual absorption coefficients of the individual boundary surface areas,

S is the total boundary surface area in square feet.

The reflected energy is $1 - \bar{a}$.

Table 4-1 gives some typical absorption coefficients for common materials. These are the percentages per square foot. These coefficients are used to calculate the absorption of boundary surfaces (walls, floors, ceilings, etc.)

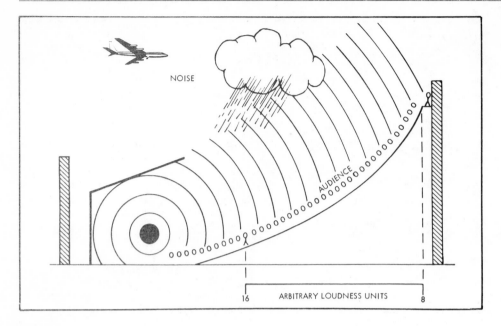

(A) Right way.

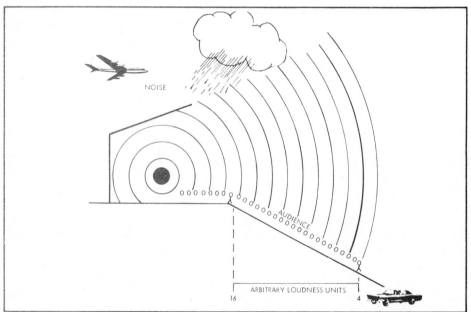

(B) Wrong way.

Fig. 4-7. Sound sources and audiences on a hill.

Table 4-2 gives typical absorption units in sabins rather than percentage figures. Sabins are either in per-unit figures or in units per length, etc.

Finally, the room will possess a reverberation time (RT_{60}). This is the time in seconds that it will take a steady-state sound, once its input power is terminated, to attenuate 60 dB. For the sake of illustration, assume a room with the following characteristics:

$$V = 500,000 \text{ ft}^3$$
$$S = 42,500 \text{ ft}^2$$
$$\bar{a} = 0.206$$
$$RT_{60} = 2.5 \text{ s}$$

The Mean Free Path

The mean free path is the average distance between reflections in a space. For our sample space:

$$\text{Mean free path} = \frac{4V}{S} = \frac{4(500,000)}{42,500} = 47 \text{ ft}$$

(4-21)

If a sound is generated in the sample space, part of it will travel directly to a listener and undergo inverse-square-law level change, etc., on its way. Some more of it will arrive after having traveled first to some reflecting surface, and still more will finally arrive having

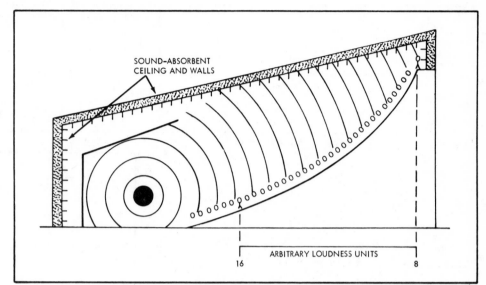

Fig. 4-8. A means for eliminating noise and weather while preserving outdoor conditions.

Table 4-1. Sound-Absorption Coefficients of General Building Materials and Furnishings

Materials	Coefficients					
	125 Hz	250 Hz	500 Hz	1000 Hz	2000 Hz	4000 Hz
Brick, unglazed	0.03	0.03	0.03	0.04	0.05	0.07
Brick, unglazed, painted	0.01	0.01	0.02	0.02	0.02	0.03
Carpet, heavy, on concrete	0.02	0.06	0.14	0.37	0.60	0.65
Same, on 40-oz hairfelt or foam rubber	0.08	0.24	0.57	0.69	0.71	0.73
Same, with impermeable latex backing on 40-oz hairfelt or foam rubber	0.08	0.27	0.39	0.34	0.48	0.63
Concrete block, coarse	0.36	0.44	0.31	0.29	0.39	0.25
Concrete block, painted	0.10	0.05	0.06	0.07	0.09	0.08
Fabrics						
Light velour, 10 oz per sq yd, hung straight, in contact with wall	0.03	0.04	0.11	0.17	0.24	0.35
Medium velour, 10 oz per sq yd, draped to half area	0.07	0.31	0.49	0.75	0.70	0.60
Heavy velour, 18 oz per sq yd, draped to half area	0.14	0.35	0.55	0.72	0.70	0.65
Floors						
Concrete or terrazzo	0.01	0.01	0.015	0.02	0.02	0.02
Linoleum, asphalt, rubber, or cork tile on concrete	0.02	0.03	0.03	0.03	0.03	0.02
Wood	0.15	0.11	0.10	0.07	0.06	0.07
Wood parquet in asphalt on concrete	0.04	0.04	0.07	0.06	0.06	0.07
Glass						
Large panes of heavy plate glass	0.18	0.06	0.04	0.03	0.02	0.02
Ordinary window glass	0.35	0.25	0.18	0.12	0.07	0.04
Gypsum board, ½ in nailed to 2 × 4's 16 in oc	0.29	0.10	0.05	0.04	0.07	0.09
Marble or glazed tile	0.01	0.01	0.01	0.01	0.02	0.02
Openings						
Stage, depending on furnishings			0.25 — 0.75			
Deep balcony, upholstered seats			0.50 — 1.00			
Grills, ventilating			0.15 — 0.50			
Plaster, gypsum or lime, smooth finish on tile or brick	0.013	0.015	0.02	0.03	0.04	0.05
Plaster, gypsum or lime, rough finish on lath	0.02	0.03	0.04	0.05	0.04	0.03
Same, with smooth finish	0.02	0.02	0.03	0.04	0.04	0.03
Plywood paneling, ⅜ in thick	0.28	0.22	0.17	0.09	0.10	0.11
Water surface, as in a swimming pool	0.008	0.008	0.013	0.015	0.020	0.025
Air, sabins per 1000 cubic feet					2.3	7.2

Table 4-2. Absorption of Seats and Audience

	125 Hz	250 Hz	500 Hz	1000 Hz	2000 Hz	4000 Hz
Audience, seated, depending on spacing and upholstery of seats	2.5-4.0	3.5-5.0	4.0-5.5	4.5-6.5	5.0-7.0	4.5-7.0
Seats, heavily upholstered with fabric	1.5-3.5	3.5-4.5	4.0-5.0	4.0-5.5	3.5-5.5	3.5-4.5
Seats, heavily upholstered with leather, plastic, etc.	2.5-3.5	3.0-4.5	3.0-4.0	2.0-4.0	1.5-3.5	1.0-3.0
Seats, lightly upholstered with leather, plastic, etc.			1.5-2.0			
Seats, wood veneer, no upholstery	0.15	0.20	0.25	0.30	0.50	0.50
Wood pews, no cushions, per 18-in length			0.40			
Wood pews, cushioned, per 18-in length			1.8-2.3			

Values given are in sabins per person or unit of seating

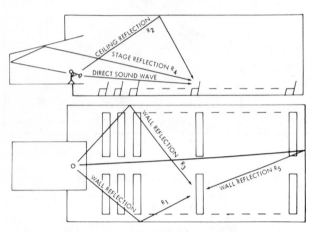

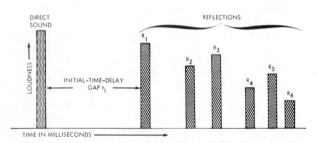

Fig. 4-9. Sound paths in a concert hall.

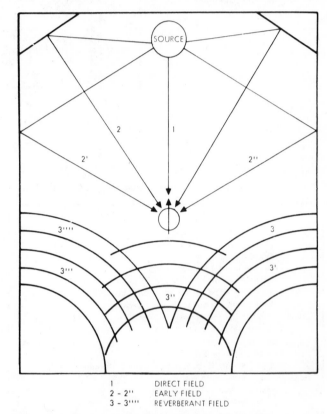

1	DIRECT FIELD
2 - 2''	EARLY FIELD
3 - 3''''	REVERBERANT FIELD

Fig. 4-10. Time relationship of direct and reflected sounds.

Fig. 4-11. Comparison of direct, early, and reverberant sound fields in an auditorium.

undergone several successive reflections (each 47 feet apart on the average). Each of these signals will have had more attenuation at some frequencies than at others due to divergence, absorption, reflection, refraction, diffraction, etc.

We can look at this situation in a different manner. Each sound made will have traveled 2.5 seconds × 1130 feet per second, or 2825 feet, before reaching inaudibility. Since the mean free path is 47 feet, then we can assume each sound underwent approximately 60 reflections in this sample space before becoming inaudible. The result is a lot different than hearing the sound just once.

The Build-Up of the Reverberant Sound Field

Fig. 4-9 shows the paths of direct sound and several reflected sound waves in a concert hall. Reflections also occur from balcony faces, rear wall, niches, and any

other reflecting surfaces. If we plot the amplitude of a short-duration signal vertically and the time interval horizontally, we can obtain a chart such as that shown in Fig. 4-10. This diagram shows that at a listener's ears, the sound that travels directly from the performer arrives first, and after a gap, reflections from the walls, ceiling, stage enclosure, and other reflecting surfaces arrive in rapid succession. The height of a bar suggests the loudness of the sound. This kind of diagram is called a *reflection pattern*, and the initial-time-delay gap can be measured from it.

Fig. 4-11 shows that the sound arriving at the listener has at least three distinct divisions:

1. The direct sound
2. The early reflections
3. The reverberant sound

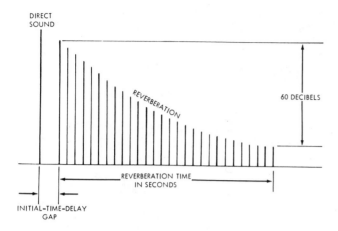

Fig. 4-12. Sound decay as measured at a listener's ears.

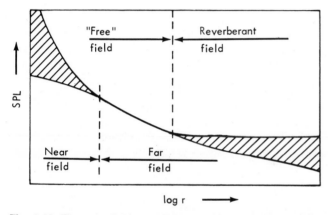

Fig. 4-13. The near field, free field, far field, and reverberant field represented graphically.

Fig. 4-12 illustrates the decay of the reverberant field. Here the direct sound enters at the left of the diagram. The initial-time-delay gap is followed by a succession of sound reflections. The reverberation time of the room is defined as the length of time required for the reverberant sound to decay 60 decibels.

We will encounter the effects of delay versus attenuation again when we approach the calculation of articulation losses of consonants in speech.

The direct sound, by definition, undergoes no reflections and follows inverse-square-law level change. The reverberant sound tends to remain at a constant level if the sound source continues to put energy into the room at a reasonably regular rate. This gives rise to a number of basic sound fields (Fig. 4-13):

1. The near field
2. The free field } far field
3. The reverberant field }

The near field does not behave predictably in terms of SPL versus distance because the particle velocity is not necessarily in the direction of travel of the wave, and an appreciable tangential velocity component may exist at any point. This is why measurements are usu-

ally not made closer than twice the largest dimension of the sound source. In the far free field, inverse-square-law level change prevails. In the far reverberant field, or diffuse field, the sound-energy density is very nearly uniform.

REVERBERATION TIME

If we return to our completely reverberant room (no absorption) and cut an opening like a large window in one wall, the sound energy can flow out the opening. The rate at which the energy escapes depends on the PWL. If the energy is halved, the rate is halved.

Now, if we doubled the volume of the room but kept the intensity of reverberant sound the same, there would be twice as much energy in the larger room, and if the window were kept the same size as before, the energy would take twice as long to escape. Therefore, we can state that the reverberation time is proportional to the volume (V) of a room. If we were to keep the room the same volume but double the area of the window, the energy would get out twice as fast. Therefore, we can state that the reverberation time is inversely proportional to the area, Sā (Sā because the area also has absorption).

$$RT_{60} = \frac{KV}{S\bar{a}} \qquad (4\text{-}22)$$

where K is the proportionality constant.

The original Sabine formula is:

$$RT_{60} = \frac{0.049V}{S\bar{a}}; \quad V = \frac{S\bar{a} \times RT_{60}}{0.049};$$

$$\bar{a} = \frac{0.049V}{S \times RT_{60}}; \quad S = \frac{0.049V}{\bar{a} \times RT_{60}} \qquad (4\text{-}23)$$

Around the turn of the century, Professor Sabine brought absorptive cushions from a good lecture hall into a reverberant lecture hall and measured the change in reverberation time for each square foot of material introduced into the hall. He found the result was a hyperbola. In honor of his work, the square-foot unit of absorption is named the *sabin*. The Sabine equation is quite accurate in rooms having a reverberation time in excess of 2 seconds, but it becomes increasingly inaccurate as the absorption coefficient approaches unity. (At one limit it predicts a reverberation time for a room with total absorption.)

THE NORRIS-EYRING EQUATIONS

While many reverberation-time equations have been proposed by Sabine, Norris-Eyring, Millington, and Fitzroy, the one receiving the widest usage is the Norris-Eyring equation. Certainly for sound-system work it is more than adequate when the absorption is *uniformly* distributed. This is the best equation for finding the true ā in actual rooms. Unfortunately, acoustical materials are rated in Sabine $\bar{a}$ rather than true $\bar{a}$. The equation may be written in the following forms:

$$V = \frac{-S \ln (1 - \bar{a}) \, RT_{60}}{0.049} \qquad (4\text{-}24)$$

$$S = \frac{0.049V}{-RT_{60} \ln (1 - \bar{a})} \qquad (4\text{-}25)$$

$$\bar{a} = 1 - e^{-\left(\frac{0.049V}{S \times RT_{60}}\right)} \qquad (4\text{-}26)$$

$$RT_{60} = \frac{0.049V}{-S \ln (1 - \bar{a})} \qquad (4\text{-}27)$$

If the room parameters are in meters instead of feet, use 0.161 instead of 0.049 as the constant.

The absorption values given by the Acoustical Materials Association are calculated as the Sabine coefficient:

$$\bar{a}_{sab} = \frac{0.049V}{S \times RT_{60}} \qquad (4\text{-}28)$$

Because we use the Norris-Eyring equations throughout an interlocked system of equations, a conversion factor must be applied to such coefficients:

$$\bar{a}_{N.E.} = 1 - e^{-\bar{a}_{sab}} \qquad (4\text{-}29)$$

If, for any reason, you wished to convert $\bar{a}_{N.E.}$ to $\bar{a}_{sab}$, then

$$\bar{a}_{sab} = -\ln (1 - \bar{a}_{N.E.}) \qquad (4\text{-}30)$$

Naturally, when calculating $\bar{a}$ from the reverberation time of a room, you do so directly in $\bar{a}_{N.E.}$. The term ln refers to the *Naperian logarithm* which has a base of 2.71828. This base is also called e. Therefore, in the $\bar{a}$ equation:

$$\bar{a} = 1 - 2.71828^{-\left(\frac{0.049V}{S \times RT_{60}}\right)} \qquad (4\text{-}31)$$

Naperian logarithms are also sometimes called *natural* logarithms or *hyperbolic* logarithms. Fig. 4-14 allows you to solve for each of these room parameters without using logarithms.

For example, assume we had gathered the data:

$$V = 500,000 \text{ ft}^3$$
$$S = 42,500 \text{ ft}^2$$
$$RT_{60} = 2.5 \text{ seconds}$$

We could then solve for $\bar{a}$ in the following manner. On the left-hand vertical scale of Fig. 4-14, locate $RT_{60} = 2.5$ seconds (halfway between 2.0 seconds and 3.0 seconds). Move across the chart horizontally to the right until you intersect the vertical line rising from the bottom scale at 500,000 ft^3. Follow the slanting line out to the number attached to it. This number (in this case 8500—halfway between 8000 and 9000) is the value of S$\bar{a}$. Therefore, if we divide S$\bar{a}$ by S we obtain:

$$\frac{S\bar{a}}{S} = \bar{a} \qquad (4\text{-}32)$$

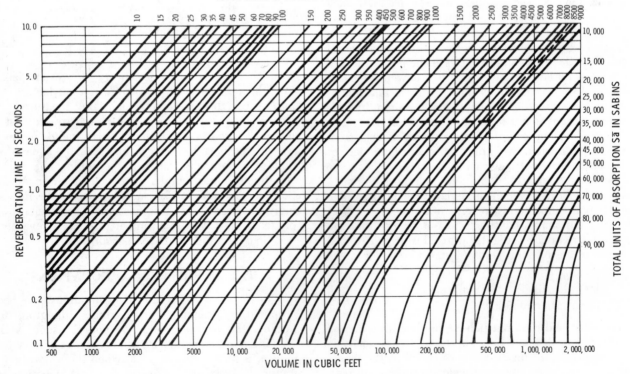

Fig. 4-14. Nomograph for solving Norris-Eyring equations.

Courtesy Hewlett-Packard

Fig. 4-15. An electronic slide rule.

or

$$\frac{8500}{42,500} = 0.20 \qquad (4\text{-}33)$$

Using an electronic calculator such as the one in Fig. 4-15, we get 0.2059, so the accuracy of the chart is quite adequate when it is used with care.

FITZROY REVERBERATION EQUATION

The Fitzroy reverberation equation is:

$$RT_{60} = \frac{0.049V}{S^2}\left[\frac{2(xy)}{-\ln(1-\bar{a}_1)} + \frac{2(xz)}{-\ln(1-\bar{a}_2)} \right.$$
$$\left. + \frac{2(yz)}{-\ln(1-\bar{a}_3)}\right] \qquad (4\text{-}34)$$

where,

V is the volume of the room in cubic feet,
S is the surface area in square feet,
xy is the height times the length (side walls),
xz is the height times the width (end walls),
yz is the length times the width (floor and ceiling),
$\bar{a}_1$ is the average absorption coefficient of *both* side walls,
$\bar{a}_2$ is the average absorption coefficient of *both* end walls,
$\bar{a}_3$ is the average absorption coefficient of the floor and ceiling.

For example, assume a small meeting room with the following parameters: length = 30 feet, width = 20 feet, height = 10 feet, ā for the side and end walls = 0.04, and ā for the floor and ceiling together = 0.80. We could calculate:

$$RT_{60} \text{ by Sabine} = \frac{0.049 \times 6000}{1000} = 0.294 \text{ s}$$
$$(4\text{-}35)$$

$$RT_{60} \text{ by Norris-Eyring} = \frac{0.049 \times 6000}{-2200 \ln(1-0.455)}$$
$$= 0.220 \text{ s} \qquad (4\text{-}36)$$

$$RT_{60} \text{ by Fitzroy} = \frac{0.049 \times 600}{(2200)^2}\left[\frac{400}{-\ln(1-0.04)} \right.$$
$$\left. + \frac{600}{-\ln(1-0.04)} + \frac{1200}{-\ln(1-0.8)}\right]$$
$$= 3.129 \text{ s} \qquad (4\text{-}37)$$

It can easily be seen that where all the absorption is on one set of surfaces, the Fitzroy equation is a wise choice; and its answer correlates with field tests.

REVERBERATION SUMMARY

It should always be considered that, insofar as the various reverberation formulas depend upon statistical averages, they presuppose a complete mixing of sound in the room. In very absorptive rooms, the sound dies away in a few reflections, and the statistical basis of the formula is weakened. Similarly, in a very large hall, because the sound cannot cross the room many times during a measured reverberation period of a few seconds, the validity of the formula is again affected.

Sabine's formula has the defect that from it a finite reverberation time can be calculated for a room with all surfaces totally absorptive, a defect from which the Norris-Eyring formula is free. Additionally, the ā found by using the Sabine formula in reverberation-chamber measurements of the absorption of materials would result in assignment of a value of 1.0 to a material that has an actual value of 0.63. The Norris-Eyring equation used under the same circumstances gives 0.63. Nevertheless, the vast majority of tested material has been assigned a Sabine ā.

In W. C. Sabine's classic 1900 paper, he found that the duration of audibility of reverberant sound in a room was largely independent of the positions of the source of sound, the observer, and the absorbent surfaces.

M. J. O. Strutt in a 1929 paper considered reverberation by regarding it as a case of free damped vibration of the volume of the air enclosed in a room. The analysis involves the general wave equations, with suitable boundary conditions imposed. Strutt regarded as unsatisfactory the theories which deal with the paths of separate sound rays. The various "eigentones" or modes of resonant vibration of the air columns in the room appear in the analysis. This analysis revealed Sabine's law as an asymptotic property to which the decay of reverberation tends as the frequency of the (forcing) sound becomes infinitely great compared with the lowest free frequency of the air itself—in other words, when the dimensions of the room become infinitely great compared with the wavelength of the sounds.

Fitzroy, on the other hand, was concerned with the discrepancies that occurred between the calculated and

Chart 4-1. Rationalized Acoustic Calculation Systems

SABINE	NORRIS-EYRING	HOPKINS-STRYKER

SABINE

$$RT_{60} = \frac{0.049V}{S\bar{a}_s}$$

$$\bar{a}_s = \frac{0.049V}{S \cdot RT_{60}}$$

$$*D_c = 0.141 \sqrt{QS\bar{a}_s}$$

$$\Delta D_x = 10 \log \left(\frac{Q}{4\pi r^2} + \frac{4}{S\bar{a}_s} \right)$$

$$\bar{a}_s = \frac{0.049V}{S \cdot RT_{60}}$$

$$\bar{a}_s = -\ln(1 - \bar{a}_n)$$

$$\bar{a}_s = \frac{-\bar{a}_R}{(\bar{a}_R - 1)} = \frac{R}{S}$$

NORRIS-EYRING

$$RT_{60} = \frac{0.049V}{-S \ln(1 - \bar{a}_n)} - \left(\frac{0.049V}{8 \cdot RT_{60}} \right)$$

$$\bar{a}_n = 1 - e$$

$$*D_c = 0.141 \sqrt{Q[-S \ln(1 - a_n)]}$$

$$\Delta D_x = 10 \log \left[\frac{Q}{4\pi r^2} + \left(\frac{4}{-S \ln(1 - \bar{a}_n)} \right) \right]$$

$$\bar{a}_n = 1 - e^{-(\bar{a}_s)} - \left(\frac{0.049V}{8 \cdot RT_{60}} \right)$$

$$\bar{a}_n = 1 - e^{-\left(\frac{\bar{a}_R}{\frac{R}{R}-1} \right)}$$

$$\bar{a}_n = 1 - e^{-\left(\frac{R}{S} \right)} = 1 - e$$

HOPKINS-STRYKER

$$RT_{60} = \frac{0.049V}{R}; \quad R = \frac{S\bar{a}_R}{1 - \bar{a}_R}$$

$$\bar{a}_R = \frac{1}{1 + \left(\frac{S \cdot RT_{60}}{0.049V} \right)} = \frac{R}{R + S}$$

$$*D_c = 0.141 \sqrt{QR}$$

$$\Delta D_x = 10 \log \left(\frac{Q}{4\pi r^2} + \frac{4}{R} \right)$$

$$\bar{a}_R = \frac{S\bar{a}_s}{S a_s + S}$$

$$\bar{a}_R = \frac{S[-\ln(1 - \bar{a}_n)]}{S[-\ln(1 - \bar{a}_n)] + S}$$

$$\bar{a}_R = \frac{1}{1 + \left(\frac{S \cdot RT_{60}}{0.049V} \right)} = \frac{R}{R + S}$$

* Additional D_c Equation:

$$D_c = 0.03121 \sqrt{\frac{QV}{RT_{60}}}$$

because $S\bar{a}$, $-S \ln(1 - \bar{a})$, and R all equal $\left(\frac{0.049V}{RT_{60}} \right)$

Sample Case Values

When:
V = 500,000 ft³
S = 42,500 ft²
RT_{60} = 2.5 seconds
Q = 5

Then:
$\bar{a}_s$ = 0.231
$\bar{a}_n$ = 0.206
$\bar{a}_R$ = 0.187
D_c = 31.17 ft
R = 9775.52 ft²

($\bar{a}_s$ = Sabine $\bar{a}$)
($\bar{a}_n$ = Norris-Eyring $\bar{a}$)
($\bar{a}_R$ = Room constant $\bar{a}$)

measured reverberation times when the absorption was not uniform. He apportioned by percentage the reverberation time of the axial modes for the vertical, lateral, and horizontal axes in the room.

It is well in considering reverberation to recognize that the idea of rays of sound is a conceptual convenience and not really how nature is operating. The modal analysis method is more exact but far too tedious to find daily use. In considering what we do with the data, the following guidelines should be of help in deciding which equation to use:

1. Use the Sabine equation in medium- to large-sized rooms where the expected $RT_{60} \geq 2.0$ seconds and the absorption is relatively uniform and usually low in value. It has the advantage of being easy to use with simple calculations, and most material ratings relate directly to it.
2. Use the Norris-Eyring equation when $RT_{60} \geq 2.0$ seconds and the additional complexity of the equation causes no problems. Always use the Norris-Eyring equation for rooms in which the expected $RT_{60} \leq 2.0$ seconds and the absorption is uniformly distributed. (See Chart 4-1 for changing values from one system to another.)
3. The Fitzroy equation is basically the Norris-Eyring equation when the absorption is uniformly distributed, but when the absorption is not uniformly distributed, it allows analysis of the 3 axial modes independently. Experience will show you that the measured reverberation time calculated with the Sabine or Norris-Eyring equation is usually longer than the calculated time whenever differences appear. The Fitzroy equation helps to rationalize these differences.

At this point, you probably are asking yourself why a sound-system engineer needs to make these calculations. The answer is that to calculate level change with increasing distance from an audio source indoors, he must know $\bar{a}$. The easiest way to obtain $\bar{a}$ in an existing space is to measure the reverberation time. You will also soon see the role reverberation plays in determining articulation losses.

LEVEL CHANGE WITH INCREASING DISTANCE FROM THE SOUND SOURCE—INDOORS

When the room is relatively regularly ratioed (that is, no major room dimension is different from any other major room dimension by more than 4 to 1 and the space has a reverberation time greater than 1.6 seconds), then we can use the following formula to obtain a relative level change from an unknown source point arbitrarily chosen.

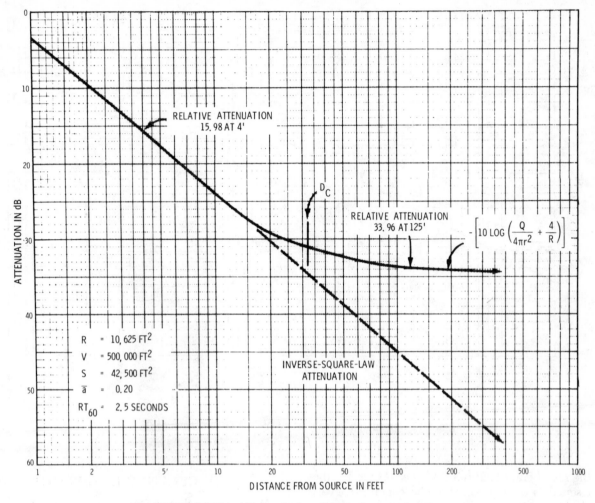

Fig. 4-16. Attenuation with increasing distance in an enclosed space.

$$\Delta D_x = -10 \log \left(\frac{Q}{4\pi D_x^2} + \frac{4}{R} \right) \qquad (4\text{-}38)$$

where,

ΔD_x is a distance converted to a dB loss figure,

D_x is the distance from the source in feet,

R is the room constant,

$R = \dfrac{S\bar{a}_R}{1 - \bar{a}_R}$,

Q is the directivity ratio.

You may use R, $-S \ln (1 - \bar{a})$, or $S\bar{a}$ depending on which reverberation-equation method you adopt.

The equation can also be solved for the distance:

$$D_x = \sqrt{\frac{Q}{4\pi \left(10^{-\frac{\Delta D_x}{10}} - \frac{4}{R} \right)}} \qquad (4\text{-}39)$$

If, in our example space, we wanted to find how much the source (Q = 5) would change level at 125 feet and we know it is putting out 90 dB-SPL at 4 feet, we would make the following calculation:

$$-10 \log \left(\frac{5}{4\pi 16} + \frac{4}{\frac{42,500 \times 0.2}{1 - 0.2}} \right) = 15.98$$

$$(4\text{-}40)$$

$$-10 \log \left(\frac{5}{4\pi 15625} + \frac{4}{\frac{42,500 \times 0.2}{1 - 0.2}} \right) = 33.96$$

$$(4\text{-}41)$$

$$33.96 - 15.98 = 17.98 \text{ dB difference} \qquad (4\text{-}42)$$

Therefore, 90 dB-SPL − 17.98 dB = 72.02 dB-SPL at 125 ft.

The reason level change does not continue in this enclosed space is that after you move far enough away from the sound source, the direct sound level, which does follow inverse-square-law level change, finally drops to the same level as the reverberant sound. At a point called the *critical distance*, D_c, the direct sound and the reverberant sound are both at the same level. Remembering that two equal SPLs add to become 3 dB greater, observe the curve of Fig. 4-16 at D_c. At 125

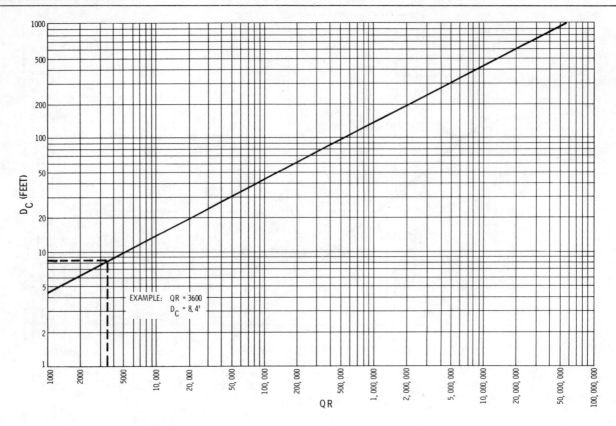

EXAMPLE: QR = 3600
D_C = 8.4'

QR

Fig. 4-17. Nomograph for converting QR into critical distance D_c.

feet, the reverberant field is 3 dB lower. At the D_c, the direct sound is 3 dB lower, but the combined levels form the curve you see at D_c.

CRITICAL DISTANCE

One of the most important concepts regarding the acoustic space you will ever encounter is D_c. First of all, consider that D_c is within 3 dB of the maximum acoustical separation you will ever get between a microphone and a loudspeaker in a given room. Again, consider that if you have a microphone in a steady reverberant field, you may wander all over the reverberant area without encountering a sudden change in level that can cause feedback. In fact, we will make use of D_c in determining the following "limits" in our design of sound systems.

1. The loudspeaker and the microphone should be at least as far apart as D_c. $D_1 \geqq D_c < 45$ ft, where D_1 is the distance between the loudspeaker and the microphone.
2. In rooms with a reverberation time exceeding 1.6 seconds, you will not be able to have any listener beyond $3.16 D_c$. As the time rises further, this multiplier will lower still further (discussed in detail under articulation losses).

CALCULATING D_C DIRECTLY

If we assume that at D_c

$$\frac{Q}{4\pi D_x{}^2} = \frac{4}{R} \tag{4-43}$$

then we can say

$$D_x{}^2 = \frac{QR}{16\pi} \tag{4-44}$$

and that

$$D_x = \sqrt{\frac{1}{16\pi}} \times \sqrt{QR} \tag{4-45}$$

Since D_x in this case $= D_c$, we can then substitute

$$D_c = 0.141 \times \sqrt{QR} \tag{4-46}$$

That this is so is evident in our sample building:

$$D_c = 0.141 \sqrt{5 \times 9775} = 31.17 \text{ ft} \tag{4-47}$$

Fig. 4-17 is a nomograph from which D_c can be found when the product QR is known.

Once you know the critical distance, you can construct a curve like that drawn in Fig. 4-16. Drop 3 dB below D_c and construct a 6-dB/double-distance line and a straight line out to greater distances; join them with a curve through D_c.

$$D_c =$$
$$\frac{\text{Dir field dB-SPL} - \text{Reverb field dB-SPL}}{20}$$

Ref dist in dir field $\times\ 10$

Still another way to arrive at D_c is

$$RT_{60} = \frac{0.049V}{R}$$

$$D_c = 0.141\ \sqrt{QR}$$

$$R = \frac{0.049V}{RT_{60}}$$

$$D_c = 0.03121\ \sqrt{\frac{QV}{RT_{60}}}$$

This method avoids having to establish which $\bar{a}$ system to use.

SENSITIVITY VERSUS EFFICIENCY LEVELS

In the "free" field (i.e., near the loudspeaker in an auditorium), a sound-level meter when placed at four feet on axis in front of the loudspeaker will read the *sensitivity* of the unit being measured. Well beyond critical distance, the microphone will read the relative efficiency or radiated power level of the unit being measured. This would suggest that the directivity index, D_I, can be used to compare the expected power-level difference between two loudspeaker drivers, either in a system or in separate systems.

The difference in the performance of two units with different values of Q can be determined by subtracting the difference in D_I between the two units from the sensitivity figure for the unit with the higher Q.

As an example, take a low-frequency driver and enclosure that has a rating of 105 dB-SPL at 4 feet from 1 watt and a Q of 5. Determine how much difference in level there will be in the reverberant field at approximately $3D_c$ between it and a high-frequency driver and horn with a rating of 110 dB-SPL at 4 feet from 1 watt and a Q of 20

$$D_I = 10 \log Q \qquad (4\text{-}48)$$

Therefore, the high-frequency unit has a D_I of:

$$D_I = 10 \log 20 = 13.01 \text{ dB} \qquad (4\text{-}49)$$

and the low-frequency unit has a D_I of:

$$D_I = 10 \log 5 = 6.99 \text{ dB} \qquad (4\text{-}50)$$

If our theorem is valid, then out in the reverberant field the difference in power levels should be:

$$\begin{aligned}
110 - 13.01 &= 96.99 \text{ dB} \\
105 - 6.99 &= 98.01 \text{ dB} \\
\text{Difference} &= 1.02 \text{ dB}
\end{aligned} \qquad (4\text{-}51)$$

(Lf speaker actually is more efficient.)

Using the classic Hopkins-Stryker equation, for a room having a room constant R of 8000 and a $3D_c$ distance of approximately 200 feet, we can write the following equations.

For the high-frequency unit:

$$4\text{-ft, 1 W level} + \left[10 \log \left(\frac{20}{4\pi 40,000} + \frac{4}{8000} \right) \right.$$
$$\left. - 10 \log \left(\frac{20}{4\pi 16} + \frac{4}{8000} \right) \right]$$

$$= 87.32 \text{ dB-SPL, the reverberant level at 200 ft} \qquad (4\text{-}52)$$

For the low-frequency unit:

$$4\text{-ft, 1 W level} + \left[10 \log \left(\frac{5}{4\pi 40,000} + \frac{4}{8000} \right) \right.$$
$$\left. - 10 \log \left(\frac{5}{4\pi 16} + \frac{4}{8000} \right) \right]$$

$$= 88.03 \text{ dB-SPL, the reverberant level at 200 ft} \qquad (4\text{-}53)$$

Then

$$87.32 - 88.03 = 0.71 \text{ dB} \qquad (4\text{-}54)$$

In determining the measurable difference in dB-SPL to be expected in the crossover region for high-frequency and low-frequency driver combinations, both the sensitivity figures and the directivity-index figures need to be taken into consideration. The directivity-index figures may be subtracted from the sensitivity of the units, and the resulting differences in power then reflect the expected level differences that should exist in the reverberant field. In most cases, this would eliminate the use of pads in crossover network systems; usually such pads are used erroneously to "match" sensitivities instead of reverberant power levels. See Fig. 4-18.

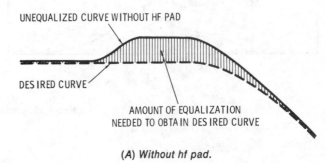

UNEQUALIZED CURVE WITHOUT HF PAD

DESIRED CURVE

AMOUNT OF EQUALIZATION NEEDED TO OBTAIN DESIRED CURVE

(A) Without hf pad.

UNEQUALIZED CURVE WITH HF PAD

DESIRED CURVE

AMOUNT OF EQUALIZATION NEEDED TO OBTAIN DESIRED CURVE

(B) With hf pad.

Fig. 4-18. Problem that can arise from using crossover pads.

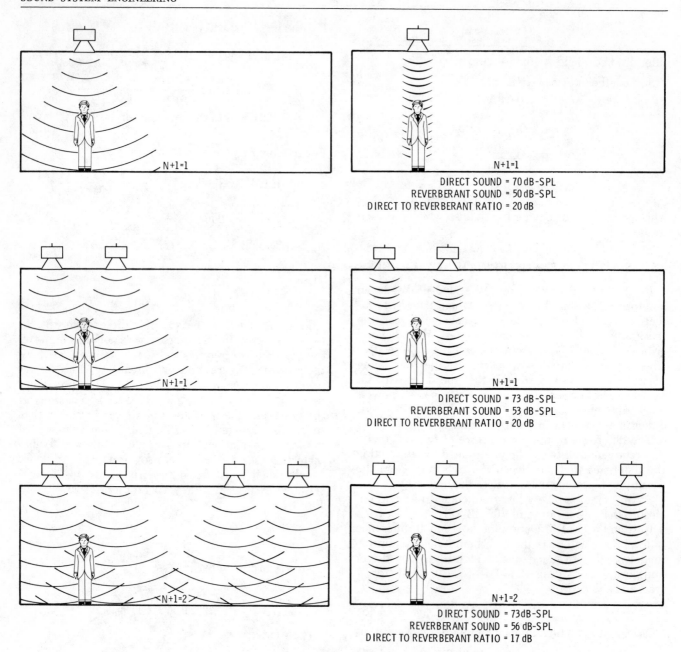

Fig. 4-19. Visualization of n + 1.

ROOM GAIN

Outdoors the level change from 4 feet to 125 feet is approximately 30 dB. Indoors in a room with a D_c of approximately 31.5 feet, the level change from 4 feet to 125 feet would be about 18 dB. The 12-dB difference is often labeled the "room gain."

Room gain is a misnomer because rooms are passive and do not have gain. What is referred to is the fact that at 125 feet in our example, the room supports the reverberant field and provides 12 dB more level to the listener than he would have received outdoors. This 12 dB is referred to as the *room gain* at that distance.

Q VERSUS R FOR CONTROLLING D_c

In examining the equation for D_c is it apparent that both Q and R have the same relative weight. This means that in a space that requires a doubling of R in order to be acceptable, you could just as well leave R alone and double Q. In typical church systems, for example, the doubling of R can easily cost $100,000 and change the entire visual appearance of the structure as well as making the music director very unhappy. Doubling Q usually costs under $10,000, and while the array may be huge, it does occupy only one spot and not whole walls and ceilings. This is a relatively new concept and not widely practiced, though certain acoustic consultants have effectively used the general idea for years. We can now enumerate a few of the factors proceeding from the existence of D_c in a space:

1. It determines maximum *acoustical* separation, hence maximum acoustic gain.
2. It determines the ratio of direct-to-reverberant sound.
3. It determines the required directivity of the loudspeaker in an already existing room.
4. It can determine the required room characteristics in a space being planned if a chosen loudspeaker is desired:

$$D_c = 0.141 \sqrt{\frac{QRM}{n+1}} \qquad (4\text{-}55)$$

$$Q = \frac{D_c{}^2(n+1)}{0.019881RM} \qquad (4\text{-}56)$$

$$R = \frac{D_c{}^2(n+1)}{0.019881\,QM} \qquad (4\text{-}57)$$

$$n+1 = \frac{0.019881\,QRM}{D_c{}^2} \qquad (4\text{-}58)$$

In these equations, $(n+1)$ is the number of loudspeaker groups; 1 is the number of loudspeakers furnishing direct sound to the listener, and n is the number of groups equal to the size of 1 that are not furnishing direct sound to the listener. (Refer to Fig. 4-19.) The quantity M is the D_c modifier. (See Fig. 4-20.)

D_c MULTIPLIERS AND DIVIDERS

Just as $n+1$ operates as a D_c divider, there are factors that can operate as D_c multipliers. Let us first take an extreme case in which the C_l contains all the useful energy, and it is aimed at an audience area that is 100% absorptive (Fig. 4-20A). Even if the room were highly reverberant, this loudspeaker would cause no reverberation. A more typical case is shown in Fig. 4-20B.

Additionally, a tilted rear wall may raise the apparent Q at the rear seats in an auditorium even further. When you measure Q in a room with a calibrated loudspeaker, the difference between what you calculate and the calibration includes all the multipliers and dividers. Therefore, such a calibrated test source allows you to do several things:

1. Measure the room constant, R, by the reverberation-time method and calculation. Then measure the apparent Q. This will include all multipliers and dividers, and by changing position of materials, position of sources, etc., you can investigate the effect of such phenomena.
2. Measure the room constant, R, by the critical-distance method using the Q of your calibrated sources in your calculations. By using this room constant, which includes all the multipliers and

dividers, you can accurately measure the axial Q of unknown sound sources.

CALCULATING RELATIVE LEVELS IN SEMIREVERBERANT SPACES

The formula for calculating relative levels in semi-reverberant spaces is:

$$\Delta D_x = -10 \log \left(\frac{Q}{4\pi D_x{}^2} + \frac{4}{R} \right)$$
$$+ \left(0.734 \, \frac{\sqrt{V}}{h \times RT_{60}} \right) \left(\log \frac{D_x > D_c}{D_c} \right)$$
$$(4\text{-}60)$$

where,

ΔD_x is the relative level in decibels,
$D_x > D_c$ is the distance from the source,
Q is the directivity factor,
R is the room constant $= s\bar{a}/(1-\bar{a})$,
V is the internal volume of the space in cubic feet or cubic meters,
h is the height of the ceiling in feet or meters,
RT_{60} is the reverberation time in seconds,
D_c is the critical distance in feet or meters.

When meters are used instead of feet in this formula,

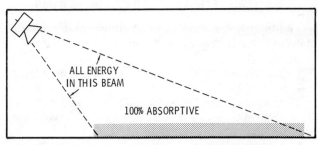

APPARENT Q = AXIAL Q $\left(\dfrac{1-\bar{a}\ \text{OF TOTAL ROOM}}{1-a\ \text{OF AUDIENCE AREA}} \right)$

EXAMPLE: AXIAL Q = 5; ROOM $\bar{a}$ = 0.01; AUDIENCE a = 1

APPARENT Q = 5 $\left(\dfrac{1-0.01}{1-1} \right)$ = ∞

(A) No reverberation.

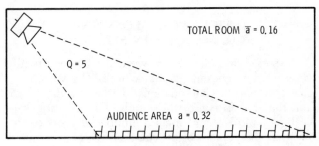

EXAMPLE: APPARENT Q = 5 $\left(\dfrac{1-0.16}{1-0.32} \right)$ = 6.18

(B) More typical case.

Fig. 4-20. D_c multipliers.

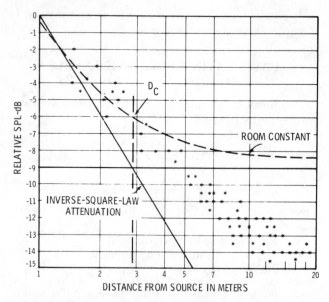

Fig. 4-21. Results of the Ogawa experiment in an odd-sized well-damped room.

replace the constant 0.734 with 1.329.

See Fig. 4-21.

FACTORS TO WATCH FOR IN ROOMS

The following factors can be serious trouble for the sound system if they are not properly controlled:

1. Curved surfaces, especially concave curved surfaces.
2. Absolutely parallel walls. Such walls cause flutter-echo. A splay of 1 inch per foot will avoid this problem.
3. Absorption on the ceiling. Unless the ceiling is very high (over 60 feet), the placement of absorption on it means the sound system has lost some useful reflecting surfaces. Absorption belongs on rear walls, rear ceilings, in the seats, etc.
4. Potential ambient noise sources—air handlers, unenclosed machinery, etc.
5. Extra wide or round audience seating.

ARTICULATION LOSSES OF CONSONANTS IN SPEECH

When we talk, the sounds we make can be broadly classified into consonants and vowels. The vowels are a, e, i, o, and u. Combinations like ba, pa, da, ta, ga, and tha contain consonant sounds. Two acoustical investigators in Holland spent a number of years resolving that the percent of articulation loss of consonants determined the articulation score in various acoustical spaces. Formulas for $\%AL_{CONS}$, the articulation loss for consonants as a percentage, were then developed and published by V.M.A. Peutz and W. Klein of Nijmegen, Holland in the December 1971 *Audio Engi-*

neering Journal. Their formulas have been adapted for this text by adding Q and presenting all their alternative forms. You will see now how useful they can be in matching the room to the sound system.

CALCULATING THE ARTICULATION LOSS OF CONSONANTS

The formula for calculating the articulation loss of consonants as a percentage is:

$$\% AL_{CONS} = \frac{641.81\,D_2^2 RT_{60}^2(n+1)}{VQM}$$

(4-61)

where,

D_2 is the distance from the loudspeaker to the farthest listener,
RT_60 is the reverberation time in seconds,
V is the volume of the room in cubic feet,
Q is the directivity ratio,
n is the number of loudspeaker groups identical to group 1,
M is the D_c modifier (usually 1 is chosen except in special instances).

The above formula is used for $D_2 \leqq D_L$, and $D_L = 3.16\,D_C$. When $D_2 \geqq D_L$, the formula becomes:

$$\% AL_{CONS} = 9\,RT_{60}$$

(4-62)

NOTE: It is necessary to assume a required signal-to-noise ratio of 25 dB to make these calculations valid.

When meters are used for distances and volumes, the constant becomes 200.

USABLE PERCENTAGES

Mr. Peutz states, "If the AL_{CONS} is below 10%, the intelligibility is very good. Between 10 and 15%, the intelligibility is good and only if the message is difficult and the speaker (talker) and/or listeners are not good will the intelligibility be insufficient. Above 15% the intelligibility is only sufficient for good listeners with speakers (talkers) and/or messages."

In comparing Peutz' and Klein's method with known data from many installations, an AL_{CONS} of 15% is considered to be a practical working limit. The basic formula can therefore be converted into the following useful forms:

Maximum D_2 that allows an AL_{CONS} of 15% =

$$\sqrt{\frac{15VQM}{641.81RT_{60}^2\,(n+1)}}$$

(4-63)

Maximum RT_{60} that allows an AL_{CNOS} of 15% =

$$\sqrt{\frac{15VQM}{641.81D_2^2\,(n+1)}}$$

(4-64)

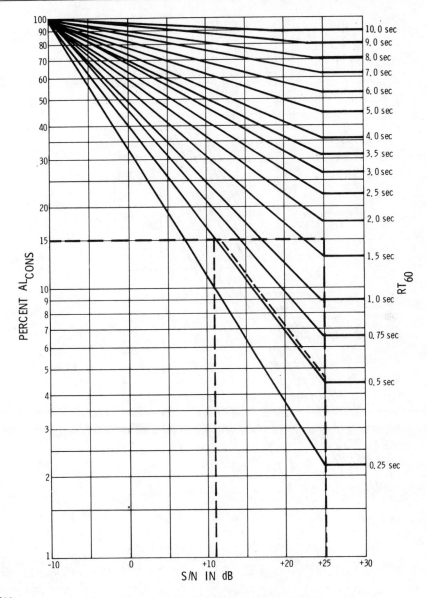

Fig. 4-22. Effect of s/n ratio on % AL_{CONS} at D_L.

Minimum V that allows an AL_{CONS} of 15% =

$$\frac{641.81 D_2^2 RT_{60}^2 \, (n+1)}{15 QM}$$

(4-65)

Minimum Q that allows an AL_{CONS} of 15% =

$$\frac{641.81 D_2^2 RT_{60}^2 \, (n+1)}{15 VM}$$

(4-66)

Other useful forms of these equations can be derived by substituting conventional RT_{60} equations in place of RT_{60}.

Min Sabine Sā for 15% AL_{CONS} = $\dfrac{1.24 \, D_2 V}{\sqrt{15 VQ}}$ (4-67)

Min Norris-Eyring Sā for 15% AL_{CONS} =

$$S \left[1 - e^{-\left(\frac{1.24 D_2 V}{\sqrt{15 VQ} \, (S)} \right)} \right]$$

(4-68)

MAXFIELD'S EQUATION

Peutz' and Klein's formula was adapted to their data from one used by Western Electric's J. P. Maxfield for finding the "liveness" of a microphone pickup for broadcasting use in the late 1930s.

$$L = \frac{1000 (RT_{60})^2 (D_S)^2}{VQ}$$

(4-69)

where D_S is the distance from the talker to the microphone.

Acceptable values of L for speech range from 0.167 to 0.666. This equation can be manipulated in the same manner as the Peutz and Klein formula.

$$\text{Max } D_S = \frac{\sqrt{L V Q}}{31.6 \, RT_{60}}$$

(4-70)

$$\text{Min } Q = \frac{1000 (RT_{60})^2 (D_S)^2}{VL}$$

(4-71)

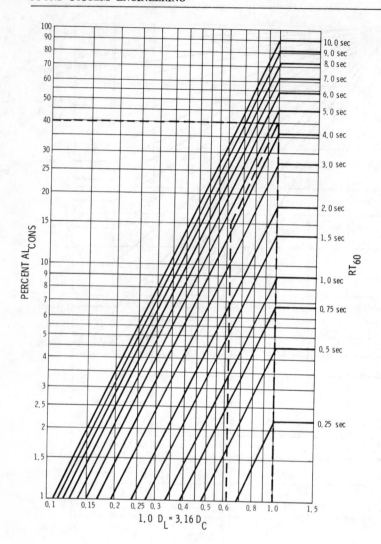

Fig. 4-23. %AL$_{CONS}$ as a function of RT$_{60}$ and distances equal to or less than D$_L$.

$$\text{Min V} = \frac{1000(\text{RT}_{60})^2(\text{D}_S)^2}{\text{LQ}} \quad (4\text{-}72)$$

$$\text{Max RT}_{60} = \frac{\sqrt{\text{L V Q}}}{31.6 \, \text{D}_S} \quad (4\text{-}73)$$

USING %AL$_{CONS}$ CHARTS

Fig. 4-22 illustrates the effect of signal-to-noise (s/n) ratio on the %AL$_{CONS}$. The AL$_{CONS}$ improves steadily with improving s/n ratio until it reaches 25 dB. After that, the articulation does not improve as the s/n is further extended.

This chart reveals that in rooms with an RT$_{60} \geqq 1.5$ seconds, we would not want to accept an s/n ratio of less than 25 dB. However, in a room of RT$_{60} = 0.5$ second, we could maintain a %AL$_{CONS}$ of 15% with only an 11-dB s/n ratio.

Fig. 4-23 illustrates the use of the %AL$_{CONS}$ formulas in a slightly simplified form. (The equations describe a curve, whereas the graph is a straight-line approximation of the formula that is on the conservative side).

These graphs, carefully studied, lead the user to a solid conceptual understanding of the ramifications of changing room and system parameters in terms of the articulation loss of consonants. Referring again to Fig. 4-23, we see a base line along the bottom, calibrated from 0.1 D$_L$ to 1.0 D$_L$ (D$_L$ means the limiting distance). The left-hand vertical scale is calibrated in %AL$_{CONS}$, and the right-hand vertical scale is calibrated in RT$_{60}$ in seconds. Here we can note that articulation losses continue to increase until D$_L$ is reached. Beyond D$_L$, the articulation losses tend to remain constant. Therefore, if we had a room with an RT$_{60} \leqq 1.6$ second and an s/n ratio of 25 dB, we could go any distance from the sound source without exceeding an AL$_{CONS}$ of 15%.

Suppose, however, that you kept the s/n ratio of 25 dB but the RT$_{60}$ rose to 4.5 seconds at D$_L$. You would follow downward between the slanting lines corresponding to 4 and 5 seconds until you intersected the 15%AL$_{CONS}$ horizontal line (or any other AL$_{CONS}$ value that you are seeking), and then drop straight down to the D$_L$ base line at 0.61 D$_L$.

By solving for x in the proportion

$$\frac{1.0D_L}{0.61D_L} = \frac{3.16 \, D_c}{x} \qquad (4\text{-}74)$$

you find that you can go $1.93D_c$ away from the sound source before exceeding $15\%AL_{CONS}$.

If $1.93D_c$ does not reach far enough to cover the last seat, the new Q required may be calculated by:

$$\text{Needed } D_c = \frac{D_2}{1.93} \qquad 4\text{-}75)$$

and

$$Q = \frac{(D_c)^2}{0.019881R} \qquad (4\text{-}76)$$

in order for $1.93 \, D_c$ to equal D_2.

These three steps can be combined into a single set of equations for finding the Q and R required to provide $15\% \, AL_{CONS}$ at D_2:

$$\text{Needed } Q = \frac{\left(\dfrac{D_2}{3.16(D_L \text{ mult})}\right)^2}{0.019881R} \qquad (4\text{-}77)$$

$$\text{Needed } R = \frac{\left(\dfrac{D_2}{3.16(D_L \text{ mult})}\right)^2}{0.019881 \, Q} \qquad (4\text{-}78)$$

where $(D_L \text{ mult})$ is the number read from the horizontal axis of Fig. 4-23.

A SAMPLE EXERCISE

To evaluate these equations, let us return to our sample acoustic environment:

$$V = 500,000 \text{ ft}^3$$
$$S = 42,500 \text{ ft}^2$$
$$\bar{a}_{N.E.} = 0.206$$
$$RT_{60} = 2.5 \text{ s}$$
$$D_2 = 125 \text{ ft}$$

First of all, we can evaluate how a talker without benefit of a sound system would do in this space. Recall that a typical male talker has a dB-SPL of 67.2 at 3.28 ft, or

$$67.2 + 20 \log\left(\frac{3.28 \text{ ft}}{2 \text{ ft}}\right) = 71.5 \text{ dB-SPL at 2 feet} \qquad (4\text{-}79)$$

This same talker has a Q of 2.5, or an angular coverage in the horizontal plane of approximately 160° (this is for speech around 2000 Hz).

We will first calculate the maximum distance from the talker at which AL_{CONS} will not fall below 15% (ignoring for the moment the need for a 25-dB signal-to-noise ratio at the same distance).

$$\text{Max dist} = \sqrt{\frac{15 \, VQ}{641.81 \, (RT_{60})^2}} \qquad (4\text{-}80)$$

or in this case:

$$\text{Max dist} = \sqrt{\frac{15 \times 500,000 \times 2.50}{641.81 \, (2.5)^2}} = 68.37 \text{ ft} \qquad (4\text{-}81)$$

The limiting distance D_L, beyond which no further loss in articulation occurs, is found by:

$$D_L = 3.16 \, D_c \qquad (4\text{-}82)$$

or

$$D_L = 3.16 \, (0.141 \sqrt{2.5 \times 11026.45}) = 73.98 \text{ ft} \qquad (4\text{-}83)$$

This means the worst of AL_{CONS} in this space for a live talker will be:

$$\%AL_{CONS} = \frac{641.81 \, (D_2)^2 \, (RT_{60})^2}{VQ} \qquad (4\text{-}84)$$

$$= \frac{641.81 \, (73.98)^2 \, (2.5)^2}{500,000 \times 2.5} = 17.56\% \qquad (4\text{-}85)$$

In the case of the required ambient noise, $D_c = 23.41$ feet, so

$$71.5 \text{ dB} - \left(20 \log \frac{23.41}{2}\right) = 50.13 \text{ dB-SPL} \qquad (4\text{-}86)$$

$$50.13 \text{ dB-SPL} - 25 \text{ dB s/n} = 25.13 \text{ dB-SPL} \qquad (4\text{-}87)$$

Therefore, if you could achieve an ambient noise level of 25.13 dB-SPL (a very, very quiet level), then this room and this talker just might get by without amplification.

It should be noted here that rarely do spaces with an RT_{60} of 2.5 seconds possess such a low ambient noise level. In general, it can be safely stated that when rooms have ambient noise levels above 45 dBA and reverberation times above 1.6 seconds, a sound system is mandatory. When rooms with RT_{60} below 1.6 seconds are noisy or too wide or will have weak talkers or poor listeners present, then sound systems are required in them as well. Conference rooms are excellent examples. Often the users are older men with advanced presbycusis (hearing loss associated with age), usually greatest at high frequencies (Fig. 4-24). In addition, they are often very quiet talkers.

CALCULATING THE MINIMUM Q

We can now calculate the minimum Q that will allow an AL_{CONS} of 15% at 125 feet in the example room.

$$\text{Min Q} = \frac{641.81 \, (D_2)^2 \, (RT_{60})^2}{15V} \qquad (4\text{-}88)$$

or

$$\text{Min Q} = \frac{641.81 \, (125)^2 \, (2.5)^2}{15 \times 500,000} = 8.36 \qquad (4\text{-}89)$$

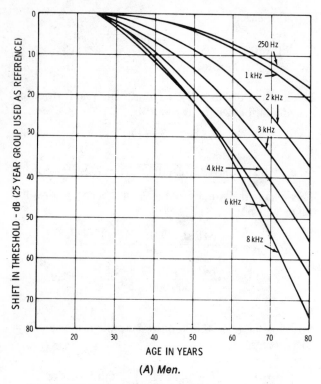

(A) Men.

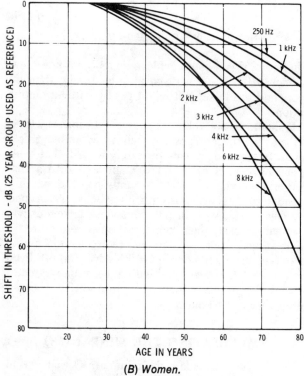

(B) Women.

Fig. 4-24. Effects of aging on hearing (presbycusis).

Therefore, if you can locate a loudspeaker with proper angular coverage specifications that also has $Q \geqq 8.36$, you can be sure of acceptable articulation at 125 feet.

There have been many striking confirmations of the accuracy of these formulas but none more so than the

experience of Ancha Electronics in Chicago. Ancha Electronics provided the rental sound system in the giant hall at McCormick Place during a Billy Graham Crusade. Bob Ancha, in the days before these formulas were available, had backed away from one of his loudspeaker arrays until his ears judged that it was getting difficult to hear. He then placed other loudspeakers in concentric circles at that distance and used time delays. The formulas yield the following result:

$$\text{Max } D_2 \text{ that allows AL}_{\text{CONS}} \text{ of } 15\% = \sqrt{\frac{15\,VQ}{641.81\,(RT_{60})^2}} \tag{4-90}$$

or, in this case

$$\text{Max. } D_2 = \sqrt{\frac{15 \times 19,702,800 \times 5.17}{641.81\,(9)^2}} = 171.44 \text{ feet} \tag{4-91}$$

The loudspeakers had actually been placed 175 feet apart.

CALCULATION OF THE MAXIMUM RT₆₀

Still another use of these very helpful equations is the determination of the limiting room parameters if an architect prefers a specific loudspeaker array for esthetic reasons. Say the architect has chosen a certain loudspeaker that has $Q = 5$ and is designing a building having a maximum distance between the preferred loudspeaker location and the farthest listener of 150 feet. You can then use the equations to inform him of the maximum RT_{60} that will allow an AL_{CONS} of 15% at 150 feet from a loudspeaker with $Q = 5$. (Assume V is 500,000 cubic feet.)

$$\text{Max } RT_{60} = \sqrt{\frac{15\,VQ}{641.81\,(D_2)^2}} \tag{4-92}$$

$$= \sqrt{\frac{15 \times 500,000 \times 5}{641.81\,(150)^2}} = 1.6 \text{ seconds} \tag{4-93}$$

The formula for D_L is:

$$D_L = 3.16\,D_c$$
$$= 3.16\,(0.141\,\sqrt{QR}) \tag{4-94}$$

If R for this room is 18,475, then

$$D_L = 3.16\,(0.141\,\sqrt{5 \times 18,475}) = 135.4 \text{ feet} \tag{4-95}$$

The desired distance falls outside D_L, and the value of AL_{CONS} is 15% only because the limit 1.6 seconds was not exceeded.

ATTEMPTING TO EQUALIZE FOR HEARING LOSS

Many times there is a tendency to attempt to adjust the amplitude response of a sound system to make it the inverse of the hearing-loss curve. This is not a good idea for several reasons:

1. Young people with normal hearing will be annoyed.
2. Older people have made mental compensation for the *gradual* onset of the loss and would also be annoyed.
3. Available high-frequency drivers would have their distortion increased noticeably with such boost.

SUMMARY

This chapter has covered the transmission of sound. You have become acquainted with calculating sound attenuation and level change under a variety of circumstances and have further found a way to calculate the effects of reverberation, directivity, and sound level on articulation losses at the listener's ears. These can now be put together into a relatively simple set of procedures for the calculation of needed acoustic gain and potential acoustic gain in our next chapter.

CHAPTER 5

Designing for Acoustic Gain

As we have seen in previous chapters, a number of factors must be present at the listener's position for easily understood communication to take place:

1. The sound must be sufficiently loud, and it must be at least 25 dB above the ambient noise level at midfrequencies (1000 Hz − 2000 Hz in rooms with $RT_{60} \geqq 1.6$ s).
2. The sound must reasonably approximate the same spectrum shape as that produced by the talker or other source.
3. The sound must reasonably approximate a ratio of direct-to-reverberant sound within the rules for acceptable articulation loss.

MAXIMUM PHYSICAL DISTANCE

If we were to use our sample acoustic environment again:

$$V = 500,000 \text{ ft}^3$$
$$S = 42,500 \text{ ft}^2$$
$$a = 0.206$$
$$RT_{60} = 2.5 \text{ seconds}$$

and were to test it for the maximum physical distance a talker and a listener could stand apart and easily be heard without a sound system, we would find that we had indeed fulfilled the three criteria mentioned above. This physical distance is typically 6 to 10 feet in an environment of the type we have chosen for our sample. For example, if we had a weak talker producing 65 dBA at 2 feet in a very quiet room, ambient noise = 28 dBA, then:

$$28 \text{ dBA} + 25 \text{ dB s/n} = 53 \text{ dBA} \qquad (5\text{-}1)$$
$$65 \text{ dBA} - 53 \text{ dBA} = 12 \text{ dB} \qquad (5\text{-}2)$$
$$2 \times 10^{\frac{12}{20}} = 8 \text{ feet} \qquad (5\text{-}3)$$

This shows that a distance of 8 feet from the talker is the maximum physical distance at which a listener can stand and be sure of hearing clearly if no sound system is present. If we had used a normal male voice level of 71 dB at 2 feet, then the maximum physical distance would have been

$$71 \text{ dBA} - 53 \text{ dBA} = 18 \text{ dB} \qquad (5\text{-}4)$$
$$2 \times 10^{\frac{18}{20}} = 16 \text{ feet} \qquad (5\text{-}5)$$

The chart in Fig. 5-1 allows these calculations to be made at a glance. "Weak voice" and "normal voice" are relatively self-explanatory. The expected voice level is a very real effect that can be relied upon in marginal communication circumstances or that must be carefully avoided in the case of noise masking systems, for example.

If a talker and a listener were 10 feet apart and you raised the noise level by means of a background masking system to approximately 58 dB-SPL overall, then your talker would involuntarily raise his voice to overcome the noise. If you were to keep the noise at 55 dBA, then masking would be effective at distances of 12 to 15 feet from the talker, who would continue to converse at his normal voice level. A talker can raise his Q slightly by cupping his hands in front of his mouth, megaphone fashion, and a listener raises his Q by cupping a hand or hands behind his ears. The limit shown for amplified speech is not due to an inability to amplify but because these levels represent dangerous SPL conditions for the listener's ears. Fig. 5-1 is a most useful chart for detailed study. It outlines the parameters of the possible and impossible sound-system solutions and is simple enough for laymen to understand during presentations of proposals, etc.

Having arrived at the maximum physical distance between a talker and a listener with no sound system present, we now adopt that distance as our goal for a successful sound system. We want this equivalent acoustic distance (EAD) to be established at our farthest listener (D_2), though he may be over one hunderd feet away.

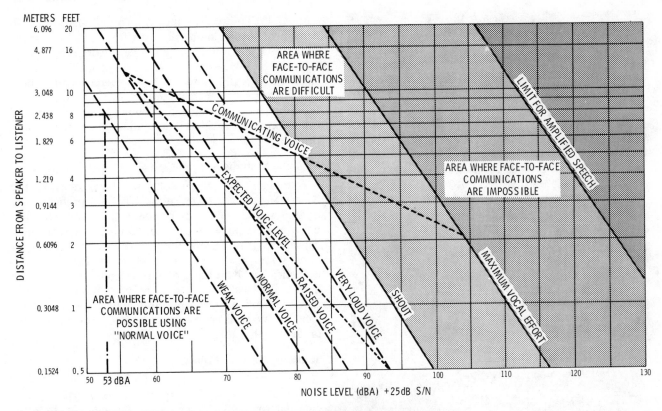

Fig. 5-1. Nomograph for finding the EAD.

MASKING SYSTEMS

Noise masking systems, or as they are identified in some specifications, *speech privacy systems,* are sound systems that utilize specially shaped random noise signals over distributed loudspeakers of very low Q to provide a controlled ambient noise level that overrides an undesired ambient noise. A masking signal is generated to override, say, the speech level from an adjacent desk area in an open-plan office by making the signal-to-noise ratio at the listener's ears too low to hear the adjacent speech level.

Level Limits

The difficulty of such systems becomes apparent when it is realized that the system must obviously have an evenly distributed level of at least 46 dBA to exceed the ordinary ambient noises present and cannot exceed 52 dBA without danger of driving a talker in its field into his "expected voice" level. Properly done, masking systems can be surprisingly acceptable to persons subjected to them, but failure to handle all of their challenges brings quick employee dissatisfaction in the business establishment where they are used. To quote from one article on the subject, "When an electronic masking system is used in an open office, it is usually advised *that the staff be kept unaware of its existence.* This obviously avoids unnecessary problems with complaints from persons using the masking system as a focus for verbal sublimation of other unvoiced minor grievances."[1]

Shaping the Noise Signal

First of all, acquire two reliable, stable noise sources, such as the General Radio 1382 noise generator. Do not be tempted to use low-cost plug-in units in the under $100 range for this work, as they are not stable enough to maintain the output level consistently over the many days and weeks they will be expected to run. Fig. 5-2A is an oscilloscope display of the output of a General Radio 1382 pink-noise generator, measured with a 32-second integration time over a 30-minute time span. Fig. 5-2B shows a display for a similar measurement of a "Brand X" pink-noise generator. Fig. 5-2C shows a display for the "Brand X" unit measured with a 32-second integration time, but in this case over a 1-hour time span.

The noise source should be set for pink noise and connected to the input of the system equalizer. The desired *acoustic* response is shown in Fig. 5-3A. It is compared (Fig. 5-3B) to commonly available test signals as viewed by a constant-percentage bandwidth analyzer (all ⅓-octave real-time analyzers are of this type). Remember this is the acoustic signal at the listener's ears.

---

[1] A. C. C. Warnock, "Acoustical Privacy in the Landscaped Office," *JASA,* Vol. 53, No. 6, 1973.

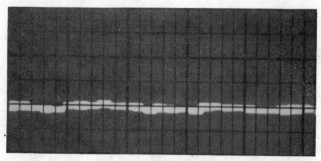

(A) GR 1382, 30 minutes.

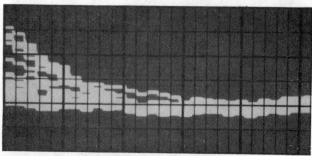

(B) "Brand X," 30 minutes.

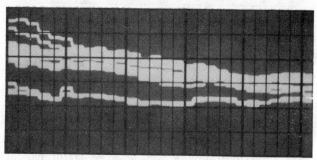

(C) "Brand X," 1 hour.

Fig. 5-2. Output spectra of pink-noise generators.

Obtaining a Diffuse Noise Field

Almost every requirement of a noise masking system is the reverse of what should be done to provide a good reinforcement or paging system. Select low-Q drivers, mount them in a good baffle facing up in the area above the suspended acoustic-tile ceiling, and let their sound pass unaided through the suspended ceiling after having first bounced off the ceiling in the plenum. No grilles of any sort should be installed in the ceiling, including cold air returns, etc., that do not have a duct attached. The suspended ceiling should have the maximum possible absorption coefficient. Lighting fixtures should be carefully arranged to avoid allowing reflections from one work area to another (they should be placed directly above the work area).

Need for Portable Screens

When the ceiling area has been made as nonreflective as possible, portable screens are also required

(Fig. 5-4). The screens should be 5 to 8 feet high with acoustical absorption on their vertical surfaces to act as both visual and aural blocks between work areas. (Less attenuation is necessary if one cannot see a conversation in progress.) Care has to be exercised that these screens are not placed directly under a hard-surfaced lighting fixture, thus negating by means of an overhead reflection the expected attenuation the panel should provide.

Masking Systems Abroad

Europeans, for the most part, have rejected the American concept of noise masking and prefer to use natural sounds of water or shape the curve of other noise makers such as air conditioning. But one must consider that in Europe the acoustical consultant exercises a far greater control over every aspect of the acoustics of the building than is accepted in the United States. For instance, European consultant V. M. A. Peutz of Holland has a portable anechoic chamber on location and tests each shipment of acoustical materials to be sure that they meet specifications.

Summary of Vital Points

1. Masking systems should be "dedicated" systems. That is, they should be used only for masking and not for background music, paging, etc. If these other functions are required, plan a separate system for them.
2. Full redundancy must be incorporated in the system (Fig. 5-5). If the system experiences a failure during the work week, then the workers become aware of its existence. Fail-safe is a must, as is planned maintenance on weekends and evenings.
3. Loudspeakers must have very low Q and be well enclosed and mounted so as to avoid structural vibrations.
4. The room ceiling must be exceptionally absorbent, and absorbent room divider screens are also required.
5. The sound system should be started around 42 dBA and brought up 1 dB per night until either a satisfactory degree of masking is achieved or 48 dBA is approached. Little is to be gained by exceeding 48 dBA.

The following publications are useful in becoming acquainted with the special vocabulary developed by certain consultants who have advised the governmental agencies eager to use such systems. (Open-plan offices sometimes save structural costs of interior walls in new government buildings and allow low-cost rearrangements.)

1. PBS-C.1 *Test Method for Direct Measurement of Speech Privacy Potential Based on Subjective Judgments.* Also ask for Appendix No. 1, *Amendments to Test Method PBS-C.1 to Include Evalu-*

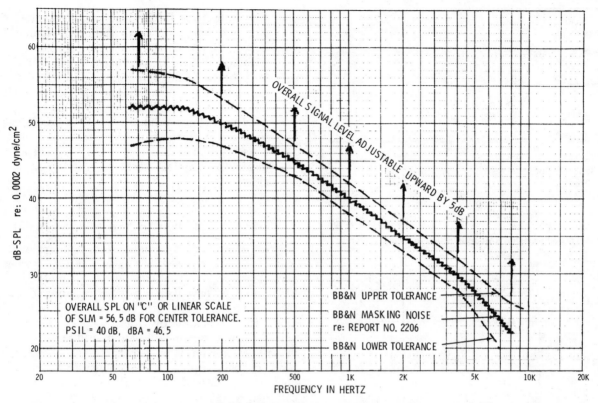

(A) BB & N suggested acoustic response.

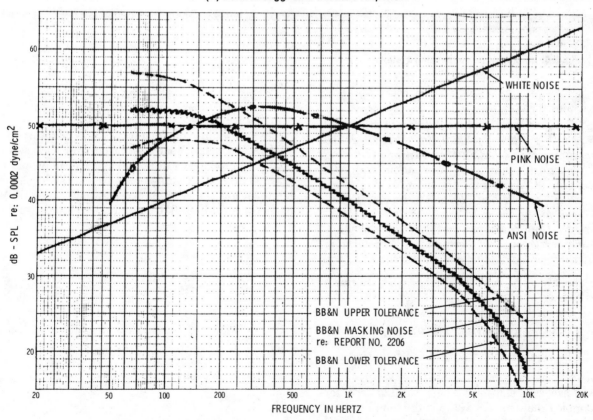

(B) Noise response curves as viewed on an analyzer using constant percentage bandwidth filters.

Fig. 5-3. Response curves for noise masking system.

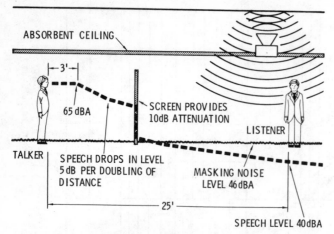

Fig. 5-4. Use of portable screen in noise masking system.

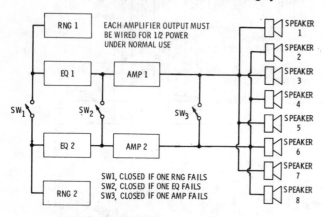

Fig. 5-5. Hookup of noise masking system.

ation of an Additional Capability for Fire Management Communication and Paging Messages.

2. *PBS-C.2 Test Method of the Sufficient Verification of Speech Privacy Potential Based on Objective Measurements Including Methods for the Rating of Functional Interzone Attenuation and NC-Background. Also ask for Appendix No. 2, Amendments to Test Method PBS-C.2 to Include Evaluation of an Additional Capability for Fire Management Communication and Paging Messages.*

3. *Guide for Acoustical Performance Specification of an Integrated Ceiling and Background System.*

All the above can be purchased from GSA, Business Services Center.

ESTABLISHING AN EAD

The EAD requires that we meet the following criteria:

1. Establish at the listener's ears (at 125 feet, for example) the same dB-SPL, via the sound system, as he would have heard at the maximum physical distance (in our sample case, the same dB-SPL as he would have heard 8 feet from the talker).

2. Establish at the listener's ears, via the sound system, the same spectrum shape he would have heard at the maximum physical distance.

3. Establish at the listener's ears, via the sound system, a ratio of direct-to-reflected sound that does not deteriorate the articulation loss of consonants by more than 15%. In other words, the equivalent acoustic distance establishes a set of conditions at some much greater distance, through the use of a sound system, similar to those that existed at some maximum physical distance without a sound system.

THE NEEDED ACOUSTIC GAIN (NAG)

Using our standard sound system notation, we can look at Fig. 5-6 and see that we have a real listener at some distance D_o. (See Appendix I, Symbols and Abbreviations.) The talker is a given distance, D_s, from the microphone. The attenuation over distance D_o minus the attenuation over distance EAD is the extra gain the sound system will be required to provide. Let us say we are outdoors and that inverse-square-law level change applies. The following distances are known: $D_s = 2$ ft, EAD = 8 ft, and $D_o = 128$ ft. We can then write:

$$NAG = 20 \log \left(\frac{D_o}{D_s}\right) - 20 \log \left(\frac{EAD}{D_s}\right) \quad (5\text{-}6)$$

or simply,

$$NAG = 20 \log D_o - 20 \log (EAD) \quad (5\text{-}7)$$

which is:

$$NAG = 20 \log 128 - 20 \log 8 = 24 \text{ dB} \quad (5\text{-}8)$$

Let us also do it the long way. If the talker produced 70 dBA at a microphone 2 feet from him, then at 4 feet he would produce 64 dBA, and at 8 feet he would produce 58 dBA. Continuing on, at 16 feet the level would be down to 52 dBA, at 32 feet it would be 46 dBA, at 64 feet it would be 40 dBA, and at 128 feet it would be

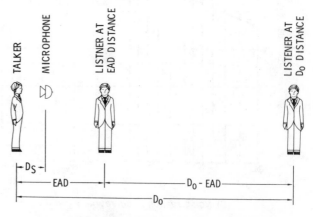

Fig. 5-6. Distances involved in determining NAG.

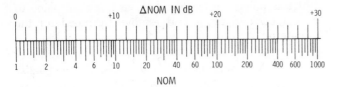

Fig. 5-7. Chart relating NOM and NOM in dB.

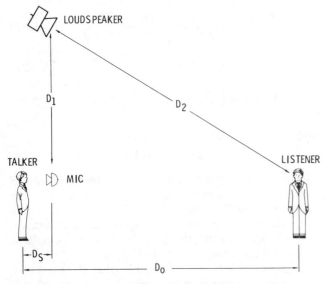

Fig. 5-8. Basic parameters of a single-source system.

34 dBA. The SPL we need is that at 8 feet, or 58 dBA. Then

$$NAG = 58\,dBA - 34\,dBA = 24\,dB \qquad (5\text{-}9)$$

We thus need 24 dB of *acoustic* gain to have an EAD of 8 feet at 128 feet.

THE NUMBER OF OPEN MICROPHONES (NOM)

If you raise two microphones to the same level in a reinforcement system, you will have to drop the overall gain 3 dB to avoid going into feedback. (Remember how decibels combine.) Since each microphone is sampling the sound field, every time you double the NOM, you will have to lower the gain 3 dB to avoid feedback (Fig. 5-7). Therefore:

$$NOM\ in\ dB = 10\log(NOM) \qquad (5\text{-}10)$$

If you intend to operate a sound system with more than one open microphone, you need to add to the gain required the decibels you will lose through having these extra microphones active.

THE FEEDBACK STABILITY MARGIN (FSM)

In the April 1955 *Journal of the Audio Engineering Society*, William B. Snow demonstrated the regenerative response characteristics of a sound reinforcement system near feedback. This paper clearly revealed that when the sound system was near feedback, the decay time of room signals passing through it increased. For example, in a room having a reverberation time of 3 seconds, with the sound system on and within a few dB of feedback, the apparent reverberation time could go to 6 or 9 or even 12 seconds. Dropping below feedback once again stabilizes the system, and the apparent and actual reverberation times become equal. An FSM of 6 dB has been found necessary by Snow (1955), Davis (1967), Mankovsky (1971), and Yamamoto (1971). We thus need to add to our required gain this 6 dB FSM.

THE NEEDED ACOUSTIC GAIN (NAG) FORMULA

We now can write a general formula for finding the needed acoustic gain of a sound reinforcement system:

$$NAG\ in\ dB = \\ \Delta D_o - \Delta EAD + 10\log(NOM) + 6\,dB\ FSM \qquad (5\text{-}11)$$

In this equation, ΔD_o and ΔEAD are the distances D_o and EAD in feet or meters converted to decibels by:

$$\Delta D_x = \\ -10\log\left(\frac{Q}{4\pi D_x^2} + \frac{4}{R}\right)\ \text{indoors, or } 20\log D_x\ \text{outdoors} \qquad (5\text{-}12)$$

$$D_x = \sqrt{\frac{Q}{4\pi\left(10^{\frac{-\Delta D_x}{10}} - \frac{4}{R}\right)}} \qquad (5\text{-}13)$$

CALCULATING POTENTIAL ACOUSTIC GAIN (PAG)

Assuming that inverse-square-law level change will serve in an outdoor situation, we can construct the set of sound-system parameters shown in Fig. 5-8. In conjunction with these calculations, we can use the nomograph in Fig. 5-9.

If the required gain ($\Delta D_o - \Delta EAD$) is 24 dB + 6 dB FSM and one microphone is open, substituting in equation 5-11 gives:

$$NAG = 24 + 0 + 6 = 30\,dB \qquad (5\text{-}14)$$

If we assign the following values to the parameters in Fig. 5-8, we can find their dB equivalents through the use of Fig. 5-9.

$$D_o = 128\,ft,\ \Delta D_o = 42\,dB$$
$$D_s = \quad 2\,ft,\ \Delta D_s = \quad 6\,dB$$
$$D_1 = \quad 45\,ft,\ \Delta D_1 = 33\,dB$$
$$D_2 = \quad 90\,ft,\ \Delta D_2 = 39\,dB$$

We can write the following formula

$$PAG = \Delta D_o + \Delta D_1 - \Delta D_s - \Delta D_2 \qquad (5\text{-}15)$$

or

$$PAG = 42 + 33 - 6 - 39 = 30 \text{ dB} \quad (5\text{-}16)$$

Since $PAG = NAG$, we have sufficient acoustic gain, SAG. We can write this another way:

$$PAG - NAG = 0 \quad (5\text{-}17)$$

If we actually write the formulas in this manner, we discover:

$$\Delta D_o + \Delta D_1 - \Delta D_s - \Delta D_2 =$$
$$\Delta D_o - \Delta EAD + 10 \log (NOM) + 6 \quad (5\text{-}18)$$

or

$$\Delta D_o - \Delta D_o + \Delta D_1 +$$
$$\Delta EAD - \Delta D_s - \Delta D_2 - 10 \log (NOM) - 6 = 0 \quad (5\text{-}19)$$

The ΔD_o's cancel, and we arrive at a most useful general formula:

$$\Delta D_1 + \Delta EAD - \Delta D_s - \Delta D_2 - 10 \log (NOM) - 6 = 0$$
$$(5\text{-}20)$$

Our original requirement was an NAG of 30 with an EAD of 8 feet and a D_s of 2 feet. We could have written the general equation in the following manner:

$$\Delta D_1 + \Delta EAD - \Delta D_s - 10 \log (NOM) - 6 = \Delta D_2$$
$$(5\text{-}21)$$

Because time delay would become a factor if we made $D_1 > 45$ feet, we chose 45 feet as a limit on D_1.

$$\text{Optimum } D_1 \geqq D_c < 45' \quad (5\text{-}22)$$

We could now write

$$\Delta 45' + \Delta 8' - \Delta 2' - 10 \log 1 - 6 = \Delta D_2 \quad (5\text{-}23)$$

or

$$33 \text{ dB} + 18 \text{ dB} - 6 \text{ dB} - 0 \text{ dB} - 6 \text{ dB} = 39 \text{ dB} \quad (5\text{-}24)$$

Looking on the dB part of the scale in Fig. 5-9, we find that 39 dB is equivalent to 90 feet.

At this point, we have arrived at a logical place to convert back to ratios and remove the need for the Δ operator.

$$\text{Maximum } D_s = \frac{D_1 \times EAD}{2D_2 \sqrt{NOM}} \quad (5\text{-}25)$$

$$\text{Minimum } D_1 = \frac{2D_s \times D_2 \times \sqrt{NOM}}{EAD} \quad (5\text{-}26)$$

$$\text{Maximum } D_2 = \frac{D_1 \times EAD}{2D_s \times \sqrt{NOM}} \quad (5\text{-}27)$$

$$\text{Minimum } EAD = \frac{2D_s \times D_2 \times \sqrt{NOM}}{D_1} \quad (5\text{-}28)$$

$$\text{Maximum } NOM = \left(\frac{D_1 \times EAD}{D_s \times 2D_2} \right)^2 \quad (5\text{-}29)$$

Caution: Indoors, no D_x can exceed D_c

$$D_x > D_c = D_c$$

In outdoor situations, simply substitute the distances directly into the equations. Indoor situations place the value of D_c as the maximum for any distance used in the equation. If an answer exceeds the D_c distance, you will need to use the Hopkins-Stryker formula in place of the simpler $20 \log D_1/D_2$.

In equation 5-24, we determined that the *maximum* D_2 distance possible is 90 feet. Why maximum distance? Let us examine what happens as we change each of these basic parameters, one at a time.

If D_1 is increased, what happens to the acoustic gain? Since the loudspeaker and microphone are separated further, the gain can be turned up more before the sound from the loudspeaker reaches the microphone at the same level as the talker's voice (unity gain). In fact, let us look at the series of level changes that both make a sound system necessary and allow it to work at all.

If, as in our example for the calculation of NAG, we again assume that the talker generates 70 dBA at a

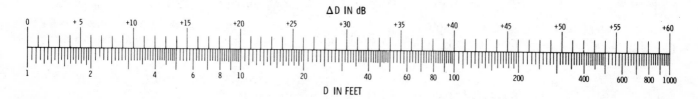

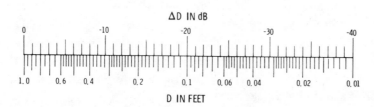

Fig. 5-9. Calculation of relative attenuation with distance (inverse square law).

microphone 2 feet in front of him, we can also assume that the loudspeaker can deliver 70 dBA also, just as feedback begins. If we work backward with inverse-square-law level change, we find that at 4 feet the loudspeaker is providing:

$$70 \text{ dBA} + 20 \log \left(\frac{45'}{4'} \right) = 91 \text{ dBA} \qquad (5\text{-}30)$$

Therefore, increasing D_1 increases the acoustic gain.

Going away from the loudspeaker in the direction of the listener, D_2, we see that at 8 feet we have 85 dBA, at 16 feet we have 79 dBA, at 32 feet we have 73 dBA, at 64 feet we have 67 dBA, and at 90 feet we have 64 dBA. Sixty-four dBA is just 6 dB greater than 58 dBA. Now, if D_2 is increased, the level at 90 feet would also decrease; therefore, increasing D_2 lowers the apparent acoustic gain.

If D_s is increased, the result is obvious. Anytime we move farther away from the microphone, we lose apparent acoustic gain.

Finally, if D_o is increased, what happens? The level change between the talker and the listener increases. Since the sound arriving from the loudspeaker has remained the same (remember we are changing only one parameter at a time), the apparent gain has increased. The formula

$$PAG = \Delta D_o + \Delta D_1 - \Delta D_s - \Delta D_2 \qquad (5\text{-}31)$$

shows by means of the signs (+ or −) which parameters will increase apparent gain if they are increased (all + signs do this) and which parameters will decrease apparent gain if they are increased (all − signs do this).

It is important to note that the *absolute acoustic gain* of the system is determined by the true *acoustical* separation between the microphone and the loudspeaker (D_1). All other parameters change the *apparent* acoustic gain (as observed by the listener).

MEASURING ACOUSTIC GAIN

It is one thing to calculate gains at the drawing-board stage of a construction project, but the real thrill comes when, after having written your calculation into a specification, many months later you actually measure the acoustic gain of the sound system after installation. The architect, engineer, owner, and other interested parties know your prediction. When your actual measurements come within ±2 dB of your calculation (which has happened in literally hundreds of jobs), these professionals have no choice but to regard you as a fellow professional.

NOTE: The potential gain figures illustrated in this chapter are dependent on the performance of room–sound-system equalization (Chapter 8) in order to insure unity gain at all frequencies of interest.

The measurement of the acoustic gain of a finished sound system is described below (see Fig. 5-10).

1. With the sound system turned off and the room made as quiet as possible (air conditioning, heating, etc., turned off), adjust the test amplifier (use pink noise as input) to give a 75-80 dBA reading over the test loudspeaker at the sound-system microphone (substitute the sound-level meter temporarily for the microphone). The microphone should be placed at its design position.
2. Carry the sound-level meter to the farthest D_2 position and measure the level from the test loudspeaker. Exercise care that the signal arriving from the test speaker is at least 6 dB greater than the ambient noise reading. Record this reading in dBA.
3. Turn on the sound system (test loudspeaker feeding a 75-80 dBA signal into the microphone) and adjust just below self-sustaining feedback (the system will ring, etc., but upon cutting off the signal, the feedback should not continue).
4. Again read the sound-level meter at the farthest D_2 position and record in dBA.
5. The reading taken with the sound system on, minus the reading taken with the sound system off, equals the total acoustic gain. The total acoustic gain should be within ±2 dB of the calculated PAG.

LIMITING PARAMETERS IN SOUND-REINFORCEMENT SYSTEM DESIGN

Certain choices of parameters limit the choice of approach to the system design. For example, if you wish to use a single-source system (and all other room parameters allow it) because of its inherently more economical approach and ability to blend acoustically with the live talker, then you cannot have an EAD of less than twice D_s. For example, if you must have a D_s of 2 feet, then the EAD cannot be less than 4 feet:

$$EAD \geqq 2 D_s \qquad (5\text{-}32)$$

Naturally, the other limit on EAD is that it not exceed D_c:

$$EAD \leqq D_c \qquad (5\text{-}33)$$

Fig. 5-10. Method of measuring acoustic gain.

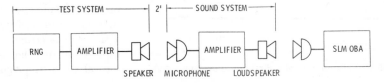

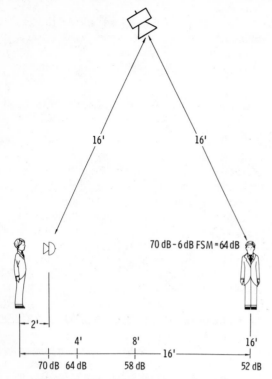

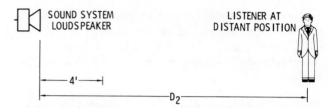

ATTENUATION OF SOUND IN dB FROM 4' IN FRONT OF LOUDSPEAKER TO LISTENER = $\Delta D_2 - \Delta 4'$

WHERE: $\Delta D_2 = -10 \log \left(\dfrac{Q}{4\pi D_2^2} + \dfrac{4}{R} \right)$

$\Delta 4' = -10 \log \left(\dfrac{Q}{4\pi 16} + \dfrac{4}{R} \right)$

Fig. 5-14. Calculation of D₂ attenuation.

This limitation $(\text{EAD} \geqq 2D_s)$ for single-source sound systems is due to the FSM. Fig. 5-11 illustrates the limiting case. When EAD must equal D_s, a distributed sound system becomes mandatory. When $D_s = \text{EAD}$, then D_1 must $\geqq 2D_2$ (Fig. 5-12). Fig. 5-13 shows how D_1 and D_2 are handled in calculating the acoustic gain of a distributed system.

HOW MUCH ELECTRICAL POWER (EPR) IS REQUIRED

While the calculation of acoustic gain is pertinent only to sound-reinforcement systems, the same techniques can be applied to finding out how to achieve a desired level at some distant point from a sound source. Rock groups, especially, make heavy demands on the power-handling capabilities of sound equipment, and the ability to predict accurately what they will get for their investment in different locations can be useful. When you have some definite acoustic sound-pressure-level (SPL) goal in mind at some given distance (D_2) from the loudspeaker, you need to know two important details:

1. The sensitivity rating of the loudspeaker, measured at 4 feet on axis when the loudspeaker is fed an input signal of one electrical watt.
2. The acoustic level change and attenuation between the loudspeaker and the farthest listener position (Fig. 5-14).

Once the desired acoustic level at the farthest listener has been determined by actual measurement, experience, calculation, etc., then the desired acoustic level plus the acoustic level change over distance D_2 equals the 4-foot rating the loudspeaker will be required to produce. For example, we desire a 90 dB-SPL program level at 128 feet (D_2). We have a loudspeaker that has a sensitivity rating of 99 dB-SPL at 4 feet from a 1-watt electrical input. What sine-wave wattage should be provided at the loudspeaker input to allow the 90 dB-SPL program level to be reached? Let us

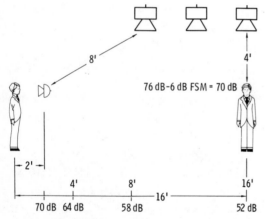

Fig. 5-11. Effect of FSM on acoustic gain.

Fig. 5-12. Requirement if D_s is equal to EAD.

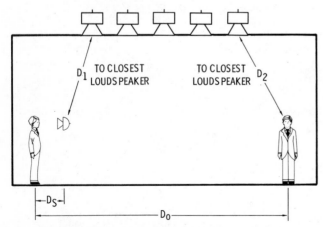

Fig. 5-13. Basic parameters of a distributed system.

further say the installation is outdoors to simplify this introductory example.

$$\text{Acoustic level change} = 20 \log \frac{128}{4} = 30 \text{ dB} \tag{5-34}$$

Adding 10 dB to allow for the difference between program levels and sine-wave levels plus 30 dB acoustic level change gives 130 dB-SPL at 4 feet from the loudspeaker. Now, if 1 watt of electrical input can produce 99 dB-SPL at 4 feet, then $130 - 99 = 31$ dB above 1 watt for the required power. Therefore:

$$\text{EPR} = 10^{\frac{31}{10}} = 1259 \text{ watts} \tag{5-35}$$

Our loudspeaker has a maximum power rating of 50 watts, so it cannot be used. We now locate a loudspeaker with a 4-foot, 1-watt rating of 113 dB-SPL.

$$130 - 113 = 17 \text{ dB above 1 watt} \tag{5-36}$$

$$10^{\frac{17}{10}} = 50 \text{ watts} \tag{5-37}$$

The first loudspeaker was a medium-efficiency loudspeaker. The second is a very high-efficiency commercial-sound type of multicellular horn system. Imagine this same requirement using a home-type low-efficiency system with a 4-foot, 1-watt rating of 89 dB-SPL:

$$130 - 89 = 41 \tag{5-38}$$

$$10^{\frac{41}{10}} = 12{,}590 \text{ watts required} \tag{5-39}$$

FINDING THE EFFICIENCY OF A LOUDSPEAKER SYSTEM

It is interesting to examine just how many acoustic watts were required at the listener's position in this case. Assume that a Q of 20 adequately covers the entire audience area. Then:

$$\begin{aligned}
\text{Acoustic watts} &= \left(10^{\frac{\text{dB-SPL} - 0.5}{10}}\right)\left(\frac{4\pi D_x^2}{Q\, 10^{13}}\right) \\
&= \left(10^{\frac{100 - 0.5}{10}}\right)\left(\frac{4\pi(128)^2}{20 \times 10^{13}}\right) \\
&= 9.175 \text{ watts} \tag{5-40}
\end{aligned}$$

Because of the high Q and efficiency (18%), this chosen combination can generate 9 acoustic watts from an input of 50 electrical watts, thereby generating the desired SPL. The equation for efficiency is

$$\% \text{ Eff} = 10^{\frac{4',\, 1 \text{ watt sens} - (10 \log Q + 107.47)}{10}} \times 100 \tag{5-41}$$

Fig. 5-15. Power amplifiers providing a total of 30,000 watts for an audio system.

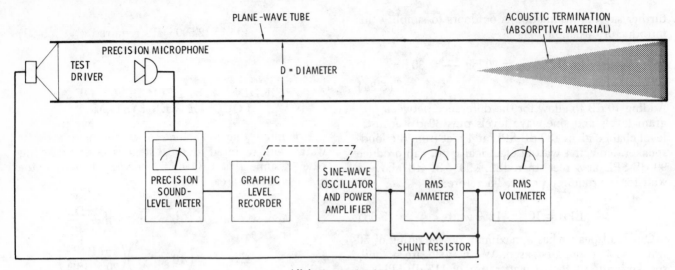

(A) Instrument setup.

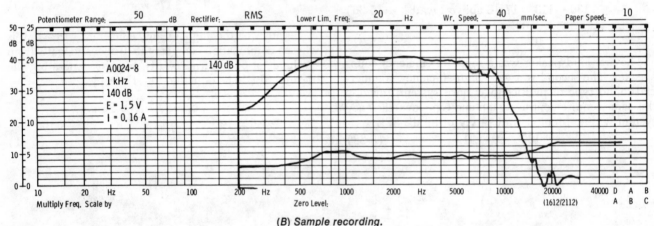

(B) Sample recording.

Fig. 5-16. Plane-wave-tube method of finding efficiency.

In the case of the low-efficiency home-type loudspeaker having a Q of 3, we can calculate:

$$\% \text{ Eff} = 10^{\frac{89 - (10 \log 3 + 107.47)}{10}} \times 100 = 0.47\% \quad (5\text{-}42)$$

You will often hear the specious argument, "Watts are cheap, so don't worry about loudspeaker efficiency." This might be partially true in very small apartment living rooms, but it is not true in commercial sound work. Fig. 5-15 shows a case in which a +3-dB mistake would have equalled 30,000 watts! The formula for calculating EPR in watts in the most direct manner is:

$$\text{EPR in watts} = 10^{\frac{(\text{Desired dB-SPL} + 10) + (\Delta D_2 - \Delta 4') - L \text{ Sens}}{10}} \quad (5\text{-}43)$$

where L Sens is the 4-foot, 1-watt rating.

This calculates the electrical power required for a given distance from the specific drivers covering that area. Power requirements usually need to be calculated area by area and then totaled for the whole system.

FINDING THE EFFICIENCY OF A COMPRESSION DRIVER USING A PLANE-WAVE TUBE

In the plane-wave tube (Fig. 5-16), all of the acoustic power passes down the tube; the surfaces of the tube present negligible absorption. Therefore, the dB-SPL measured is representative of the total circular area surrounding the test microphone (installed in the interior of the tube near the driver). The electrical input power in watts is calculated as the product of the voltage to the driver (rms volts), the current to the driver (rms amperes), and the cosine of the phase angle between them (power factor).

It is then necessary to convert the dB-SPL to acoustic watts. This is done by finding the dB-SPL for which there is a direct relationship to acoustic watts, according to the formula:

$$\text{dB-PWL} = 10 \log \frac{\text{Acoustic watts}}{10^{-12} \text{ watts}} \quad (5\text{-}44)$$

So, acoustic watts $= 10^{\text{dB-PWL}/10} \times 10^{-12}$ watts.

Further, since the dB-SPL $\cong$ dB-PWL at 0.282 meter, we need to convert the circular area we have into an equivalent spherical area, and, using the radius of that sphere as an equivalent measuring distance, find the inverse-square-law spreading in decibels for a sphere with a radius of 0.282 meter. (This is legitimate because both the circular area and the equivalent spherical area will have the same dB-SPL, hence the same power passing through their surfaces.)

If we assume the diameter, D, for the plane-wave tube and express it in centimeters, we can say that the radius of an equivalent sphere would have to be:

$$r = 0.25D \qquad (5\text{-}45)$$

Then the dB-PWL at 0.282 meter would be (remember, at 0.282 meter dB-SPL $\cong$ dB-PWL):

$$\text{dB-SPL} = \text{dB-SPL}_{\text{meas}} - 20 \log \frac{0.282}{\frac{0.25D}{100^*}} \qquad (5\text{-}46)$$

$$\text{dB-SPL}_{\text{meas}} - 20 \log \frac{28.2}{0.25D} = \text{dB-PWL} \qquad (5\text{-}47)$$

* Area is in square centimeters, and we need the radius in meters.

Having obtained dB-SPL, we can go back to the basic equation and find acoustic watts:

$$10^{\frac{\text{dB-PWL}}{10}} \times 10^{-12} \text{ watt} = \text{Acoustic watts} \qquad (5\text{-}48)$$

and

$$\% \text{ Eff} = \left(\frac{\text{Acoustic watts}}{\text{Electric watts}} \right) \times 100 \qquad (5\text{-}49)$$

These separately derived equations combined become:

$$\% \text{Eff} = \frac{10^{\frac{\text{dB-SPL} - 20 \log \left(\frac{28.2}{0.25D} \right)}{10}} \times 10^{-12} \text{ watt}}{(EI) \, PF} \times 100 \qquad (5\text{-}50)$$

where,

dB-SPL is the level at the precision microphone in the plane-wave tube,

D is the diameter of the tube in centimeters,

E is the rms voltage,

I is the rms current,

PF is the power factor (cosine of phase angle θ).

Example:

dB-SPL = 140, E = 1.5 V rms, I = 0.16 A rms, PF = 1

$$\% \text{Eff} = \frac{10^{\frac{140 - 20 \log \frac{28.2}{0.25 \times 2.54}}{10}} \times 10^{-12}}{1.5 \times 0.16 \times 1} \times 100 = 21.33\% \qquad (5\text{-}51)$$

FINDING THE MAXIMUM PROGRAM LEVEL FROM THE AVAILABLE WATTAGE

Quite often there must be a compromise between what is desired and what is attainable. It is especially important to know, in the case of an existing system, what you should be able to measure as a maximum program level at D_2. The formula for this is:

$$\text{Max Program Level} = 10 \log \left(\frac{\text{Watts Available}}{10} \right) - (\Delta D_2 - \Delta 4') + L \text{ Sens} \qquad (5\text{-}52)$$

Again, using our "outdoor" example for ease of calculation, we find:

$$\text{Max Program Level} = 10 \log \left(\frac{50 \text{ watts}}{10} \right) - (42 - 12) + 113 = 90 \text{ dB-SPL} \qquad (5\text{-}53)$$

Fig. 5-17 allows you to convert watts to dB with a reference of 1 watt. This is now the *average program level*. The peak power levels will be 10 dB higher (100 dB-SPL). This means that with this power in this environment, you should never see swings on a sound-level meter *above* 90 dB-SPL on program material. When the sound-level meter hits 90 dB-SPL on program material, the amplifier is putting out 50+ watts on the peaks of that material.

SUMMARY

We have applied our knowledge of the effect of the environment on a sound system, to calculate accurately the acoustic gains and losses relative to different posi-

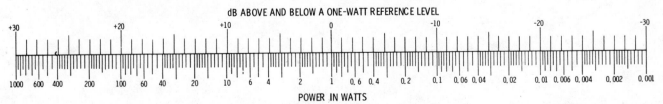

dB ABOVE AND BELOW A ONE-WATT REFERENCE LEVEL

POWER IN WATTS

Fig. 5-17. Decibels relative to 1 watt.

tioning of the talker, the microphone, the loudspeaker, and the listener. Calculation of EAD, followed by the derivation of NAG, led us to the usefulness of the PAG formula. The $NAG - PAG = 0$ concept allowed direct computation of the desired unknown. Converting back to ratios at that point allowed calculation without the need of logarithms.

A development of the same data required for these acoustic gain calculations was evolved to allow EPR and efficiency to be calculated. The difference between loudspeaker efficiency and sensitivity should have become apparent to you. Now that you have a working knowledge of these basic parameters, we can look at hardware for their fulfillment and manipulation.

CHAPTER 6

Interfacing the Electrical and Acoustical Systems

Having reached a relationship among the loudspeaker, microphone, talker, and listener that allows the desired acoustic gain, we must turn our attention to the practical realization of this relationship. Our next concern is what happens to the signal from the acoustic input, into the microphone, through the electrical gains and losses of the sound-system components, until sufficient power reaches the loudspeaker array. Additionally, the acoustic coverage density and uniformity of the loudspeaker array will determine the accuracy of our predictions for any given location.

THE MICROPHONE AS THE SYSTEM INPUT

There are many excellent texts on how microphones transduce acoustic power into electrical energy. These same texts develop the combination of the pressure microphone and the velocity (gradient) microphone into a cardioid microphone. If you are not familiar with these interesting problems, the bibliography (Appendix II) contains a list of excellent references.

The problem is to integrate a commercial-type microphone into a workable sound system. To do this requires that you measure certain parameters of the microphone to gain the information you require. Some manufacturers issue reasonably accurate data; most don't. To avoid trying to guess which ones, at which times, measure any microphones intended for use in a serious professional sound-recording or sound-reproducing system yourself.

MICROPHONE SENSITIVITY

To determine the electrical input level to a sound system, you need to know the electrical output generated by the microphone when placed in a known SPL.

Courtesy General Radio Co.

Fig. 6-1. A sound-level meter.

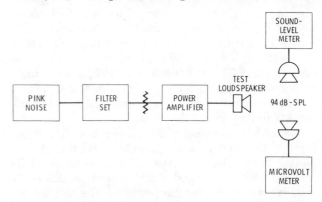

Fig. 6-2. Measurement of microphone sensitivity.

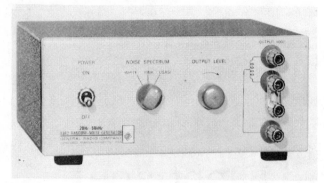

Courtesy General Radio Co.

Fig. 6-3. A random-noise generator.

Courtesy General Radio Co.

Fig. 6-4. A frequency-selective ac microvoltmeter.

Fig. 6-5. A high-pass–low-pass filter.

Courtesy United Recording Electronics Industries

The use of 94 dB-SPL (10 dynes/cm² SPL) is recommended. While 74 dB-SPL (1 dyne/cm² SPL) is also commonly used, it is harder to employ in the field because of its closeness to typical ambient noise levels.

Everyone seriously interested in the professional sound business should own or have easy access to a precision sound-level meter (SLM). An SLM (Fig. 6-1) is required to measure ambient noise; to calibrate sources; to serve as an input for frequency-response, reverberation-time, time-delay, distortion, and acoustic-gain measurements; and for many other uses.

In setting up the microphone measurement system shown in Fig. 6-2, you will require a random-noise generator (Fig. 6-3), a microvoltmeter (Fig. 6-4), a high-pass and a low-pass filter set (Figs. 6-5 and 6-6), a power amplifier, and a well-constructed test loudspeaker in addition to the SLM.

A specific measuring point (about 5 to 6 feet) in front of the loudspeaker is selected, and the SLM is placed there. The system is adjusted until the SLM reads 94 dB-SPL (a band of pink noise from 250 Hz to 5000 Hz is excellent for this purpose). The microphone to be tested is now substituted for the SLM. The open-

circuit voltage reading of the microphone output is taken with the microvoltmeter.

$$S_V = 20 \log E_O - \text{dB-SPL} + 74 \qquad (6\text{-}1)$$

where,

S_V is in dB referenced to 1 volt for a 1 dyne/cm² SPL (74 dB-SPL) acoustic input to the microphone,

E_O is the output of the microphone in volts,

dB-SPL is the level of the actual acoustic input.

If, for example, we gave a microphone an acoustic input of 94 dB-SPL (10 dynes/cm²) and read an electrical output of 0.001 volt (1 millivolt), we would then calculate:

$$S_V = 20 \log 0.001 - 94 + 74$$
$$= -80 \text{ dB/1 volt/1 dyne/cm}^2 \qquad (6\text{-}2)$$

This is read as "minus eighty dB referenced to one volt referenced to one dyne per square centimeter."

The calculation can be performed graphically with the aid of Fig. 6-7.

We need to know the rating of this microphone in terms of dBm. That is, if we assign an equivalent dBm rating to the microphone and connect it to an amplifier with a gain of 40 dB as measured by the insertion gain method, will we be able to predict the amplifier output level, and will the microphone dBm rating match the input overload dBm specification given for the amplifier?

$$S_P = S_V - 10 \log Z + 44 \text{ dB} \qquad (6\text{-}3)$$

where,

S_P is the equivalent dBm rating for an acoustical input of 94 dB-SPL (10 dynes/cm²),

Z is the *measured* impedance of the microphone (most manufacturers' specifications use the *rated* impedance).

Assume our example microphone (0.001 volt from 94 dB-SPL acoustic input) has an impedance of 200 ohms. We can write:

$$S_P = -80 - 10 \log 200 + 44 = -59 \text{ dBm}/10 \text{ dynes/cm}^2 \qquad (6\text{-}4)$$

This is read as "minus fifty-nine dBm referenced to ten dynes per square centimeter." (See Fig. 6-8.)

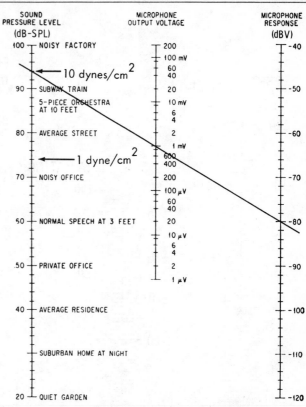

Fig. 6-7. Microphone-output nomograph.

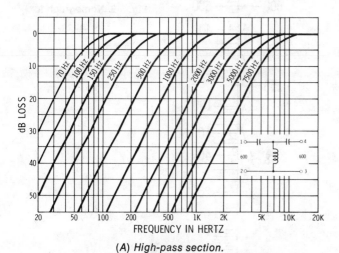

(A) High-pass section.

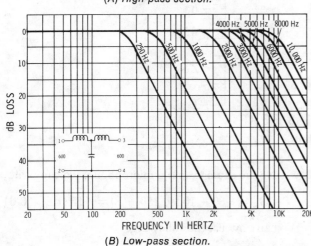

(B) Low-pass section.

Courtesy United Recording Electronics Industries

Fig. 6-6. Response characteristics of a passive filter set.

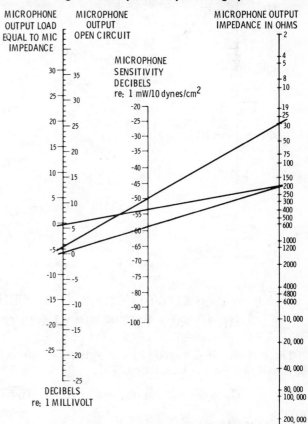

Fig. 6-8. A method of rating a microphone in terms of "equivalent" power output.

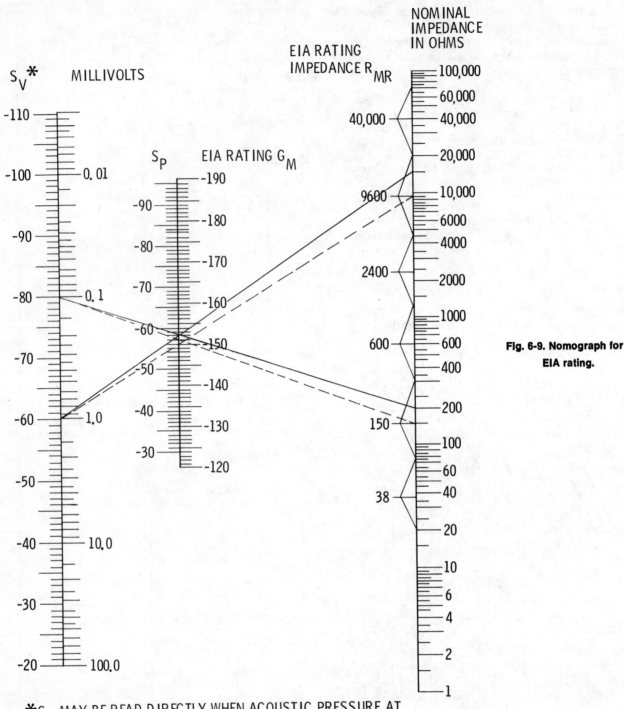

Fig. 6-9. Nomograph for EIA rating.

*S_V MAY BE READ DIRECTLY WHEN ACOUSTIC PRESSURE AT MICROPHONE DIAPHRAGM = 1 dyne/cm^2 (74 dB-SPL)

There is one final method of specifying microphone sensitivity called the EIA rating.

$$G_M = S_V - 10 \log R_{MR} - 50 \text{ dB} \qquad (6\text{-}5)$$

where,

    G_M is the EIA rating,

    R_{MR} is the center value of the nominal impedance range (see Fig. 6-9).

If we use the same example microphone, we can write:

$$G_M = -80 - 10 \log 150 - 50 = -152 \text{ dB} \qquad (6\text{-}6)$$

We can now list the following:

Open-Circuit Voltage (0 dB = 1 volt per microbar): −80 dB

Power Level (0 dB = 1 milliwatt per 10 micro-bars): −59 dBm

EIA Rating (0 dB = EIA Standard SE-105, Aug. 1949): −152 dB

All three ratings are for the same microphone.

If for some reason a microphone is measured into a load equal to its impedance, remember that its open-circuit voltage rating is 6-dB higher.

Open-Circuit Voltage Response Formulas

$$S_V = 20 \log E_O - dB\text{-}SPL + 74 \qquad (6\text{-}7)$$

$$E_O = 10^{\frac{S_V + dB\text{-}SPL - 74}{20}} \qquad (6\text{-}8)$$

$$dB\text{-}SPL = 20 \log E_O - S_V + 74 \qquad (6\text{-}9)$$

Power-Level Response Formulas

$$S_P = S_V - 10 \log Z + 44 \qquad (6\text{-}10)$$

$$S_V = S_P + 10 \log Z - 44 \qquad (6\text{-}11)$$

$$Z = 10^{\frac{S_V - S_P + 44}{10}} \qquad (6\text{-}12)$$

EIA Rating Formulas

$$G_M = S_V - 10 \log R_{MR} - 50 \qquad (6\text{-}13)$$

$$S_V = G_M + 10 \log R_{MR} + 50 \qquad (6\text{-}14)$$

$$R_{MR} = 10^{\frac{S_V - G_M - 50}{10}} \qquad (6\text{-}15)$$

R_{MR} DEFINED

Ranges		Values Used
20 Ω −	80 Ω =	38 Ω
80 Ω −	300 Ω =	150 Ω
300 Ω −	1250 Ω =	600 Ω
1250 Ω −	4500 Ω =	2400 Ω
4500 Ω −	20,000 Ω =	9600 Ω
20,000 Ω −	70,000 Ω =	40,000 Ω

1 dyne per square centimeter (1 dyne/cm²) = 1 microbar

Just by being an impedance, a microphone generates thermal noise. If no acoustic signal were present, the microphone would still produce a minute output voltage. The thermal noise relative to 1 volt is −198 dB at 1 Hz bandwidth and 1 Ω impedance. Therefore, we can write:

$$TN/1 \text{ volt} = -198 \text{ dB} + 10 \log (\text{BW in Hz}) + 10 \log Z \qquad (6\text{-}16)$$

Thermal noise relative to 1 volt is converted to EIN in dB by the formula:

$$EIN \text{ in dB} = -198 \text{ dB} + 10 \log (\text{BW in Hz}) + 10 \log Z - 6 - 20 \log 0.775 \qquad (6\text{-}17)$$

The impedance (Z) is 600 ohms in this case.

Taking our sample microphone with its S_V of −80 dB, we can see that for a bandwidth of 30 to 15,000 Hz and an impedance of 200 ohms we would have:

$$-198 \text{ dB} + 10 \log 14970 + 10 \log 200 = -133 \text{ dB/1 volt} \qquad (6\text{-}18)$$

or

$$-198 \text{ dB} + 10 \log 14970 + 10 \log 600 - 6 - 20 \log 0.775 = -132 \text{ dBm} \qquad (6\text{-}19)$$

The signal-to-noise ratio becomes:

$$133 - 80 = 53 \text{ dB} \qquad (6\text{-}20)$$

or

$$132 - (59 + 20) = 53 \text{ dB} \qquad (6\text{-}21)$$

This is the signal-to-noise ratio if the acoustic input to the microphone is 74 dB-SPL. If the acoustic input were, for example, a rock singer at 120 dB-SPL, then the s/n ratio becomes 53 + (120 − 74) = 99 dB. The output level of the microphone, however, now is −59 dBm + (120 − 94) = −33 dBm. The trick is to choose a microphone sensitivity that allows an acceptable s/n ratio at the same time it also allows acceptable dynamic range. When microphones with too high sensitivity are used, input pads (bridging type) have to be used at the mixer amplifier. When the sensitivity chosen is too low for the task at hand, the s/n ratio may suffer. A careful evaluation of the sensitivity actually required for a given performer can ensure the optimum operation of a sound system.

The question now becomes, "Which method am I to use in my design work?" For almost all system design, as opposed to component design, the open-circuit power response is needed, except when the microphone will actually work into its rated impedance. Normally, professional equipment is rated at a nominal input impedance of 150 ohms and has an actual input impedance 10 times that value. Some of the older ribbon microphones, etc., used to work into a terminated 30-ohm input. The method using decibels relative to one volt for an SPL of 1 dyne/cm² is useful to the component designer. He can then solve this kind of problem: "I wish to work as low as 40 dB-SPL with a microphone having a rating of −60 dBV. What minimum input voltage must my preamplifier handle?" The solution is:

$$e_m = 10^{\frac{dB\text{-}SPL - 74 + dBV}{20}} \qquad (6\text{-}22)$$

or

$$e_m = 10^{\frac{40 - 74 + (-60)}{20}} = 0.00002 \text{ volt, or } 20 \ \mu V \qquad (6\text{-}23)$$

This may be found on the nomograph of Fig. 6-7 by placing one end of a straightedge at −60 dBV and the other end at 40 dB-SPL, thereby intersecting 20 microvolts on the center scale.

Having found the open-circuit power response of our "example" microphone is −59 dBm in an acoustic field of 94 dB-SPL, we can then place an SLM in front of the lecturer, preacher, rock-and-roll performer, etc., and see what input levels the preamplifier needs to handle. See Table 6-1.

Table 6-1. Typical Preamplifier Input Levels

	dB-SPL at Mic	Mic Elec Output	+ 10 dB
Lecturer	70	—83 dBm	—73 dBm
Preacher	85	—68 dBm	—58 dBm
Rock-and-Roll	115	—38 dBm	—28 dBm

It is important to recognize that the method of measuring sensitivity we have chosen is an on-axis measurement and does not necessarily apply at high or low frequencies or at differing polar angles. Even omnidirectional microphones become directional at higher frequencies (Fig. 6-10A). Also shown are the classic bipolar response (Fig. 6-10B) and the combination, electrically, of a bipolar and pressure response into a cardioid pattern (Fig. 6-10C).

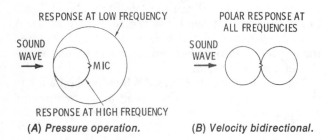

(A) Pressure operation.   (B) Velocity bidirectional.

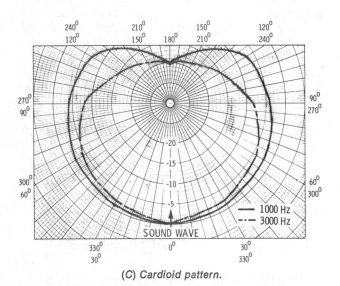

(C) Cardioid pattern.

Fig. 6-10. Basic microphone polar responses.

OMNIDIRECTIONAL OR CARDIOID

A vast amount of sales literature promises feedback control through the use of cardioid microphones. After learning how to maximize the acoustic gain, you are ready to understand that in a well-designed system an omnidirectional microphone should give greater acoustic gain than a similar cardioid-type mechanism. Why? First, because the omnidirectional microphone will be smoother in frequency response (Fig. 6-11). This shows two condenser-type microphones from the same manufacturer with only the microphone "buttons" interchanged.

Fig. 6-12 depicts the rather complete manufacturer's data on a well-designed, dual, dynamic cardioid microphone.

Just how important is a good cardioid microphone? It is vital if:

1. A nearby noise (less than D_c from the microphone) needs to be discriminated against, or occasionally selected; e.g., NOALA.
2. You must work at a $D_1 < D_c$ and you can orient the pattern of the microphone advantageously.

Cardioid microphones should be used with caution for:

1. Flush mounting or floor mounting where you wish to pick up the additional acoustic gain available from such mounting.
2. Lavaliers.
3. Very close talking.

Examples of microphones are shown in Fig. 6-13. Fig. 6-13A shows an omnidirectional microphone that may be used as a measuring microphone or for recording or sound-system purposes. The high-quality directional, studio and recording microphone in Fig. 6-13B features smooth amplitude response. Fig. 6-13C shows a microphone often used by entertainers.

It is surprising what a wide range of available microphones can be made to work very satisfactorily in high-quality systems when they can be matched to each other and the system. Much of the talk regarding "this microphone picks up better" or "this microphone reaches farther," etc., has to do with some feature of the system far remote from the microphone, but triggered by connecting differing microphones.

A classic example of 20 years ago was the widespread popularity of a foreign condenser microphone system among recording engineers because of its "superior presence." When the foreign manufacturer issued a technical letter describing the difference between the termination of his microphone in the European manner and the American method, he spoiled the market because the "superior presence" then disappeared. (An equalizer could have been used to restore it.)

A popular foreign electret microphone exhibits differing frequency response using different batteries. In one case, a pair of these were tested. One was essen-

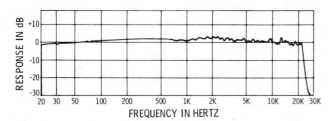

(A) Frequency response of omnidirectional microphone system.

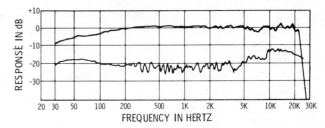

(B) Frequency response of cardioid system (showing front-to-back discrimination.

(C) Polar characteristics of cardioid microphone.

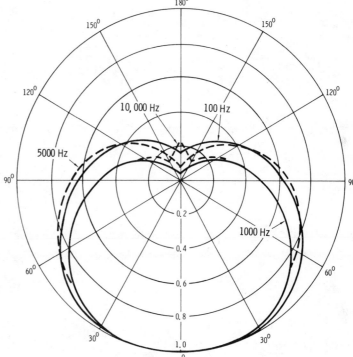

Fig. 6-11. Comparison between omnidirectional and cardioid microphones.

tially flat in acoustic response, and an identical one had an 8-dB hump at 8 kHz. When their batteries were interchanged, the microphone that formerly had the flat response then had the 8-dB hump at 8 kHz, and the other microphone was uniform in response.

MEASURING THE FREQUENCY RESPONSE AND DIRECTIONAL CHARACTERISTICS OF A MICROPHONE

Interesting as it is, the manufacturer's data should not be used other than as a general guide to selection for further tests. The recommended test setup is shown in Fig. 6-14. The heart of this test system is the real-time audio spectrum analyzer (RTA), shown in Fig. 6-15. The RTA allows you to see in "real time" amplitude versus frequency at 30 frequencies simultaneously. The test loudspeaker is first brought into a "flat" acoustical response through equalization while the SLM feeds the RTA. Once this calibration has been per-

formed, the microphone can be connected to the preamplifier, and its response to the calibrated sound field can be viewed on the screen of the RTA.

You can now view the frequency response and relative sensitivity of each microphone compared to the other microphones, and best of all, the relative directional response of each microphone compared to the other microphones. The failure to match microphones carefully in stage systems and conference systems, where NOM's are high, can lead to substantial loss of acoustic gain that cannot be regained economically in the equalization process.

REVIEW OF MICROPHONE SENSITIVITY

Let us review what we need to know about microphones to allow us to proceed with the design of the electrical gain of a sound system:

1. We find the "open-circuit power sensitivity" over a band of 250 Hz to 5000 Hz.

2. We verify that the frequency response of the microphone is typical for its type and that the microphone is matched in response to the other microphones to be used with it.

3. We make sure that the polar response allows us useful frontal coverage and that the microphone is matched in response to the other microphones with which it is to be used.

When you use this method of microphone selection, you will find that many mysterious variances you formerly encountered when working with sound systems have disappeared.

DIVISION OF ELECTRICAL GAINS AND LOSSES

In a typical sound system, there are components that provide gain (symbolized as in Fig. 6-16A), and there are components that present loss (symbolized as in Fig. 6-16B). We now need to discuss the distribution of these gain and loss "blocks" throughout a practical sound system.

Gain "blocks" are available in increments as small as 30 dB and as large as 100 dB. Very useful gain increments fall in the 40-dB area. If a high s/n ratio is to be maintained with variable gain blocks (mixers, power amplifiers with gain control, etc.) while a proper peaking factor and low distortion are preserved, proper setting of the variable gain control is mandatory. In the case of fixed gain blocks, variable or fixed loss blocks will need to be inserted as required.

Loss blocks can be attenuators, mixing networks, equalizers, pads, etc. A rough rule of thumb for a typical sound system is that after you have algebraically totaled all the gains and losses, you should have an overall gain figure of approximately 115 dB. This can be seen by assuming that our microphone calculated at the beginning of the chapter (−59 dBm in a sound field of 94 dB-SPL) receives an acoustic input of 88 dB-SPL. Then 94 dB − 88 dB = 6 dB, and −59 dBm − 6 dB = −65 dBm. If the sound system has a 100-watt output (+50 dBm), then we need 115 dB of gain to get from the level at the mixer input to the level at the loudspeaker input at full power.

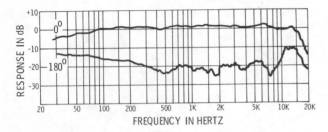

(A) Frequency response.

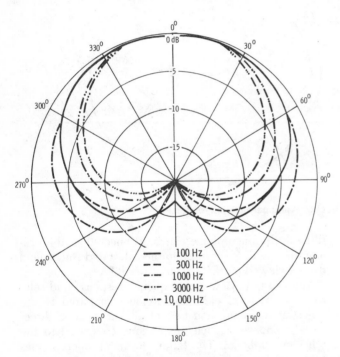

(B) Cardioid polar pattern.

——	100 Hz
– – –	300 Hz
–·–·–	1000 Hz
–··–··–	3000 Hz
······	10,000 Hz

The microphone shall be of the cardioid type employing dual dynamic moving coil cartridges. Each cartridge shall be shock mounted. Frequency response shall be uniform from 40 to 16,000 Hz. The output level shall be at least −53 dBm/10 dynes/cm² and the nominal impedance shall be 200 ohms balanced to ground. Average front-to-back discrimination shall be 20 dB over the range of 40 to 16,000 Hz. A humbucking coil shall be used to ensure hum of not greater than −120 dB when referenced to 10⁻³ gauss.

(C) Architect's and engineer's specifications.

Fig. 6-12. Typical response curves and specifications for a quality microphone.

A TYPICAL MIXER AMPLIFIER

A typical mixer amplifier has the following specifications:

Gain	87 dB
Power output	+18 dBm (with low distortion)
Output noise	80 dB below full output

We know we must allow 10 dB as a peak factor, so the −65 dBm program level out of the microphone should cause the output of the mixer to reach +8 dBm. Therefore, we need to adjust the overall gain of the mixer to 73 dB. (The attenuators in the mixer can be set back approximately 87 − 73 = 14 dB of working loss.) Let us suppose, for the moment, that we are going to connect the output of this mixer directly to the input of a power amplifier having the following characteristics:

$$\text{Power output} = 100 \text{ watts} = 50 \text{ dBm}$$
$$\text{Gain} = 64 \text{ dB}$$

This means the amplifier will reach full output from 50 dBm − 64 dB = −14 dBm. Again, to provide our 10-dB peaking factor, the most output we would want

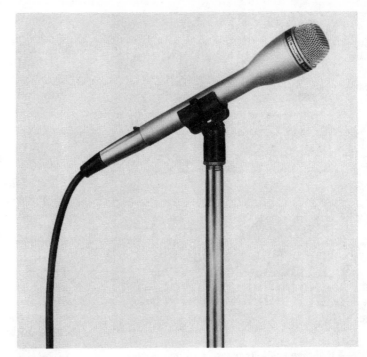

(A) Omnidirectional microphone.

(B) Directional microphone.

(C) Entertainer's microphone.

Courtesy Shure Brothers Inc.

Fig. 6-13. Examples of microphones.

Fig. 6-14. Method of measuring frequency and polar response of a microphone in the room where it is to be used.

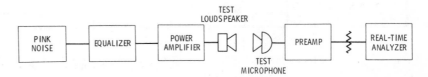

Fig. 6-15. A real-time audio-frequency spectrum analyzer.

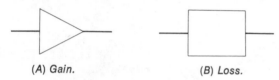

(A) Gain.   (B) Loss.

Fig. 6-16. Symbols for components that present gain or loss.

to see at the output of the power amplifier would be +40 dBm (10 watts) of program material. Therefore, the maximum input power would be:

$$-14 \text{ dBm} - 10 \text{ dB} = -24 \text{ dBm} \qquad (6\text{-}24)$$

The mixer amplifier is putting out a program level of +8 dBm, and it should continue to do so in order to ensure the maximum s/n ratio; so we need to insert +8 to −24 dB (32 dB) of attenuation in the form of a pad or an input attenuator. This set of circumstances is illustrated in Fig. 6-17. Note that the pad has replaced the gain overlap.

A MORE COMPLICATED SYSTEM

Fig. 6-18 illustrates a more complex system, and the graph below the block diagram is an example of a gain chart. In first inspecting the total losses in the system (10 + 14 + 14 + 14 = 52 dB), you would immediately recognize that you had exceeded the gain overlap available in the mixer and amplifier of the previous example. This immediately tells you that you need a line amplifier. It is highly desirable never to come closer than 10 dB to the original input level at any point in the system beyond the input (so that the noise voltages do not become additive—two equal noise levels add to increase the noise 3 dB). For this reason, the required gain block is placed between two loss blocks rather than following the last gain block. Observe too, that the second gain block is also adjusted to its highest program level that still leaves it a 10-dB peaking factor. Finally, as the input level reaches overload at the output of the mixer, so does every other active element in the system. This is the desired goal of a well-designed electrical system—that all sections of it reach overload simultaneously. This allows all parts of the system to be operated as far as possible above the noise floor, and in well designed equipment it should mean that careful control of noise at the input determines the overall signal-to-noise ratio.

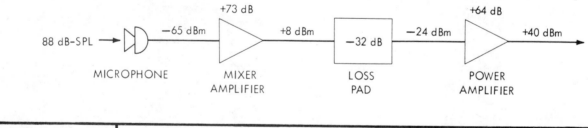

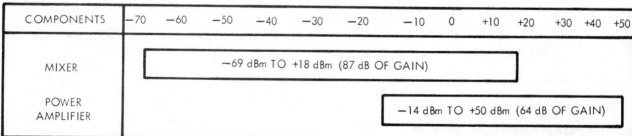

GAIN OVERLAP = −14 TO +18 = 32 dB

Fig. 6-17. Illustration of gain overlap.

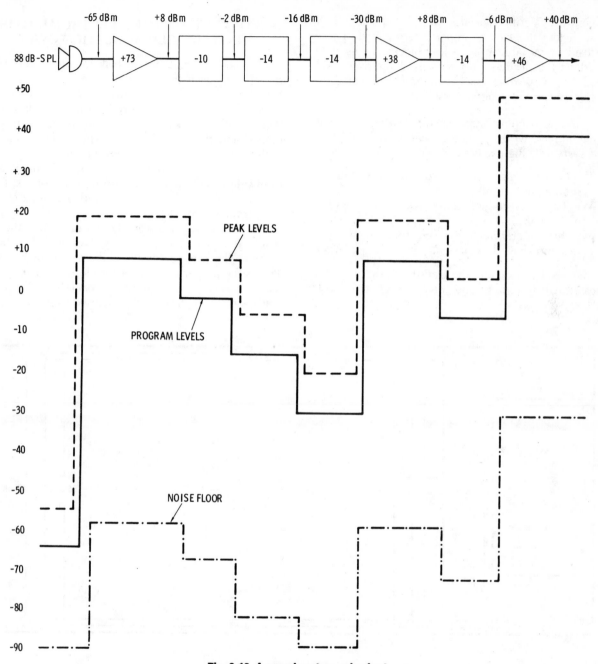

Fig. 6-18. A sound-system gain chart.

SUMMARY OF ELECTRICAL GAIN ADJUSTMENTS

To realize a high signal-to-noise ratio, low distortion, and an adequate peaking factor while handling the distribution of gain and loss blocks throughout the sound system, the following sequence should be used:

1. At the diaphragm of the microphone, measure the dB-SPL that is equal to the customer's requirements, and convert it to the electrical output of the microphone in equivalent dBm.

2. To stay well above system noise and to allow the use of VI meters on program material, adjust each gain block to the highest output consistent with the required 10-dB peaking factor. Start at the microphone and proceed in order through the system until the power amplifier is reached.

3. Insert additional gain blocks whenever the inserted loss exceeds the gain overlap.

4. If variable gain blocks are used, make the final program level adjustments at the final power-amplifier gain control.

5. If fixed gain blocks are used, substitute fixed or variable loss blocks in place of the absent gain

controls. Verify that the output impedances of such loss blocks are properly terminated. These fixed or variable passive loss blocks are used to adjust the desired output levels of the fixed gain blocks to 10 dB below maximum output capabilities on normal program material.

Before approaching system equalization methods and techniques, we have only to look at the final link in our system in slightly greater detail.

1. We have examined the environment in which the system exists and operates.
2. We have determined the needed and possible acoustic gains.
3. We have determined the electrical gains and losses and their distribution.

We now need to examine the transducer that couples the electrical system to the environment—the loudspeaker system.

CONVERTING THE ELECTRICAL GAIN INTO USABLE ACOUSTIC POWER

The most difficult design task facing a professional sound engineer is that involving the loudspeaker array. If system equalization is to bring the acoustic response at all frequencies to a predetermined relationship, thereby allowing the acoustic gain formulas to fulfill their calculations, then the acoustic coverage must be uniform over the entire audience area.

What is considered uniform? Plus or minus 2 dB from side-to-side and ±2 dB from front-to-back, for an extreme variation in any major audience area of 8 dB (i.e., from 250 to 5000 Hz). See Fig. 6-19.

The easiest way acoustically, but invariably the most costly, is to use a high-density overhead distribution system. The proper density is illustrated in Fig. 6-20. This is the proper density pattern for a distributed system using very high-quality coaxial 8″, 12″, or 15″ loudspeakers, each properly enclosed as well. Fig. 6-21

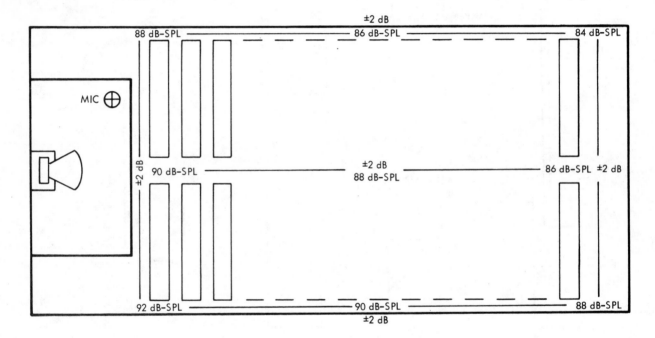

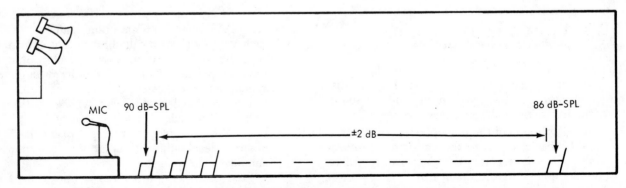

Fig. 6-19. Maximum permissible coverage variations in an auditorium.

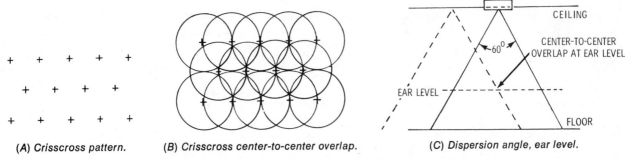

(A) Crisscross pattern.   (B) Crisscross center-to-center overlap.   (C) Dispersion angle, ear level.

Fig. 6-20. Proper distribution density in an overhead distributed sound system.

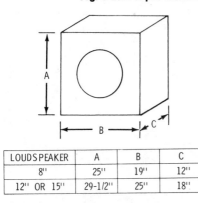

LOUDSPEAKER	A	B	C
8''	25''	19''	12''
12'' OR 15''	29-1/2''	25''	18''

Fig. 6-21. Preferred back box sizes for high-quality speakers in distributed systems.

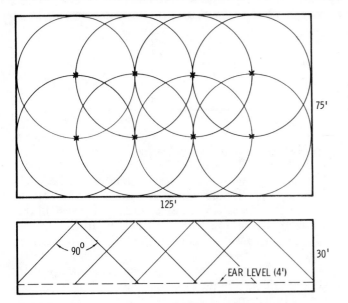

Fig. 6-22. Actual layout of example room.

gives the dimensions of such enclosures. These are infinite-baffle enclosures filled completely with absorbent material and designed to be mounted up in the ceiling behind a grille. If loudspeakers of the proper quality are chosen and the high density is adhered to, you can count on not exceeding ±2 dB in any area they cover. (You can test the quality of the loudspeaker quickly with pink noise and a real-time analyzer on a sample mounted in the ceiling of your shop to see if the fre-

quency response changes more than 4 dB at any frequency between 250 and 5000 Hz as you move off-axis.)

A quick check of the required density of loudspeakers can be obtained by the following formula; the result should be verified later by an actual speaker layout.

$$N = \frac{3 \, (\text{Ceiling area in ft}^2)}{2\pi \left[(\text{Ceil ht} - 4') \tan \dfrac{\text{Angle}}{2} \right]^2} \quad (6\text{-}25)$$

where N is the number of loudspeakers required for center-to-center overlap. (See Table 6-2). For example, in a room 30 feet high, 75 feet wide, and 125 feet long, with a loudspeaker that has a true 90° coverage angle:

$$N = \frac{3(75 \times 125)}{2\pi \left[(30 - 4) \tan \dfrac{90}{2} \right]^2} \cong 7 \quad (6\text{-}26)$$

Fig. 6-22 shows an actual layout for the example room.

An older method of checking coverage was to use the 4000-Hz octave on a sound-level meter to check distribution. This is a quick way to detect major flaws in an existing system you may be inspecting, but the accurate way is to check simultaneously all the ⅓-octave bands from 250 Hz to 5000 Hz by using the RTA. (Several successful sound contractors have filled the ceilings of their shops with speakers to provide coverage of ±2 dB for demonstration purposes. Then if the contractor has a client who feels he doesn't want to pay for good coverage, the contractor can demonstrate how ±4, 6, or 8 dB sounds.)

Some designers strike on the idea that if they aim the loudspeakers at the walls or ceilings they can take advantage of the uniformity of the reverberant field. They do indeed get smooth distribution but poor articulation because they do not meet the requirement that $AL_{CONS} = 15\%$. Therefore, it is important that you achieve good, smooth distribution while maximizing the direct sound to each audience area.

LOUDSPEAKER PLACEMENT

Single-source systems are preferred in most auditorium situations because of their economy and their naturalness. Vertical displacement of the loudspeaker as opposed to horizontal displacement takes advantage of

Table 6-2. Area Covered by Ceiling-Mounted Loudspeakers and Number Required for Even Distribution

Ceiling Height Minus Four Feet (Listener Height)	Area in ft² Covered by a Loudspeaker Having a Total Coverage Angle of 60°	Number of Loudspeakers per 1000 ft² in Order for the Edge of One Pattern to Reach the Center of the Other	Area in ft² Covered by a Loudspeaker Having a Total Coverage Angle of 90°	Number of Loudspeakers per 1000 ft² in Order for the Edge of One Pattern to Reach the Center of the Other
3.0	9	166	28	52
3.5	12.6	119	38	40
4.0	16.5	91	50	30
4.5	21.2	71	63	24
5.0	28.5	52	78	20
5.5	32.2	47	95	16
6.0	38.5	39	114	13
6.5	45.5	33	133	11
7.0	50.0	30	153	10
7.5	58.0	26	177	9
8.0	65.5	23	200	8
8.5	75	20	227	7
9.0	85	18	256	6
9.5	95	16	282	6
10.0	106	14	314	5
10.5	116	12	346	5
11.0	128	11	380	4
11.5	142	10	415	4
12.0	154	10	452	4
12.5	163	9	490	3
13.0	176	9	530	3
13.5	190	8	570	3
14.0	206	7	620	3
14.5	220	7	660	3
15.0	235	6	710	2
15.5	254	6	760	2
16.0	271	6	810	2
16.5	287	5	860	2
17.0	308	5	910	2
17.5	327	5	970	2
18.0	345	4	1020	2

Chart courtesy of Vic Hall, Communications Co., San Diego

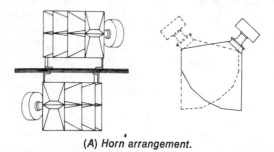

(A) Horn arrangement.

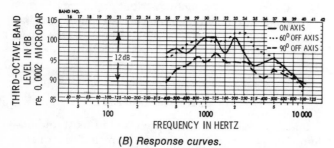

(B) Response curves.

Fig. 6-23. On-axis and off-axis response of two horns stacked vertically and splayed horizontally.

the listener's inability to localize sound sources displaced vertically. Because the listener's ears are in the horizontal plane, the slightest motion of the head allows accurate localization of horizontal displacements of the sound source. Because of this and because of the interference patterns created by hearing from a limited number of sources slightly displaced, the location of loudspeakers on either side of a stage opening, or down side walls, always produces poorer intelligibility than can be achieved in the same space with a single source, centrally located.

Locating the single source on the center line of the room is always beneficial because the reflections of sound from the source will then be symmetrical, allowing greater acoustic gain and smoother distribution. One very common mistake, when wider coverage is required, is to place the loudspeakers or horns side by side. This placement usually *narrows* the horizontal coverage by acting like a "line source" in the horizontal plane. Correct and incorrect methods are shown in Figs. 6-23 and 6-24, respectively, which include the resulting on-axis and off-axis responses.

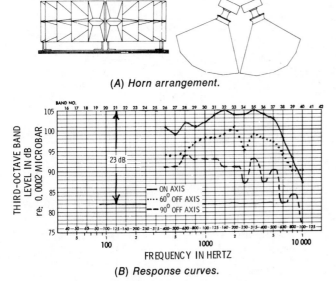

(A) Horn arrangement.

(B) Response curves.

Fig. 6-24. On-axis and off-axis response of two horns in a side-by-side arrangement.

In an effort to give the "far-throw" horn more level, it used to be common practice to "pad down" the "near horn." That is, a power T-pad would be inserted in the horn circuit covering the nearest part of the audience, and, for example, 6 dB more power would be fed to the horn aimed at the rear of the audience area in hopes of compensating somewhat for the effects of inverse-square-law level change (this does work outdoors).

Today we know that what we need to do is increase the Q of the "far-throw" horn, which also raises its directivity index and the ratio of direct to reflected sound at the listener. Since the power to both horns remains the same, the reverberant level also remains the same because the two horns divide the electrical input power between them and distribute it to where it can do the most good. The reverberant field is the sum of all acoustical power put into it. When you reach the required dB-SPL with lower acoustic power (by raising the Q), you also lower the reverberant field. In practical cases, it is fairly safe to say that the transducer with the lowest Q, at equal power with

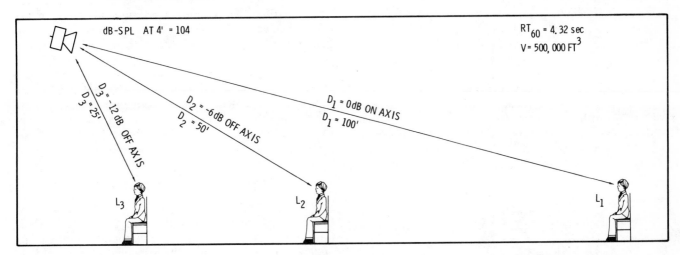

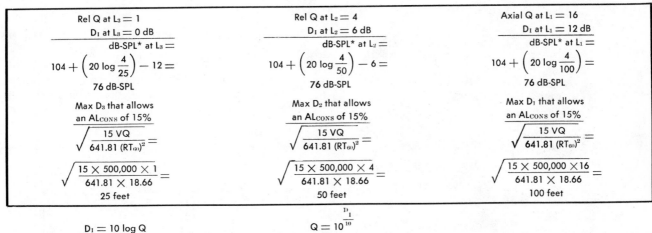

Rel Q at L_3 = 1	Rel Q at L_2 = 4	Axial Q at L_1 = 16
D_I at L_3 = 0 dB	D_I at L_2 = 6 dB	D_I at L_1 = 12 dB
dB-SPL* at L_3 =	dB-SPL* at L_2 =	dB-SPL* at L_1 =
$104 + \left(20 \log \dfrac{4}{25}\right) - 12 =$	$104 + \left(20 \log \dfrac{4}{50}\right) - 6 =$	$104 + \left(20 \log \dfrac{4}{100}\right) =$
76 dB-SPL	76 dB-SPL	76 dB-SPL
Max D_3 that allows an AL_{CONS} of 15%	Max D_2 that allows an AL_{CONS} of 15%	Max D_1 that allows an AL_{CONS} of 15%
$\sqrt{\dfrac{15\,VQ}{641.81\,(RT_{60})^2}} =$	$\sqrt{\dfrac{15\,VQ}{641.81\,(RT_{60})^2}} =$	$\sqrt{\dfrac{15\,VQ}{641.81\,(RT_{60})^2}} =$
$\sqrt{\dfrac{15 \times 500,000 \times 1}{641.81 \times 18.66}} =$	$\sqrt{\dfrac{15 \times 500,000 \times 4}{641.81 \times 18.66}} =$	$\sqrt{\dfrac{15 \times 500,000 \times 16}{641.81 \times 18.66}} =$
25 feet	50 feet	100 feet

$$D_I = 10 \log Q \qquad Q = 10^{\frac{D_I}{10}}$$

When the proper Q is chosen for the last seat and the off-axis response of the loudspeaker is used to obtain even coverage, articulation is solved at the same time.

* The dB-SPL values are for the direct sound levels.

Fig. 6-25. Loudspeaker orientation—ideal case.

other transducers, controls the reverberant level for a given room constant (R).

Fig. 6-25 illustrates loudspeaker orientation (ideal case).

In overhead distributed systems, a special consideration has to be given to the number of loudspeakers. Critical distance becomes:

$$D_c = 0.141 \sqrt{\frac{QR}{n+1}} \qquad (6\text{-}27)$$

where n is the number of loudspeakers of equal acoustic output that do not provide direct sound to the listener. If 1 is 5 speakers as in a distributed system, then n is the number of groups of five each, but not counting the original group of five.

The formula may be solved for each of the other quantities:

$$Q = \frac{D_c^2(n+1)}{0.019881\,R} \qquad (6\text{-}28)$$

$$R = \frac{D_c^2(n+1)}{0.019881\,Q} \qquad (6\text{-}29)$$

$$n+1 = \frac{0.019881\,QR}{D_c^2} \qquad (6\text{-}30)$$

Every time the number of loudspeakers that are on at the same level is doubled, the reverberant level is raised by 3 dB. Also, for every doubling of the number of loudspeakers heard directly by the listener, the level of the direct sound rises 3 dB. So it is only the loudspeakers covering other areas that contribute to a

Courtesy Lubell Laboratories

Fig. 6-26. An underwater transducer.

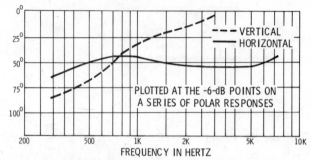

Fig. 6-27. Angular distribution of a horn.

higher reverberant level. This can limit D_2 more than would at first be suspected when distributed sound systems are installed in highly reverberant gymnasiums, etc. Again, high-density coverage becomes a critical parameter.

UNDERWATER SOUND

When high-quality sound is required underwater (competitive and synchronized swimming, scuba instruction, very large pools), the underwater transducer shown in Fig. 6-26 may be used. A single unit of this type replaces over 100 underwater loudspeakers of the type formerly available, at only twice the price per unit. One of these units provides sufficient level in an Olympic-sized pool. Sound waves are strong enough that one can "feel" the sound; thus communication is possible to swimmers executing any stroke and is effective during turns and for underwater movies.

VARYING THE Q OF AN ARRAY

If you cannot find, for example, a sufficiently narrow vertical coverage angle (a quite common problem), a line array can be constructed. The sound column using cone-type loudspeakers is the least efficient form of line array because:

1. The horizontal angle remains that of any typical cone, 180°.
2. The vertical angle starts at 180° for one cone, and, even if each doubling of the number of cones halved the vertical angle, 8 cones would still only reach a vertical angle of 22.5° (Q = 16).

As a matter of fact, no practical cone-type column reaches a useful Q of 10. Now, let us consider a line

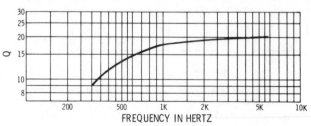

Fig. 6-28. Plot of Q for horn of Fig. 6-27.

array of four horns. The horizontal angle is approximately 50° through the speech range, and the vertical angle approximates 25° to 30° through the same region. Due to slight rear lobes, etc., the Q averages around 20 through the same region (see Figs. 6-27 and 6-28). A difference in Q of 2 to 1 means that the critical distance, D_c, is 1.4 times greater than whatever it was at the lower Q. When such an in-line array of horns is combined with an *unenclosed* line array of large cones having heavy absorption wrapped around the rear side, thus turning the pattern into a cardioid, the resulting overall loudspeaker system can penetrate almost twice as far into reverberant space with clarity than any other type of system. Such arrays require careful equalization and sharp low-frequency cutoff below 150 Hz (better than 18 dB/octave). Fig. 6-29 shows such an array installed on a temporary hoist for a demonstration in a very reverberant church. The church purchased it and a whole system to go with it, praising the fact that it let them hear clearly at last (the fourth sound system purchased).

In large arenas, you often need penetration and wide distribution. These quite contradictory requirements can be met remarkably well by using a helix line array. When the helix array is properly designed, the horns should be aligned edge-to-edge, rather than overlapped as in Fig. 6-30. A number of useful techniques have proven worthwhile in the adjustment of arrays:

1. Always adjust and get desired levels and coverage with that part of the system covering the farthest listener first.
2. Always have each area individually at the level and coverage you desire before attempting any combination of them.
3. When wide horizontal or vertical angles are needed, stack and splay sectoral- or radial-type horns. See Figs. 6-31 and 6-32.

Fig. 6-29. A high-Q loudspeaker array on demonstration in a church auditorium.

Fig. 6-30. The wrong way to stack and splay. The horns should not overlap.

Fig. 6-31. A set of professional compression drivers with their associated sectoral-type horn.

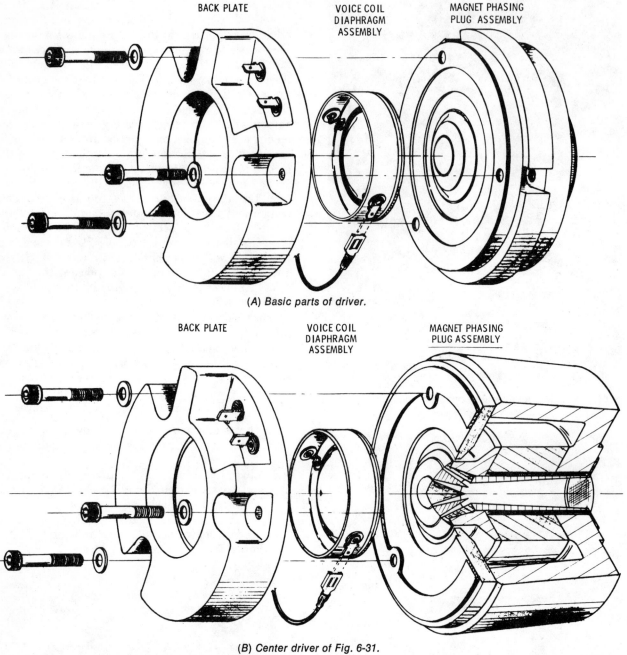

BACK PLATE   VOICE COIL DIAPHRAGM ASSEMBLY   MAGNET PHASING PLUG ASSEMBLY

(A) Basic parts of driver.

BACK PLATE   VOICE COIL DIAPHRAGM ASSEMBLY   MAGNET PHASING PLUG ASSEMBLY

(B) Center driver of Fig. 6-31.

Courtesy Emilar Corp.

Fig. 6-32. Exploded views of compression drivers.

4. Use multicellular-type horns for narrow coverage problems. You may stuff up to half the cells on a multicell if they are not covering useful audience area, but you need the remainder of the cells for useful coverage.

5. Slight reorientations of horns will often make dramatic changes in the smoothness of distribution, due to the complex reflection patterns usually present. Time and care should be exercised to ensure that you really do have optimum positioning of each part of an array. Measurements made with an RTA, while adjustments are made, allow thousands of views of the response relative to positioning that would not have been practical in the past.

6. Treat second arrays with time-delay units, and treat the areas they cover as if they were separate auditoriums, remembering that the reverberant field will rise 3 dB when it is necessary to run both arrays at near equal power.

7. Make every effort to get the proper array (usually large) into the proper position (often in conflict with some visual decoration) by early discussion

Fig. 6-33. A large, high-Q array integrated into the architecture of a church.

Courtesy Knowles Electronics, Inc.

Fig. 6-34. Subminiature loudspeakers.

of the need and by challenging the architect for a creative housing for the array.

Fig. 6-33 shows a large array, properly positioned, which has been turned into a decorative asset in a church.

At the other extreme in size, Fig. 6-34 shows subminiature loudspeakers for use in pew-back systems and similar applications.

SUMMARY

We have discussed the calculation of the electrical gain of the sound system in terms of transducers, active gain devices, passive loss devices, and their combination into a workable chain. We can now proceed to those specific techniques that help integrate each of the components chosen. Theory without the practical techniques of interconnection, measurement, and adjustment all too often remains theory instead of practice, and this is a practical text.

CHAPTER 7

Installing the Sound System

It is not the purpose of this chapter to provide technician-level training in how to solder, cable, pull wire, install terminal boards, etc. There are excellent trade schools that specialize in such training. (Also see Appendix III.) What does need more discussion than it usually gets is the need for the design engineer to troubleshoot large, complex systems and find grounding oversights, impedance mismatches, level misadjustments, wiring placement errors, etc. This chapter is devoted to a discussion of such problems.

CIRCUIT LEVELS

In professional sound systems, it is customary to categorize circuits in the following manner:

1. Microphone wiring (−80 dBm to −20 dBm).
2. Line-level wiring (−20 dBm to +30 dBm). To telephone engineers, this becomes a maximum level of 0 dBm.
3. High-level wiring (+30 dBm and above; i.e., all loudspeaker circuits).
4. Ac power wiring.
5. Dc control wiring or emergency power wiring (relays, batteries, etc.)

Line-level wiring and dc control wiring can be cabled together if necessary, but all other categories must be kept physically isolated from each other.

In many cases, categories 1, 2, and 5 can use cable such as Belden 8451. Category 3 can use cable such as Belden 8434, when the correct wire gauge is available. Cables in category 4 should meet all local and national electrical codes. A typical routing of circuits is shown in Fig. 7-1. The reason for such care in isolating circuits is the desire for stability in the system. A microphone circuit next to a loudspeaker circuit can "feed across" (crosstalk), actually causing the start of an oscillation which, thereafter, may be self-sustaining.

A good first check to make on a sound system being worked with the first time is to feed in a sine-wave signal from an audio oscillator (Fig. 7-2) and attach an oscilloscope (Fig. 7-3) across the output of the power amplifier or amplifiers. In 90% of the cases, it is then necessary to do a step-by-step elimination of parasitic oscillations; the circuit isolation should be checked first. Once circuit isolation has been eliminated as a cause of system instability, then the grounding and shielding system is inspected.

GROUNDING AND SHIELDING

Several convenient rules can be formulated concerning signal shields and how they should be handled. The rules listed below are quite general but are effective in large systems.[1]

1. Each separable environment (signal or power) should be enclosed in one single electrostatic enclosure (shield).
2. The shield for each signal environment should be tied *once* and *only once* to the zero-potential point within that environment.
3. The shield tie should be arranged so that the unwanted signal currents drain toward ground and do not flow in signal conductors.

Examples of how shielding termination is handled in equipment with balanced inputs and outputs, either rack mounted or not rack mounted, are shown in the diagrams of Fig. 7-4.

Some test instruments must have the third wire on the power plug lifted, or they will cause trouble across balanced lines (e.g., oscilloscopes across balanced 70-volt loudspeaker lines).

It is necessary to attach the shields at both ends of the short runs to the chassis of the filter set when components are in separate carrying cases.

---

[1] The Trompeter Electronics, Inc. catalog contains very useful information on grounding and shielding. Write Trompeter Electronics, Inc., 8936 Comanche Ave., Chatsworth, Calif. 91311.

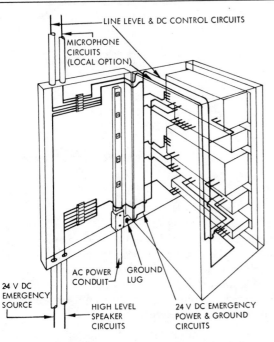

Fig. 7-1. Cable routing in equipment rack.

Courtesy General Radio Co.

Fig. 7-2. A low-distortion, stable-impedance audio oscillator with sine-wave or square-wave output.

GROUNDING PRACTICES

In rack mounting, a heavy insulated wire is run from each chassis to the common rack ground, which in turn is led to a true water-pipe ground connection. The absolute need for a good, solid connection to a water-pipe ground cannot be emphasized too greatly. There is sometimes confusion as to how to connect one system (console, power-amplifier racks, recording equipment) to another. The connection must be made through repeat coils, isolation transformers, etc., which remove dc coupling, or else one system must outrank the other and supply the ground. It is recommended that transformers be used and the shield of the interconnecting lines be tied to a unit-ground bus at *one end only* (use the amplifier input end whenever possible).

Most sound-system equalizing filters are constructed with one side grounded, making them unbalanced to ground. To use these filters in a balanced system with a minimum of hum and interference pickup, multiple grounds must be avoided. Where filter sets are at a distance from the amplifiers associated with them, or where it is desired to patch filter sets into other circuits on certain occasions, it is best to provide isolation transformers in and out of the filter set.

It cannot be overemphasized that, in general, ground and distribution buses should be made of solid copper wire with an insulated covering. Chance grounds must be avoided because ground loops will result. Bare wires and buses may be used where the particular conductor is rigid and supported in midair within an amplifier, rack, or console, and where many subwires connect to the bus. Connections made with a subwire of smaller diameter than a bus should be made by wrapping the subwire around the bus, then soldering by heating the *bus* until applied solder flows smoothly throughout the coiled unit. A large-wattage iron or gun should be used. The best possible solder connections must be made to avoid contact resistance or interface resistance. The dc resistance of a ground bus should never exceed 0.1 ohm.

When wiring and cabling the sound system, you should be careful to ensure that every shield is carefully insulated from every other shield or that every shield is completely bonded to all other shields. Intermittent or partial shield connections are particularly troublesome. Low-level circuits (less than −20 dBm) should have the shields insulated from all conduits and from each other.

Courtesy Hewlett-Packard

Fig. 7-3. An oscilloscope suitable for audio work.

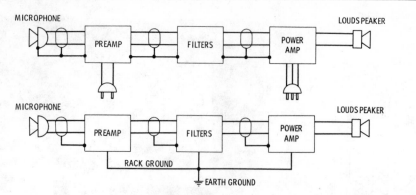

(A) Equipment in separate cases.

(B) Equipment in a rack.

Fig. 7-4. Examples of connections of shields to chassis.

SERVING CABLE

Since the shield surrounding any run of cable should be terminated only at one end, it is mandatory that the other end of the cable be properly "served." This means that the shield is properly trimmed back and carefully insulated with either a plastic cap or plastic tape. All wiring should be formed and carried as a cable. Cable-form bar construction for rack-mounted equipment is shown in Fig. 7-5.

USEFUL WIRING CONCEPTS

Whenever possible, the central grounding position serving a number of separate ground-bus systems should be located to allow equal distances from all racks or consoles concerned. It is desirable that the lengths (and hence the resistances) of all of the ground-bus systems be as equal as possible. In consoles, grounding should be done as close as possible to the inputs to avoid rf pickup. The General Radio Model 1650 impedance bridge allows easy measurement of resistances as low as 0.1 ohm, and it may be used to verify that the ground system is adequate.

Always search out a cold-water-pipe ground—gas pipes, hot-water pipes, etc., are often insulated from ground at some point. Do not use the telephone-service ground or the power-company ground because these are potential sources of interference from one of the devices connected to these services.

In wiring a typical equalized sound system, the following check list is useful:

1. If it isn't supposed to be insulated, ground it! (This refers to all metal ware, chassis racks, table trim on consoles, etc.)
2. The attachment to the bus of all power-supply ground returns should be farthest from the input terminals. In consoles, just the reverse is usually done due to rf-pickup problems.
3. A separate, insulated solid wire should be run from the input terminals (same point as internal ground bus) of each piece of equipment to what is known as the rack or unit ground. The chassis is the equipment shield. The lowest-inductance connection for the chassis is the rack. Each chassis should be checked for continuity to the rack at the time of mounting. A good rack ground is needed. It should consist of the shortest possible length of large-gauge wire or shield braid.
4. The shield of any cable which connects to a terminal block should be grounded to the terminal-block ground bus.

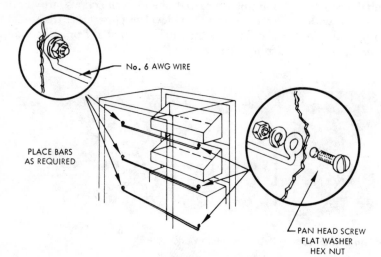

Fig. 7-5. Cable-form bar construction.

5. If a cable connects to a jack field but not to a terminal block, the shield should be grounded to the jack-field ground bus.

6. Any miscellaneous equipment such as VI-meter panels, line attenuators, filters, etc., should have their metal frames, chassis cabinets, and the like tied through separate insulated wires to the nearest unit ground bus.

7. Each unit ground bus should continue unbroken to the central ground point (use a single piece of wire). This point should be located near the physical center of the equipment area so that the ground distribution buses (which connect the various subsystems into a single system) will all have approximately the same length.

8. A cold-water-pipe ground should be established and checked for a resistance value of less than 0.1 ohm.

9. Circuits should be carried in conduits and cables, and arranged for proximity according to the signal levels for which they are intended.

10. All shields should be properly served at one end and terminated at the other end. No shield should be used to carry current.

11. Cables carrying circuits of differing levels should be kept at least two inches from each other. When it becomes necessary for them to cross, a loop is formed that allows the two-inch separation as they cross paths.

12. All cables should be carefully trimmed, and unshielded lengths should be kept to an absolute minimum.

When grounding practices are not followed and shielding is neglected or incorrectly used, then any of the waveforms shown in Fig. 7-6 may appear on the screen of an oscilloscope connected across the output of a power amplifier.

For those desiring to delve more deeply into the art and science of grounding, the references contained in the special list at the end of Appendix II should prove useful.

IMPEDANCE MATCHING

Next to the decibel, impedance is probably one of the most often used terms in the audio engineer's vocabulary. Also in common with the decibel, the word "impedance" rarely can be even defined properly by its user. Even less often is impedance handled correctly in sound systems.

In the audio industry, many of the best practitioners are largely self-taught. Yet, a sampling of questions based on a practical system problem immediately stumps a majority of the recent electrical engineering graduates from state universities. Therefore, more discussion of common practices and malpractices can be profitably carried on.

Impedance Defined

What is impedance? Is it resistance? "Sort of," reply some. Many a technician has put an ohmmeter across the voice coil of a 16-ohm loudspeaker and been surprised to read 4.5 ohms or less. What has he read with the ohmmeter? The dc resistance of the voice coil. Is this the impedance? No.

Now, let us use a bridge circuit to read the ac resistance (R) of the loudspeaker. Is this the impedance? No, but it is part of the impedance.

Then, what is impedance? It will be defined as the total opposition, including resistance and reactance, a circuit offers to the passage of *alternating* current.

What are these words, "opposition" and "reactance"? We all know what resistance is. Opposition means resistance, restraint, hindrance, etc. From this we can conclude that in alternating-current circuits there exists some other resistance-like component, and this additional restraint which adds to that of the ac resistance is called *reactance*.

There are two kinds of reactance, capacitive reactance (X_C) and inductive reactance (X_L). Reactance varies with frequency, whereas ac resistance tends to

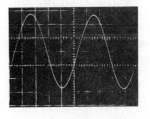

(A) *Pure sine wave.*

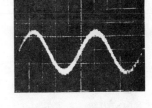

(B) *Noise on sine wave.*

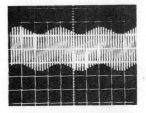

(C) *Hum riding on sine wave.*

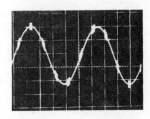

(D) *Rf bursts on sine wave.*

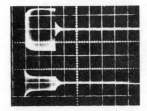

(E) *Ringing of filters with a less than critical bandwidth.*

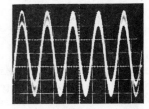

(F) *Oscillation or rf riding on sine wave.*

Fig. 7-6. Undesired waveforms from output of power amplifier (compared with desired sine wave).

stay the same with frequency (certainly over the audio range).

Now, let us add two more terms to our collection and proceed to measure an impedance. Let us designate the *impedance* Z and the *power factor* PF. With this addition, we can now list the terms we have developed:

$$R = ac\ resistance$$
$$X = Reactance = X_L - X_C$$
$$X_C = Capacitive\ reactance$$
$$X_L = Inductive\ reactance$$
$$Z = Impedance$$
$$PF = Power\ factor$$

If we now measure voltage and current in a real circuit, we will find that when an inductor-like device is in the circuit, the current lags behind the voltage in phase and that when a capacitor-like device is in the circuit, the current leads the voltage in phase.

Making Reactance Visible

By setting up a standard way of plotting reactances, we can see plots of their action and interaction. We can do this with rectangular coordinates. Components that are 90° apart in phase are represented by vectors that are 90° apart (Fig. 7-7). From Fig. 7-7, we can write the following formulas for impedance:

Cartesian Form

$$Z = R + jX \qquad X = X_L - X_C \qquad (7\text{-}1)$$

This describes how to plot the action on the chart shown. The j tells us that X is 90° away from R.

Polar Form

$$Z = \sqrt{R^2 + (X_L - X_C)^2} \qquad (7\text{-}2)$$

$$Impedance\ phase\ angle = arc\ tan\ \frac{X_L - X_C}{R} \quad (7\text{-}3)$$

$$PF = cos\ (Phase\ angle) = \frac{R}{Z} \qquad (7\text{-}4)$$

$$R = Z \times PF \qquad (7\text{-}5)$$

$$Z = \frac{R}{PF} \qquad (7\text{-}6)$$

These equations describe how to obtain the magnitude of the impedance vector and the phase angle between it and 0° on the ac-resistance axis.

It can be seen by inspection of Fig. 7-7 that when phase angles are small, the impedance value approaches the ac resistance value, and, conversely, when phase angles are large the reactive component must be carefully measured. The performance of transformers, loudspeaker voice coils, etc., exemplifies conditions in which there are large phase angles. Link circuits, passive attenuators, etc., normally exhibit small phase angles. In most normal audio work, it is the magnitude of the impedance (the length of vector Z) that is of importance in terms of building out, terminating, or

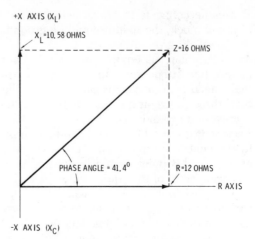

Fig. 7-7. Calculation of impedance.

matching impedances. Only rarely will the typical audio engineer have good reason actually to measure the phase angle, but he should know what it is. (A loudspeaker has a "blocked" impedance—cone cannot move—and a motional impedance. When the loudspeaker impedance does not rise or fall with a change in frequency, it is essentially resistive within that frequency range. The ac resistance plus the motional impedance equals the total impedance measured.)

Let us look at an open circuit and a matched circuit (Fig. 7-8). For each circuit:

$$E_L = E_S \frac{R_L}{R_L + R_S} \qquad (7\text{-}7)$$

Assume E_S is 1 volt in each case. Then for the open circuit (Fig. 7-8A):

$$E_L = 1 \frac{100,000}{100,130} \cong 1 \qquad (7\text{-}8)$$

For the matched circuit (Fig. 7-8B):

$$E_L = 1 \frac{130}{260} = 0.5 \qquad (7\text{-}9)$$

The ratio of the two load voltages, converted to decibels, is:

$$20\ log\ \frac{0.5}{1} = -6\ dB \qquad (7\text{-}10)$$

This example shows that a quite normal source in a sound system (many mixers have 130-ohm outputs)

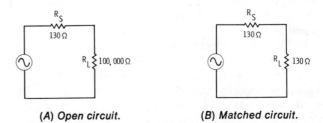

(A) Open circuit. *(B) Matched circuit.*

Fig. 7-8. Comparison of open circuit and matched circuit.

which is developing 1 volt across an open circuit (very high load impedance compared to the source impedance) will drop 6 dB in level when a load impedance equal to the source impedance is provided. This is one of the reasons dynamic microphones rated at 150-ohms input impedance are connected to mixers that present essentially an open-circuit termination (usually 3000+ ohms) in order to improve the signal-to-noise ratio by approximately 6 dB. This also means, however, that in the construction of microphone pads it is necessary to make them bridging-type pads. That is, the microphone looks into 3000 + ohms, but the first stage of the mixer looks back at 150 ohms. (Microphone pads are used when the performer's acoustic input to the microphone results in an electrical output that would overload the input of the mixer at the first stage.)

The same principle can be used in measuring the true output impedance of a power amplifier. Refer to Fig. 7-9.

$$Z_o = \frac{R_1 R_2 (E_1 - E_2)}{E_2 R_1 - E_1 R_2}$$

$$= \frac{E_1 - E_2}{\dfrac{E_2}{R_2} - \dfrac{E_1}{R_1}} \qquad (7\text{-}11)$$

For ease of calculation, make the larger resistance R_1. When open-circuit voltage E_o can be measured directly, $E_1 = E_o$, and the formula becomes:

$$Z_o = \frac{E_o R_2}{E_2} - R_2 \qquad (7\text{-}12)$$

In the special case where R_1 is infinite and R_2 is selected so that $E_2 = 0.5 E_o$:

$$Z_o = R_2 \qquad (7\text{-}13)$$

Some amplifiers approach zero ohms output impedance. If no change is measurable, the output impedance is zero ohms.

The first way of measuring the magnitude of the impedance is shown in Fig. 7-10. Turn the decade resistor box to its highest resistance (i.e., 100,000 ohms). Then read the open-circuit voltage on the ac vtvm. Next adjust the decade resistor box downward in resistance until the ac vtvm reads 6 dB below the reading for open circuit. The total resistance reading of the decade resistor box now equals the magnitude of the source impedance.

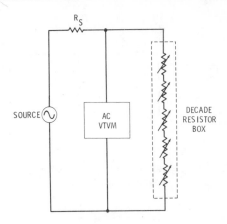

Fig. 7-10. Method of finding impedance magnitude with decade resistor box and ac vtvm.

When it is desired to know the magnitude of the impedance, the inductive reactance, the capacitive reactance, and the phase angle, the standard CRL type of impedance bridge is the obvious choice. The unit in Fig. 7-11 has provisions for external oscillator connections as well as a 1000-Hz internal oscillator. Since it can measure R directly as ac resistance and can measure L and C, it is easy to convert to X_L and X_C by the formulas:

$$X_L = 2\pi fL \qquad (7\text{-}14)$$

and

$$X_C = \frac{1}{2\pi fC} \qquad (7\text{-}15)$$

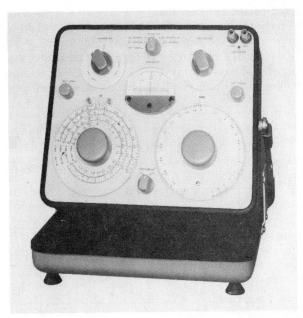

Courtesy General Radio Co.

Fig. 7-11. A standard type of impedance bridge.

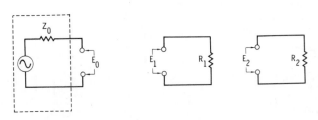

Fig. 7-9. Measuring power-amplifier output impedance.

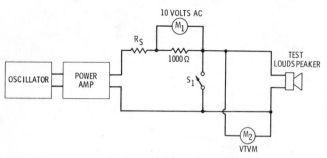

Fig. 7-12. The constant-current method of measuring loud-speaker impedance.

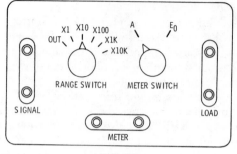

(A) Panel.

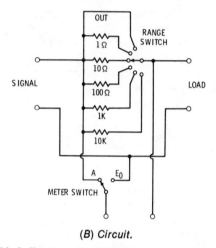

(B) Circuit.

Fig. 7-14. A direct-reading impedance-measuring device.

where,
  f is the frequency in hertz,
  L is the inductance in henrys,
  C is the capacitance in farads,
  X_C is the capacitive reactance in ohms,
  X_L is the inductive reactance in ohms.

Often these are found indirectly by measuring storage factor (Q) or dissipation (D); $Q = X/R = 1/D$, and $D\sqrt{1 + D^2} = PF = \cos\theta$.

From the knowledge of R, X_L, and X_C, the phase angle can be calculated from equation 7-3.

The Constant-Current Method of Measuring Impedance

Fig. 7-12 illustrates the circuit for measuring imped-ance by what is called the "constant-current" method. The amplifier used as a test source is made into an es-sentially constant-current generator. The 8-ohm tap of a conventional power amplifier usually has an actual output impedance well less than one ohm. Through the use of the 1000-ohm resistor in series with the test load, such a generator is created.

The procedure is as follows. First, close S_1 and adjust the power-amplifier gain for a 10-volt indication at M_1. Then open S_1 and read the voltage on M_2. Finally, mul-tiply the M_2 voltage by 100 to obtain the impedance (values to 100 ohms). (The impedance of most loud-

speakers is 100 ohms or less. The nominal output im-pedance of the power amplifier is 8 ohms.)

Many manufacturers use a graphic level recorder in place of M_2 and obtain automatic impedance plots, such as that shown in Fig. 7-13.

Calibrating to any reference Z, the difference in deci-bels between the reference Z and any other Z can be calculated by:

$$Z = \text{Reference } Z \times 10^{\frac{\pm dB}{20}} \qquad (7\text{-}16)$$

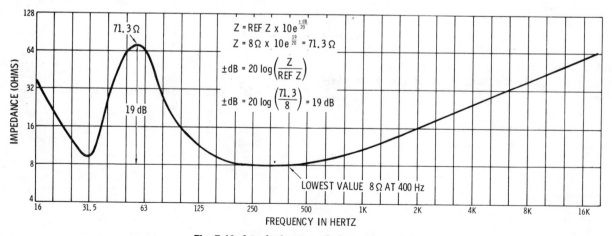

Fig. 7-13. A typical automatic impedance plot.

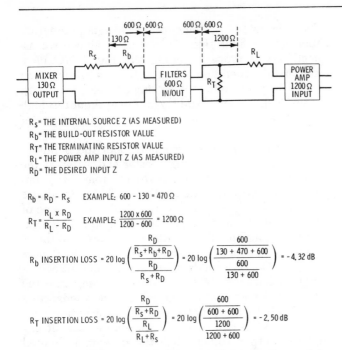

R_s = THE INTERNAL SOURCE Z (AS MEASURED)
R_b = THE BUILD-OUT RESISTOR VALUE
R_T = THE TERMINATING RESISTOR VALUE
R_L = THE POWER AMP INPUT Z (AS MEASURED)
R_D = THE DESIRED INPUT Z

$R_b = R_D - R_S$ EXAMPLE: 600 - 130 = 470 Ω

$R_T = \dfrac{R_L \times R_D}{R_L - R_D}$ EXAMPLE: $\dfrac{1200 \times 600}{1200 - 600}$ = 1200 Ω

R_b INSERTION LOSS = $20 \log \left(\dfrac{\dfrac{R_D}{R_S + R_b + R_D}}{\dfrac{R_D}{R_S + R_D}} \right)$ = $20 \log \left(\dfrac{\dfrac{600}{130 + 470 + 600}}{\dfrac{600}{130 + 600}} \right)$ = - 4.32 dB

R_T INSERTION LOSS = $20 \log \left(\dfrac{\dfrac{R_D}{R_S + R_D}}{\dfrac{R_L}{R_L + R_S}} \right)$ = $20 \log \left(\dfrac{\dfrac{600}{600 + 600}}{\dfrac{1200}{1200 + 600}} \right)$ = - 2.50 dB

Fig. 7-15. Calculation of build-out and termination resistor values and insertion losses.

and, if the impedance is known, to find the dB difference between it and the reference Z, then:

$$\pm \text{dB difference} = 20 \log \dfrac{Z}{\text{Ref } Z} \qquad (7\text{-}17)$$

Fig. 7-14 describes an impedance tester designed by Ed Lethert of Northwest Sound Service, Minneapolis, for use in installing and maintaining motion-picture-theater sound systems. There are direct-reading impedance meters such as the one made by Sennheiser Electronic Corporation in West Germany. This unit includes three oscillator frequencies and a set of charts for finding X_L and X_C, if desired. Magnitude, Z, is read directly on the meter. (Refer to Fig. 9-5.)

Many loudspeaker designers use the GR ZY impedance bridge, now available only on the used equipment market. In any case, there are today rapid, accurate, and reliable measuring tools available to the professional audio engineer.

Using Impedance Measurements in Impedance Matching

Having obtained the measurement, what do you do with it? The most frequent use of an impedance measurement is in matching the measured value to some desired value. Fig. 7-15 illustrates a typical situation for the sound-system installer. A set of passive equalizers is placed in a link circuit between a mixer and a power amplifier. The output of the mixer is labeled 600 ohms; however, a quick measurement reveals it is really 130 ohms. The passive filter set needs to be fed from a true 600 ohms; 470 ohms in series with 130 ohms adds up to 600 ohms. (Balanced circuits would have half

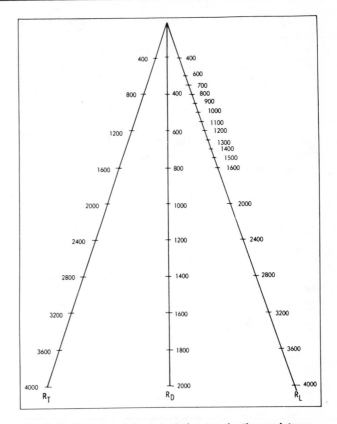

Fig. 7-16. Nomograph for calculating termination resistance.

this value in each leg.) We have added extra loss in the circuit, and we need to know how much it is when we adjust gains and losses for the system as a whole. The solution is worked out at the bottom of Fig. 7-15.

Now, we have an additional problem. The output of the passive filter set should also see 600 ohms. The input to the power amplifier is also labeled 600 ohms, *and it should be that value.* Most often it is not, due to the way the gain potentiometer is wired. A quite typical case is the 1200 ohms shown in Fig. 7-15. Because this input impedance is higher than the desired value, it should be shunted with a terminating resistor. Fig. 7-15 shows the calculation, and Fig. 7-16 is a nomograph which permits the solution of the same problem by placing a straightedge from R_L across R_D to read R_T. Fig. 7-15 shows the calculation of the loss caused by the insertion into the circuit of this terminating resistor.

Consequences of Failing to Provide Matching

In the case of passive filters, equalizers, and attenuators, the result of failure to provide proper build-outs and terminations is shown in Figs. 7-17, 7-18, and 7-19.

Fig. 7-17A shows a low-pass pi filter. This is not a constant-impedance network, since at some high frequency the capacitors across the input and output legs will become the equivalent of a short circuit. High-pass filters exchange the positions of the inductors and capacitors and would present a very low impedance at some low frequency.

In the case of the three-element circuit shown in Fig. 7-17A, each element should provide 6 dB per octave of attenuation for a total combined attenuation of 18 dB per octave (Fig. 7-17B). This would be true whenever the filter was connected to a matched source (assume it sees a matched load).

If this filter were to be connected to a zero-impedance source, then the input capacitor of the filter would have no effect since, by definition, the output voltage of a zero-impedance source is not affected by load. In this case, the filter would be reduced to a two-element filter of the L type providing only 12 dB per octave of attenuation (Fig. 7-17B).

A side effect of connecting some amplifiers to such a load without using build-out resistors would be the increase in intermodulation distortion from signals appearing on the slope of the cutoff region where the filter represents a downward mismatch to the amplifier.

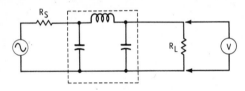

(A) Circuit diagram.

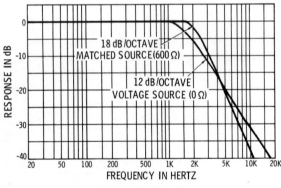

(B) Matched load.

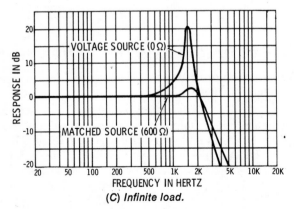

(C) Infinite load.

Fig. 7-17. Effect of termination on pi network.

Now, let us look at the effect of changing the termination of the filter since, in the cases above, we assumed it was properly terminated. Fig. 7-17C illustrates first the condition of being attached to a matched source, but an infinite load impedance. A +3 dB "bump" is the penalty paid for failure to shunt this high impedance with a terminating resistor of the proper value.

If we were, however, to ignore both the build-out resistor and the terminating resistor and arrive at the condition where the filter was driven from a zero-impedance source and loaded with an infinite-impedance load, then the upper curve in Fig. 7-17C is the type of "out-of-control" situation we can encounter. If we examine the diagram for this filter, we can see that this is a logical outcome of the failure to match impedances correctly. The series inductance and the output capacitor of the filter form a series-resonant circuit across the output of the generator. The current at resonance is limited only by the Q of the coil. Since the output voltage appears across one leg of the series-resonant circuit, the output voltage, like the current, is limited only by the Q of the coil. When a load is placed across the output, this tends to reduce the Q and limit the voltage rise. If the source resistance is raised from zero, it will limit the current at resonance and hence limit the voltage rise across the output.

What can we learn from this basic example? That a simple pi filter needs to have both its input and its output impedances matched carefully if its design parameters are to be properly employed.

Fig. 7-18 shows a similar analysis for a T network. Fig. 7-18B shows the results of connecting the filter to a matched load and first measuring it with a matched source attached and then with a zero-impedance source attached. In this case, the zero-impedance source causes a rise of approximately +3 dB prior to cutoff. This is caused by the resonance of the first two elements of the filter.

Fig. 7-18C shows the drastic effects of operating this filter without proper termination. If the source is matched but the output is not, the attenuation rate is reduced from 18 dB per octave to 12 dB per octave. If this filter is left with an infinite load impedance and also connected to a zero-impedance source, then the unhappy effects of the upper curve of Fig. 7-18C are the result.

Once again, we can learn from these examples that pi and T networks should be carefully matched to their source and output for smoothest response and accurate ultimate attenuation.

Our third example is the bridged-T constant-impedance network with limiting action (Fig. 7-19). This circuit family has widespread usage today in room–sound-system equalizers. Because the resistors in these networks sufficiently control the coil Q, the response of such a circuit is virtually unchanged by mismatch of source or load impedance.

Figs. 7-19B and 7-19C show how the response of these circuits is unaffected by zero-impedance sources or infinite-impedance loads. It is still wise to build out and terminate such circuits because the usual practice is to employ either pi or T networks in the same link circuit for cutoff filters, etc.

Having examined these sample cases, we can now list three main reasons for making impedance measurements in audio link circuits:

1. To aid in gain calculations.
2. To calculate the proper build-out resistor value.
3. To calculate the proper terminating resistor value.

Loudspeaker Impedance

When you are involved in the everyday matching of a loudspeaker to an amplifier, knowledge of where the *lowest* point is in the impedance curve becomes important. On one occasion, a manufacturer of musical-instrument loudspeakers quoted a higher value of

impedance by two to one, to make it seem that their loudspeaker was more sensitive than one of their competitor's, which had been given an accurate impedance specification. Ask yourself, is the higher output you hear from one loudspeaker really greater because of sensitivity, or is the impedance rating incorrect?

Unfortunately, just the connection of a loudspeaker with a specified impedance to a power amplifier with the same impedance tap available is not as straightforward as it might appear. What if you want a four-woofer system? For example, suppose the four woofers are 8 ohms each (a common case nowadays due to transistor amplifiers). Two of them in parallel have a combined impedance of 4 ohms, and four of them in parallel have an impedance of 2 ohms. But the amplifier has only 4-, 8-, and 16-ohm taps. By connecting to the 8- and 16-ohm taps (no connection to the common or "0" tap), you get approximately 1.4 ohms, which is safely below the 2 ohms required, yet still close enough to deliver adequate power to the loudspeakers. Connecting across the 4-ohm and 8-ohm taps gives less than 1 ohm. Now you can connect sixteen 16-ohm loudspeak-

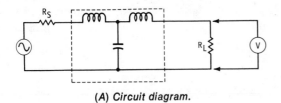

(A) Circuit diagram.

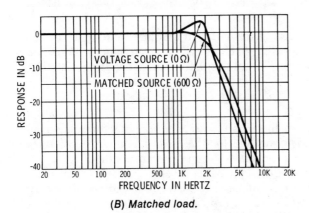

(B) Matched load.

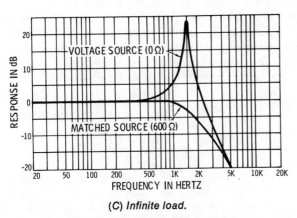

(C) Infinite load.

Fig. 7-18. Effect of termination on T network.

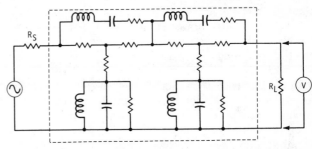

(A) Circuit diagram.

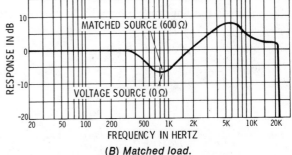

(B) Matched load.

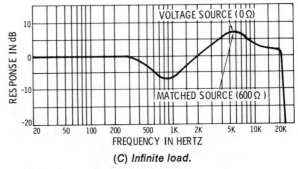

(C) Infinite load.

Fig. 7-19. Effect of termination on bridged-T network.

117

ers or eight 8-ohm loudspeakers in parallel without the need for 70-volt transformers.

Another approach for twenty-plus dollars is to buy a high-quality autoformer and "step up" the 2 ohms formed by connecting the loudspeakers in parallel back to 8 ohms. Fig. 7-20 details all the available impedances at the output of a conventional amplifier output transformer and all available impedance ratios a typical high-quality autoformer allows.

Impedance Matching 70-Volt Lines

Many believe that with a 70-volt system all that needs to be done is to ascertain the total power available from the amplifier and be sure not to exceed it when adding transformers with so many watts assigned to the voice coil attached to each secondary. Just pick power on the primary and voice-coil impedance on the secondary and keep adding transformers until all their powers equal the total power available. A panacea? Unfortunately, no. Seventy-volt distribution systems have garnered a reputation for poor quality out of all proportion to the simple reasons why this occurs. First of all, this simplified method forgets to account for *possible insertion losses* of the transformers themselves.

Two major possibilities enter into the calculation of the effect of the insertion loss of a 70-volt transformer on the planning of the electrical power required (EPR) from the power amplifier or amplifiers.

In the first case, the manufacturer of the transformer recognizes that the loudspeaker ought to receive the power stated on the primary taps of the transformer, since the sound-system designer will have planned his required sound levels on the basis of that wattage value to his loudspeakers. This manufacturer states what the insertion loss is (usually in decibels) and, just as important, adjusts the windings internally to compensate

for the stated insertion loss, thereby insuring that the stated primary wattage appears at the loudspeaker terminals. When this is the case, the actual primary impedance, Z, of the transformer can be found. Where the transformer insertion loss is compensated for in the transformer windings:

Total pwr in dBm =
Pwr to spkr in dBm + pwr loss in trans in dB $\qquad$ (7-18)

Total pwr in watts =
(Pwr to spkr in watts) (Pwr loss in trans as a ratio)
$$\qquad (7\text{-}19)$$

$$Z = \frac{(70.7)^2}{\text{Total pwr in watts}}$$

$$= \frac{5000}{\text{Pwr to spkr in watts} \times 10^{\frac{\text{Insertion loss in dB}}{10}}}$$
$$\qquad (7\text{-}20)$$

For example, if we had a transformer with a 10-watt primary tap and a 1.5-dB insertion loss, what would be the true primary impedance, and how many loudspeakers could be used safely with a 100-watt amplifier?

$$\text{Total pwr} = \text{Pwr to spkr} \times 10^{\frac{\text{Insertion loss in dB}}{10}}$$

$$= 10 \times 10^{\frac{1.5}{10}} = 14.13 \text{ watts}$$
$$\qquad (7\text{-}21)$$

Dividing the 100-watt amplifier output by 14.13 watts indicates that a total of seven loudspeakers may be used. The true primary impedance is:

$$Z = \frac{5000}{14.13} = 354 \text{ ohms} \qquad (7\text{-}22)$$

In the second case, the manufacturer has made no compensation for the insertion loss. One of the problems this manufacturer presents is the fact that the 70-volt line impedance seems correct when measured with an impedance meter, but the acoustic output is too low. In a typical case, the insertion losses can be quite high, but for the sake of an example, let us again choose an insertion loss of 1.5 dB. This time the primary impedance remains at its rating (usually), and the power at the secondary taps is what is off by 1.5 dB. Where the transformer insertion loss is not compensated for in the transformer windings:

$$\text{Pwr to spkr in watts} = \frac{\text{Pwr drawn by trans in watts}}{\text{Pwr loss in trans as a ratio}}$$

$$= \frac{10}{10^{\frac{1.5}{10}}} = 10 \times 10^{\frac{-1.5}{10}} = 7.08 \text{ watts}$$
$$\qquad (7\text{-}23)$$

If you attempt to get 10 watts out at the secondary, remember that the additional power you add will also

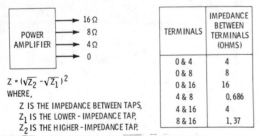

$$Z = (\sqrt{Z_2} - \sqrt{Z_1})^2$$
WHERE,
Z IS THE IMPEDANCE BETWEEN TAPS,
Z_1 IS THE LOWER - IMPEDANCE TAP,
Z_2 IS THE HIGHER - IMPEDANCE TAP.
DCR OF WINDINGS CHOSEN MUST BE 5% OR LESS OF Z CALCULATED.

TERMINALS	IMPEDANCE BETWEEN TERMINALS (OHMS)
0 & 4	4
0 & 8	8
0 & 16	16
4 & 8	0.686
4 & 16	4
8 & 16	1.37

(A) Amplifier output.

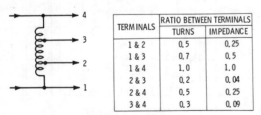

TERMINALS	RATIO BETWEEN TERMINALS	
	TURNS	IMPEDANCE
1 & 2	0.5	0.25
1 & 3	0.7	0.5
1 & 4	1.0	1.0
2 & 3	0.2	0.04
2 & 4	0.5	0.25
3 & 4	0.3	0.09

(B) With autoformer.

Fig. 7-20. Matching of impedances.

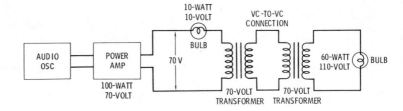

Fig. 7-21. A transformer "truth box."

suffer 1.5 dB degradation, so that 14.13 watts are required at the primary in order for 10 watts to be obtained at the secondary.

Usually, line losses are ignored as well. Therefore, it is almost certain that connecting an impedance bridge to a 70-volt system will result in reading an impedance *lower* than the rating of the amplifier. This is why the low-impedance, no-transformer method mentioned above is attractive; you buy heavier copper instead of transformers.

Reactive 70-Volt Transformers

As if things weren't bad enough, the majority of 70-volt transformers offered are of poor quality and highly reactive at lower and higher frequencies. An eye-opening test is to take any two identical transformers you commonly use and wire them "back to back" from voice coil to voice coil. Connect one of the 70-volt windings to the 70-volt output of a 100-watt power amplifier. Connect the other 70-volt winding to a standard 110-volt 60-watt light bulb. Put a 10-volt 10-watt bulb in series with the line coming from the power amplifier. Connect an audio oscillator to the input of the power amplifier. Setting the oscillator to 1000 Hz, adjust the amplifier gain until the light bulb lights up to just below normal brightness (70 volts). The small bulb will either not light or be very dim. Now, sweep the audio oscillator down in frequency. As the frequency lowers, the large bulb will go out (no power being delivered to the load), and the small bulb will glow brighter and brighter until it may burn out. (The transformer reactance has caused the equivalent of a short circuit of the amplifier output.) See Fig. 7-21 for the details of this demonstration.

At this point, you should begin to appreciate what these transformers are doing to the amplifier every time the program material contains any bass power. That this condition is all too prevalent is shown in Fig. 7-22, which shows how the impedance of one type of 70-volt transformer varies with frequency. Often, the amplifier manufacturer is falsely blamed for making unreliable amplifiers that burn up too easily. The only safe recourse for the amplifier manufacturer is to raise the cost of his units to the level where he can afford to build in the capability to work into a short circuit without damage. Much design time and money is wasted in this manner because sound engineers won't, don't, or can't measure impedance correctly.

Fig. 7-23 illustrates a typical 70-volt distribution system and indicates how the powers chosen are actually

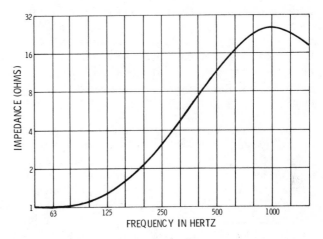

Fig. 7-22. Impedance variation encountered with one type of 70-volt transformer.

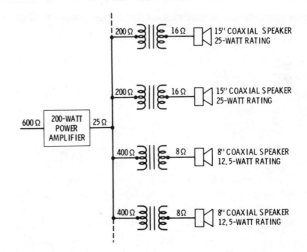

Fig. 7-23. A 70-volt distribution system illustrating typical values of impedances.

impedance choices. In high-quality transformers, the insertion loss is compensated for in the windings; therefore, the loudspeaker actually receives the power indicated. This means that each transformer draws slightly more power from the line than is indicated and that the final impedance will be too low if an attempt is made to add up powers equal to the amplifier power. In most cheap units, the power indicated on the label is not the power received; hence, the dB-SPL falls lower than calculated. While the impedance reads correctly, the acoustic output is too low for the available power.

Unauthorized-Tap Detector

The "sure kill" for unauthorized taps on 70-volt lines starts with the assumption that the unauthorized taps are speakers (8, 4, or 3.2 ohms) that have been added without 70-volt line-speaker matching transformers and thus are causing problems with power-amplifier output mismatching. An ac impedance measuring device (bridge or tester) can be used to verify that the 70-volt speaker line causing problems is not shorted but does have a low-impedance (approximately 3 or 8 ohms) load on it. A "kill" then would consist of connecting a filament-transformer secondary to the 70-volt line and plugging the primary into an available 120-volt ac power outlet for a few moments. An autotransformer, if used, should be isolated.

One caution is suggested by the following experience. A tv repairman was called to service an extensive distributed paging and music system at a ski resort. He soon discovered that the only speaker working had no transformer and that those not working all had transformers. "Naturally," he disconnected all the transformers. Be sure to check a couple of your own loudspeakers first before using this "cure."

Because the frequency is 60 Hz, the secondary ac voltage should be not much more than 12 volts for 70-volt lines feeding inexpensive 70-volt line matching transformers of limited frequency response and efficiency and speakers of about 10-watts program-material capacity (for example, Muzak® systems using Muzak®-supplied components). For 70-volt line transformers tapped at 4 watts, the power applied to 8-ohm speakers would be less than 0.2 watt, but the power applied to 8-ohm speakers tapped directly across the 70-volt line without 70-volt line transformers would be about 18 watts. For 4-ohm speakers, 36 watts would be applied, and for 3.2-ohm speakers, 45 watts would be applied.

This should be enough to either burn out the voice coils of the unauthorized loudspeakers or make them "try to climb out of the ceiling." If the voice coils do not burn out, plugging the filament transformer into the ac power outlet again should cause the unauthorized loudspeakers to announce their locations loudly.

To protect the filament transformer, a ⅜-ampere slow-blow fuse should be placed in series with the primary (Fig. 7-24). To give an indication that the 70-volt line is cleared, a 0.5-ohm, 25-watt wirewound power resistor should be placed in series with the secondary of the 4-ampere filament transformer and the 70-volt line. With the voltmeter test leads placed across the resistor, a sudden drop in voltage across the resistor would be an indication that the low-impedance load on the 70-volt line had been cleared.

For 70-volt loudspeaker lines feeding higher-quality 70-volt line transformers and speakers of more than 20 watts program-material capacity, a higher ac secondary voltage could be used, but it should not exceed 25 volts. For 25 volts, the transformer should have a current rating of 8 amperes or more. The primary fuse should have a 1.5-ampere rating, and the secondary 0.5-ohm series resistor should have a 100-watt rating. With 25 volts, the power applied to 8-ohm loudspeakers would be about 78 watts, and the power applied to 3.2-ohm loudspeakers would be about 195 watts.

Testing of 70-Volt Line During Installation

A 70-volt line can be checked out continuously while speakers with 70-volt transformers are connected to the line. To do this, two 10-ohm, 100-watt power resistors are connected in series with the 8-ohm output of a power amplifier and the 70-volt line being installed (Fig. 7-25). Music or noise is fed into the amplifier, and the volume control is adjusted so that a level is obtained that is not objectionable at 1 foot from the loudspeakers being connected to the 70-volt line.

If the 70-volt line is shorted or a 70-volt transformer is installed backward, the sound level from the previously installed loudspeakers will drop drastically, but the amplifier output is protected by the 20 ohms of series resistance. The amplifier should be protected from driving an open line by paralleling two 50-ohm, 100-watt power resistors across the 8-ohm output ahead of the series resistors (100-watt resistors should be used with a 200-watt amplifier). These four power resistors could be mounted by themselves in a 5″ × 7″ × 2″ or larger aluminum chassis box or mounted in a box with the circuit of an impedance-measuring device.

70-Volt Check List

Among the reasons 70-volt distributed systems are rather universally considered good only for background music, restaurants, etc., and not for auditoriums and arenas are the following unfavorable factors:

1. Failure to use overhead distribution.
2. Failure to achieve density of coverage.

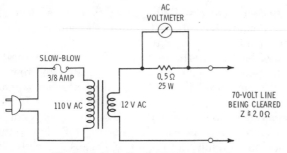

Fig. 7-24. Unauthorized-tap detector.

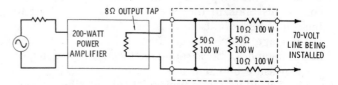

Fig. 7-25. Tester for 70-volt loudspeaker lines.

3. Failure to use heavy-duty, high-quality coaxial loudspeakers.

4. Failure to enclose the loudspeakers properly.

5. Failure to measure the transmission-line impedance to ensure that it is equal to or greater than the amplifier output impedance.

6. The proclivity of a distributed system to acquire unauthorized taps on it.

7. Such systems are more costly when properly done.

If all of these negative factors are resolved, then an overhead distributed system has only item 7 against it.

A ballroom with three hundred 15-inch coaxial loudspeakers powered by 7500 watts is a genuine entertainer- and customer-pleaser. Hotel ballrooms, meeting rooms, night clubs, and other environments where the stage may be set up literally anywhere require well-designed distributed systems. When the density of coverage is high, the acoustic gain is high, and the live source is not intensely directional, time delay can be avoided at surprising distances.

Matching Crossover Networks to Drivers

Still another area of unhappy impedance experiences is that of failing to ensure that each leg (high-frequency leg and low-frequency leg) of a crossover network is properly terminated (Fig. 7-26). All too frequently, the autotransformers are used as level adjusters rather than as impedance matchers, with the resultant difficulties shown in Fig. 7-27, as compared to the desired result in Fig. 7-28.

Biamplification

In a biamplification system, the active or passive crossover network is connected ahead of the power amplifiers; Fig. 7-29 represents a typical system. You do not have to listen very long to such a system to recognize that it sounds much "cleaner" than the same loudspeakers driven through a passive crossover network connected to the amplifier output. Why this is so, however, has not been so "cleanly" described, and some incorrect reasons have appeared in print from time to time.

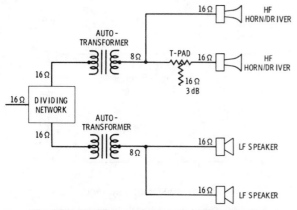

Fig. 7-26. Typical crossover-network termination.

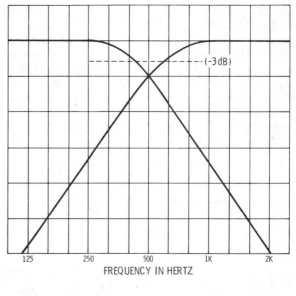

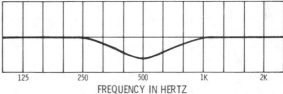

(A) Driver impedance less than network impedance.

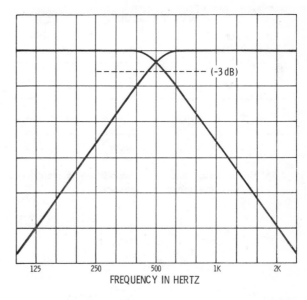

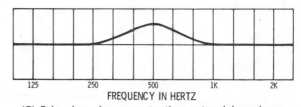

(B) Driver impedance greater than network impedance.

Fig. 7-27. Results of improper use of autotransformers with crossover network.

Fig. 7-30 shows the circuitry involved in a conventional system (Fig. 7-30A) and in a biamplified system (Fig. 7-30B). Fig. 7-31 illustrates the harmonics generated by overdriving the power amplifier at a low frequency, first at 6 dB (Fig. 7-31A) and then at 20 dB (Fig. 7-31B). In the biamplified system, the high-frequency harmonics generated in the low-frequency amplifier do not go anywhere but to the woofer, which has a rolloff characteristic that attenuates them. The high-frequency signal remains untouched.

An easy demonstration of this is to set up a conventional system in the manner shown in Fig. 7-32. You will find that the very offensive buzz tone is gone; this is what biamplifying does for a sound system.

Some rules for biamplification systems are:

1. Be sure the input to the passive 600-ohm crossover is correctly built out and that each output leg is correctly terminated.
2. Put a passive level control in front of the line-level crossover network, because the amplifier gain controls are no longer available for that purpose—they are now "balance" controls.
3. Provide protection against low frequencies in the high-frequency driver line about one octave *below* the crossover frequency of the 600-ohm passive network used in the link circuit. This is often a simple capacitor of the nonpolarized, oil-filled motor-starting variety. This saves the high-frequency drivers if catastrophic amplifier failure occurs.

The value of the protection capacitor may be found as follows:

1. Choose the −3 dB frequency (f), usually one octave below the regular crossover point.
2. Choose the impedance (of the loudspeaker line) in ohms (Z).
3. Choose X_C in ohms ($X_C = 2Z$ in matched case, and $X_C = Z$ in unmatched case).

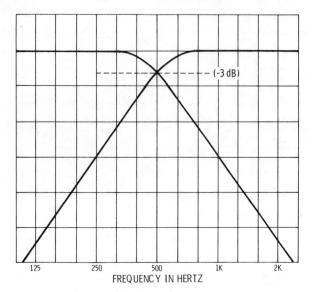

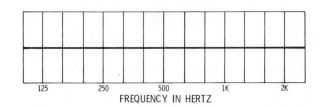

Fig. 7-28. Result when the driver impedance is matched to the network impedance.

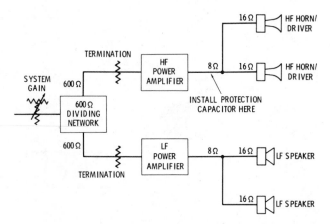

Fig. 7-29. The handling of network terminations in a typical biamplification system.

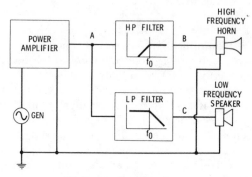

(A) Conventional system.

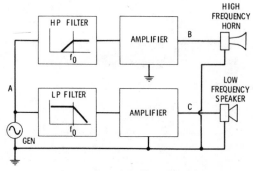

(B) Biamplification system.

Fig. 7-30. Crossover methods in sound systems.

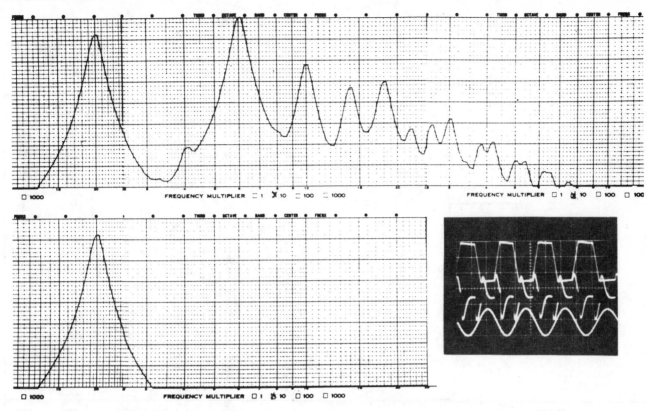

(A) Spectra of single-amplifier (upper) and biamplified (lower) systems 6 dB into clipping at 200 Hz.

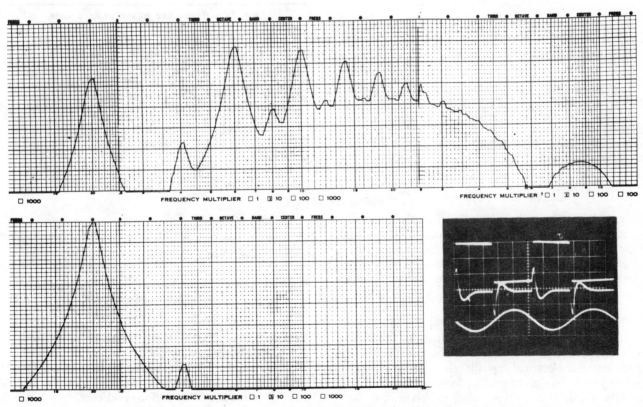

(B) Spectra of single-amplifier (upper) and biamplified (lower) systems 12 dB into clipping at 200 Hz.

Fig. 7-31. Effects of overdriving amplifier.

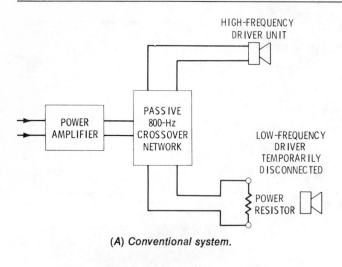

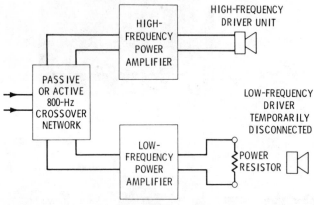

(A) Conventional system.

(B) Biamplification system.

Fig. 7-32. Demonstration of the benefits of biamplification.

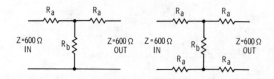

Loss in dB	R_a	R_b	Loss in dB	R_a	R_b
0.5	18	10,000	0.5	8.2	10,000
1	33	5,100	1	18	5,100
2	68	2,700	2	33	2,700
3	100	1,600	3	51	1,600
4	130	1,200	4	68	1,200
5	160	1,000	5	82	1,000
6	200	820	6	100	820
7	220	680	7	110	680
8	240	560	8	130	560
9	270	470	9	150	470
10	300	430	10	150	430
12	360	330	12	180	330
14	390	240	14	200	240
16	430	200	16	220	200
18	470	150	18	220	150
20	510	120	20	240	120
22	510	100	22	240	100
24	510	75	24	270	75
26	560	62	26	270	62
28	560	47	28	270	47
30	560	39	30	270	39
32	560	30	32	270	30
34	560	24	34	270	24
36	560	18	36	270	18
38	560	15	38	270	15
40	560	12	40	300	12
Values used are 5% EIA Values.		If $Z \neq 600\,\Omega$ divide all values by $\frac{600}{Z}$.		For loudspeaker circuits use adjustable wirewounds.	

Fig. 7-33. Resistance values for fixed pads.

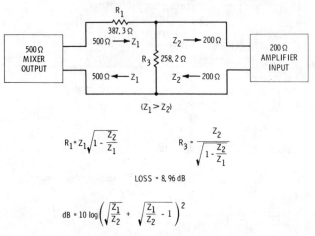

$(Z_1 > Z_2)$

$$R_1 = Z_1 \sqrt{1 - \frac{Z_2}{Z_1}} \qquad R_3 = \frac{Z_2}{\sqrt{1 - \frac{Z_2}{Z_1}}}$$

LOSS = 8.96 dB

$$dB = 10 \log \left(\sqrt{\frac{Z_1}{Z_2}} + \sqrt{\frac{Z_1}{Z_2} - 1} \right)^2$$

Fig. 7-34. Conventional minimum-loss pad for matching 500-ohm output to 200-ohm input.

4. Choose either matched (source Z = load Z) or unmatched (source Z ≪ load Z) case.

For example, assume the loudspeaker impedance is 8 ohms and the amplifier output impedance is 0.1 ohm. Therefore the desired X_C is 8 ohms. If f is 250 Hz,

$$C = \frac{10^6}{2\pi f X_C} = \frac{10^6}{2\pi \times 250 \times 8} = 80\ \mu F \qquad (7\text{-}24)$$

Biamplification systems offer significantly lower distortion, much easier control of acoustic levels, and greater versatility regarding number and type of drivers used at any one time. Today, this method is virtually the only choice for high-level rock entertainment systems.

Fixed Power Pads

Quite often in the course of designing and constructing a complex single-source array, it becomes necessary to change the electrical input levels to differing horns and drivers as well as to provide losses in 600-ohm link circuits. To do this, we use either unbalanced or balanced fixed pads. Suppose you need a 6-dB unbalanced pad for a 16-ohm circuit. Fig. 7-33 shows that for a 600-ohm circuit the required resistance values are $R_a = 200$ ohms and $R_b = 820$ ohms. To find the values for a 16-ohm circuit, divide by 600/Z, or in this case 600/16 = 37.5. The needed values are then 5.3 ohms for R_a and 21.9 ohms for R_b. (For various pad configurations and the corresponding design equations, refer to number 127 in Appendix VIII.)

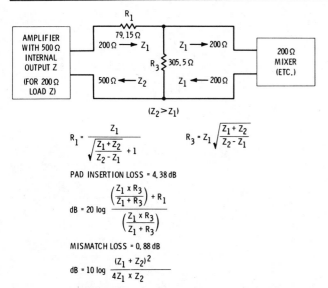

$$R_1 = \frac{Z_1}{\sqrt{\frac{Z_1 + Z_2}{Z_2 - Z_1}} + 1} \qquad R_3 = Z_1 \sqrt{\frac{Z_1 + Z_2}{Z_2 - Z_1}}$$

PAD INSERTION LOSS = 4.38 dB

$$dB = 20 \log \frac{\left(\frac{Z_1 \times R_3}{Z_1 + R_3}\right) + R_1}{\left(\frac{Z_1 \times R_3}{Z_1 + R_3}\right)}$$

MISMATCH LOSS = 0.88 dB

$$dB = 10 \log \frac{(Z_1 + Z_2)^2}{4 Z_1 \times Z_2}$$

Fig. 7-35. Impedance-correcting pad for use when internal output impedance is higher than load impedance.

Minimum-Loss Matching Pads

Figs. 7-34, 7-35, and 7-36 give, in detail, the construction of minimum-loss matching pads for unequal impedances. Fig. 7-34 shows conventional minimum-loss pads for matching 500 ohms to 200 ohms. Fig. 7-35 illustrates the design of an improved impedance-correcting circuit for matching impedances when the internal output impedance is higher than the load impedance, and Fig. 7-36 gives the design for the reverse situation. If a loss greater than the minimum loss calculated for these pads is desired, then a conventional loss pad may be added to them.

Ralph W. Townsley's book *Passive Equalizer Design Data* is a must for any serious student of impedance matching and passive networks. (See the bibliography in Appendix II.)

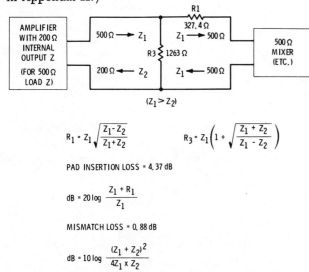

$$R_1 = Z_1 \sqrt{\frac{Z_1 - Z_2}{Z_1 + Z_2}} \qquad R_3 = Z_1 \left(1 + \sqrt{\frac{Z_1 + Z_2}{Z_1 - Z_2}}\right)$$

PAD INSERTION LOSS = 4.37 dB

$$dB = 20 \log \frac{Z_1 + R_1}{Z_1}$$

MISMATCH LOSS = 0.88 dB

$$dB = 10 \log \frac{(Z_1 + Z_2)^2}{4 Z_1 \times Z_2}$$

Fig. 7-36. Impedance-correcting pad for use when internal output impedance is lower than load impedance.

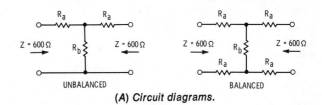

(A) Pad elements.

1 dB = 1	18 dB = 15 + 1 + 2
2 dB = 2	19 dB = 15 + 2 + 2
3 dB = 1 + 2	20 dB = 15 + 5
4 dB = 2 + 2	21 dB = 15 + 5 + 1
5 dB = 5	22 dB = 15 + 5 + 2
6 dB = 5 + 1	23 dB = 15 + 5 + 1 + 2
7 dB = 5 + 2	24 dB = 15 + 5 + 2 + 2
8 dB = 5 + 2 + 1	25 dB = 15 + 10
9 dB = 5 + 2 + 2	26 dB = 15 + 10 + 1
10 dB = 10	27 dB = 15 + 10 + 2
11 dB = 10 + 1	28 dB = 15 + 10 + 1 + 2
12 dB = 10 + 2	29 dB = 15 + 10 + 2 + 2
13 dB = 10 + 1 + 2	30 dB = 15 + 10 + 5
14 dB = 10 + 2 + 2	31 dB = 15 + 10 + 5 + 1
15 dB = 15	32 dB = 15 + 10 + 5 + 2
16 dB = 15 + 1	33 dB = 15 + 10 + 5 + 1 + 2
17 dB = 15 + 2	34 dB = 15 + 10 + 5 + 2 + 2
	35 dB = 15 + 10 + 5 + 1 + 2 + 2

(B) Combinations of elements.

Fig. 7-37. Method of assembling pads in 1-dB increments.

A Six-Element Universal Test Pad

An easy way to handle the installation of a needed pad in 1-dB increments to 35 dB is shown in Fig. 7-37. Carrying a half-dozen sets of six simple pads allows their combination into almost any value desired. Both unbalanced and balanced configurations are shown in Fig. 7-38. Normally, the nearest 5% value suffices, but where precision is desired, use the 1% value nearest to that shown in Fig. 7-38B.

A Bridging Attenuator Box

One of the most useful devices a sound-system engineer can possess is a bridging attenuator box that allows him to feed balanced or unbalanced; high-impedance or low-impedance; high-, medium-, or low-level signals to his console from any location that has a nom-

(A) Circuit diagrams.

UNBALANCED				BALANCED		
Loss in dB	R_a	R_b		Loss in dB	R_a	R_b
1 dB	34.5	5208		1 dB	17.25	5208
2 dB	68.8	2582		2 dB	34.4	2582
5 dB	168.1	987.6		5 dB	84.1	987.6
10 dB	312	421.6		10 dB	156	421.6
15 dB	418.8	220.4		15 dB	209.4	220.4

Use 5% values and grind to exact value using impedance bridge (or use nearest 1% value).

(B) Resistor values.

Fig. 7-38. Details of pad elements.

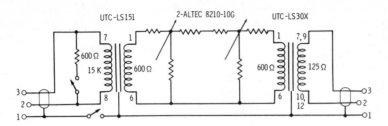

Fig. 7-39. Bridging attenuator box.

inal 150-ohm balanced microphone low-level input. The circuit in Fig. 7-39, contributed by Steven Hodge, allows just such versatility.

The unit provides both isolation and as much attenuation as required. The output of the unit is designed to be used with any balanced microphone-level input. The procedure for using the attenuator box is to set both attenuators until you have a usable signal at the output. This attenuator box has been used on all types of speakers and line-level signals coming from a variety of equipment ranging from the cells of optical sound-projector equipment to guitar amplifiers. Although the cost of such a unit is substantial, it is well worth it in that it enables you to hook up a variety of equipment quickly and without difficulty.

The Sescom Model SM-1 Split Matcher can serve as the nucleus of a "bridging box." It has been designed to allow an electric instrument to be plugged into and out of it back to the amplifier of the instrument, while providing another output at microphone impedance to the console of the sound system. The addition of an adjustable pad at the output of the Split Matcher gives an effective bridging box (60K input, 150-250 Ω output, −10 dBm input level).

Hybrid Transformers

Telephone companies, motion-picture dubbing console constructors, and knowledgeable sound engineers use hybrid transformers to obtain impedance matching to long telephone lines, studio lines, etc. Fig. 7-40 illustrates the useful properties of these units. Hybrid transformers allow interesting signal divisions and combinations while maintaining impedance matching between differing circuits.

A signal arriving at the lower left termination of the schematic in Fig. 7-40 will be transferred to the upper

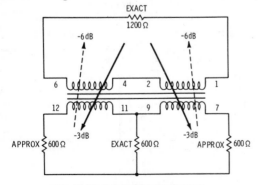

Fig. 7-40. A hybrid transformer.

load, and none of this signal will appear in the lower right termination. If the signal arrives at the lower right termination, it will be transferred to the upper load also, and none of it will appear at the lower left termination. In order to obtain these characteristics, the balancing resistor connected to the center point of the transformer winding must be set to the proper value relative to the upper termination. (In the case of long transmission lines with complex impedances, precision balance networks can replace the balance resistors. Impedances of 300, 600, 900, 1200 ohms, etc., are routinely handled by readily available hybrids.)

To understand better the operation of this device, assume a signal originates from the lower left, and assume the impedance looking into 11-12 to be exactly equal to the value of the 600-ohm balancing resistor. If this is so, then the voltage drop from 12 to 11 will be exactly duplicated across 9 and 7, which would *seem* to induce a voltage in the circuit of the lower right termination. This is not the case, however, since this voltage is exactly equal but opposite in phase to the drop across the balancing resistor. Therefore, no voltage is available to cause current through the lower right termination. One half the voltage (−6 dB) is lost in the resistor; therefore, the signal being transferred to the upper load is at −6 dB.

In the case where the signal comes into the hybrid through the upper termination, the two lower loads can be considered in series, and consequently no voltage appears across the balancing resistor. Therefore, there is no voltage loss in transmission. However, because of the equal division of the upper signal between the lower right and the lower left loads, each load will receive one half the power, or 3 dB less than the original.

Conclusion

This section has touched on the basics of impedance measurement, calculation, matching, and transformation. It has not covered the real complexities that a professional transmission engineer, for example, wrestles with, but it has dealt with the areas of greatest aggravation for the average sound engineer.

FUNDAMENTALS OF TIME DELAY

Natural time delays are always present in a sound system because of the finite speed of sound in air. On occasion, we introduce additional time delay in a sound system through placement, time-delay devices, or reflections. There are both the absolute delay (that which occurs due to total distance traveled plus total time delay introduced) and relative delay (the apparent delay between any two sound sources) at the listener's position. Additional changes in acoustic level may be "traded off" against differences in delay time to allow a listener greater latitude in acceptable parameters before annoyance. Fig. 7-41 illustrates some basic time-delay and level-versus-delay experiments (Fay-Hall, Henry, Haas, etc., effect).

Time-Delay Calculations

With the advent of digital time-delay devices offering wide frequency response and dynamic range at inaudible distortion levels, it is desirable to include the benefits of such components in the design of modern sound systems. In order to apply these components intelligently, the designer and user need a basic understanding of how the velocity of sound changes with temperature, how the time sound takes to travel relates to the distance traveled, and how to make time-delay measurements. All the necessary equations are shown in Chart 7-1.

Example 1—If the direct sound travels 125 feet (D_D) and the reflected sound travels 160 feet (D_R), what is the time interval at the listener's ears between the arrival of the direct sound and the arrival of the first reflection? (The room temperature is 80°F.)

$$V = 49 \sqrt{459.4 + 80°} = 1138 \text{ ft/sec} \quad (7\text{-}25)$$

$$\frac{x \text{ ms}}{\text{ft}} = \frac{1}{1138 \text{ ft/s}} \frac{1000 \text{ ms}}{\text{s}} = 0.879 \text{ ms/ft} \quad (7\text{-}26)$$

$$D_R (0.879) - D_D (0.879) = 160 (0.879) - 125 (0.879)$$
$$= 30.77 \text{ ms} \quad (7\text{-}27)$$

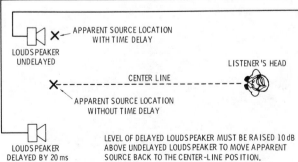

Fig. 7-41. Basic time-delay and level-versus-delay experiments.

Chart 7-1. Temperature, Time, and Travel Equations

Temperature Equations

$$V = 49 \sqrt{459.4 + °F}$$

where,

V is the velocity in feet per second,
°F is the Fahrenheit temperature.

$$49 \sqrt{459.4 + 72.42} = 1130 \text{ ft/s}$$

$$°F = \frac{V^2}{49^2} - 459.4$$

$$\frac{1130^2}{49^2} - 459.4 = 72.42°$$

Time Equations

$$\frac{x \text{ ms}}{\text{ft}} = \frac{1}{V} \frac{1000 \text{ ms}}{\text{s}}$$

where V is the velocity in feet per second.

$$\text{Time in ms} = \text{Distance} \frac{x \text{ ms}}{\text{ft}}$$

$$\frac{1}{1130 \text{ ft/s}} \frac{1000 \text{ ms}}{\text{s}} = \frac{0.885 \text{ ms}}{\text{ft}}$$

$$100 \text{ ft} \times 0.885 \text{ ms/ft} = 88.5 \text{ ms}$$

Travel Equations

$$\frac{x \text{ ft}}{\text{ms}} = V \frac{1}{1000 \text{ ms}}$$

where V is the velocity in feet per second.

$$\text{Distance} = \text{Time in ms} \frac{x \text{ ft}}{1 \text{ ms}}$$

$$1130 \text{ ft/s} \frac{1s}{1000 \text{ ms}} = 1.13 \text{ ft/ms}$$

$$88.5 \text{ ms} \times 1.13 \text{ ft/ms} = 100 \text{ ft}$$

Conventional Distance, Velocity, and Time Equations

$$D = VT; \quad V = \frac{D}{T}; \quad T = \frac{D}{V}$$

where,

D is the distance,
V is the velocity,
T is the time.

$$3000 \text{ mi} \cong 186,000 \text{ mi/s} \times 0.016 \text{ s}$$

$$186,000 \text{ mi/s} \cong \frac{3000 \text{ mi}}{0.016 \text{ s}}$$

$$0.016 \text{ s} \cong \frac{3000 \text{ mi}}{186,000 \text{ mi/s}}$$

$$\frac{1000 \text{ ms}}{\text{s}} \frac{0.016 \text{ s}}{1} = 16 \text{ ms}$$

Example 2—By using tone-burst signals of short duration (10 ms typically), it is possible, through using an oscilloscope either with a camera or with variable persistence, to measure the time interval between a direct sound and a reflection. See Fig. 7-42. The oscilloscope may be set up to trigger when sound first reaches the test microphone (to measure the time difference between the direct sound and reflections) or to trigger when the tone-burst generator keys the audio oscillator (to measure the length of time it takes the direct sound to reach the test microphone from the sound source). Once you have measured the time delay, usually in

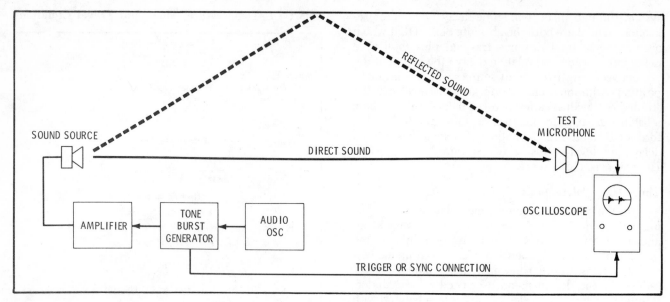

Fig. 7-42. Measuring time delay.

milliseconds, and converted it to an equivalent distance in feet, the detection of likely surfaces becomes the drawing of an arc having that radius and the position of the measuring microphone as the center. All surfaces that the arc contacts become possible reflectors, and where multiple surfaces are suspect, the movement of the microphone toward one of them quickly confirms or eliminates it as the reflector.

For example, if the direct sound took 78 ms to reach the listener and the reflection arrived 36 ms later, this means that the extra distance the reflection traveled in our example room was:

$$\text{Distance} = \text{Time in ms } \frac{\text{x ft}}{1 \text{ ms}}$$
$$= 36 \text{ ms } \frac{1.138 \text{ ft}}{\text{ms}} = 41 \text{ ft} \qquad (7\text{-}28)$$

One caution is to be aware of the fact that the reflected sound may have undergone more than one reflection in arriving at the listener's position. When all nearby surfaces fail to intersect properly with the arc drawn, it may need to be subdivided into likely multiple reflections. Again, movement of the test microphone is highly useful to determine experimentally the direction from which the sound was last reflected.

Example 3—Imagine that you are at the drawing-board stage of an auditorium and find that the balcony overhangs the rear seats on the main floor in a way that precludes these seats from receiving direct sound from a well designed single-source system on the centerline of the auditorium. You wish to place supplementary horns flush into the front of the balcony bottom area to cover the rear seats under the balcony. The distance from the front single-source array to the position where you want to put the supplementary loud-

speakers is 85 feet. For normal room temperature (72.42°F), what time delay to the supplementary loudspeakers should you provide?

$$\text{Distance} \times \frac{\text{x ms}}{\text{ft}} = 85 \times 0.885 = 75.23 \text{ ms}$$
$$(7\text{-}29)$$

You now add 20 ms to this figure in order to achieve what is called the Fay-Hall, Haas, etc., effect. When both loudspeakers, without delay, produce approximately equal SPL at the listener's ears, the introduction of $D_2 + 20$ ms of delay to the loudspeaker nearest the listener moves the apparent source of all sound to the undelayed loudspeaker (Fig. 7-43). So the total time delay you would provide would be

$$75.23 + 20 = 95.23 \text{ ms} \qquad (7\text{-}30)$$

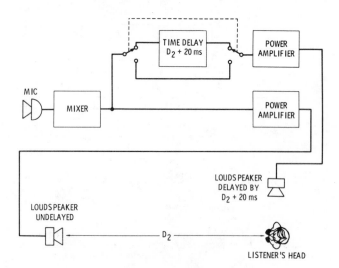

Fig. 7-43. Auditory inhibition effect.

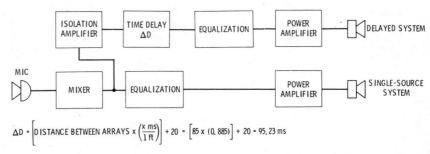

Fig. 7-44. Introduction of time delay into a sound system.

$$\Delta D = \left[\text{DISTANCE BETWEEN ARRAYS} \times \left(\frac{x \, ms}{1 \, ft}\right)\right] + 20 = \left[85 \times (0.885)\right] + 20 = 95.23 \, ms$$

See Fig. 7-44. Sometimes slight variation of the 20 ms is necessary because of reflected energy, etc.

Example 4—Fig. 7-45 illustrates how to obtain a natural time delay by making D_2 20 ms greater than D_o (at 72.42°F this means D_2 should be 1.13×20 ms = 22.6 feet greater than D_o). This would mean that the listener, hearing the talker's live voice first, would identify the talker as the source even when the reinforcement from the loudspeaker was reaching his ears at a level up to 10 dB higher.

Example 5—Fig. 7-46 illustrates the Doak and Bolt delay-versus-level criteria. The chart in Fig. 7-46B shows the "trade-off" between relative levels at the listener's ears and time delay. For example, if, due to distance, the natural delay between sound source 1 and sound source 2 at the listener's ears were 200 ms we would need to make sound source 2 approximately 25 dB above sound source 1 at the listener's ears in order not to annoy more than 10% of the audience in that area.

A very sophisticated use of time delay and level versus time delay is in the masking of an echo. Fig. 7-47 illustrates a possible case. The time the sound takes to travel from source 1 to the listener is $90 \times 0.885 = 79.65$ ms. The path the sound echo takes is $(175 + 90) \times 0.885 = 234.53$ ms. Therefore, at the listener's ears a relative delay of $234.53 - 79.65 = 154.88$ ms is heard (a definite discrete echo). Since the echo is the result of sound being focused by the concave surface area shown at the rear of the auditorium, it is apparent only in a limited audience area. If a local loudspeaker is provided in that area and its total delay at the listener's ears is made 20 ms behind the arrival of the sound from the main loudspeaker in the front of the auditorium, the listener is not aware of its presence. The total delay of the sound reaching the listener from source 2 is therefore $79.65 + 20 = 99.65$ ms. The actual delay inserted in the electrical circuit is 99.65 ms less 17.7 ms (the equivalent of 20 feet in milliseconds), or 81.95 ms. The time difference between the arrival of this sound

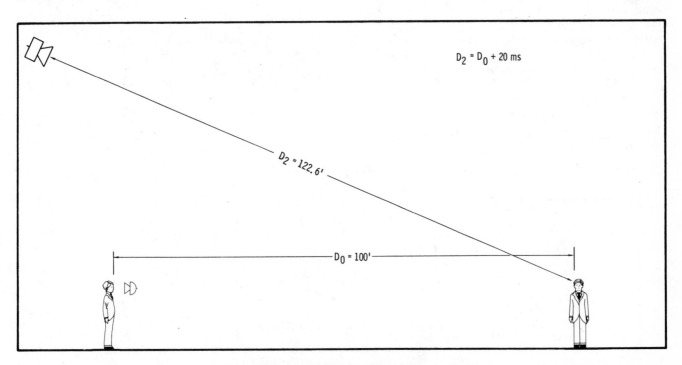

Fig. 7-45. Using natural time delay.

(A) Relative delay at listener.

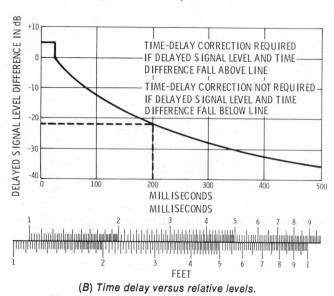

(B) Time delay versus relative levels.

Fig. 7-46. Doak and Bolt delay-versus-level criteria.

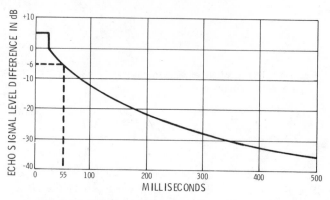

Fig. 7-48. Relative levels versus time delay of echo.

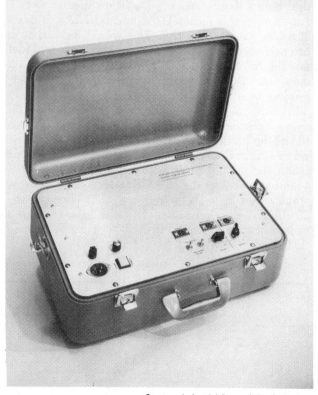

Courtesy Industrial Research Products, Inc.

Fig. 7-49. Time-delay test set.

and the arrival of the echo is $234.53 - 99.65 = 134.88$ ms. Using the Doak and Bolt 10% annoyance chart (Fig. 7-48), we find that if we make the local loudspeaker approximately 15 dB higher in level than the echo, we will have succeeded in masking the echo from the listener (enter the chart at 134.88 ms on the ms scale, and read 15 dB on the left scale).

A good, basic understanding of these simple but important relationships is vital to the creative design of sound systems today. Time-delay relationships complete the chain of necessary criteria for the proper placement of a loudspeaker.

1. Location allows an AL_{cons} of 15% or less at D_2.
2. Location allows PAG = NAG.

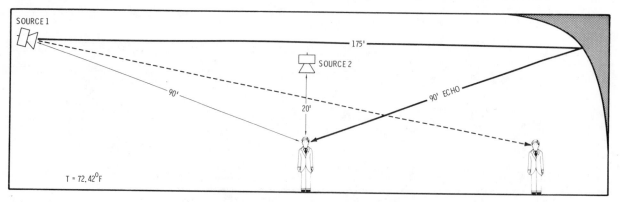

Fig. 7-47. Using time delay to "mask" an echo.

Fig. 7-50. An industrial-type digital time delay.

Courtesy Industrial Research Products, Inc.

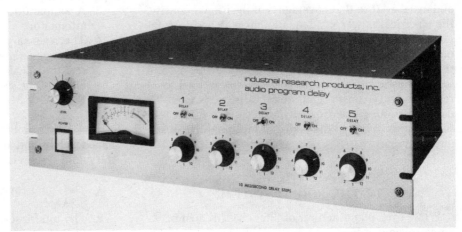

Fig. 7-51. A studio-type digital time-delay device.

Courtesy Industrial Research Products, Inc.

3. Location ensures that no time delay shall exceed 40 ms (approximately 45 feet) at either the listener's location or the performer's location without sufficient remedial measures (earphones for the announcer at a basketball arena, monitor loudspeakers for rock-and-roll performers, or similar facilities).

Time-Delay Units

Figs. 7-49, 7-50, and 7-51 show commercially available time-delay units. The time-delay test set in Fig. 7-49 allows two channels of delay variable in 10-ms steps up to 120 ms. Fig. 7-50 shows a typical industrial-type digital time delay that incorporates plug-in cards to change the amount of delay desired (ideal to leave on the job). A typical studio-type digital time delay which allows up to five channels for special effects is shown in Fig. 7-51.

PROOFING THE INSTALLED SYSTEM

The oscilloscope and oscillator are used first to check stability and to set levels. Always remember to have both the oscilloscope and voltmeter across any circuit to be checked to ensure that the voltage read is from the intended waveform.

In setting levels, proceed from the speech input to the power-amplifier output. During this, inspect all terminations and build-outs.

Having determined that the system is stable, matched, and operating at designed levels, you can then proceed to the measurement of its acoustic gain (see Chapter 5). In each case above, the foreknowledge gained from careful, accurate design methods guides you into the predicted performance and quickly alerts you to any deviations from design.

After all of these tests are completed, the sound system is ready for equalization.

131

CHAPTER 8

Equalizing the Sound System

At this point, if you have designed a system capable of benefiting from equalization and have constructed and installed it so that coverage is of the proper density, the electrical power is adequate and matched to sufficiently efficient transducers able to absorb it, and the entire system is free from hum, noise, oscillations, and rf interference, you are ready to equalize this system to its acoustic environment to ensure the specified tonal response and acoustic gain at each listener's ears. To do this requires insertion of the necessary filters into the sound system and the taking of meaningful acoustic measurements.

INSERTING THE FILTERS IN THE SOUND SYSTEM

While each manufacturer of filters has his own packaging scheme, it is wise to organize the available filters into a master test set as diagrammed in Fig. 8-1. Typically, a master test set consists of the following items:

1. The required fractional-octave filters.
2. A high-pass, low-pass filter set.
3. A comparator switch with its associated calibrated attenuator.
4. The necessary terminals to allow interposition of noise generators, sine-wave generators, meters, real-time analyzers, etc., either before or after the filters. One such assembled test set is shown in Fig. 8-2.

Test sets can be totally passive, totally active, or mixed active and passive. The placement of filters in the sound system is dependent on the following factors:

1. The gain overlap between components (Fig. 8-3A).
2. The total insertion loss of all the filters combined (Fig. 8-3B).
3. The differing sources (Fig. 8-4).
4. The differing outputs (Fig. 8-5).

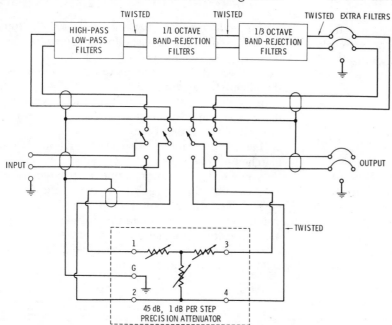

Fig. 8-1. Diagram of a master test set.

Fig. 8-2. Master test set of the type in Fig. 8-1.

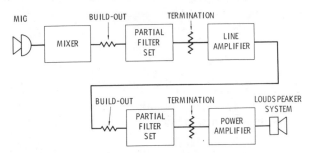

(A) Use of a full filter set.

(B) Use of partial filter sets.

Fig. 8-3. Insertion of filter sets into typical link circuits.

Build-out and termination resistors may cause additional losses in link circuits and should be accounted for.

WHAT IS ROOM–SOUND-SYSTEM EQUALIZATION?

Equalization is as old as audio. Tape recording makes good use of equalization to avoid noise. The very low frequencies and the high frequencies are boosted in the record mode (Fig. 8-6). When the inverse response is applied during playback, the result is a uniform overall signal response and a more uniform s/n ratio. Carrying this concept further, you can see the result of combining conventional equalization methods with sound-system–room equalization (Fig. 8-7).

You learned in Chapter 6 that the true loop gain figure is determined by the separation of the loudspeaker and microphone and that the effect of critical distance acts as a limit on this separation. Fig. 8-8 is a step-by-step example of how unavailable acoustic gain, due to feedback caused by the highest amplitude present, can be made available by equalizing all frequencies (making them equal in amplitude response).

It can also be seen that acoustic gain restoration covers the entire spectrum. Examination on a frequency-by-frequency basis reveals that at low frequencies the modes are spaced apart and at higher frequencies they overlap into a continuous spectrum shape.

The total number of room modes (N) up to a given frequency (f_c) is found by:

$$N = 4V \left(\frac{f_c}{C}\right)^3 \qquad (8\text{-}1)$$

where,

N is the number of modes,
V is the volume of the room in cubic feet (room has a regular shape),
f_c is the upper frequency limit in hertz,
C is the velocity of sound in feet per second.

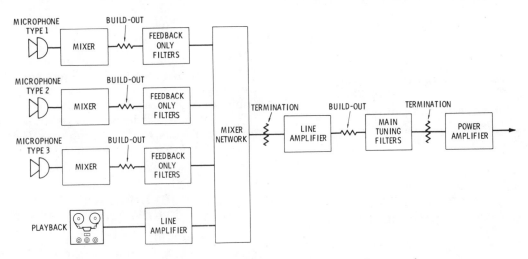

Fig. 8-4. Equalization of multiple microphones having major differences in response.

133

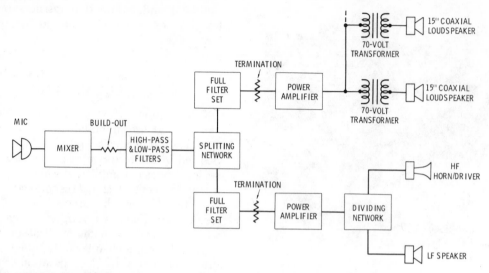

Fig. 8-5. Equalization of multiple loudspeaker types having major differences in response.

S/N NOT CONSTANT WITH FREQUENCY

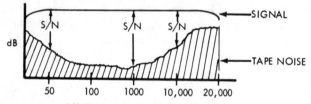

(A) Tape signal relative to tape noise.

EQUALIZER CHARACTERISTIC
INSTALLED IN RECORDING EQUIPMENT

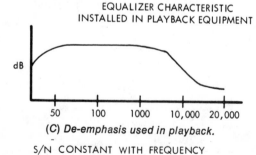

(B) Pre-emphasis used in recording.

EQUALIZER CHARACTERISTIC
INSTALLED IN PLAYBACK EQUIPMENT

De-emphasis used in playback.

(C) De-emphasis used in playback.

S/N CONSTANT WITH FREQUENCY

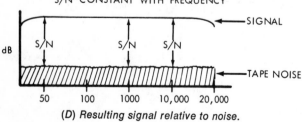

(D) Resulting signal relative to noise.

Fig. 8-6. Purpose of electronic equalization in tape recording.

and where

$$f_c > \frac{4C}{V^{1/3}} \qquad (8\text{-}2)$$

EXAMPLE:

$$4(500{,}000)\left(\frac{500}{1130}\right)^3 = 173{,}262 \text{ modes} \qquad (8\text{-}3)$$

Since in this case

$$\frac{4(1130)}{(500{,}000)^{1/3}} = 56.95 \text{ Hz} \qquad (8\text{-}4)$$

expression 8-2 is satisfied.

When the frequency is sufficiently high so that N is large, the number of modes per hertz is given by:

$$\frac{\text{Modes}}{\text{Hz}} = \frac{12Vf_c{}^2}{C^3} \qquad (8\text{-}5)$$

EXAMPLE:

$$\frac{12(500{,}000)(500)^2}{(1130)^3} = \frac{1040 \text{ Modes}}{1 \text{ Hz}} \text{ at 500 Hz} \qquad (8\text{-}6)$$

What the filters operate on are not room modes but clusters of room modes. The filters are used to shape the upper envelope of the modes. It has been remarkably well substantiated that the narrowest intervals necessary in equalizing sound systems for acoustic gain are approximately ⅓-octave intervals. Note that almost none of the band-rejection filters so spaced are ⅓-octave filters; most are closer to ¹⁄₁₀-octave.

SOUND REPRODUCTION IN MOTION-PICTURE THEATERS

Figs. 8-9, 8-10, and 8-11 illustrate a "systems" approach taken to the use of equalization in motion-picture theaters. This particular description (included

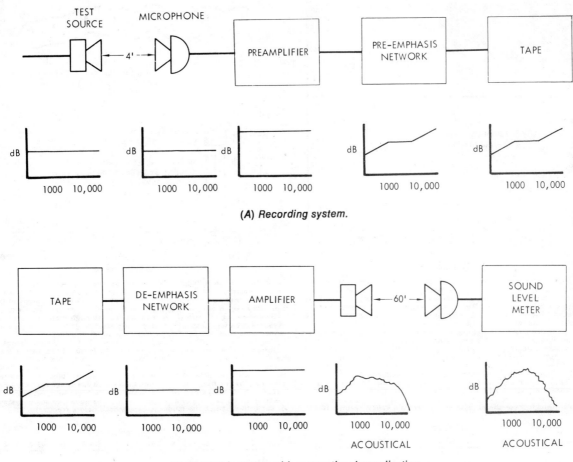

(A) Recording system.

(B) Playback system with conventional equalization.

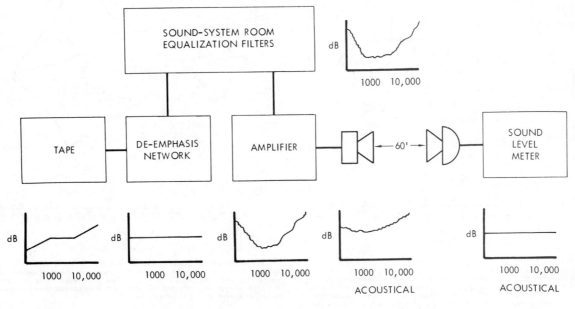

(C) Playback system with sound-system–room equalization.

Fig. 8-7. Typical recording and playback system equalizations.

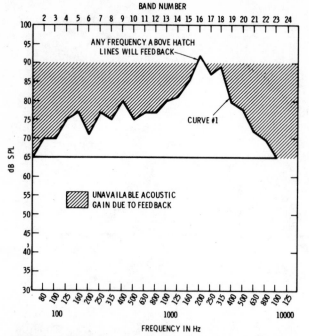

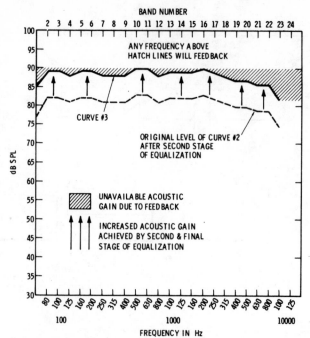

(1) A typical situation that can occur in an auditorium. The hatched line near the top of the chart represents the sound pressure level necessary to cause feedback. Where this line falls is a direct function of the distance between the microphone and the loudspeaker. It will fall lower when they are placed closer together (less potential acoustic gain) and higher (more potential acoustic gain) when they are separated.

The black line shows the sound pressure level output of the loudspeaker if a signal equal in level at all frequencies is connected to the input of sound system. The irregularity of the output is partly due to the inability of the loudspeaker to respond perfectly uniformly to a uniform input signal, and partly — the major part — due to the effect of the room itself on the acoustic output of the loudspeaker. In this case feedback will occur, first at 2000 Hz, where the peak is situated, since any attempt to raise the gain — increase the level of all frequencies at the same time — will find this peak to be the first frequency to push above the limit line. To follow this example through these charts, assume the acoustic gain measures 10 dB.

(3) Additional "smoothing" of the curve can allow greater acoustical gain at the majority of frequencies. However, further "smoothing," even if perfectly done, would yield only 1 or 2 dB at the very most throughout the frequency region of critical importance for speech (see hatched area).

By comparing (3) with (2) we can see that, through the vital frequency response area for speech, for example, the acoustic gain at all frequencies is increased from 300 to 3000 by, typically, 10 dB or more.

Originally, only 2000 Hz could be brought to 90 dB-SPL before feedback occurred; now all frequencies can be brought to 90 dB-SPL before feedback. For example, in "C" above middle "C" was limited to 75 dB-SPL compared to 2000 Hz which could reach 90 dB-SPL. In other words, 2000 Hz controlled or dictated the maximum level for all other frequencies. (3) shows that no frequency has more than a 2 dB advantage over any other frequencies. Since we had 10 dB acoustic gain to begin with, we will easily measure 20 dB or more of acoustic gain with the equalized sound system, or subjectively twice the loudness experienced before feedback.

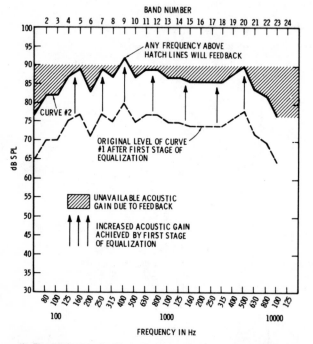

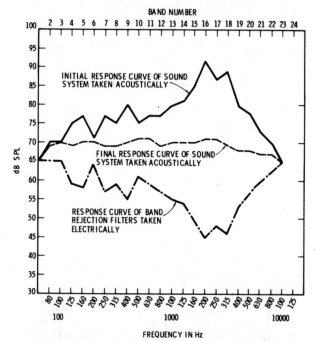

(2) The original curve #1 (dashed line) after the peaked area between 2000 and 3150 Hz has been made equal (equalized) to the majority of the other frequencies. The arrows indicate how all these frequencies may now be raised simultaneously in gain before the new peak at 400 Hz pushes above the hatch lines and causes feedback. The number of decibels at each frequency between the dashed curve and the solid curve represents the increased acoustic gain made possible by this first stage of sound system equalization.

(4) The electrical response curve of the critical band rejection filters (bottom curve) join together to form the inverse of the loudspeaker-room response curve (top curve). As this inverse filter response is included in the total sound response, the resultant is the smoothed over-all acoustic response shown by the middle curve.

Fig. 8-8. How equalization raises acoustic gain.

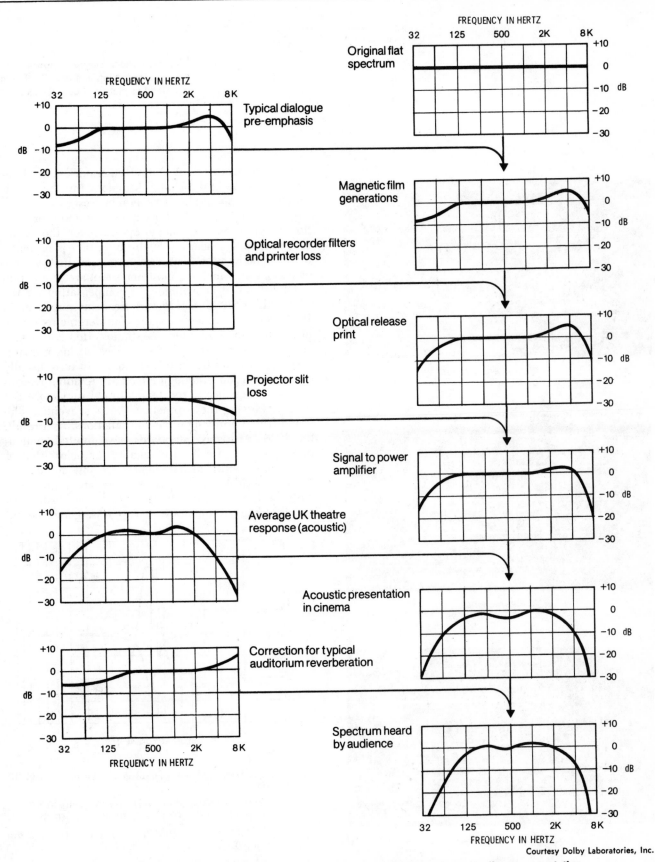

Courtesy Dolby Laboratories, Inc.

Fig. 8-9. Evolution of "Academy" optical sound track from original recording to audience presentation.

137

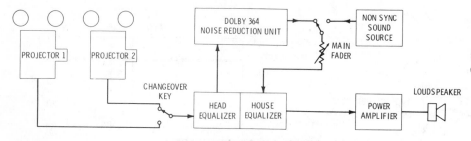

Fig. 8-10. Block diagram showing use of noise reduction and equalization in motion-picture sound system.

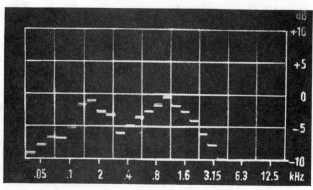

(A) Without equalization.

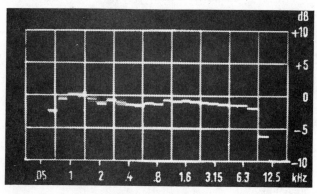

(B) Flat response.

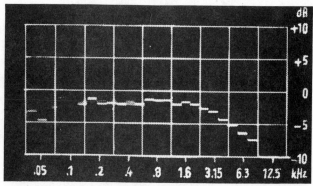

(C) Desired response.

Courtesy Dolby Laboratories, Inc.

Fig. 8-11. Typical response curves for a motion-picture theater.

through the courtesy of Dolby Laboratories, Inc.) refers to theaters in the United Kingdom, but the principles involved should be of general interest.

A basic requirement for accuracy in sound reproduction is uniform frequency response over the entire range of human hearing. Such uniformity is normally unavailable in most theater sound systems for a variety of reasons, of which the most important are production practices aimed at matching or compensating for the standards of the Motion Picture Academy published in 1938. As these standards require considerable reduction in output at high frequencies, studios often find it necessary to emphasize high frequencies during preparation of the sound track; this emphasis, in turn, usually causes distortion. Although aimed at providing reasonable sound quality in theaters with old projectors and sound systems, these practices have prevented film sound from improving in new installations. As a result, the 1938 "Academy" standards have limited motion-picture sound to a level of quality far below that of other media with which audiences are now familiar.

When optical sound tracks are made and reproduced with the Dolby noise-reduction system, the disturbing effects of background noise are suppressed, and the full

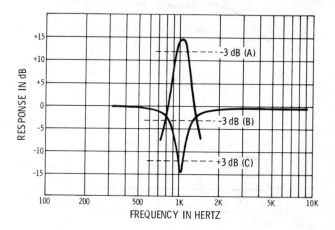

1. THE BANDWIDTH OF A BANDPASS FILTER IS MEASURED 3 dB BELOW ITS CENTER-FREQUENCY LEVEL (A).

2. THE BANDWIDTH OF A BAND-REJECTION FILTER IS MEASURED 3 dB BELOW THE NORMAL LEVEL BEFORE THE FILTER IS INSERTED (B).

3. ON OCCASION INDIVIDUALS HAVE CHOSEN TO DEFINE THE BANDWIDTH OF A BAND-REJECTION FILTER AS "UP 3 dB FROM THE CENTER NOTCH" (C).

Fig. 8-12. Measuring the bandwidth of a filter.

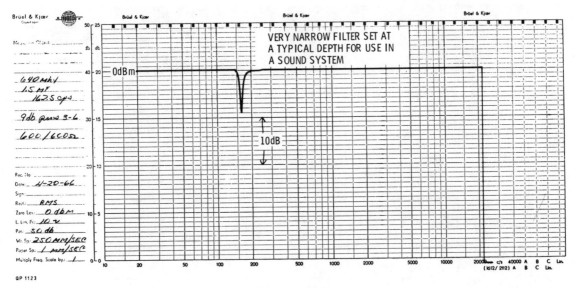

(A) Typical depth.

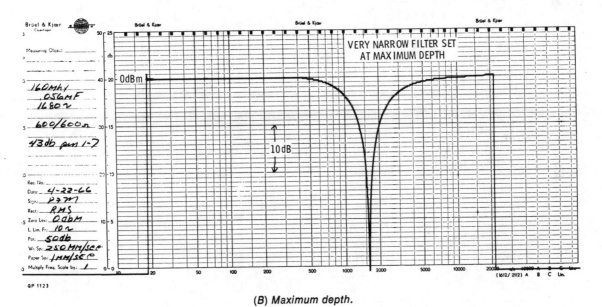

(B) Maximum depth.

Fig. 8-13. Response curves of very narrow-band filters.

capability of optical sound recording can be used. Audiences gain maximum benefit from the process when the frequency range available from the sound system in the theater is extended and as uniform as possible. Fortunately, the sound in most theaters can be improved in this respect without replacement of existing equipment, or with only minor additions to the loudspeaker complement, through use of the Dolby E2 cinema equalizer. Used in conjunction with the Dolby 364 noise reduction unit (Fig. 8-10), the E2 offers improved fidelity from simple optical sound tracks. Used with films which are not Dolby-encoded, or which are old or worn, the Dolby 364 provides

"Academy" response with optional dynamic noise reduction, by push-button selection.

Fig. 8-11 represents typical house curves, as shown on the screen of a real-time analyzer, which illustrate the degree of control over theater sound which the E2 permits. Response before installation of the E2 is shown in Fig. 8-11A; Fig. 8-11B demonstrates that the equalizer range allows essentially flat response to be achieved. The desired curve, which rolls off smoothly at 3 dB/octave at high frequencies, is shown in Fig. 8-11C. The response can be made as uniform as is necessary, and is mainly limited by the power-handling abilities of the speakers used.

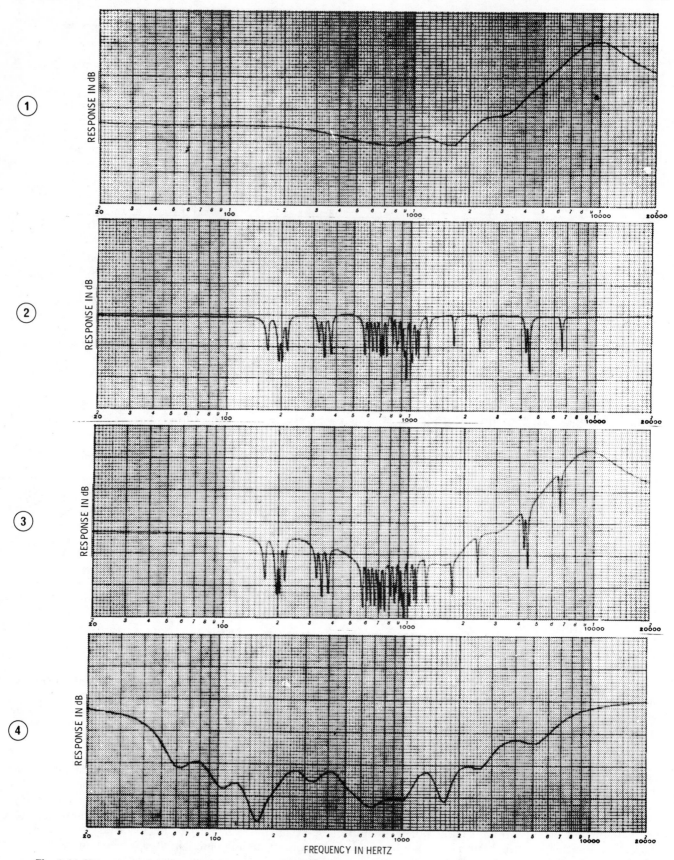

Fig. 8-14. Very narrow-band equalization (1, 2, and 3) and typical combining-type filter equalization of same system (4).

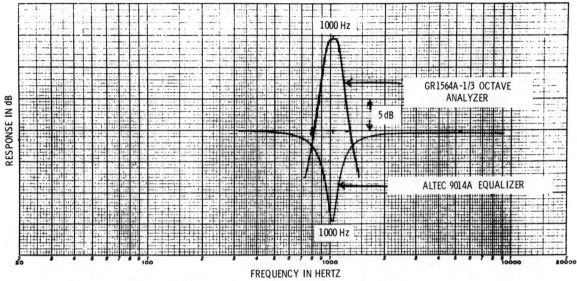

Fig. 8-15. Narrow-band combining-type band-rejection filter section compared to 1/3-octave bandpass filter section.

BANDWIDTH OF FILTERS

The meaning of the bandwidth of a filter is shown in Fig. 8-12. Much controversy has centered about the use of narrower filters for correcting "room modes," etc. There are many who feel it is not possible to either:

1. Raise the acoustic gain additionally by using filters narrower than $\frac{1}{10}$ octave.

2. Improve the articulation-loss-for-consonants percentage by using filters narrower than $\frac{1}{10}$ octave.

What is meant by the term "very narrow-band filters" is shown in Fig. 8-13.

When the filters employed are spaced at greater octave intervals, i.e., 2/3, 1/2, 1/1, or 1.5/1, they gradually become a form of tone control but no longer can "shape" detailed inverse curves. If the problem at hand is basically a series of constant slopes and the filters match the slopes, this is a fortunate situation.

The earliest method of sound-system–room equalization employed individual broadband networks to shape a rough inverse of the house curve (curve 1 in Fig. 8-14). This was followed by the insertion one at a time of very narrow notch filters at the predominant feedback frequencies (curve 2 in Fig. 8-14). When the two sets of filters were electrically combined, the response was like curve 3 in Fig. 8-14. Curve 4 in Fig. 8-14 is the replacement tuning finally put in the job after the

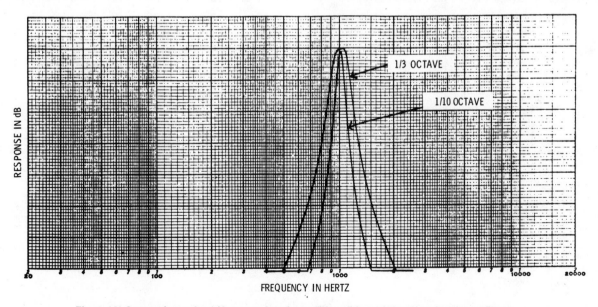

Fig. 8-16. Comparison of a 1/3-octave bandpass filter with a 1/10-octave bandpass filter.

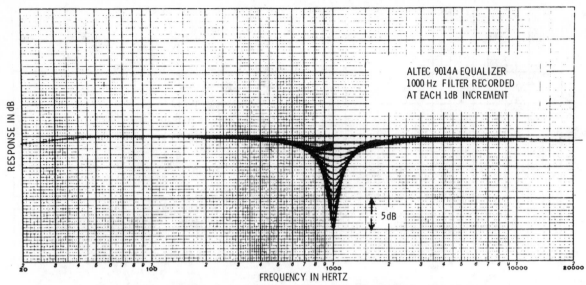

Fig. 8-17. Response of a narrow-band band-rejection filter at each of its 14 steps.

advent of ⅓-octave spaced bridged-T filter sets. Note how the same overall gain restoration is provided by either type of filter, but that the ⅓-octave spaced filter set removed feedback at many frequencies by changing the slope rate instead of depressing the amplitude. It is important to remember that the sound-system deviations from uniformity in a system worth equalization are quite correctable by the slope-rate changes available in the ⅓-octave spaced filter sets.

CHARACTERISTICS OF SUCCESSFUL FILTERS

Let us compare an ISO ⅓-octave bandpass filter with a ⅓-octave spaced band-rejection filter (Fig. 8-15). By further comparing the two basic bandpass filter shapes, both ⅓-octave and ¹/₁₀-octave, we see

that the inverse of the ¹/₁₀-octave response most closely approximates the response of the band-rejection filter (Fig. 8-16). Looking at a single filter section and recording each of its 1-dB steps, we get a series of curves as shown in Fig. 8-17. If we were to record each filter section in a set of 24 such filters, by setting each filter for maximum rejection and then restoring it to zero before recording the next filter section set at its maximum rejection, we would obtain the set of curves shown in Fig. 8-18. If we were to turn all 24 filter sections to maximum rejection at the same time, we would discover their most important property—they combine (Fig. 8-19). Note also that in combining they are essentially additive (their combined depth exceeds 20 dB at the bottom of the ripple). Fig. 8-20 shows in detail how they combine. The narrower curve is 1000 Hz set

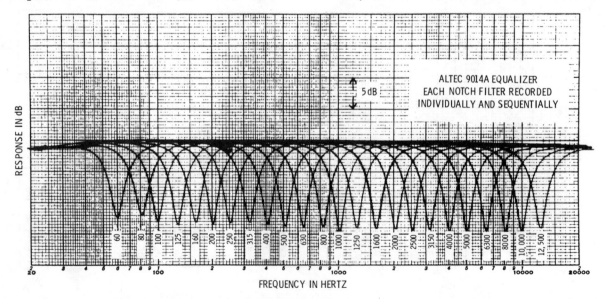

Fig. 8-18. A series of narrow-band sections recorded one at a time, sequentially.

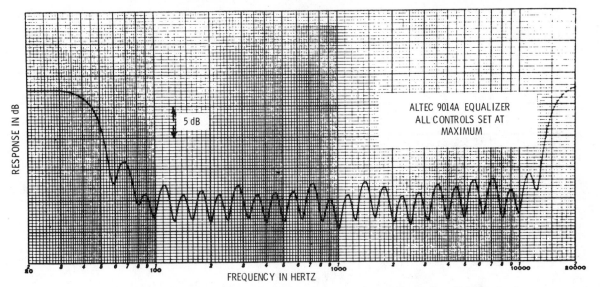

Fig. 8-19. Series of narrow-band sections all turned to maximum attenuation simultaneously.

at −6 dB. The wider curve is 800 Hz at −2 dB, 1000 Hz at −2 dB, and 1250 Hz at −2 dB. Here they have combined to become 6 dB deep, and the center of the curve is at the middle of the three. It is not difficult to imagine the complexity of combining 14 to 24 of these sections all at different levels to appreciate that some form of real-time observation is required to comprehend thoroughly what is going on.

Fig. 8-21 shows the electrical response of a set of filters on an actual job. Fourteen sections were employed at the frequencies and levels indicated. Note that at 160 Hz the filter is at −10 dB but the curve due to combination effects is at −18.5 dB. The real test is to compare the inverse of the filter response with the acoustic response before equalization. This is done on

a ⅓-octave basis in Fig. 8-22. Filters producing the type of response we have just looked at can be either passive or active.

Fig. 8-23 shows a comparison of the electrical amplitude response of a set of Boner very narrow-band filters and a set of critical-bandwidth combining filters after adjustment on the same job.

The bridged T (passive) and twin T (active) circuits (Figs. 8-24 and 8-25, respectively) are without insertion loss until deliberate loss is put in, and, in the active circuit, the same unit usually has gain makeup for the filters, making it a zero-loss device. The passive version is further distinguished by having a constant input and output impedance, and it normally requires only proper termination.

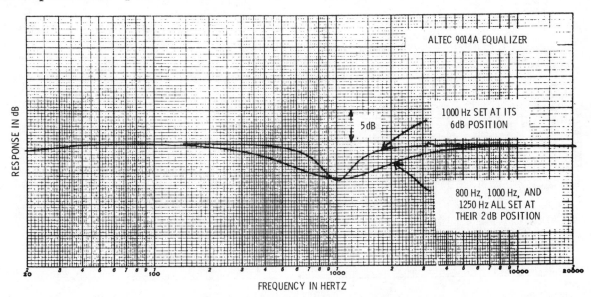

Fig. 8-20. Response of a 1000-Hz section with 6-dB attenuation compared with the response of a combination of 800-Hz, 1000-Hz, and 1250-Hz sections with 2-dB attenuation each.

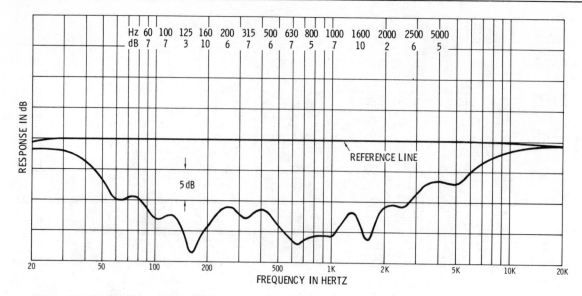

Hz	60	100	125	160	200	315	500	630	800	1000	1600	2000	2500	5000
dB	7	7	3	10	6	7	6	7	5	7	10	2	6	5

Fig. 8-21. Example of 14 narrow-band filter sections in combination to form inverse of raw house curve.

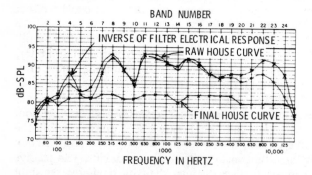

Fig. 8-22. Example of correlation between raw house curve and inverse of filter electrical response curve.

FILTER TRANSFER CHARACTERISTICS

The transfer characteristics of band rejection, minimum phase filters are shown in Fig. 8-24B.

Going back to our earlier example of the combining power of these filters, in terms of amplitude, we see an example of their combining power in terms of phase (Fig. 8-25B). The steeper the amplitude slope rate, the steeper the rate of phase change.

Fig. 8-26 shows all filters at −1-dB amplitude and the resultant phase characteristic. Fig. 8-27 shows the same information for −4-dB settings.

Again, taking a practical example, Fig. 8-28A shows the equalized and unequalized response of the left

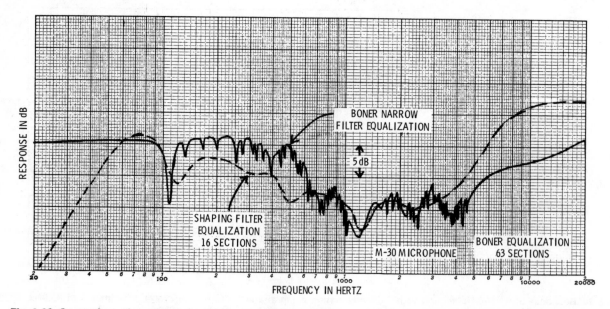

Fig. 8-23. Comparison of response of a set of very narrow-band filters and a set of critical-bandwidth combining filters.

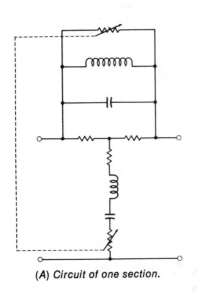

(A) Circuit of one section.

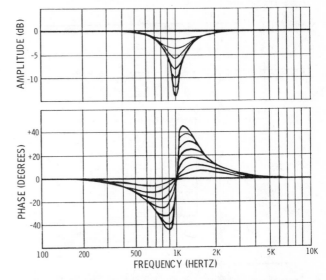

(B) Amplitude and phase characteristics of one section.

(C) One section of prototype combining or shaping critical band filter.

Fig. 8-24. Bridged-T configuration for tandem filter sections.

channel of a monitor system. Fig. 8-28B shows the same information for the right channel.

Fig. 8-29A shows the electrical amplitude response of the corrective filters, and Fig. 8-29B shows the phase response of each channel.

MINIMUM-PHASE FILTERS

A minimum-phase filter introduces the minimum possible phase shift but still retains the corrective amplitude change. It is also obvious that the relative phase

between channels is virtually identical. It is this careful band-by-band resolution of phase that so many listeners have dubbed as the "sharp focus" that equalization seems to produce in sound systems already relatively smooth in an amplitude sense.

Richard C. Heyser has pointed out that, "Highly important to a loudspeaker's ability to produce accurate sound, when it has been properly equalized, is that of minimum phase change. A minimum-phase-change loudspeaker is one which, when all amplitude response variations are removed by conventional resistance,

145

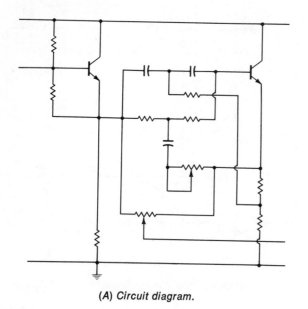

(A) Circuit diagram.

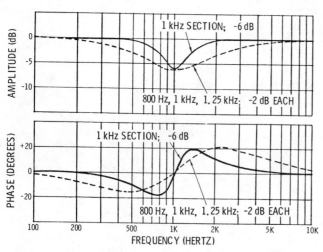

(B) Amplitude and phase characteristics.

Fig. 8-25. Active configuration for tandem filter sections.

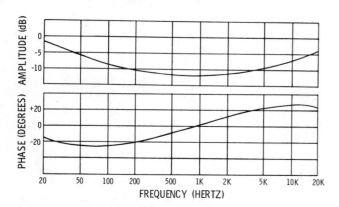

Fig. 8-26. Combined phase and amplitude response, all sections set for −1 dB.

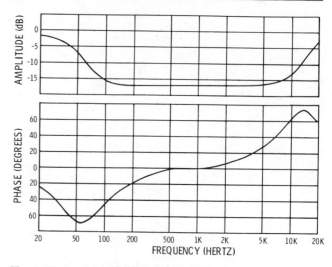

Fig. 8-27. Combined phase and amplitude response, all sections set for −4 dB.

capacitance, and inductance networks, has the minimum possible phase shift over the frequency spectrum. Properly designed equalizers for balancing the amplitude response *will also automatically balance the phase response for a minimum phase loudspeaker.*" (Italics added.) Also, "A nonminimum-phase loudspeaker will usually exhibit frequency-response difficulties which can be associated with *time delay* effects which, in turn, *cannot* be corrected with conventional passive or active equalization."

Turning to Frederick E. Terman's *Radio Engineers' Handbook*, in the chapter on circuit theory we find the *phase area theorem:*

$$\int_{-\infty}^{+\infty} B\,du = \frac{\pi}{17.37}(A_\infty - A_0) \qquad (8\text{-}7)$$

where,

B is the phase shift in radians,

u is $\ln \frac{f}{f_0}$, where f is the actual frequency and f_0 is any convenient reference frequency,

A_∞ is the attenuation in dB at infinite frequency,

A_0 is the attenuation in dB at zero frequency (not at frequency f_0).

Terman says of the relation described by this equation, "The total area under the phase characteristics, when plotted on a logarithmic frequency scale, depends only upon the difference between the transmission (or attenuation) at zero and infinite frequency, and does not depend in any way upon the way in which the transmission varies between these limits; nor does it depend upon the physical configuration of the network, provided a minimum-phase-shift structure is employed. . . . [This] means, for example, that if a network is employed to change the transmission from one fixed value to another fixed value and if, at the same time, the maximum phase shift that can be permitted at any

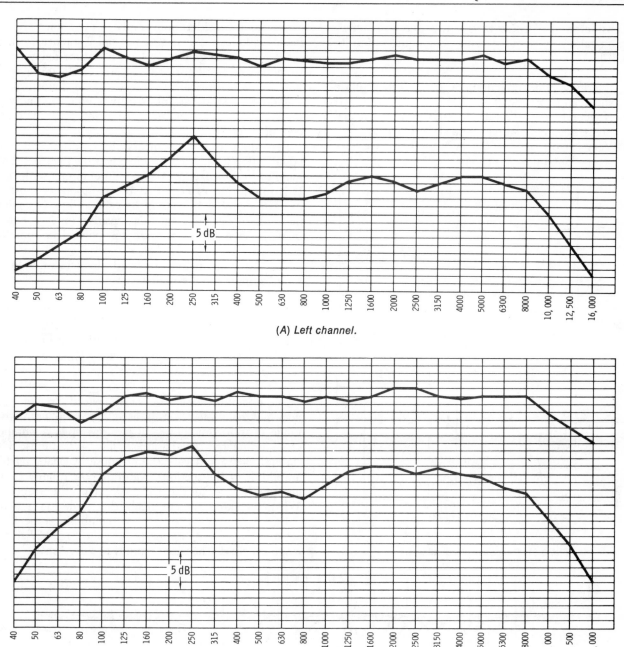

(A) Left channel.

(B) Right channel.

Fig. 8-28. Equalized and unequalized response of a monitor system.

frequency is limited to some relatively low value, then the region where the attenuation is changing must be spread out over a sufficiently wide frequency range so that the necessary area can be obtained under the phase curve without this curve having a maximum exceeding the allowable value. This fact is of considerable significance in connection with the design of feedback amplifier systems, since here the transmission around the feedback loop must have associated with it a phase shift that is always less than 180°, even when the transmission is varying."[1]

Mr. Terman goes on to show that phase shift is a function of attenuation slope and that ". . . the shape of the weighting function [associated with the slope-rate equation] is such that changes in the slope of the attenuation characteristic at frequencies close to the reference frequency have far more effect on phase shift than do changes in the slope of the characteristic at more remote frequencies."

[1] Frederick E. Terman, *Radio Engineers' Handbook* (New York: McGraw-Hill Book Company, Inc., 1943), pp. 218-219.

Consideration of these facts causes the wary engineer engaged in sound-system–room equalization to avoid:

1. Bandpass filter configurations, because their phase shift can go over 360°.
2. Noncombining discrete filters, because mutual phase accommodation cannot take place.
3. Very narrow bandwidths, because they have very steep slope rates.

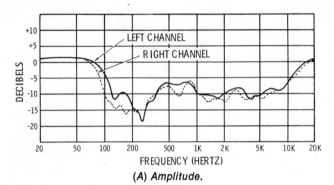

(A) Amplitude.

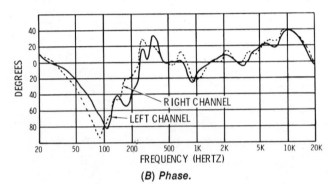

(B) Phase.

Fig. 8-29. Response of equalizers.

These same considerations apply to the choice of professional loudspeakers, and the only practical advice the authors can give is to look into time-delay spectrometry and fast Fourier analyzers (costly at this writing) or else critically observe which loudspeakers sound better after careful amplitude equalization with the correct type of combining filter set. (A trained ear *can tell*.)

Recording-studio engineers have often rejected equalization when their problem was the fact that their monitor loudspeaker was a nonminimum-phase device. It is interesting to note that the loudspeaker most in use as a monitor, in spite of its venerability, is a minimum-phase device. Ears this sensitive deserve better than to have to *compensate* for polydriver monitor systems.

We can sum up the preferred characteristics for a sound-system–room equalizer:

1. Each should be a constant-impedance, combining type of filter.
2. Each should be of the minimum-phase type.
3. Each should have approximately $\frac{1}{10}$-octave filters spaced at $\frac{1}{3}$-octave intervals.

Fig. 8-30 illustrates a $\frac{1}{3}$-octave spaced filter set that does not combine. In this case, the total corrective range is approximately 8 dB before ripple. A number of experimenters try bandpass filter sets (Figs. 8-31 through 8-35) and vary the response by changing the amplitude of the sections. Naturally, the quality is not acceptable due to the steep skirts of the response. When the skirts are not steep, the resolution is poor.

Fig. 8-36 shows a one-octave combining-type filter set suitable for use in a master test set. Fig. 8-37 shows response charts for three models of filter sets.

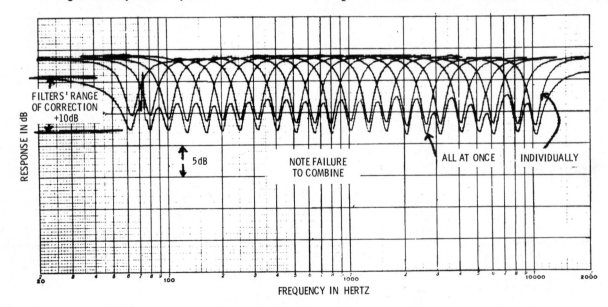

Fig. 8-30. Response of a noncombining narrow-band filter set (1/3 octave).

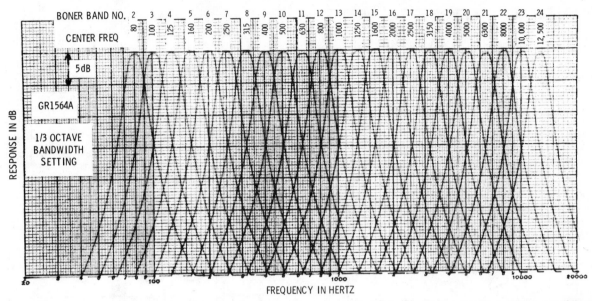

Fig. 8-31. Response of a typical contiguous bandpass filter set (normally used for analyzing signals but not equalizing them).

FILTER TRANSIENT RESPONSE

Very narrow-band filters exhibit what is called "ringing." Ringing is due to the time constant of the filter circuit. It takes a certain length of time to charge the circuit upon application of the signal and an equal amount of time to discharge the circuit upon cessation of the signal. Fig. 8-38 shows waveforms for two types of filters. Fig. 8-38A is for a constant-K type with the source waveform shown at the top and the output waveform when the filter is set for −6 dB shown at the bottom. Fig. 8-38B shows the source "pulled" into ringing by the load when the filter output is set for −6 dB on a "narrow-band" type.

COMBINING FILTER SECTIONS

Another not-too-well understood feature of combining filters is their ability to be used in tandem to twice the depth attained singly (Fig. 8-39). Note in Fig. 8-39 that the filters can combine into level differences exceeding 40 dB (a power difference of 10,000 to 1). Fig. 8-40 illustrates the response of two 1000-Hz filters in tandem with the first 14 steps on one and second 14 steps on the second in addition to the first set. A maximum depth of −28 dB is attained. Fig. 8-41 shows the response of two filters side-by-side plus two more identical filters in tandem. Fig. 8-42 illustrates how changing amplitude can change the frequency of the

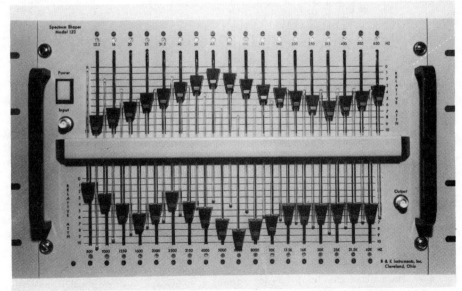

Fig. 8-32. Example of a bandpass filter set.

Courtesy B & K Instruments, Inc.

149

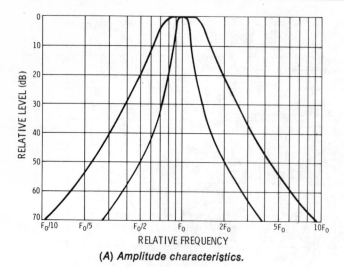

(A) Amplitude characteristics.

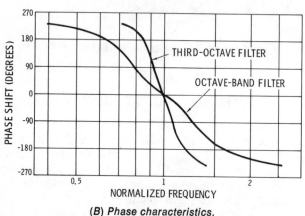

(B) Phase characteristics.

Fig. 8-33. Transfer characteristics of high-quality octave and 1/3-octave bandpass filters.

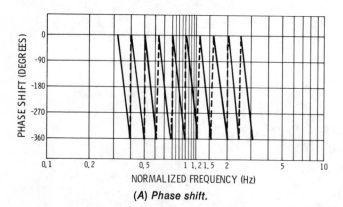

(A) Phase shift.

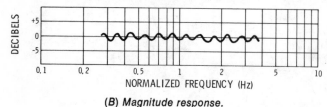

(B) Magnitude response.

Fig. 8-34. Normalized characteristics for several 1/3-octave-band filter channels.

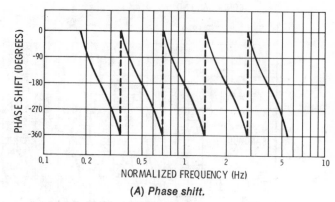

(A) Phase shift.

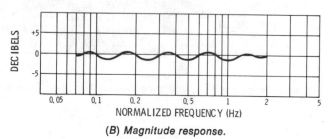

(B) Magnitude response.

Fig. 8-35. Normalized characteristics for several octave-band filter channels.

dip point. Starting with side-by-side tandem filters and then partially removing only one of the tandem filters, note how the dip point swings toward the deeper of the tandem units. Actually, the center of the dip point is "tunable" between any two 1/3-octave center frequencies by relative adjustment of the amplitudes of adjacent filters.

It can be seen that the combination of equalizers can be quite complex. It is not something done by taking one or two acoustical response curves and then adjusting the filter set "by feel." It is hard enough to do with the correct tools; it is nearly impossible with inadequate tools.

INCREASING SLOPE RATES

In very noisy industrial paging systems, it is often desirable to achieve very sharp cutoffs at each edge of the spectrum in use. This saves putting out power at frequencies where it adds more to the reverberant energy than it does to the message being delivered. The combining action of 1/3-octave spaced filters can also steepen the slope rate of a conventional cutoff filter set. Fig. 8-43 illustrates the response of a standard 18-dB/octave cutoff filter set adjusted to cutoff frequencies of 500 Hz and 5000 Hz (note the −3-dB points of the response). By adding in tandem 1/3-octave filters for one octave above and below the cutoff frequency, each section adjusted for its maximum attenuation, cutoff rates can be achieved that exceed 150 dB/octave.

Fig. 8-36. A combining type filter set.

Courtesy Shure Brothers Inc.

Normally, any slope rate greater than 18 dB/octave is to be avoided, but on rare occasions such as +9 second spaces with noise levels in excess of 90 dBA, it becomes the only way to communicate at all, and the "ringing" of the steep slopes is less of a problem, relatively, than adding power to the reverberant space in the room. It is only normal to assume that the number and type of devices proposed to be useful in sound-system–room equalization will continue to increase and that the information presented here will help you analyze their usefulness.

CRITICAL BANDWIDTHS

One final comment regarding filter bandwidths: After the discovery of the ringing problem in the very narrow type of notch filter and the gradual development of lower-electrical-Q, minimum-phase-shift networks, it was of great interest to find that the bandwidth which avoided the ringing problem coincided with what is called "the critical bandwidth." The critical bandwidth is that bandwidth within which the human ear cannot detect spectrum shape when listening to complex sounds. As the years since this discovery have proven repeatedly in several thousand sound systems, this was indeed a point of diminishing return so far as decreasing bandwidth was concerned. Experience shows that the ⅓-octave spacing is the optimum spacing interval. It is interesting to note that for different reasons, nearly 40 years of measurement work in architectural acoustics has led workers in that field to decide that ⅓-octave spacing offers the necessary resolution for their measurements.

ADJUSTING THE EQUALIZERS

Having designed an excellent system, chosen the correct equalizer, and installed the equalizer in the proper link circuit or circuits, you then have only to carry out a procedure that will result in correct and efficient adjustment of the filters.

One easy way to raise acoustic gain quickly, without regard to specific overall spectrum shapes, is to perform a "feedback" tuning. Fig. 8-44 shows the interconnection of the necessary test equipment to a simple sound system. The sound system is *gently* brought into feedback and stabilized at as low a level as possible. The oscillator is then swept until an identifiable Lissajous pattern is developed (Fig. 8-45). Upon observing the ratio above or below zero beat, you can rapidly dial in the exact zero-beat frequency. Then go to the nearest frequency available on the master test set. If the feedback occurs exactly between two of the available center frequencies on the master test set, attenuate both frequencies at the same time, centering on the in-between feedback frequency. No more insertion should be used than is necessary to cause the feedback to stop —usually 1 to 3 dB and almost never more than 3 dB. The tuning proceeds in this manner, taking one feedback at a time, until you see that you are essentially repeating the initial starting pattern or until a very low and very high feedback frequency occur. After every 5 or 6 feedback adjustments, stop and "talk" the system. You should hear both gain and quality improve. Actually, any point where the acoustic gain is satisfactory to you and where the quality is acceptable can be the stopping point. If you have calculated the PAG, then reaching that figure clearly tells you that you have finished.

This method was widely used at the beginnings of equalization in rooms, but it is used today only as an emergency measure. A far better way has almost entirely replaced this older method, though this method is still the only way to do tunings in areas having extremely high ambient noise levels.

USING THE REAL-TIME ANALYZER IN EQUALIZATION

Watching each interaction as it occurs and being able to correct for mistakes as they appear on the screen is the advantage of real-time analysis. When the first real-time analyzer was developed and shown in 1968, it was hard to believe that the 20 minutes per house curve was being reduced to 20 milliseconds per house curve. Transient effects that formerly had escaped our attention when running so-called "average response" house curves were now seen in operation.

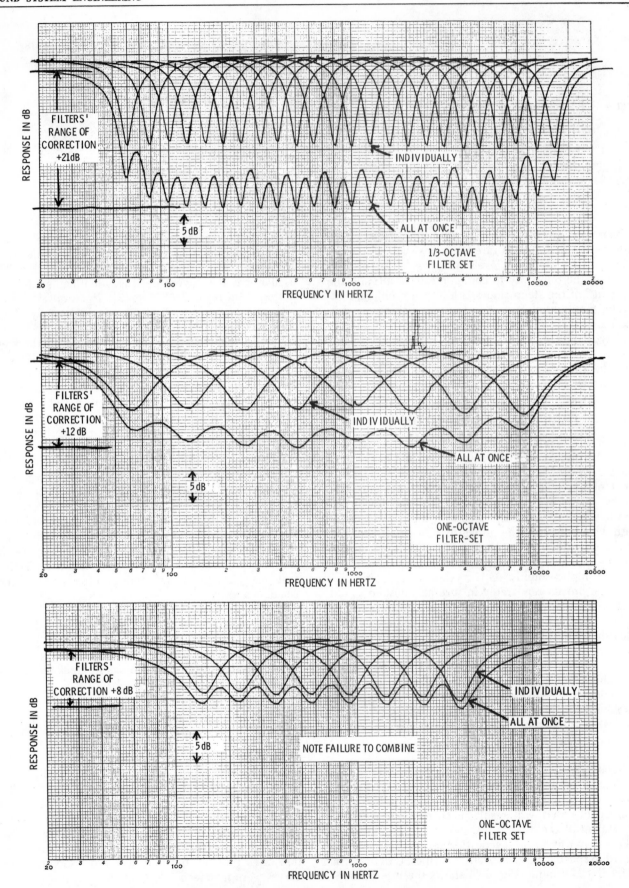

Fig. 8-37. Response charts for three filter sets.

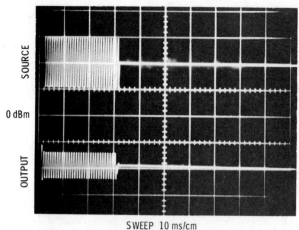

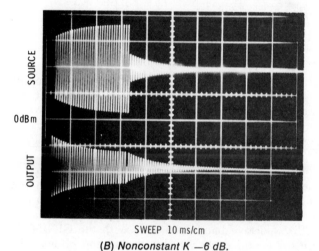

SWEEP 10 ms/cm

(A) Constant K —6 dB.

SWEEP 10 ms/cm

(B) Nonconstant K —6 dB.

Fig. 8-38. Illustration of ringing that occurs when nonconstant-K filter of very narrow bandwidth is employed.

At a famous recording studio during a demonstration of equalizing monitor loudspeakers, a diaphragmatic absorption was traced to a loose "sound-lock" door. Upon holding the door tightly shut, an 80-Hz notch in the house curve disappeared.

TUNING FOR PLAYBACK

Several hundred tunings have shown it is always best to start with the highest point on the given house curve. It is important to remember that for the first three steps on any of the narrow-band filters *five bands will be affected*—the band the filter is centered on plus two above and two below the center frequency. This means that when peaks are next to dips in the house curve, the entire area may need to be lowered initially by the filter centered on the peak frequency before the filter becomes narrow enough to control only one band. Normally, such lowering becomes part of the overall broadbanding needed to achieve final balance.

It is best not to introduce corrections too rapidly with any one filter at the onset; just barely pull down the highest peak until it is even with the bands nearest it. This usually causes a readjustment of the entire area followed by the same gradual procedure at the next peak presented. It does not take long to find out that no one can hope to understand equalization completely without a lot of experience on the job with a real-time analyzer. Many engineers set up a test system and hold informal contests to see who can master a smooth, efficient tuning the fastest. Such practice can lead to very impressive on-the-job performance at times when the customer is watching.

As the tuning proceeds, opportunities to lower areas will offer themselves. Careful choice of the correct filters will result in all of these filters being at a narrow

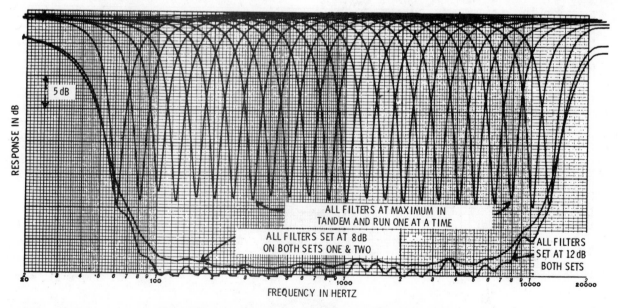

Fig. 8-39. Combining effects of tandem narrow-band sections.

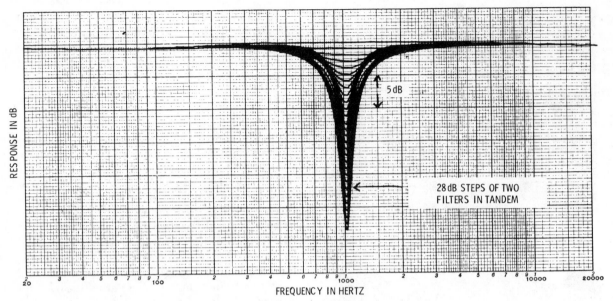

Fig. 8-40. Response of tandem sections of two 1000-Hz filters adjusted one step at a time.

enough setting (past 3 dB) to allow detailed finishing of the final curve. If, near the end of the tuning, a bump exists in the curve and use of a particular filter that has not been used before puts in too wide a correction, the best policy is to wipe out the whole tuning and start over again. During the second tuning, be more careful in the initial choice of the filters so as to allow the detailed correction of the desired bands near the conclusion of the tuning.

Of course, attention must be paid to avoid tuning in the null of a standing-wave pattern. A short walk with the microphone of the analyzer, especially in a small control room, is fascinating, instructive, and necessary.

Similar care should be observed in the handling of dips in the response of a loudspeaker and a room caused by diaphragmatic action of some boundary surface. This is identifiable when, after all the bands around the dips are brought down, they still fall the same number of dB below the surrounding bands. Do not chase it on down, because that will only increase the insertion loss of the total equalization with but negligible improvement in the response. The correct method is to drive the loudspeaker-room combination with $\frac{1}{10}$-octave bands of noise. With the GR 1564A, use the continuously variable tuning and observe the effect on the real-time analyzer to find the frequency where the absorption of the signal is greatest; then use

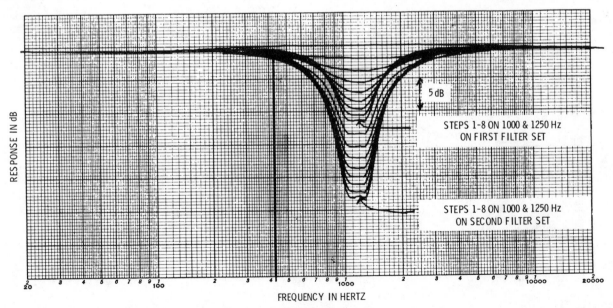

Fig. 8-41. Response of tandem filter sections of 1000 and 1250 Hz with only the first 8 steps of each section used.

154

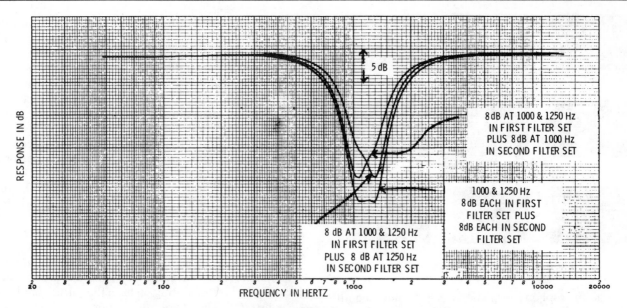

Fig. 8-42. Effect of changing amplitude on frequency of dip point.

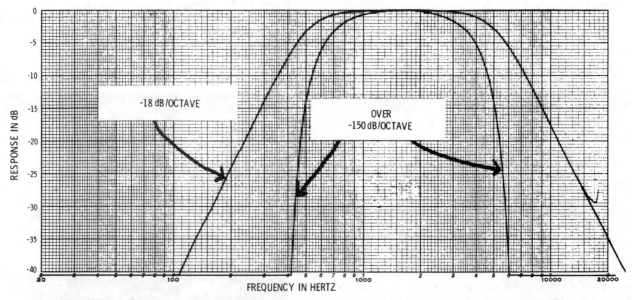

Fig. 8-43. An example of using narrow-band filters to increase the slope rate of a set of cutoff filters.

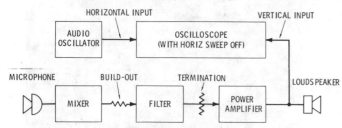

Fig. 8-44. Test-equipment hookup to sound system for finding feedback frequencies.

your fingertips and feel all the surfaces of the space, including walls, doors, windows, etc. You will feel the offending surface vibrating in sympathy with the test signal. Hannon Engineering of Los Angeles, in equaliz-

ing the Decca Records studios, was able to find a walled-over window area, unknown to the studio users, that was the cause of a deep dip in the response curves. Naturally, such a scientific approach to a studio problem leaves a highly favorable impression with the customer.

TUNING A REINFORCEMENT SYSTEM

Up to this point, essentially nonregenerative sound systems have been discussed—that is, acoustic feedback has not been a factor in their tuning. When an open microphone is used, several additional conditions complicate the tuning procedure:

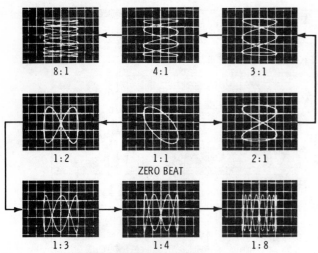

Fig. 8-45. Typical Lissajous figures.

1. The microphone response is usually not smooth, especially in the case of cardioid microphones.
2. The multipath long-time-interval reflections, with their varying amplitude and phase, become part of a regenerative system as the overall gain is increased.
3. The listening area is spread over a wider range with a typical reinforcement system than with a typical playback system.

It is normal practice to start the tuning of a reinforcement system in the same way as for a playback system—i.e., smoothing the house curve by placing the measuring microphone in a typical listener position in the audience area. It is a good idea to do this even before checking the distribution of the loudspeaker array and then have someone "walk" the test microphone while you watch the screen on the real-timer analyzer. This is a much more rigorous way to learn the fine art of loudspeaker coverage and leads to correct methods more quickly than using the 4000-Hz octave band filter by itself. This procedure makes it very obvious why horns should be stacked and splayed instead of placed side by side. Naturally, it is futile to attempt to equalize a sound system that will not hold the house curve over the majority of the listening area.

It is always of great interest to examine the difference between the house curve thus tuned in the audience area and the house curve observed at the location where the microphone used in the sound system is to be placed. When the sound-system microphone is located in an area with a lower room constant (more liveness) than the area where the audience is seated (e.g., where the stage house is large and live, and the audience area is highly absorptive), quite different house curves can be expected at the two locations. Because the real-time analyzer allows economical inspection of these situations, it should be possible to gain a great deal more insight into the behavior of sound systems in rooms during the coming years.

Having worked out the distribution and the smoothing of the house curve, you are then left with the problems of the actual microphone response (as used in the space) plus the advantages or disadvantages of its position relative to the loudspeaker, audience area, and immediate reflecting surfaces. We have all learned that sound-system microphones can vary over a wide range of useful amplitude characteristics. There is also the irrational to consider—when the performer prefers a certain shape, size, color, trade name, or personal microphone.

If the microphone is located where $D_1 < D_c$ and tuned for maximum gain, it will be sensitive to being moved. If it is placed so that $D_1 \geqq D_c$, it will be almost completely insensitive to location changes so far as maximum acoustic gain is concerned.

On a number of occasions, the effect of mounting a microphone a foot or two away from a reflecting surface versus flush-mounting on or in the surface has been demonstrated. The phase cancellation that occurs when a microphone is mounted on a stand is easily visible on the real-time analyzer if you use as a sound source a loudspeaker equalized to a "flat" response and move the microphone away from its stand and down to the reflecting surface. Fig. 8-46 shows a series of response curves made at positions from 17 inches above a surface (curve A) to flat on the surface (curve E). Note how two different distinct reflection cancellations move upward in frequency as the surface is approached (deliberate offset was introduced with a calibrated attenuator). Note also that curve D crosses curve C and touches curve E. In churches, flush-mounting of an omnidirectional condenser microphone in the top of the altar allows substantially more speech energy to arrive at the microphone diaphragm. In some cases, the increase is as much as 6 dB, due to the fact that at the boundary surface there is a coherent addition of the reflection and the direct sound, causing a pressure dou-

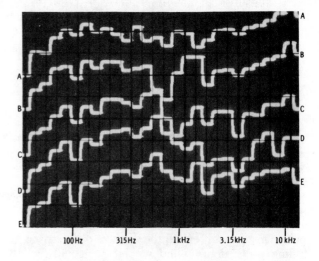

Fig. 8-46. Response curves for various distances between microphone and surface.

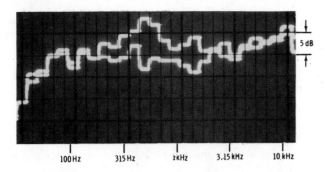

Fig. 8-47. Response curves for two positions of microphone.

bling. Fig. 8-47 shows two curves made with a measuring microphone. The lower trace was made with the microphone 17 inches from the surface; the upper trace is for the flush-mounted position. Note the increased gain from 250 to 2000 Hz, the speech region.

If it is desired to measure the frequency response of the sound-system microphones, a high-quality loudspeaker capable of being tuned to ±1-dB uniformity should be used. The sound-system loudspeaker is not normally a good choice because of its remote location. For best results, a distance of 10 feet between the loudspeaker and microphone is suggested as a good standard distance. Use of this distance will allow meaningful comparison of data taken at many locations.

If the sound-system microphone has rough response, and maximum acoustic gain is the main desire, then it should be introduced into the measuring chain. If the sound system is smoothed with the sound-system microphone as the measuring microphone, you should be near maximum gain. This will not be so if the acoustic environment where the microphone is actually to be used is essentially different from the environment at the loudspeaker location.

The ultimate test of whether or not you have achieved the maximum acoustic gain is to take a feedback threshold response and see if further increases in gain are possible (Fig. 8-48).

In dealing with feedback, experimental use of the controls can be most useful. You may be well into a tuning and have a feedback mode come up squarely on 1000 Hz; however, experience has shown it is wise to try both the 800-Hz and 1250-Hz controls as well. In many cases, an additional 3 dB of attenuation of the

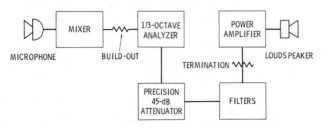

Fig. 8-48. Test-equipment hookup for performing feedback-threshold response plots.

1000-Hz control will be necessary to handle the feedback, but only 1 or 2 dB of the 800- or 1250-Hz control may be needed. The reason for this is associated with the need to change the slope rate of the filter correction curve in the 1000-Hz region; hence the phase is changed rather than the amplitude. In any case, it has been proven that the most accurate matching of the inverse electrical-response curve of the filter with the raw house curve occurs when such details are applied.

A REAL-TIME REGENERATIVE-RESPONSE METHOD OF EQUALIZING A SOUND SYSTEM

One of the earliest demonstrations of the effect of operation near regeneration on the measured frequency response of a sound reinforcement system was by William B. Snow before the February 1954 meeting of the Audio Engineering Society in Los Angeles. Snow recorded on a high-speed graphic level recorder the dramatic amplitude changes that occurred in the overall amplitude-versus-frequency response as the reinforcement system was brought nearer and nearer regeneration.

Almost a decade later, this same method was used with a manually operated oscillator to identify those frequencies whose amplitude responded unduly to the approach of the regeneration point of the sound system. Shock excitation was employed to observe the increased decay periods of frequencies that otherwise would not feed back upon being increased in gain but were unduly affected by the approach of the system regeneration point. Snow's paper had also demonstrated this point, proving that such frequencies, when shock excited near regeneration, could take as much as 4 to 6 times as long to decay as the same frequencies required when they were excited well below the regeneration point (-12 dB).

Degree of Correction Necessary

Clearly evident in this process is the fact that below regeneration the amplitudes of the frequencies involved are of the order of 1 or 2 dB higher than other nearby frequencies. As these frequencies approach regeneration, their amplitudes can "swell" to +20 dB or more. (Naturally the sound system must supply the power for this regeneration, as the room cannot—it is passive. The room can provide nulls and modes, but not amplification.) If, before regeneration is approached, one of these frequencies has its amplitude brought to uniformity with the remainder, then upon approaching regeneration again, this frequency will not "swell" in amplitude.

The ability to make the needed controlling corrections at a magnitude associated with the nonregenerative state of the system was first observed by the authors in 1966 and was presented as a paper, "Adjustable ⅓ Octave Band Notch Equalizer for Minimizing Detrimental Interaction Between a Sound System and Its

Acoustic Environment[2]," at the September 1967 meeting of the SMPTE in Chicago and the AES in New York in October as part of a demonstration of a minimum-phase, band-rejection filter set capable of continuous adjustment from 63 Hz to 12,500 Hz. The content of the paper is summarized briefly in the following paragraph.

"Each section of a special passive constant-K equalizer consisting of 24 notch filters centered on each of the standard ISO center frequencies for ⅓-octave bands consists of a notch filter adjustable in 1-dB steps to a maximum of 14 dB. The shape of the notch is approximately the inverse of that encountered in commercially available ⅓-octave bandpass filter sets used in acoustical measurement work. Each section of the equalizer is contiguous with those on either side of it, allowing continuous correction slopes to be formed. Conventional frequency-response analysis with pink noise and ⅓-octave bandpass filters is used, followed by feedback reduction through attenuation of the specific feedback frequency. The feedback-threshold method of analysis for achieving maximum acoustic gain in a re-enforcement sound system is discussed."

Boosting filters cause new regenerative frequencies to appear. When a boost filter is employed to attempt to lift a diaphragmatic absorption, it causes two bumps and a dip where formerly only a dip appeared. Reflections in a room can come together +3 dB max but ∞ dB rejection in a room.

Sound-System Equalization in Real Time

At the spring 1969 meeting of the AES in Los Angeles, the authors demonstrated the use of a ⅓-octave real-time audio-frequency spectrum analyzer in equaling a sound system to unity gain at all frequencies. (The real-time analyzer had been used by the authors since June 1968 for proprietary sound-system equalization.) This demonstration was accomplished in a 20-minute session with large-screen television, allowing the audience to watch the equalization process on the screen of the analyzer. An A-B test was made to show the increased gain of the equalized system over the "raw" system, and a computer was used to verify that the potential and measured gain correlated.

Since that time, the combining-type band-rejection filter has been used in well over 90% of the equalized sound systems. Most of those using the discrete-filter approach today use the combining filters for the major portion of the tuning, especially in the critical articulation region from 1500 to 3000 Hz, and then drop in a few discrete filter sections below 1500 Hz to correct what is referred to as "room ring modes" (identified by C. P. Boner as those frequencies that, near regeneration, cause the signal to have a period several times longer than that for nearby frequencies).

[2] Loudspeaker Q plus equalizer versus R. The value of R controls modal amplitudes; so can the equalizer, indirectly.

There are problems inherent in trying to correct those frequencies that are excessively "lively" near regeneration:

1. Unnecessary amplitude correction caused by mistaking the regeneration amplitude for the true amplitude.
2. Failure to understand the phase relationship of these signals to those that will feed back naturally upon raising the system gain.
3. Misidentifying them as eigen wavelengths. We actually "tune" the upper envelope of a series of "piled-up" modes.

Earlier Techniques

Until real-time analyzers were available for under $5000 (1970), early equalization work was predominately done by repeatedly raising the gain of the sound system until feedback occurred and adjusting the appropriate filter to reduce the system amplitude at that frequency. One or 2 dB at the very most is necessary to bring the system back to stability. By repeating this for 20-30 feedbacks, it is possible to raise the acoustic gain of a sound-reinforcement system to within a few decibels of unity gain at all frequencies. While this method is an excellent way to increase gain with a nominal amount of test equipment, it leaves the overall tonal balance to the ear of the practitioner. Those with perfect pitch often exhibit a nonuniversal taste, and those with a taste that agrees with the majority of listeners are not often gifted with perfect pitch.

When real-time analyzers became available, this problem was handled by adjusting the sound system to the desired overall tonal balance visually and taking typically seven or eight feedbacks in order to raise the gain (usually to allow the adjustment of the overall response characteristic to the inverse of the response of the microphone). Then the sound system was shock excited with program material to see if one of the ⅓-octave bands of the real-time analyzer was slow to decay as compared to an adjacent band. This method works quite well, depending on the skill and intuition of the practitioner to choose the filters employed by the "least amplitude" method, and it yields an audible improvement in sound quality. The greatest difficulty lies in detecting exactly which filter at which amplitude is correct during the shock excitation of the system with typical program material. And, what might be correct for one user needs readjustment for another. Some practitioners use discrete filters to chase these elusive longer decay frequencies. A good choice of discrete filters is shown in Fig. 8-49.

A New Technique

Careful thought and experimentation regarding what needed correcting and what was needed to do that correction led to the following considerations:

1. The variability in the "correction" process was directly due to the variability in the shock-excitation signal, namely, "typical" program material (usually the operator's voice).

2. The inability to "guess" in adjusting the overall tonal balance which filters interacted with which frequencies and with which phase relationship.

3. A desire to be able to shock-excite the entire band-pass.

The solution came from considering these problems. The test signal of pink noise equally excites all frequencies. Bringing the system to within a few decibels of regeneration allows the room and sound system to "display" which frequencies are unduly sensitive to approaching regeneration including those due to phase as well as amplitude.

The sound system is fed an input of pink noise, and its "raw" response is observed through a measuring microphone in the audience area attached to the input of the real-time analyzer. The performer's microphone is then brought up in level until a hollow ringing tone is heard. The most regenerative frequencies will now reveal themselves in their optimum order of correction. Every adjustment of the filter, as well as its total effect on the house curve, is viewed on the screen of the real-time analyzer. The house curve being equalized is never out of sight. By exerting the least amplitude change in collapsing the large regenerative swellings, a tuning considerably superior to that formerly attained using the older methods is achieved.

Playback Systems

This same technique can be startlingly effective in the equalization of sound reproduction systems or sound synthesizing systems. In this case, instead of using a performer's microphone to achieve regeneration, the calibrated measuring microphone is simultaneously used for both room-response measurement and regeneration. Multichannel systems tuned using this technique are characterized by superior spatial geometry as well as improved tonal response. The improved reproduction of geometry is believed to be due to the

Courtesy United Recording Electronics Industries
Fig. 8-49. A highly useful 1/6-octave discrete filter set for use in addition to the "combining" 1/3-octave set.

better acoustic phase response between channels at the listener's position, and while only a small area so benefits, it is usually only the mixer's general area that has to be covered in the typical studio monitoring-room situation. Some unusually extended-range systems may now feed back at frequencies well above audibility (in one case above 30,000 Hz), and care must be taken to use a low-pass filter in conjunction with either the sound system or the measuring system.

SUMMARY OF RTA APPLICATION

From these notes on the use of the real-time analyzer, it can be seen that the following list of uses is just a beginning for the imaginative sound contractor:

1. House curves made with measuring microphone.
2. House curves made with sound-system microphone.
3. Examination of distribution of all frequencies at differing locations at the same time.
4. Examination of the house curve at the performer's location.
5. Response curves of the filter settings.
6. Detection of feedback frequencies.
7. Frequency response of microphones to be used in the sound system.
8. Examination of cross talk between lines.
9. Setting levels throughout sound system both electrically and acoustically.
10. Detection of resonating surface areas by means of observing the effect of manual damping of the vibrating surface.

Pink noise (equal energy per octave) is used rather than white noise (equal energy per hertz) because the bandpass filters used in the typical RTA are constant percentage bandwidth rather than constant bandwidth. This means that a white-noise signal put into a constant-percentage bandwidth analyzer would have a +3-dB-per-octave rise with increasing frequency. (The filters grow wider with increasing frequency, thereby summing more hertz at the same level.) Pink noise on a per-hertz basis decreases 3 dB per octave; therefore, pink noise matches constant-percentage bandwidth response, allowing a "flat" response across the screen of an RTA (Figs. 8-50, 8-51, 8-52, and 8-53).

THE TUNING ENVIRONMENT

Fig. 8-54 reveals many of the acoustic fields that can be equalized. In one case, whenever the tuning was made uniform to the desired house curve (Fig. 8-55), there was not enough acoustic gain in the audience area. When the acoustic gain was raised by the feedback method, the shape of the house curve in the audience area was unacceptable. Analysis with an RTA revealed that the loudspeaker array mounted in the proscenium area was not properly shock mounted and

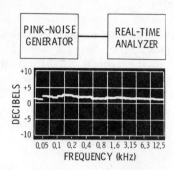

Fig. 8-50. Pink noise as it appears when displayed on the screen of a real-time analyzer.

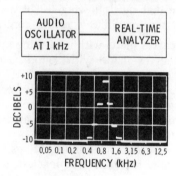

Fig. 8-51. A sine wave as it appears when displayed on the screen of a real-time analyzer.

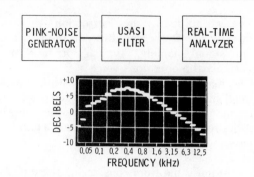

Fig. 8-52. USASI or ANSI noise as it appears when displayed on the screen of a real-time analyzer.

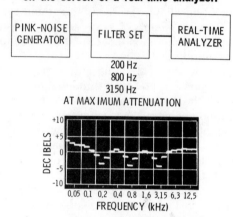

Fig. 8-53. Signal through three band-rejection filters as viewed on the screen of a real-time analyzer.

was causing the arch structure to reradiate a signal downward to the microphones, causing premature feedback. When this large array was properly shock mounted and properly isolated in the proscenium arch area, then the house curve could be shaped as desired, and the acoustic gain could be brought to its potential at the same time.

Being alert to each of these acoustic fields can solve many problems that seem mysterious when considered in the context of a single field. Often, you will equalize in more than one of the fields at the same time. For

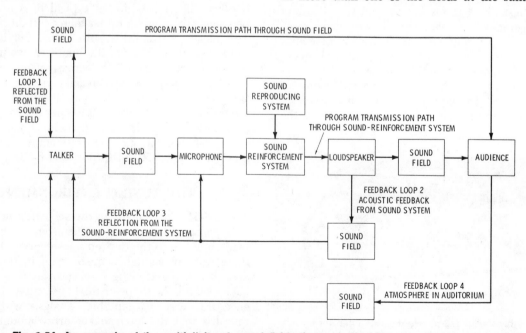

Fig. 8-54. An example of the multiplicity of sound fields that can affect how you choose to equalize.

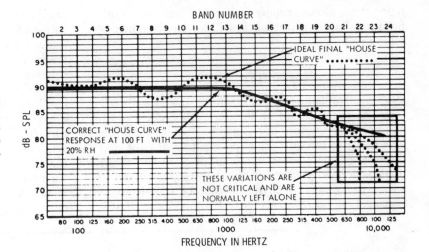

Fig. 8-55. A suggested weighting to the equalized response of a sound system in a large auditorium (about 100 feet from the sound system) that has wide audience acceptance. At a shorter distance from the sound source, there would be proportionately less high-frequency rolloff.

example, you will equalize the main system for the audience, the foldback system for the entertainer, a delayed under-balcony system for a distributed system, and separate equalization for a time-delayed portion of the main system. Some of these are in the direct field and some in the reverberant field. No one, as yet, has all the answers to applying equalization to the fantastic variety of sound systems being designed today. Mask-

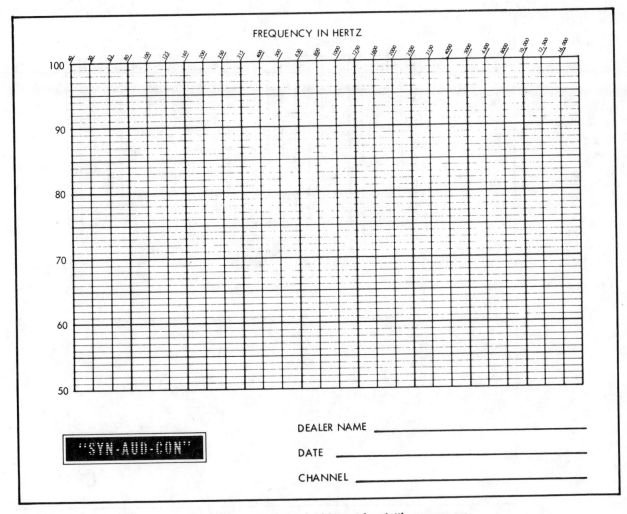

Fig. 8-56. A suggested standard format for plotting responses.

ing systems alone become fascinating projects requiring precision equalization to achieve totally undetectable masking.

PROXIMITY MODES

The microphone proximity effect, traditionally referred to in the technical literature, is the effect of increased bass response in the microphone as the talker gets closer to the unit. This remains true of most unidirectional microphones today and is often effectively used by trained performers to enhance their otherwise weak bass tones. Since the advent of sound-system equalization, however, we have become aware of still another effect of the proximity of large bodies (performers) on a typical cardioid microphone. That is the increased tendency to feedback at some key midrange frequency where the system is otherwise stable until the microphone is approached. You can use your hands cupped around the microphone to bring the system into feedback and can adjust the level of feedback by "playing" the microphone. In adjusting the appropriate filter, care should be taken not to carry the adjustment too far. The idea is to correct the tendency of the microphone to cause instability when it is approached by the performer and not to remove all tendency toward feedback even when the microphone is completely encircled by a closed hand.

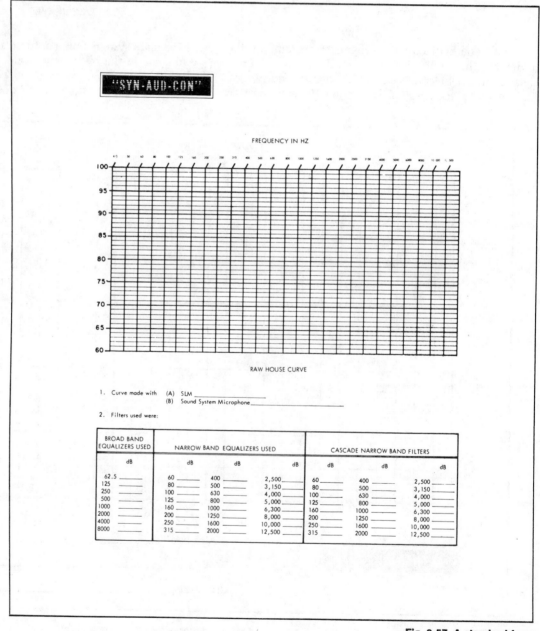

Fig. 8-57. A standard form

CHECKING MICROPHONE POLARITY

Suprisingly, one minor checkout prior to equalization time that often is overlooked is the poling of the microphones in a multimicrophone system. The easiest way to accomplish this is to arbitrarily assume that the first microphone you pick up is correctly poled. Holding it in one hand and the second microphone in the other hand, bring them closer and closer together while talking into them (such as "one-one-one"). They are in phase if the apparent bass response increases as they are brought closer together in front of your mouth. They are out of phase if the bass weakens as they are brought together. In any case, be sure to check this important factor before equalizing. The Shure Model A15PR phase reverser is invaluable in this work. Be careful before you rewire microphones; the patch cords could be miswired.

LOUDSPEAKER POLARITY

In examining the "raw" response of a loudspeaker array, pick the poling that gives the most usable response through the crossover region. True phasing can enter in here, as well as polarity, and great care should be exercised in the relative positioning of horns to each other, especially the spacing and positioning of the high-frequency elements in relation to the low-fre-

---

3. High pass cutoff _____ Hz.

4. Low pass cutoff _____ Hz.

5. Physical Measurements

D_s = _____ ft. Q = _____

D_1 = _____ ft. $\%A_{L_{CONS}}$ = _____

D_2 = _____ ft. RT_{60} = _____ s

D_0 = _____ ft. V = _____ ft^3

D_c = _____ ft. S = _____ ft^2

NOM = _____   EAD = _____ ft

R = _____ ft^2

6. Calculated acoustic gain potential _____ dB.

7. Measured acoustic gain _____ dB.

8. Subjective response of customer and observers was

(A) Excellent _____

(B) Good _____

(C) Fair _____

(D) Unacceptable _____

Comments _____

_____

_____

_____

_____

_____

9. Sound system components

(A) Source _____

_____

(B) Electronics _____

_____

(C) Transducers _____

_____

10. Single line block diagram (one channel only)

Name _____

Company _____

Date _____

Job No. _____

for records keeping.

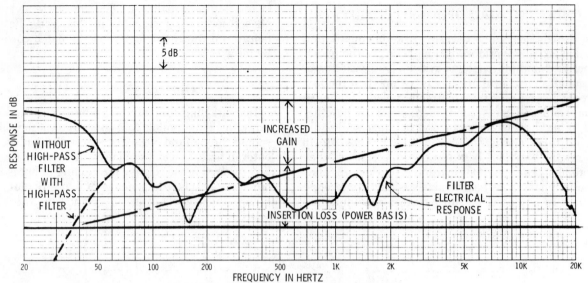

Fig. 8-58. Insertion loss and increased gain.

quency elements. Remember, out in the audience area there will be phase relationships between direct and reflected sound as well as those between two direct sound sources. The real-time analyzer is invaluable for examining the potential variations and their effects on the audience area. John Hilliard's paper entitled "Notes on How Phase and Delay Distortions Affect the Quality of Speech, Music and Sound Effects" (1964 IEEE Transactions on Audio) is of particular interest on this subject.

CHARTS AND RECORD KEEPING

We all learn from experience, and in sound-system–room equalization, it is essential that you keep records of your jobs, or each one will be your first one. The need for standard frequency-response charts is obvious. Fig. 8-56 shows such a standard chart that has vertical and horizontal scales that match those found on the standard logarithmic charts used in level recorders, etc. This allows overlaps to be made between your recorded

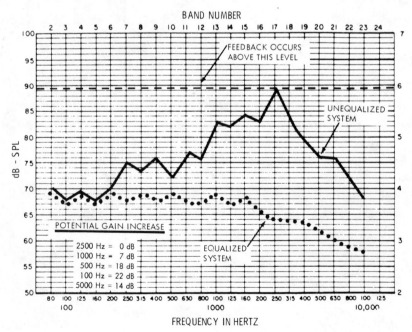

Fig. 8-59. How to calculate the potential acoustic gain increase (the unrealized acoustic gain).

data and machine-run curves of your filter settings. Fig. 8-57 illustrates a standard reporting form that records invaluable data for future reference, be it for maintenance of the system or for checking the validity of a new theory using your own recorded data as checks.

DEMONSTRATING THE EQUALIZATION

Depending, of course, on the need for equalization in a given sound system (how rough the house curve is without equalization), you may or may not want to make a demonstration with the equalizers first switched out of the system and then switched into the system. Occasionally, the switch goes from total unintelligibility to startling clarity. More normally (or we never could have sold sound systems before equalization came along), the equalization modestly raises the gain, fills out the rough spots in the response, and is essentially the icing on a well-baked cake. In about one case out of 100, switching in the equalizer results in no discernible audible difference. If so, rejoice, and go home with congratulations for having done an exceptional design, installation, and check-out of a sound system. To make the comparison, the attenuator in the master test set is turned to maximum attenuation. The switch is set to the equalized position, and the sound system is adjusted to where feedback just starts. The switch is then thrown to the unequalized position, and the attenuator is adjusted until feedback again just starts. You can now lower the master gain control on the sound system 6 dB. This means that when you switch back and forth between equalized and unequalized, each position is just 6 dB below feedback. At this point, the number of decibels read on the attenuator on the master test set can be divided into two categories:

1. Approximately one half of the value is the insertion loss of the filters.

2. Approximately one half the value is the increase in acoustic gain over whatever existed before the tuning began. See Fig. 8-58.

The total acoustic gain is equal to the acoustic gain in the raw system plus the increase in acoustic gain obtained from using the filters. It is of interest to note that it is possible to have an increase in acoustic gain but not necessarily an increase in loudness at the same time. Remember the Fletcher-Munson characteristics of the human ear; if the increase in gain is at low frequencies only, the change in loudness may barely be perceptible.

One look at the "raw" house curve allows immediate calculation of the "potential acoustic gain increase"—that is the unavailable acoustic gain at other frequencies than the feedback frequency (Fig. 8-59).

SUMMARY

There is no substitute for experience in this new technique. It is best to practice with standard small systems in your back room many times before attempting a job in public. It must always be remembered that equalization is used to ensure that all frequencies can reach unity gain at the same time. If the system does not have smooth coverage, then only a limited area has the benefit of the increased gain. If the electrical gain of the system cannot support the acoustic gain requirements, equalization is again in vain. When all facets of a sound system are handled professionally, equalization guarantees the calculated result.

The process of equalization applied to a misdesigned or misinstalled system magnifies the faults present; the difference between properly covered areas and dead spots is now greater; hum, noise, etc., are louder; feedback may occur from cross talk as well as room reflections. Really good results from equalization tell the world you have done the entire job well.

CHAPTER 9

Instrumentation

Instrumentation is used to measure room parameters before the design begins; it is used to compute design factors; it is used to install the system; and finally, it is used to operate and maintain the system. The greatest single division between professional work and nonprofessional work in the commercial sound business is the use and understanding of basic audio and acoustic instrumentation. Lord Kelvin wrote, "I often say that when you measure what you are speaking about, and can express it in numbers, you know something about it; but when you cannot measure it, when you cannot express it in numbers, your knowledge is of a meager and unsatisfactory kind. It may be the beginning of knowledge but you have scarcely, in your thought, advanced to the stage of Science whatever the matter may be . . . ."

BASIC ELECTRONIC INSTRUMENTS

While it is difficult to imagine, there are professional sound engineers who do not own an audio oscillator, ac vtvm, or oscilloscope. These three instruments are as basic as a soldering iron, electrical tape, screwdrivers, etc. The quality of the instruments is every bit as important as the kind of instruments. For example, the oscillator (Fig. 9-1) should have a constant-impedance output (most do not) so that an attenuator reading between it and the measured device can be relied on. It should hold its output impedance (usually 600 ohms) uniform at zero output for noise measurements. It must, of course, have low distortion (less than 0.1%) with both sine-wave and square-wave outputs.

The voltmeter should be capable of reading down to a millivolt. It should have an input impedance of at least 25 megohms (typically in parallel with 80 pF and independent of the attenuator setting). Highly desirable are the selective voltmeters such as that shown in Fig. 9-2. (This instrument can also be a signal source when used with a random-noise generator.) The scales should include both voltage and dB markings.

The oscilloscope (Fig. 9-3) can be any high-quality, low-frequency model, but the voltage range should go below 1 millivolt, and the sweep speeds per division should be 10 microseconds to 0.1 second. Naturally, a calibrated graticule, an external horizontal input, and amplitude-selection triggering are musts. Variable persistence, single sweep, dual trace, and differential inputs are useful. Whenever possible, it is suggested that a camera be included at the time the scope is purchased, to enable records to be made of data measured.

Another basic electronic instrument that is indispensable to the professional sound engineer is the impedance bridge. This invaluable instrument should be used before every interconnection of components in a sound system. You should always know:

1. The exact impedance of the link circuits.
2. The impedance of the output line being attached to the power amplifiers.
3. The impedance at the input of the crossover network.
4. The exact termination and buildout of each passive device inserted.

A very useful bridge is shown in Fig. 9-4.

Fig. 9-5 shows a compact tester designed for the quick and easy measurement of impedance. Because of the small signal that it applies to the device under test, this tester may be used for impedance measurements on microphones, magnetic recording heads, microphone transformers, and any other device that would be damaged by the application of a large test signal, as well as for resistance, capacitance, and inductance measurements of the more usual kind. It has three audio test frequencies, selected by push button, and gives a direct reading of impedance in ohms on the meter. A change of frequency shows whether the impedance is inductive or capacitive, and reference to the nomogram supplied with the instrument gives the actual value of the component under test. The test frequencies are 250 Hz, 1 kHz, and 4 kHz. The range of

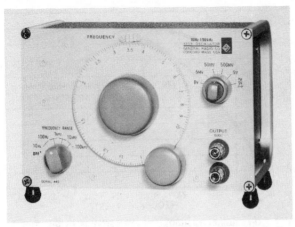

Courtesy General Radio Co.

Fig. 9-1. An audio oscillator.

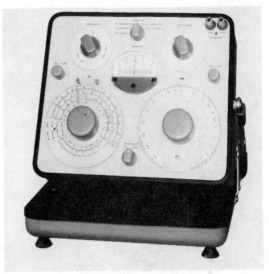

Courtesy General Radio Co.

Fig. 9-4. An impedance bridge.

Courtesy General Radio Co.

Fig. 9-2. A tunable voltmeter.

Courtesy Hewlett-Packard

Fig. 9-3. An oscilloscope.

Courtesy Sennheiser Electronics Corp.

Fig. 9-5. The ZP 2 impedance tester.

measurement is 1 ohm to 1 megohm, in twelve push-button–selected ranges.

The internal transistorized oscillator applies a small signal to the device under test. The alternating current through the test device is amplified by the internal transistorized amplifier and applied to the meter. For stability, range selection is achieved by the alteration of the turns ratio of two transformers. Changes of sen-

sitivity of the instrument with time can be checked by reference to one standard component and the sensitivity corrected if necessary by a front-panel control. The single recalibration will hold good for all twelve ranges. Power is supplied from an internal 9-volt dry battery.

BASIC ACOUSTIC INSTRUMENTS

Many sound contracting firms own good basic acoustical measuring equipment. First and foremost is an accurate, reliable, well-calibrated sound level meter or SLM (Fig. 9-6). It should include all standard weight-

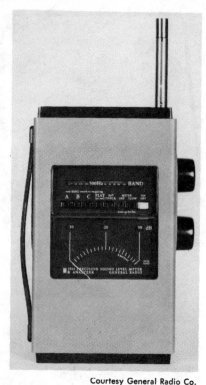

Courtesy General Radio Co.

Fig. 9-6. A sound level meter.

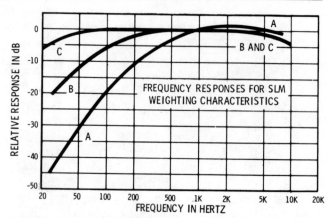

Fig. 9-7. Frequency-response characteristics in the American National Standard Specification for Sound Level Meters, ANSI-S1.4-1971.

ings plus an octave-band analyzer. Impact calibration is vital if you intend to do noise measurements in addition to your sound work. Condenser-type microphones are a necessity because you will use the SLM as a secondary standard for the calibration of microphones and loudspeakers (see Fig. 9-7).

An acoustic noise source is necessary (the oscillator is not usable in typical room measurements because of standing-wave patterns and room-mode distribution). Because of the rapidly increasing use of real-time audio-frequency analyzers, it is wisest to purchase a noise source that includes pink noise. Some instrumentation used in early equalization work had a white-noise source and achieved a "pink" noise equivalent by

varying the bandwidth and amplitude of the analyzing bandpass filter set used with the noise source. This is all right until the day you wish to use any other analyzer and find that to do so requires a conversion from white noise to pink noise. The noise generator shown in Fig. 9-8 includes white, pink, and USASI (now called ANSI) noise. It offers a 600-ohm output, either balanced, unbalanced, or with floating output levels adjustable from −48 dBm to approximately +12 dBm.

NOISE MEASUREMENTS

In addition to making possible precision sound-system measurements, a precision sound level meter allows the engineer to make noise surveys. Fig. 9-9 shows a family of noise-criteria curves, and Table 9-1 lists typical applications of these curves.

Fig. 9-10 is a chart for predicting the annoyance caused by various sound levels. To use the chart, locate in the curved grid at the bottom the point corresponding to the sound levels of the noise under consideration, and project directly above it into the first of the six correction sections bounded by the horizontal lines. When

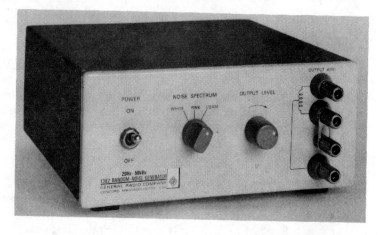

Fig. 9-8. A random-noise generator.

Courtesy General Radio Co.

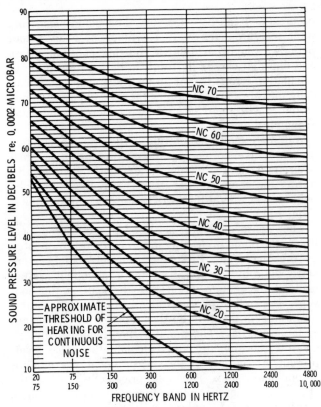

Fig. 9-9. Noise-criteria curves.

Table 9-1. Typical Application of Noise-Criteria Curves

Type of Space	Recommended Curve
Broadcast Studios	NC 15-20
Concert Halls	NC 15-20
Legitimate Theaters (500 Seats—No Amplification)	NC 20-25
Music Rooms	NC 25
School Rooms (No Amplification)	NC 25
Television Studios	NC 25
Apartments and Hotels	NC 25-30
Assembly Halls (With Amplification)	NC 25-35
Homes (Sleeping Areas)	NC 25-35
Motion-Picture Theaters	NC 30
Hospitals	NC 30
Churches (No Amplification)	NC 25
Courtrooms (No Amplification)	NC 25
Libraries	NC 30
Restaurants	NC 45
Coliseums (For Sports Only With Amplification)	NC 50

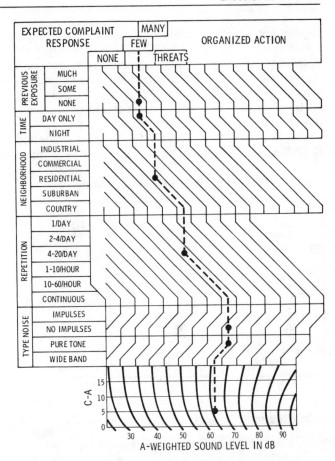

Fig. 9-10. Annoyance of neighborhood sound levels.

entering a correction section, follow the lane entered until reaching a position opposite the condition listed at the left which applies to the neighborhood noise under consideration; then proceed vertically, disregarding lanes, until the next section is reached. In this way, work upward through the lanes of the correction sections until reaching the response to be expected at the top. For example, if truck movements at a new loading station are to be cued by a whistle that will produce 65 dBA and 70 dBC at the nearest homes 10 to 15 times per day, then few complaints would be expected (according to the dashed line traced through the chart).

The following material on noise measurements is included courtesy of the General Radio Co.

In addition to the normal noise survey of building sites, race tracks, etc., there is the federal activity in this area. There is still no general agreement as to exactly how much noise, what type of noise, or what durations of exposure to noise constitute a health hazard. But a legal definition of excessive noise has been established and probably will be the accepted guide for some time to come.

The definition comes in the form of safety regulations issued by the U.S. Department of Labor under the Walsh-Healey Public Contracts Act. Early in 1969, Section 50-204.10 was added to this act which, for the first time, provided noise limits beyond which manufacturers were compelled to take steps to protect their employees' hearing. Although the Walsh-Healey Act applies only to manufacturers selling to the federal government goods valued in excess of $10,000 or services valued in excess of $2500, more recent legislation has extended the coverage to all industries involved in interstate commerce.

This later measure, the Occupational Safety and

Health Act, OSHA (public Law 91-596), which was signed into law in December 1970, also encourages industrial plants to purchase equipment both for noise measurement and monitoring and for workers' protection through periodic audiometer tests of their hearing. It also authorizes the establishment of a large organization to administer and enforce the standards.

The Walsh-Healey exposure limits, as incorporated in OSHA, are given in Table 9-2. The exposures given

Table 9-2. Noise Exposure Limits

Band	Noise Level (dBA)	Maximum Exposure (Hours)
	Under 90	Unlimited
A	90 to 92	6
B	92 to 95	4
C	95 to 97	3
D	97 to 100	2
E	100 to 102	1.5
F	102 to 105	1
G	105 to 110	0.5
H	110 to 115	0.25
	Above 115	None

are those permissible for a normal 8-hour working day. When the noise consists of differing levels throughout the day, the combined effect is considered as follows:

$$C_T = (C_A/6 + C_B/4 + C_C/3 + C_D/2 + C_E/1.5 +$$
$$C_F/1 + C_G/0.5 + C_H/0.25) \times 100 \qquad (9\text{-}1)$$

where,

C_T is the total cumulative noise exposure (level/time) expressed as a percent (100% is the maximum allowed),

C_A, C_B, etc., are the total times the noise level is in band A, B, etc.

These limits are based on tests that have established that, for every halving of the duration of exposure, the intensity of exposure can be increased 5 dBA without an increase in the risk of noise-induced hearing losses. The noise levels are specified as dBA because A-weighted levels have been found to correlate well with hearing loss.

One way to make noise measurements to the OSHA criteria is by means of a sound-level meter. Its small size and battery power make it ideally suited to surveys of an industrial plant for quick identification of areas of potentially harmful noise. In areas where the noise remains constant for substantial periods of time, the SLM can also be used to compute the amount of exposure, as shown in the preceding formula.

Where the noise levels vary, the sound-level meter may not be practical for determining cumulative noise exposure. Here, the operator must not only measure more than one noise level (with the probability of several different range settings), he must also time the duration of each level so the total combined noise ex-

posure (C_T) can be calculated. This could mean constant measurements and recordings over an 8-hour period—a somewhat difficult and time-consuming task and one that can easily result in data-transcription or calculation errors. Use of an instrument that automatically measures and computes the total exposure, in accordance with the OSHA table, is a more practical and economical method.

Automatic noise monitoring is the practical solution to cumulative noise-exposure measurements in areas where noise levels fluctuate above and below 90 dBA during the course of the day. This is the philosophy behind the General Radio 1934 noise-exposure monitor (Fig. 9-11).

The exposure monitor is placed in the desired location in the plant, preferably in the area most frequented by the employees. In some cases, this can be more easily done by the use of a remote microphone, especially if the monitor itself is to be kept in the floor supervisor's office. At the start of the day, an operator pushes one of the push buttons representing the length of the work day. The monitor then begins to detect, measure, accumulate, and calculate the noise levels present. At the end of the measurement, the monitor automatically stops. The operator can check the results at any time, even before the measurement is complete. By pushing one of two buttons, he can read the percent of noise exposure or the percent of test time that has accumulated (if he pushes the percent of test time button halfway through lunch, for example, the display will read 50%). If he chooses, he can wait until the next day to read and record the percent of noise exposure at the same time he initiates another measurement.

In many working environments, it may not suffice to measure noise exposure at a fixed location for the duration of a workday. This is evident when you consider

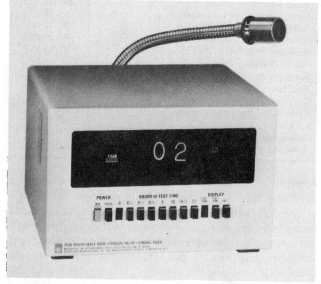

Fig. 9-11. A noise-exposure meter.

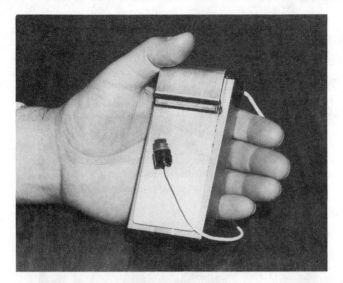

(A) Dosometer unit.

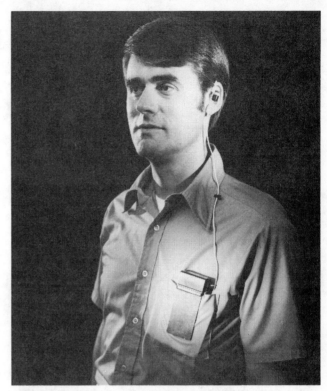

(B) Subject wearing unit.

(C) Readout device.

Fig. 9-12. A noise dosometer.

the worker who moves about to several locations in the course of his duties or performs a variety of operations during the day, each generating different noise levels.

The practical way to measure the noise exposure in these circumstances is with a noise-exposure monitor that can be worn by the worker and which moves about with him during the day. The General Radio 1944 noise-exposure monitor (Figs. 9-12A and 9-12B) is a wearable instrument that weighs less than eight ounces and is small enough to fit into a shirt pocket.

The 1944 is a complete monitor with a built-in microphone and its own battery power. It detects noise, weights it, and accumulates total noise exposure for the workday, based on OSHA criteria. In order to provide tamper-proof operation, there are no displays or visible controls on the unit.

Retrieving the information detected and stored in the monitor is accomplished with the companion noise-exposure indicator (Fig. 9-12C). At the end of the workday, the wearable monitor is plugged into the indicator. A button is pressed, and the cumulative noise

exposure is displayed on a light-emitting-diode readout. The number displayed represents the accumulated percentage of noise exposure a worker has experienced, 100% being the maximum permissible in accordance with OSHA. A lamp on the indicator is energized in the event that 115 dBA has been exceeded at any time during the work period.

A simple and convenient means of periodically checking calibration is a must when noise-exposure measurements are made. The 1944 indicator unit contains a built-in calibrator to permit rapid calibration verification at the start and end of each day's measurements.

BUILDING A PINK-NOISE FILTER

Many engineers possess noise generators that put out only white noise (constant energy per hertz). The filter shown in Fig. 9-13, when placed at the output of such a generator, changes the white noise into pink noise (constant energy per octave). The proper test signal

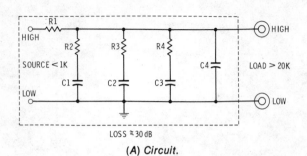

(A) Circuit.

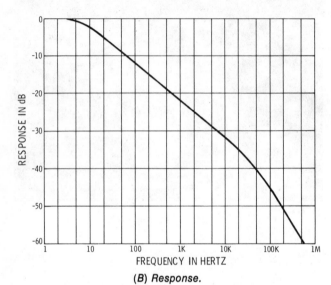

(B) Response.

C1	0.649 μF,	±2%, 100 Vdcw, COP-24
C2	0.287 μF,	±2%, 100 Vdcw, COP-24
C3	0.0866 μF,	±2%, 100 Vdcw, COP-24
C4	0.0442 μF,	±2%, 100 Vdcw, COP-24
R1	6.49 K,	±1%, 1/8 W, REF-60
R2	3.09 K,	±1%, 1/8 W, REF-60
R3	953 Ω,	±1%, 1/8 W, REF-60
R4	309 Ω,	±1%, 1/8 W, REF-60

NOTE: REF = Resistor, film; COP = Capacitor, plastic

(C) Parts list.

Fig. 9-13. Pink-noise filter.

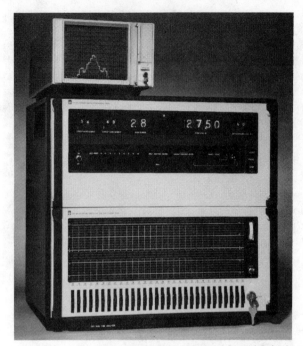

Courtesy General Radio Co.

Fig. 9-14. A real-time analyzer.

Courtesy Communications Co., Inc.

Fig. 9-15. A lower-cost real-time analyzer.

for all loudspeaker testing using real-time analyzers is pink noise. White noise delivers excessive power at the highest frequencies and can damage drivers. This pink-noise filter is an RC low-pass filter with a slope of −3 dB per octave from 20 Hz to 20 kHz and a slope of −6 dB at higher frequencies. For shielding, the case of the filter is grounded to the low input and output terminals. The output of the pink-noise filter will be approximately 30 dB below its input, and the level in each 1/3-octave band will be approximately 17 dB below that. Thus, when the output meter of the random-noise generator indicates 3 volts, the output of the filter will be approximately 0.1 volt, and the level in each 1/3-octave band will be approximately 15 millivolts. (The

design of this filter is given courtesy of General Radio Co.)

REAL-TIME AUDIO-FREQUENCY SPECTRUM ANALYZERS

It really is not possible to become "expert" at sound-system–room equalization without the use of a real-time analyzer (RTA). The use of one of these devices (Fig. 9-14) allows literally 30 times the number of response curves to be viewed in the same time it took to make just one curve by the conventional serial-analyzer method. Their high cost is the only present deterrent to much wider usage, though hundreds are in use by professional sound engineers around the United States. Fig. 9-15 shows one of the least expensive real-time analyzers available to the professional sound engineer. Any available oscilloscope can be used as its display.

The potential purchaser of one of these valuable tools is cautioned to beware of the vibration-type narrow-band real-time analyzers and the various poorly thought-out designs that suffer from a variety of resolution, display, reliability, and calibration problems.

Fig. 9-16 shows the contrast between signals as seen on an oscilloscope and on the screen of a real-time analyzer. The time functions represent the oscilloscope display, and the power spectra represent the RTA display. Fig. 9-17 represents a series of spectra over a time period.

INTERNATIONALLY PREFERRED FREQUENCIES AND EXACT NUMBER VALUES FOR THEM

In working with equalizers and analyzers, many engineers wonder how the center frequencies for such components are selected, what their bandwidths are, and how 1-Hz equivalents can be obtained. The following data give the formulas and tables relating to such devices. Table 9-3 lists preferred frequencies for labels,

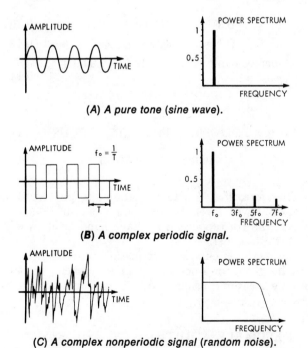

(A) A pure tone (sine wave).

(B) A complex periodic signal.

(C) A complex nonperiodic signal (random noise).

Fig. 9-16. A comparison of data presented by an oscilloscope and a real-time analyzer.

Table 9-3. Preferred Frequencies for Labels

Preferred Frequencies	1/1 Oct	1/2 Oct	1/3 Oct
16	x	x	x
18			
20			x
22.4		x	
25			x
28			
31.5	x	x	x
35.5			
40			x
45		x	
50			x
56			
63	x	x	x
71			
80			x
90		x	
100			x
112			
125	x	x	x
140			
160			x
180		x	
200			x
224			
250	x	x	x
280			
315			x
355		x	
400			x
450			
500	x	x	x
560			
630			x
710		x	
800			x
900			
1000	x	x	x
1120			
1250			x
1400		x	
1600			x
1800			
2000	x	x	x
2240			
2500			x
2800		x	
3150			x
3550			
4000	x	x	x
4500			
5000			x
5600		x	
6300			x
7100			
8000	x	x	x
9000			
10,000			x
11,200		x	
12,500			x
14,000			
16,000	x	x	x

and Table 9-4 lists internationally preferred ISO numbers. Note that the use of spectrum level corrections applies only to measurements of broadband noise signals and not to sinusoidal signals.

Table 9-4. Internationally Preferred ISO Numbers (Renard Numbers)

1/12 Octave 40 Series	1/6 Octave 20 Series	1/3 Octave 10 Series	1/2 Octave 6-2/3 Series	2/3 Octave 5 Series	1/1 Octave 3-1/3 Series	Exact Value
1.	1	1	1	1	1	1.000000000
1.06						1.059253725
1.12	1.12					1.122018454
1.18						1.188502227
1.25	1.25	1.25				1.258925411
1.32						1.333521431
1.4	1.4		1.4			1.412537543
1.5						1.496235654
1.6	1.6	1.6		1.6		1.584893190
1.7						1.678804015
1.8	1.8					1.778279406
1.9						1.883649085
2.	2	2	2		2	1.995262310
2.12						2.113489034
2.24	2.24					2.238721132
2.36						2.371373698
2.5	2.5	2.5		2.5		2.511886423
2.65						2.660725050
2.8	2.8		2.8			2.818382920
3.						2.985382606
3.15	3.15	3.15				3.162277646
3.35						3.349654376
3.55	3.55					3.548133875
3.75						3.758374024
4.	4	4	4	4	4	3.981071685
4.25						4.216965012
4.5	4.5					4.466835897
4.75						4.731512563
5.	5	5				5.011872307
5.3						5.308844410
5.6	5.6		5.6			5.623413217
6.						5.956621397
6.3	6.3	6.3		6.3		6.309573403
6.7						6.683439130
7.1	7.1					7.079457794
7.5						7.498942039
8.	8	8	8		8	7.943282288
8.5						8.413951352
9.	9					8.912509312
9.5						9.440608688

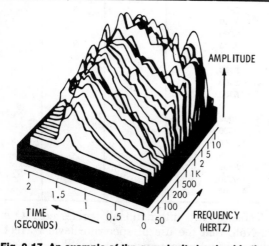

Fig. 9-17. An example of the complexity involved in the analysis of transient sounds.

Fractional-Octave Formulas

True $\frac{1}{3}$-octave center frequencies $= 2^{1/3} \times 2^{1/3} \ldots \times 2^{1/3}$ (9-2)

Exact-value ISO center frequencies =

$$10^{\frac{1}{\text{N Series}}} \times 10^{\frac{1}{\text{N Series}}} \ldots \times 10^{\frac{1}{\text{N Series}}} \quad (9-3)$$

Bandpass of fractional-octave filters:

Lower limit $= 0.5^{0.5 \text{ (Octave fraction)}} \times f_c$ (9-4)

Upper limit $= 2^{0.5 \text{ (Octave fraction)}} \times f_c$ (9-5)

-3-dB Bandwidth = Upper limit $-$ Lower limit (9-6)

where f_c is the center frequency.

Spectrum level correction $= 10 \log (\text{Bandwidth})$ (9-7)

Examples

EXAMPLE 1:

Find the bandwidth and spectrum level correction for the 1000-Hz $\frac{1}{3}$-octave band:

$$0.5^{0.5(1/3)} \times 1000 = 890.9 \text{ Hz} \quad (9-8)$$

$$2^{0.5(1/3)} \times 1000 = 1122.46 \text{ Hz} \quad (9-9)$$

$$1122.46 - 890.9 = 231.56 \text{ Hz} \quad (9-10)$$

$$10 \log 231.56 = 23.65 \text{ dB} \quad (9-11)$$

(This value is subtracted from the measured value to obtain the 1-Hz value.)

EXAMPLE 2:

A set of 1-octave data is available. It is desired to replot it in $\frac{1}{3}$-octave levels. (Assume relatively wideband noise data.)

$$0.5^{0.5(1/3)} \times 1000 = 890.9 \text{ Hz} \quad (9-12)$$

$$2^{0.5(1/3)} \times 1000 = 1122.46 \text{ Hz} \quad (9-13)$$

$\frac{1}{3}$-octave bandwidth $= 1122.46 - 890.9 = 232 \text{ Hz}$ (9-14)

$$0.5^{0.5(1/1)} \times 1000 = 707 \text{ Hz} \quad (9-15)$$

$$2^{0.5(1/1)} \times 1000 = 1414 \text{ Hz} \quad (9-16)$$

1-octave bandwidth $= 1414 - 707 = 707 \text{ Hz}$ (9-17)

$$10 \log \frac{707}{232} = 4.84 \text{ dB} \quad (9-18)$$

Therefore, the $\frac{1}{3}$-octave material is plotted at a 4.84-dB lower level. If the data were in $\frac{1}{3}$-octave bands, the corresponding 1-octave band levels would be 4.84-dB higher.

Noise-criteria curves, noise-masking curves, etc., are usually given for 1-octave center frequencies but are usually measured using $\frac{1}{3}$-octave real-time analyzers, etc.

DESIRABLE ADDITIONS TO THE BASICS

With the addition of a tone-burst generator (Fig. 9-18), it becomes possible to put coherent bursts

Fig. 9-18. A tone-burst generator.

through the system. This allows measurements of the ratio of direct-to-reflected sound, the time delay between sounds, and the location of undesirable reflecting surfaces. This highly useful instrument is a logical addition to the oscillator, oscilloscope, and camera.

When working with architects, engineers, consultants, and knowledgeable owners, it becomes very worthwhile to be able to give them well-documented reports. A graphic level recorder, with the necessary plug-ins, will allow documentation to be made of the following parameters:

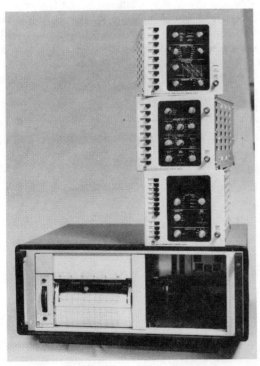

Fig. 9-19. A high-speed level recorder.

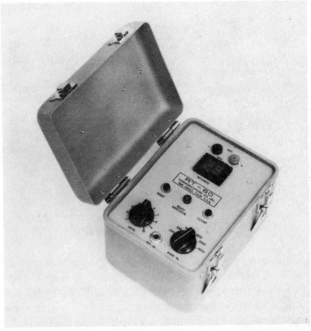

Fig. 9-20. A digital-readout reverberation-time meter.

1. Measurement of reverberation time.
2. Measurement of the electrical response of filters, amplifiers, etc.
3. Measurement of the final acoustic response in ⅓-octave form.
4. Measurement of the distribution of coverage.
5. Measurement of the thd.

A camera and RTA allow documentation of items 2, 3, 4, and 5.

These measurements allow the fortunate user to include tight documentation clauses in a specification he happens to write, and it is a rare user who doesn't want accurately detailed data. Fig. 9-19 shows a level recorder that has interchangeable function modules that allow sine-wave, noise, and time-base measurements to be made with a single basic unit.

Fig. 9-20 shows a less expensive alternative to a level recorder for obtaining reverberation times. The unit illustrated has solid-state circuitry and a digital read-out. Center frequencies of the ⅓-octave bandpass filter are 250, 500, 1000, 2000, and 4000 hertz.

One other type of "instrument" is increasingly finding its way into the professional engineer's tool kit. That is the electronic calculator-computer (Fig. 9-21). In terms of the design portion of a sound system, it changes hours of calculation into fractions of a minute. It also is one of the finest self-teachers a "late starter" in mathematics is likely to encounter. After one of these units has been programmed directly from its own keyboard, the sequences can be recorded on magnetic cards, allowing rapid re-entry of the program as desired (Fig. 9-22). Digitizers are available which allow any

Courtesy Hewlett-Packard

Fig. 9-21. A desk-top computer.

Courtesy Hewlett-Packard

Fig. 9-22. Use of magnetic card to store computer program.

complex curve to be resolved into its original coordinates (Fig. 9-23). These can be used to generate complex data from field measurements, with nontechnical personnel to do the processing. Plotters allow raw coordinate data to be plotted as graphs (Fig. 9-24).

At the very least, any professional in the sound business should acquire one of the scientific-type hand-held calculators. The model shown in Fig. 9-25 possesses an operational stack that allows equations to be entered like the reading of English sentences. The authors suggest considering only those units that have a minimum of four registers plus Lukasiewicz reverse Polish notation operational stacks.

USING INSTRUMENTS EFFECTIVELY

We have now listed the main instruments of use to a professional sound engineer. It is worthwhile to discuss the major everyday use of such instruments and some of the methods of interconnection commonly employed. As you unpack each electronic component destined for a sound system, it should go on the bench and be hooked up to a suitable resistance load. The audio oscillator should be connected to the input, and the oscil-

loscope and voltmeter should be connected to the output (Fig. 9-26). Each loudspeaker, along with its crossover network or its transformer (in the case of 70-volt units), should be tested as shown in Fig. 9-27.

The electronic component is tested for gain, stability, noise, etc., first with the resistive load and then with the actual load. All kinds of problems can be detected by these simple tests: bad connections that occurred during shipment, rubbing voice coils, mislabeled transformers, low output, hum problems, noise problems, distortion problems, etc. Either quick repairs can be made or warranty claims can be made to the manufacturer.

In looking at rooms already in existence, you need to know the volume, surface area, and reverberation time. The high-speed graphic level recorder or reverberation-time meter is used in conjunction with the random-noise generator, tunable voltmeter, and a test-system power amplifier and loudspeaker (Fig. 9-28). You are then able to use your calculator-computer to find a, R, %AL$_{CONS}$, D$_c$, D$_L$, etc.

Fig. 9-29 shows optimum values of RT$_{60}$ at 500 Hz, and Fig. 9-30 shows optimum reverberation times for other frequencies. Note how closely this curve agrees

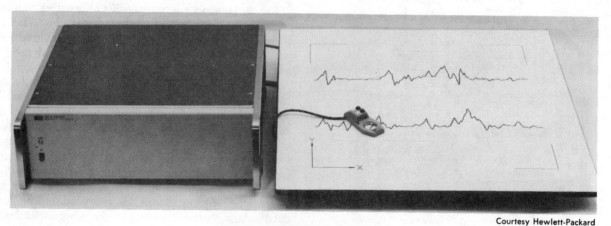

Courtesy Hewlett-Packard

Fig. 9-23. Example of a digitizer.

Fig. 9-24. Plotter for recording equations in the computer in visual form.

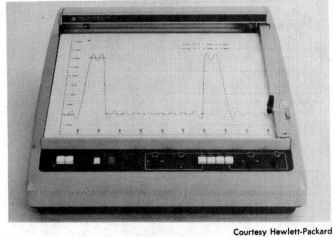

Courtesy Hewlett-Packard

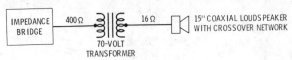

(A) Speaker and transformer.

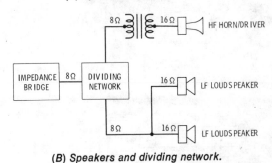

(B) Speakers and dividing network.

Fig. 9-27. Use of impedance bridge to inspect the load to be attached to the power amplifier.

Courtesy Hewlett-Packard

Fig. 9-25. A scientific-type hand-held calculator.

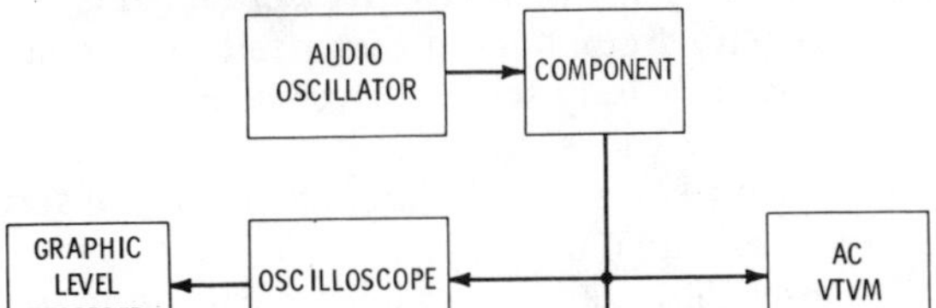

AUDIO OSCILLATOR → COMPONENT

GRAPHIC LEVEL RECORDER ← OSCILLOSCOPE ← AC VTVM

RESISTIVE LOAD

Fig. 9-26. Measurement of frequency response of a component.

with what the $\%AL_{CONS}$ formula reveals about the usable acoustic limits even though the two views were arrived at separately over a fifty-year period.

During system installation, the voltmeter is used to measure levels across the impedances measured by the bridge. The oscilloscope displays instabilities related to misgrounding or incorrect shield terminations. After the system is wired and the electrical levels are set,

then the acoustic equipment is used to set acoustic levels, check coverage, and measure acoustic gain. Fig. 9-31 shows the method of plotting house curves.

If there is trouble with echos or reflections and it becomes necessary to find out which surfaces are causing the problem, or if it is desired to check exactly the phase between a high-frequency and low-frequency loudspeaker, then the tone-burst generator is used (Fig. 9-32).

DESIGNING INSTRUMENTATION INTO THE SOUND SYSTEM FOR EASE OF MAINTENANCE AND OPERATION

Many a well-designed reinforcement and playback sound system gains a bad reputation after a short period of operation because of operator confusion regarding all features of a complex system, or because of inadequate maintenance, again due to the complexity of a large system. Fig. 9-33 illustrates one potential aid in such cases. When the audio oscillator is the source, the oscilloscope and ac vtvm can be switched to the

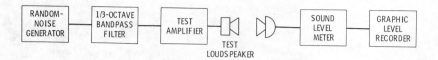

Fig. 9-28. Method of measuring reverberation time.

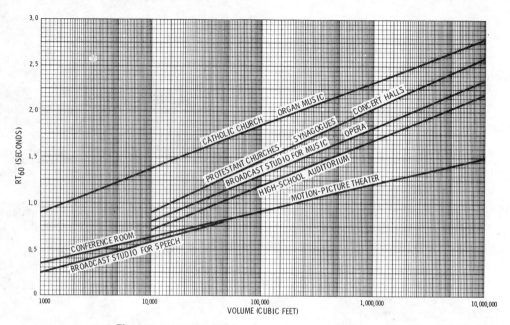

Fig. 9-29. Optimum RT$_{60}$ versus room volume at 500 Hz.

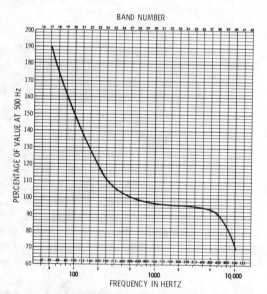

Fig. 9-30. Optimum RT$_{60}$ versus frequency as a percentage of the value of RT$_{60}$ at 500 Hz.

output of each section of the sound system in turn for checking output levels, distortion, hum, noise, etc. By using random noise as a source and by switching the real-time analyzer to each output, it is possible to see the frequency response. A test microphone position is established in the auditorium, and the acoustic response of each part of the loudspeaker array can be observed by switching; thus any faulty drivers are quickly detected by the change in their recorded frequency response or overall level. The operator of such a system can have many alternative components in the rack, to "patch" around those that need maintenance, and he knows precisely which driver needs a new diaphragm, etc. He can even touch up equalization just before a performance and see the results on the screen of his own real-time analyzer.

Other tests these same instruments can be used for include:

1. Measurement of sound absorption using a reverberation chamber.

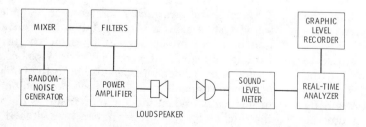

Fig. 9-31. Plotting of house curves.

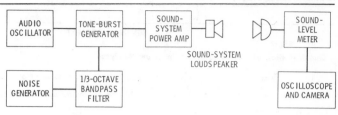

Fig. 9-32. Measurement of delay time of reflected sound and/or ratio of direct to reflected sound.

2. Measurement of transmission loss of materials located between two test rooms.
3. Site selections by making ambient noise-level surveys.
4. Measurement of Q, DI, PWL, etc., of a device.
5. Polar responses.
6. Alignment of tape recorders.

TEST ROOMS AND SPACES

Of great use to the professional sound engineer is a diffuse reverberant space for testing loudspeakers and microphones. This typically can be a garage area, warehouse space, or similar hard-surfaced room where the absorption of the material of each surface is about the same. Lucky indeed are those professionals who recognize the need for and have the means to obtain their own anechoic chamber. Many sound men have constructed semianechoic rooms by using simple frameworks in a quiet area and enclosing the framework with glass-wool material. Such simple spaces can be useful in determining directivity indexes at higher frequencies (above 500 Hz). For those with access to a quiet countryside area, outdoor testing can be very effective. Usually, the device to be tested is buried in the ground and facing upward, or it can be hung from a pole, platform, or other suspension arrangement.

Using the formula

$$D_c = \text{Ref dist} \times 10^{\dfrac{\text{Reference dist dB-SPL} - \text{Reverb dist dB-SPL}}{20}}$$

$$(9\text{-}19)$$

followed by

$$Q = \frac{(D_c)^2}{0.019881R} \qquad (9\text{-}20)$$

we can calculate Q for a loudspeaker in a semireverberant room. In using this simple testing method, the following precautions help make the data more reliable:

1. Make the reverberant dB-SPL measurement at least $2D_c$ from the loudspeaker for a Q that is as large as you reasonably might encounter. For example, if $Q = 30$ and $R = 1864$,

$$2D_c = 2 \times 0.141 \sqrt{30 \times 1864} = 66.7 \text{ ft} \quad (9\text{-}21)$$

2. Pick a reference distance that will allow at least 10-dB difference between the reference-distance dB-SPL and the reverberant-distance dB-SPL (provided you do not have to go closer to the loudspeaker than its largest dimension in so doing).

3. Pick an acoustic environment that is very "live" (in excess of 3 seconds), reasonably symmetrical (equal height, width, and depth dimensions) and with equally reflective surfaces (no single, large surface should have an ā that is greatly different from that of any other large surface).

As an example, we can work out the 2000-Hz Q for a sample horn. The reference distance is 8 feet, the reference dB-SPL value is 75 dB, and the reverberant dB-SPL value is 68.5 dB. Then:

$$D_c = 8 \times 10^{\dfrac{75 - 68.5}{20}} = 16.9 \text{ ft} \qquad (9\text{-}22)$$

$$Q = \frac{(16.9)^2}{0.019881 \times 1864} = 7.71 \qquad (9\text{-}23)$$

Note that for each frequency there is a different R to be used.

One of the main reasons for manufacturers to publish Q data for their loudspeakers is to allow the sound engineers to measure the Q multiplying effects of loudspeaker placement, angle of incidence in covering absorptive areas, and combinations of loudspeakers into common arrays.

When field measurements of Q are made in semireverberant spaces, it becomes important, then, to counteract such multipliers (unless you actually seek to measure them) during the measurement of a loudspeaker with an unknown Q. One way to accomplish this is to measure, using a loudspeaker having a known

Fig. 9-33. A method of including basic test instruments in a sound system to improve maintenance and operation.

SEMINAR FORMAT

Demonstration of Real-Time Audio-Spectrum Analyzer

1. Sine-wave signals into B input contrasted to waveform as seen on a regular oscilloscope.

2. Random-noise generator into B input with the following spectrum displayed:

    A. White Noise

    B. Pink Noise

    C. ANSI Noise

Checking of Amplifier Electrical Response

1. Action of bass and treble controls displayed.

2. High-cut filter response checked.

Testing of Loudspeaker Acoustical Response

Comparison evaluation of up to six different loudspeaker systems.

Equalization

1. On a typical loudspeaker system.

2. Listening comparison in and out of circuit with recorded program material.

3. Feedback mode tuning.

4. Proximity mode tuning.

5. Diaphragmatic action investigation.

Critical Distance (D_c) Discussion

1. Relationship to surface area and average acoustical absorption coefficient.

2. Importance of %AL$_{CONS}$ rule for maximum distance from proposed loudspeaker location to the most distant listener location.

Needed System Acoustical Gain Considerations

1. Potential Acoustical Gain (PAG).

2. Needed Acoustical Gain (NAG).

Geometric Projections

Actual working out of typical examples by participants.

Question and Answer Period

Fig. 9-34. Sample format for an in-house seminar.

Q, the apparent room constant $R = S\bar{a}/(1 - \bar{a})$ for each octave band in which the Q of the unknown loudspeaker will be measured. If, for example, we were to measure a reference-distance dB-SPL of 90 at 5 feet and a reverberant dB-SPL of 80 for the 2000-Hz octave band with a loudspeaker that had a Q of 5 as specified by its manufacturer from anechoic measurements of its polar response, we could then calculate:

$$D_c = 5 \times 10^{\frac{90-80}{20}} = 15.8 \, \text{ft} \qquad (9\text{-}24)$$

$$R = \frac{D_c{}^2}{0.019881 \, Q} = \frac{15.8^2}{0.019881 \times 5} = 2515 \, \text{ft}^2 \qquad (9\text{-}25)$$

This R now includes the result of any Q multipliers that might be present and acting on the calibrated loudspeaker. We can assume that if this R is now used in the measurements of the critical distance for the unknown loudspeaker, we can calculate Q free of multiplier effects, as it remains a constant for each measurement. In measuring the unknown loudspeaker:

$$Q = \frac{D_c{}^2}{0.019881 \, R} \qquad (9\text{-}26)$$

and if $D_c = 30$ for unknown loudspeaker at 2000 Hz, then:

$$Q = \frac{(30)^2}{0.019881 \times 2515} = 18 \qquad (9\text{-}27)$$

This same method can be used to find R multipliers.

EDUCATIONAL USES OF INSTRUMENTATION

Selling truly professional sound systems becomes a matter of educating a succession of people. An architect, engineer, auditorium manager, arena owner, etc., does not have the time or desire to become an expert in sound systems but rather is seeking an expert he can rely on to give him meaningful advice. One way to assure such an individual of what he is to expect from you is to have him with you when you establish the EAD in an existing building. Have him walk away from the quiet talker until he decides he is at the maximum distance. Let him read the SLM that tells you the dB-SPL required at EAD. Walk with him back to the proposed D_2 point and remeasure. Explain that the difference in dB that he sees and hears is the acoustic gain figure you are going to write into the specification and that if he really desires to hear as clearly at D_2 as he did at EAD, then *he* must stand by the fulfillment of that requirement. If you have a real-time analyzer at this same demonstration, show him the changes that the room causes as the distance is increased from the loudspeaker, and when you have the time, demonstrate how an equalizer can correct it. Then point out that any successful bidder should be required to have the same equipment if he is to be sure to obtain the same results. Each specification clause that you can tie down by such educational demonstrations ensures that you will not be bidding against unqualified, unequipped "fast talkers" with a lower price for an inadequate job.

IN-HOUSE SEMINAR

One very competent firm in the midwest has developed a continuing series of informative seminars, aimed at architects, engineers, and customers, that serves the following major purposes:

1. Introduces the attendee to the company, its personnel, and its facilities.
2. Introduces the attendee to the sights and sounds of the basic parameters we work with, such as frequency, amplitude, absorption, reflections, etc.
3. Familiarizes the attendee with the terms used in specifications and their meanings in terms of audible changes in the quality of the desired sound—terms such as Q, D_c, AL_{CONS}, PAG, NAG, EPR, etc.
4. Encourages the attendee to supervise the tests of systems himself because he now knows what to expect and is capable of recognizing right and wrong approaches.

Such sessions should not mix personnel from different firms together, as that makes it more difficult for the attendee to ask questions when a peer from another firm is present. An informal conference-table meeting in a room sufficiently large to allow testing, with a simple sandwich-type meal served as you work, allows everyone to be at ease and in his best learning mood. A very successful format for such meetings is shown in Fig. 9-34.

If you have not conducted such seminars before, you will find that your own personnel will become highly involved and increase their abilities to communicate the vital basics to each nontechnical customer with whom they deal.

SUGGESTED REFERENCES

It is recommended that the serious professional own and use the following references as adjuncts to his use of instrumentation:

Don Davis, *Acoustical Tests and Measurements* (Indianapolis: Howard W. Sams & Co., Inc., 1965).
Leo L. Beranek, *Acoustic Measurements* (New York: John Wiley & Sons, Inc., 1949) (an older book, but full of excellent basic material).
Bernard M. Oliver and John M. Cage, *Electronic Measurements and Instrumentation* (New York: McGraw-Hill Book Co., 1971).
Arnold P. G. Peterson and Ervin E. Gross, Jr., *Handbook of Noise Measurement* (General Radio Co.).

These references proceed from the simplest basic hookup information to the most sophisticated measure-

Table 9-5. Instrument Manufacturers

Company Name and Address	Items Available
General Radio Co. 300 Baker Ave. Concord, Mass. 01742	Acoustic instruments, acoustic books and manuals, newsletters, electronic equipment and components
Brüel and Kjaer Instruments Inc. 5111 West 164th St. Cleveland, Ohio 44142	Acoustic instruments, acoustic books, manuals, newsletters, electronic equipment and components
Hewlett-Packard Co. 1501 Page Mill Road Palo Alto, Calif. 94304	Electronic equipment, components, books, newsletters, computers, calculators
Sennheiser Electronic Corp. 10 West 37th St. New York, N.Y. 10018	Microphones, electronic instruments and components
Communications Company 3490 Noell St. San Diego, Calif. 92110	Reverberation meter, real-time analyzer, pink-noise "plug-in" generator
Tektronix, Inc. P.O. Box 500 Beaverton, Oregon 97005	Oscilloscopes, electronic components, newsletters, audio test sets.

ments likely to be encountered outside of a "state-of-the-art" breakthrough group.

Table 9-5 lists some instrument manufacturers of interest to sound-system engineers, along with some of the items available from these companies.

SUMMARY

An engineer who thoroughly masters the mathematical aspects of the decibel, and who learns all basic measurement methods and the instrumentation necessary to make them, needs only day-to-day experience with actual systems to grow rapidly into a genuine audio expert. Many otherwise very talented technicians miss meaningful breakthroughs, either because they cannot analyze theoretical information in its mathematical form or because they fail to measure a phenomenon encountered by ear while working with a practical system. While the human ear remains the most deli-cate and versatile audio instrumentation available for the detection of an effect, the subsequent measurement of that effect generates the data that allows the human mind to evaluate and discover interrelationships other-wise hidden to the senses. It has been truly stated that "when we can measure something (the problem), we know something about it." All else is hypothetical.

CHAPTER 10

Sample Design Applications

It is now time to consider how to utilize the approaches discussed in this text and apply them to practical jobs. Sometimes the design problems are simple, but the engineering realization of them is both complicated and expensive. At other times, the design approach is laborious and full of complicating detail, but it leads to insights allowing great savings in material, time, and cost.

One great temptation is to assume that "this job looks like the one we did last month, so we won't need to do all that calculation again." This kind of thinking usually precedes "disasters" such as finding a 10-dB difference in power required because of an oversight a full design review would have uncovered, or an "n + 1" that destroys intelligibility in a large convention center where the R could have been properly adjusted had it been realized what effect n + 1 was going to have on the "apparent" Q.

INDIANAPOLIS AND ONTARIO SPEEDWAYS

Here the problem is simple and the answer strains the state of the art. The problem is cars that at 10 feet read 120 dBA (thanks to the turbocharger, they have become quieter during the past few years). This 120 dB occurs at the same distance from the potential listener that would be suitable for a desirable loudspeaker location. Fig. 10-1 shows the sensitivity data published by one manufacturer of high-powered drivers and horns. Fig. 10-2 explains how the information shown in Fig. 10-1 was obtained. The sound pressure level (SPL) is measured 4 feet from the mouth of the specified horn, and on its principal axis. If the SPL is measured with a sound level meter (SLM), it will be convenient to use the "rms slow" position to average the fluctuations. If an anechoic environment is not available, measurements should be made outdoors. The input signal is a band of pink noise generated by filtering the output of a GR 1382A random noise generator through a bandpass filter, properly terminated with 600 ohms and set to pass frequencies ranging from 500 Hz

to 3000 Hz. The input power is defined to be one watt delivered to the nominal driver impedance, i.e., 4 volts rms for 16-ohm drivers, 2.83 volts rms for 8-ohm drivers, and 2 volts rms for 4-ohm drivers.

Data made using noise sources is particularly useful because it is easier to duplicate in the field. It also in-

Driver	Horn	Electrical Input Power	SPL at 30 Ft	SPL at 10 Ft	SPL at 4 Ft
291-16	203B	40 watts	110.0 dB	119.5 dB	127.5 dB
291-16	203B	1 watt	94.0 dB	103.5 dB	111.5 dB
290E	203B	100 watts	110.5 dB	120.0 dB	128.0 dB
290E	203B	1 watt	90.5 dB	100.0 dB	108.0 dB
730C	203B	75 watts	110.5 dB	120.0 dB	128.0 dB
730C	203B	1 watt	92.0 dB	101.5 dB	109.5 dB
291-16	803B	40 watts	109.0 dB	118.5 dB	126.5 dB
291-16	803B	1 watt	92.5 dB	102.0 dB	110.0 dB
290E	803B	100 watts	109.0 dB	118.5 dB	126.5 dB
290E	803B	1 watt	89.0 dB	98.5 dB	106.5 dB
730C	803B	75 watts	109.0 dB	118.5 dB	126.5 dB
730C	803B	1 watt	90.5 dB	100.0 dB	108.0 dB
291-16	1003B	40 watts	106.5 dB	116.0 dB	124.0 dB
291-16	1003B	1 watt	90.5 dB	100.0 dB	108.0 dB
290E	1003B	100 watts	107.0 dB	116.5 dB	124.5 dB
290E	1003B	1 watt	87.0 dB	96.5 dB	104.5 dB
730C	1003B	75 watts	107.0 dB	116.5 dB	124.5 dB
730C	1003B	1 watt	88.5 dB	98.0 dB	106.0 dB
291-16	1203B	40 watts	103.5 dB	113.0 dB	121.5 dB
291-16	1203B	1 watt	88.0 dB	97.5 dB	105.5 dB
290E	1203B	100 watts	104.5 dB	114.0 dB	122.0 dB
290E	1203B	1 watt	84.5 dB	94.0 dB	102.0 dB
730C	1203B	75 watts	104.5 dB	114.0 dB	122.0 dB
730C	1203B	1 watt	86.0 dB	95.5 dB	103.5 dB
291-16	311-60	40 watts	110.0 dB	119.5 dB	127.0 dB
291-16	311-60	1 watt	94.0 dB	103.5 dB	111.5 dB
290E	311-60	100 watts	110.5 dB	120.0 dB	128.0 dB
290E	311-60	1 watt	90.5 dB	100.0 dB	108.0 dB
730C	311-60	75 watts	110.5 dB	120.0 dB	128.0 dB
730C	311-60	1 watt	92.0 dB	101.5 dB	109.5 dB
291-16	311-90	40 watts	106.5 dB	116.0 dB	124.0 dB
291-16	311-90	1 watt	90.5 dB	100.0 dB	108.0 dB
290E	311-90	100 watts	107.0 dB	116.5 dB	124.5 dB
290E	311-90	1 watt	87.0 dB	96.5 dB	104.5 dB
730C	311-90	75 watts	107.0 dB	116.5 dB	124.5 dB
730C	311-90	1 watt	88.5 dB	98.0 dB	106.0 dB

Fig. 10-1. Sample field repeatable sensitivity measurements.

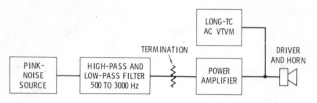

Fig. 10-2. Method of obtaining measurements
shown in Fig. 10-1.

cludes approximately an 11-dB crest factor, thereby supplying the necessary peak factor for program material. In looking at Fig. 10-1, we see that the driver labeled 290E and the horn labeled 203B give a full-power output of 128 dB-SPL at 4 feet with 100 watts. With compression in a communications-type system, 6 dB down could be achieved and it still would be possible to talk over the system with sufficient clarity. Therefore, the maximum program level to be expected at 4 feet is 132 dB-SPL. Four feet in front of the loudspeakers is 14 feet from the track, so the car has a level there of:

$$120 \text{ dB} + 20 \log \frac{10}{14} = 117 \text{ dB-SPL} \qquad (10\text{-}1)$$

Thus, we should have at the listener's ears a 15-dB advantage for the speech signal over the noise of the cars. Remember that outdoors we can easily accept a 10-dB signal-to-noise ratio according to the Peutz articulation equations. If several hundred loudspeakers are required, then the total power requirement equals many thousands of watts. At Ontario (Fig. 10-3) it is 30,000 watts, and at Indianapolis (Fig. 10-4), it is almost 25,000 watts.

Engineering problems included special 200-volt distribution systems requiring 200-volt transformers, custom mountings for the loudspeakers, etc. In one case, $\frac{1}{3}$-kW amplifiers were used, and in the other, 5-kW amplifiers were used.

HIGH POWER INDOORS

Carrying the same problem (high ambient noise levels) indoors, so to speak, we can find ourselves today in very large aircraft hangers and assembly plants, because 747s are indeed very large aircraft. Again, a careful measurement of the problem precedes thoughtful design. Fig. 10-5 shows a test equalization-measuring session in a large aircraft hanger on a major airfield. For the sake of our design example, let us say the hangar is 1000 feet long by 500 feet wide by 100 feet high and has an RT_{60} at 1000 Hz of 9 seconds. Assume the ambient noise level from the motor-generator systems used in the maintenance of the aircraft reaches 75 dBA.

$$V = 1000 \times 500 \times 100 = 50{,}000{,}000 \text{ ft}^3 \quad (10\text{-}2)$$

$$
\begin{aligned}
2(1000 \times 500) &= 1{,}000{,}000 \\
2(500 \times 100) &= 100{,}000 \\
2(1000 \times 100) &= 200{,}000 \\
\hline
S &= \overline{1{,}300{,}000} \text{ ft}^2
\end{aligned}
\qquad (10\text{-}3)
$$

Fig. 10-3. The 30,000 watts of audio amplification for the Ontario Motor Speedway being tested in the contractor's shop.

Fig. 10-4. The lineup of power amplifiers used at the Indianapolis Motor Speedway.

Then

$$\bar{a} = 1 - e^{-\frac{0.049(50{,}000{,}000)}{1{,}300{,}000(9)}} = 0.189 \qquad (10\text{-}4)$$

Because of the high ambient noise level, we would require 100 dBA at the listener's ears in order to have a % AL_{CONS} of 15% (25 dB s/n ratio required). If we were to stack four of the drivers and horns of the type in the previous example, we would have a power-handling capacity of 400 watts and a Q of 18. Using the EPR formula, we would find:

$$EPR = 10^{\frac{(100 + 10) + 27.5 - 115}{10}} = 178 \text{ watts} \qquad (10\text{-}5)$$

The 115-dB figure for loudspeaker sensitivity is due to the stacking of four units, which yields a D_I advan-

Fig. 10-5. A measuring session in a large aircraft hanger.

Fig. 10-6. A highly reverberant church containing an equalized sound system.

tage of approximately 3 dB above a single unit (one-half the vertical angle because of the stacking). Since these units represent about as powerful and directional an array as it is possible to achieve in the present economy, it becomes apparent that an increase of but 3 dB in the ambient noise level would exhaust our capability to provide clear communication in this situation:

$$\text{Max dB-SPL}_{\text{prog}} = 10 \log\left(\frac{400}{10}\right) - 27.5 + 115$$

$$= 103 \text{ dB-SPL} \qquad (10\text{-}6)$$

If, for example, the ambient noise level rose to 90 dBA, an rf pocket-paging unit should be considered, though even then it might not be heard in such an ambient noise, and a unit with a light might be required. The 25-dB s/n ratio can be short when outdoors, provided the maximum levels observed are not continuous. Indoors, it requires strict adherence in almost every case. In very large spaces with high reverberation times, it is often necessary to tandem filter sets to counteract the tremendous effect the room exerts on the driver response.

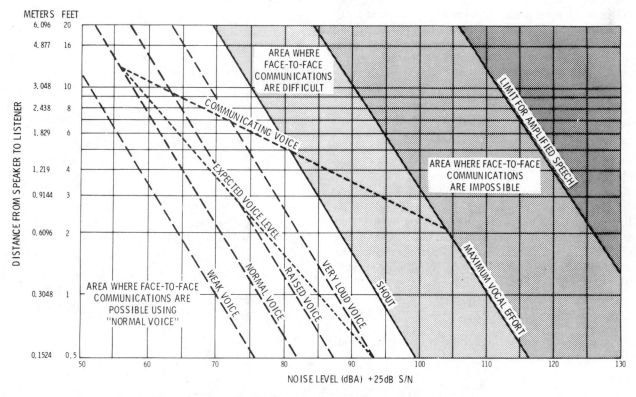

Fig. 10-7. EAD for varying ambient noise levels.

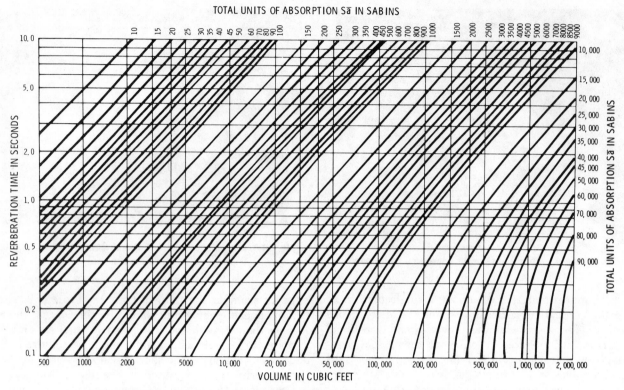

Fig. 10-8. Nomograph for reverberation calculations using the Norris-Eyring equations.

A CHURCH REINFORCEMENT SYSTEM

Here is a typical problem: a rather reverberant catholic church in which the worshipers had not heard the sermon in English even though the priest had been speaking it for a year (Fig. 10-6). The parameters were:

$$V = 500,000 \text{ ft}^3$$
$$S = 42,500 \text{ ft}^2$$
$$RT_{60} = 4.5 \text{ seconds}$$

Let us first approach this design using the charts provided in this text.

If the ambient noise level reads 35 dBA, we can then add 25 dB for our required s/n ratio and look up 60 dBA on the EAD chart (Fig. 10-7). This reveals that we would prefer an EAD of 8 feet. On Fig. 10-8, the intersection of 4.5 seconds and 500,000 ft³ is nearest the Sā = 5000 line, but a bit above it, so we choose Sā = 5100. Dividing, we find:

$$\bar{a} = \frac{S\bar{a}}{S} = \frac{5100}{42,500} = 0.12 \qquad (10\text{-}7)$$

At this point, we know the Sabins in the space equal 5100, and we can calculate:

$$R = \frac{S\bar{a}}{1 - \bar{a}} = \frac{5100}{1 - 0.12} = 5795 \qquad (10\text{-}8)$$

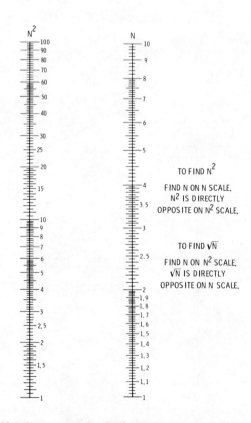

TO FIND N^2

FIND N ON N SCALE.
N^2 IS DIRECTLY
OPPOSITE ON N^2 SCALE.

TO FIND $\sqrt{N}$

FIND N ON N^2 SCALE.
$\sqrt{N}$ IS DIRECTLY
OPPOSITE ON N SCALE.

Fig. 10-9. Nomograph for finding the square root of a number.

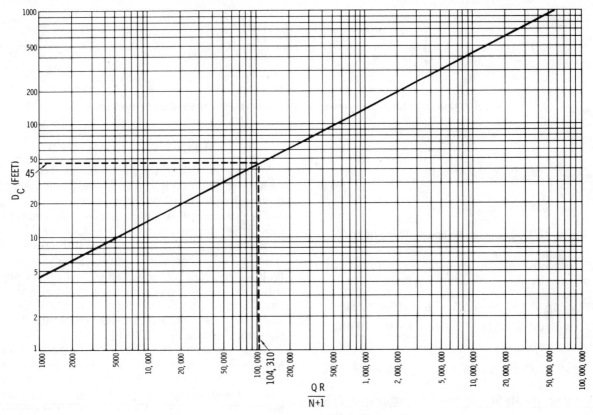

Fig. 10-10. Nomograph for critical distance D_c.

Having made a choice of a desirable D_2 distance, for example 100 feet, we can solve for the minimum Q that would allow an AL_{CONS} of 15%:

$$\text{Min Q} = \frac{641.81 \ (D_2)^2 (RT_{60})^2}{15V}$$

$$= \frac{641.81 \ (10,000) \ (20.25)}{15(500,000)} = 17.33$$

$$(10\text{-}9)$$

We again select from what is available in loudspeakers and pick Q = 18. If we wanted to find the new % AL_{CONS}, we would use:

$$\% \ AL_{CONS} = \frac{641.81 \ (D_2)^2 \ (RT_{60})^2}{VQ}$$

$$= \frac{641.81 \ (10,000) \ (20.25)}{500,000(18)} = 14.44\%$$

$$(10\text{-}10)$$

We can further calculate the maximum RT_{60} allowable with this room to still have an $AL_{CONS} = 15\%$ (Fig. 10-9):

$$\text{Max RT}_{60} = \sqrt{\frac{15VQ}{641.81 \ (D_2)^2}}$$

$$= \sqrt{\frac{15(500,000) \ 18}{641.81 \ (10,000)}} = \sqrt{21} = 4.58$$

$$(10\text{-}11)$$

With the aid of Fig. 10-10, we can calculate D_c:

$$D_c = 0.141 \ \sqrt{QR}$$

$$= 0.141 \ \sqrt{104310} = 45 \ \text{ft} \qquad (10\text{-}12)$$

and

$$D_L = 3.16 \ D_c = 142.2 \ \text{ft} \qquad (10\text{-}13)$$

We now need to convert the distances into their equivalent attenuations expressed in decibels. You will see that while the computer uses the long form, it is simpler for us to use the approximation that the inverse square law works until we reach D_c and that no further attenuation exists beyond D_c. To aid us, we can use the conversion nomograph in Fig. 10-11. In this case, we will use no decibel number greater than 33 dB because that is opposite the D_c distance of 45 ft. We can write:

Distance	Attenuation
EAD 8 ft	18 dB
D_1 35 ft	31 dB
D_2 100 ft	33 dB

and using the nomograph in Fig. 10-12 we can write:

$$\text{NOM} = 1; \quad dB = 0$$

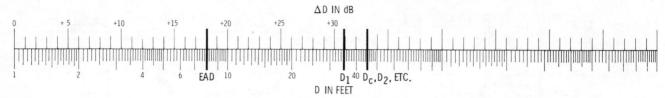

Fig. 10-11. Nomograph for converting distance into relative attenuation in decibels.

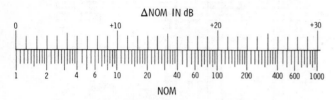

Fig. 10-12. A nomograph for finding 10 log NOM.

Using our acoustical-gain formula, we can then write it to solve for D_s:

$$\Delta D_s = \Delta EAD + \Delta D_1 - \Delta D_2 - 6 - 10 \log NOM$$
$$= 18\,dB + 31\,dB - 33\,dB - 6 - 0 = 10\,dB$$

$$(10\text{-}14)$$

Looking at 10 dB on the conversion nomograph (Fig. 10-11), we find that D_s can equal just over 3 feet. Suppose we wish 80 dB-SPL at the farthest listener (D_2) and that we have chosen a loudspeaker system having a sensitivity figure of 99 dB-SPL at 4 feet with 1 watt of electrical input. We can then write:

$$EPR = (dB\text{-}SPL_{max} + 10) + (\Delta D_2 - \Delta 4') - (L\,Sens)$$
$$= (80 + 10) + (33 - 12) - 99 = 12\,dB \quad (10\text{-}15)$$

Looking at Fig. 10-13, we can see that 12 dB = 15 watts.

For the maximum dB-SPL$_{prog}$ we can use the formula:

$$dB\text{-}SPL_{prog} = (Watts\ avail\ re\ 1\ watt)$$
$$- (\Delta D_2 - \Delta 4') - 10\,dB + (L\,sens)$$
$$= 14\,dB - (33 - 12) - 10\,dB + 99$$
$$= 82\,dB\text{-}SPL$$

$$(10\text{-}16)$$

This simplified method has seen wide use by approximately 200 sound firms over the past several years on literally thousands of jobs and is considered reliable and accurate.

USING THE COMPUTER

We can now go through this exact design using a computer. The example calculations shown here were obtained with an HP 9820 computer.

For this example, suppose that, by measurement, you found the internal volume (V) and the total boundary surface area (S). You then measured the reverberation time (RT_{60}) either with a graphic level recorder, with an RT_{60} meter, or by ear and stopwatch. The computer, using the Norris-Eyring equation, calculates the average absorption coefficient ($\bar{a}$) plus the total absorption units in Sabins ($S\bar{a}$) and the room constant (R). These results are shown in Fig. 10-14.

Next, you enter the desired distance between the loudspeaker location and the most remotely located listener (D_2), and the computer, using the data already stored, calculates the minimum Q that will allow an AL_{CONS} of 15%. You select the Q available, and the computer calculates the new AL_{CONS} in percent and continues on to show the maximum RT_{60} that will allow an AL_{CONS} of 15% in that room using that Q. Critical distance (D_c) and the limiting distance (D_L) are then calculated. The resulting printout is shown in Fig. 10-15.

The computer now requires two of the following three parameters: EAD, D_1, or D_s. You can choose the required EAD from the chart; D_1 is chosen by available location in this case; an operator can run the system, ensuring an NOM of 1. Therefore, the computer tells you that the priest can stand 2½ feet away from the microphone and create an 8-foot EAD at 100 feet (Fig. 10-16).

The computer is now ready to calculate the basic electrical power required (EPR) formulas in which you supply the maximum program level in dB-SPL desired at the D_2 listener's ears (Fig. 10-17). You also supply the loudspeaker sensitivity at 4 feet with 1-watt input. The computer calculates the EPR to deliver the required SPL at the specific distance. You then supply

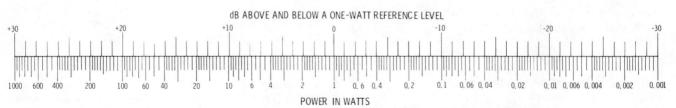

Fig. 10-13. Nomograph for converting power to decibels with a reference level of 1 watt.

```
SYN-AUD-CON
SOUND SYSTEM
DESIGN PROGRAM

V IN CU.FT.=
        50000.000
S IN SQ.FT.=
        42500.000
ABS.COEF.=
        0.000
RT60 IN SECS.=
        4.500
ABS.COEF.=
        .120
SABINS IN SQ.FT.
        5110.142
R IN SQ.FT.=
        5808.554
```

Fig. 10-14. Computer printout of absorption coefficient, absorption, and room constant.

```
D2 IN FT.=
        100.000
MIN.Q FOR
AL-CONS=15%
BECOMES
        17.329
Q SELECTED=
        18.000
SELECTED Q
GIVES AN
AL-CONS% OF
        14.441
WITH SELECTED
Q & D2
MAX.RT60 IN SEC
FOR AL-CONS=15%
BECOMES
        4.586
DC IN FT.=
        45.592
DL IN FT.=
        144.071
```

Fig. 10-15. Computer printout of additional quantities.

the total electrical power available, and the computer calculates the maximum possible program level at D_2 (remember, program level is peak power minus 10 dB). A 25-watt amplifier will do the job. The computer, using the longer attenuation formulas, has produced the more accurate design, but the closeness of agreement between it and the manual method is substantial. Of course, the computer is much faster (takes about 1 minute per design after data is gathered).

```
EAD IN FT.=
        8.000
D1 IN FT.=
        35.000
DS IN FT.=
        0.000
NOM=
        1.000
MAX.DS IN FT.=
        2.647
```

Fig. 10-16. Computer printout of maximum D_s.

```
MAX.SPL AT D2=
        80.000
(L)SENS. =
        99.000
E.P.R.IN WATTS=
        13.652
WATTS AVAIL.=
        25.000
MAX.PROG.LEVEL
IN DB-SPL=
        82.627
```

Fig. 10-17. Printout of computer EPR calculations.

Newer programs under study use $-S \ln(1 - \bar{a})$ in place of R for even greater theoretical occuracy.

A CONFERENCE SYSTEM

Now that you have seen the general application of the principles we have been discussing and one of the computer formats for them, we can apply the same technique to a very complex type of system design—the conference room. Fig. 10-18 shows an exceptionally large system of this type. This 35-microphone system uses approximately 46 loudspeakers. Fig. 10-19 illustrates a semiflush-mount microphone with its special shock mounting, the microphone mute for telephone calls, and the microphone switch.

Fig. 10-20 shows one commercial solution to obtaining the advantages of flush mounting. The Shure Models S53P and S55P stands are designed specifically for "distant pickup" microphone situations, where the distance from source to microphone is greater than the height of the source from the floor. When a conventional microphone stand is used as in Fig. 10-20B, reflections from the floor arrive out of phase at the microphone and cancel out certain groups of tones. If the microphone is placed on the floor, as in Fig. 10-20C, these cancellations cannot occur, and the tonal balance is similar to a close microphone technique. To be effective, this stand must support the microphone as close to the floor as possible without touching (approximately ⅛ inch). It must also provide excellent shock isolation so that floor vibrations are not introduced into the microphone.

Fig. 10-18. Example of a large conference room.

Fig. 10-19. Microphone can be taken from mounting and close-talked when two conference rooms are interconnected.

Fig. 10-21 shows a control system for the chairman of the conference. One excellent design idea in systems of this type is to cross-connect microphones to loudspeakers in order to increase D_1. Naturally, the NOM should be kept as low as possible, and either an automatic mixing device or a block-out that prevents more than two open microphones from operating at one time is necessary. Suppose, for example, we have the following set of parameters: $V = 15,000$ ft³; $S = 4,700$ ft²; $RT_{60} = 0.25$ second. We could work with the computer to acquire the data in Fig. 10-22.

Note the NOM of 2 in Fig. 10-22. The use of a device like the Shure Voicegate (Fig. 10-23) and a priority system could keep the NOM this low.

There is never any margin for error in conference systems, and at their very best they require a very careful integration of the room design with the sound system. When two conference rooms are interconnected via common carrier, much attention must be paid to the termination equipment. Fig. 10-24 shows the interconnection of conference rooms via four-wire to four-wire terminating sets or via two-wire to two-wire terminating sets. Four-wire to two-wire connections may also be used. Avoid two-wire interconnections whenever possible, but when you must use them, be sure they are dedicated circuits (your use only). When two-wire circuits are used, the hybrid transformers will determine the overall gain, because even hybrids with carefully adjusted balance networks typically have 10-15 dB transhybrid losses.

ROOM CONSIDERATIONS IN CONFERENCE SYSTEMS

Hard-surfaced tables reflect sound usefully back to the hearers. So do overhead reflector panels above the middle of the table. Walls that tilt very slightly inward with increasing height can help. End walls should be "deadened," as should the parts of the ceiling not used for reflection. Floors should be carpeted to reduce the

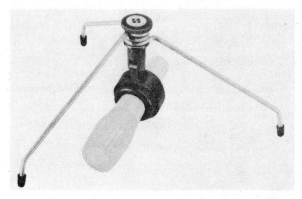

Courtesy Shure Brothers Inc.

(A) Microphone stand.

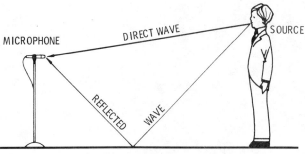

(B) Microphone on conventional stand.

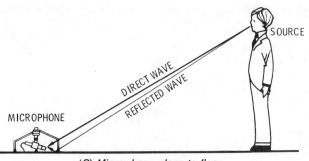

(C) Microphone close to floor.

Fig. 10-20. Microphone operation near floor.

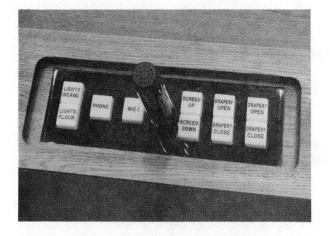

Fig. 10-21. Chairman's microphone position.

noise of shuffling feet, chairs being moved, etc. As mentioned earlier, the room constant should allow the critical distance to be approximately equal to the maximum D_1 distance you can conveniently obtain. The use of subminiature loudspeakers (Fig. 10-25) can often reduce both D_s and D_2, since these devices can be both microphone and loudspeaker through the use of a voice switch.

ARENA SYSTEMS

Large arenas require very careful design analysis because the bidding for them is usually very competitive, and any mistakes turn the job into a "perpetual upkeep" assignment for the contractor involved. Arrays are often of enormous size (many tons), reverberation times are high, and power requirements are astronomical.

Systems of the type shown in Fig. 10-26 can be fascinating projects; volumes of 9,000,000 ft³ are encountered with boundary surface areas of 300,000 ft² and reverberation times of 3.5 seconds when the arena is full of people. Here again, let us use the computer to see the nature and value of the problems that we can encounter. It should be stressed that while we illustrate here a finally accepted program, the real usefulness of the computer is not the nice presentation of the finished calculation but the ability to have made dozens of such sets in the full examination of the potential problems.

The results for a large arena are shown in Fig. 10-27. Note that in these very large buildings if you can get a 25-dB s/n ratio, a very low Q can be used. Usually the s/n ratio limits the % AL_{CONS} and not the reverberation time. The total lack of acoustical control in the space can't be tolerated, but greater margins are allowable so long as $n + 1$ is observed and the change in "apparent" D_c is noted. The EAD must be low to ensure a 25-dB s/n ratio (naturally, when the crowd screams, the % AL_{CONS} suffers). Fortunately, announcers must talk close to the microphone to escape noise as well. The indicated EPR is per area of coverage. With the arena separated into eight zones, the total EPR becomes 1416 watts. With large woofer bins at lower sensitivities than the horns, a 6-dB margin is conservative, for a total of 5664 watts.

In really huge arenas, the interplay between D_2, coverage, $n + 1$, etc., leads to very large arrays distributed and on time delay. Fig. 10-28 shows an example of a very large semidistributed system. Digital time delay on a ring of large loudspeakers allowed a reduction in D_2 for many listeners. (Note the large central cluster in the center of the dome.)

DESIGNING A "ROCK" MUSIC SYSTEM

One factor that is fundamental to the successful design of a "rock" music system is the ability of that system to deliver sound *to the performer's location* with a

191

```
SYN-AUD-CON
SOUND SYSTEM
DESIGN PROGRAM


V IN CU.FT.=
        15000.000
S IN SQ.FT.=
         4700.000
ABS.COEF.=
            0.000
RT60 IN SECS.=
             .250
ABS.COEF.=
             .465
SABINS IN SQ.FT.
         2185.609
R IN SQ.FT.=
         4085.428
D2 IN FT.=
           45.000
RT60<1.5 SECS.
AL-CONS<15%
Q SELECTED=
            3.000

DC IN FT.=
           15.610
DL IN FT.=
           49.327
EAD IN FT.=
            8.000
D1 IN FT.=
           15.000
DS IN FT.=
            0.000
NOM=
            2.000
MAX.DS IN FT.=
            1.863
MAX.SPL AT D2=
           80.000
(L)SENS. =
           96.000
E.P.R.IN WATTS=
            3.641
WATTS AVAIL.=
            8.000
MAX.PROG.LEVEL
IN DB-SPL=
           83.419
```

← Note that the computer detects that RT_{60} is below 1.5 seconds and % AL_{CONS} is all right. N+1 not a factor because of low RT_{60}.

← D_1 must be made to take advantage of this.
Room must be "deadened" until D_C = a desirable D_1 distance.

← D_1 does match D_C (which is probably even greater and uses the third attenuation formula).

← 2 feet is adequate if talkers face microphones.

← This is watts per speaker (46 x 8 = 368 watts total).

Fig. 10-22. Computer data for conference room.

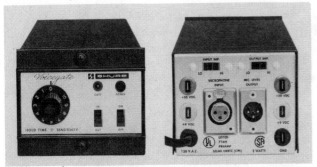

Courtesy Shure Brothers Inc.

Fig. 10-23. Device that automatically reduces microphone gain 16 dB in absence of speech input.

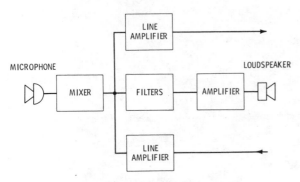

(A) Four-wire dedicated interconnection.

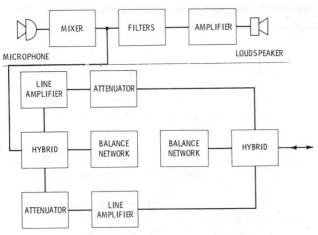

(B) Two-wire dedicated interconnection.

Fig. 10-24. Interconnection of conference rooms.

frequency and dynamic range stimulating to the performer and precisely informative so that he can judge his performance and make "real-time" corrections. In the past, extensive use has been made of stage monitors by knowledgeable sound engineers who learned to accept that coverage of the performer had precedence over coverage of the audience. This is not an unreasonable requirement when it is realized that the audience attends the concert to witness an artistic experience. Perfect acoustic coverage of the audience, if the performance is poor, is unsatisfactory to the audience,

Courtesy Knowles Electronics, Inc.

Fig. 10-25. Subminiature loudspeakers suitable for "in-chair," "pew-back," or "shirt-collar" mounting.

whereas quite uneven acoustic coverage will be tolerated at a concert where the performers have really "turned on" and "done their thing," stimulated by a much sought after, seldom found, combination of the right music, a receptive audience, and a sound that bathes them physically as well as aurally.

During the early 70s, this led to a duality of sound systems. One was the house system, and the other was the monitor system. The groups attempting to use the same equipment for both requirements usually ended up with a split array on each side of the stage, relying on the side lobes of the main array to help the performer hear and feel the bass while using floor monitors to fill in the rest.

The desire to feel as well as hear led to quite high midrange sound levels in order to bring the bass up to the desired level. Loudspeakers with high Q gave higher output on-axis but did not sound musical to the performer. Equalization applied to the house system often ensured that the sound system drew all the power at the low-frequency end of the spectrum and often overdrove the conventional woofers adapted to this service.

A New Engineering Approach to Musical Problems

The rock-system audio engineer has to, first, have the artistic desire and, second, possess the creative ability to translate such desires into realizable hardware. Alembic, Inc. in San Francisco has approached this seemingly contradictory set of artistic desires versus acoustic limitations and found the following answers:

1. Recognizing that the task of the sound system is no longer simply to amplify the artist but to become an extension of the artist's instrument, be it wind, string, vocal, etc., Alembic worked out the necessary direct pickup of the instrument by installing magnetic pickups directly in the instruments and by using instrumentation-type microphones in a differential connection for the vocal effects, thus connecting the artists directly to the

Fig. 10-26. A massive arena array capable of handling several thousand watts of audio power.

electronics of the proposed system. To vary gain, the dc polarizing voltage of the microphones is varied, changing the microphone sensitivity.

Special completely nonacoustical guitars were built. All acoustic output from the guitar is suppressed, and thus it is less subject to feedback as well. For the piano, a capacitive pickup with polarized plates above the strings is used.

2. Having effectively eliminated feedback by reducing D_s to the irreducible minimum, Alembic was then able to consider the ideal loudspeaker system. Such a system would:

A. Bathe the performer in a physical and aural environment that he could control emotionally and physically with his musical instrument. (When you have a mixer in the audience, the performer loses control of his expression.)

B. Allow each performer to maximize his acoustic needs in terms of his individual performance as well as ensure that he is a coordinated part of the ensemble as a whole.

C. Allow the audience to hear the sound system, not as a reinforcement system but as a musical instrument in its own right. True stereo geometry can be achieved visually and aurally for all listeners for both the sound source and the performer.

D. Provide the necessary hardware to support tomorrow's creative experimentation with computer-controlled synthesizers.

E. Eliminate intermodulation between instruments by the use of separate systems.

The result is shown in Fig. 10-29. Each performer has parts of the array dedicated to his requirements, but with all the parts useful and coordinated in much the same way a classic pipe organ is utilized. Note the reverse application of directivity techniques. Because this is a musical use, high Q values for high frequencies are avoided as carefully as possible, but low and middle frequencies are assisted materially by the use of line radiators.

All parts of the array are separately amplified, with equalization applied not for acoustic gain, but for tonal requirements. Obviously this system is a gigantic monitor system. It consists of 480 speakers integrated into its own 40,000 pound stage and sound tower. The stage measures 56 feet wide by 42 feet deep, is erected 7 feet above the floor level, and is backed by a sound wall 38 feet in the air. It can be assembled for a performance in 15 hours. This $350,000 sound system not only solves the stage-monitor problem, but it also gives substantially better sound at reasonable levels in the audience area. A typical audience-area level is 110 dBA, and the

```
SYN-AUD-CON
SOUND SYSTEM
DESIGN PROGRAM


V IN CU.FT.=
      9000000.000
S IN SQ.FT.=
      300000.000
ABS.COEF.=
      0.000
RT60 IN SECS.=
      3.500
ABS.COEF.=
      .343
SABINS IN SQ.FT.
      102885.954
R IN SQ.FT.=
      156588.467
D2 IN FT.=
      145.000
MIN.Q FOR
AL-CONS=15%
BECOMES
      1.224       For a single-speaker array
Q SELECTED=
      5.000       Because N+1 ≅ 4
SELECTED Q
GIVES AN
AL-CONS% OF
      3.673       Or with N+1 = 4   AL CONS = 15%
WITH SELECTED
Q & D2
MAX.RT60 IN SEC
FOR AL-CONS=15%
BECOMES
      7.073       For a single speaker only
DC IN FT.=
      124.762     Or where N+1 = 4, D_C = 62.38 feet
DL IN FT.=
      394.249     Or where N+1 = 4, D_L = 197.12 feet
EAD IN FT.=
      2.000
D1 IN FT.=
      65.000
DS IN FT.=
      0.000
NOM=
      1.000
MAX.DS IN FT.=
      .611
MAX.SPL AT D2=
      100.000
(L)SENS. =
      115.000
E.P.R.IN WATTS=
      177.922
WATTS AVAIL.=
      400.000
MAX.PROG.LEVEL
IN DB-SPL=
      103.540
```

Fig. 10-27. Printout of computation results for a large arena.

system feels far more powerful than the midrange screamers putting out 120 to 125 dBA under the same conditions. The bass has very low distortion and is quite powerful. Auditorium managers are impressed with the fact that it can "free up" as many as 400 paying seats in the typical arena as compared with more conventional systems. Such systems require approximately 10,000 watts of audio power.

Some of the engineering problems to be considered are:

1. Determining the acoustic power each performer individually requires, what directivity factor is best at which frequencies, and what role the array design should play in tonal balance versus the ability to equalize.
2. What problems will develop when the ensemble is used in a typical environment (excessively live, reflective, and noisy)?
3. The physical housing, transportation, and maintenance of so much equipment. What standardizations and redundancies can be achieved to assist in the logistical task?

Interesting theoretical questions present themselves: Is this array "1" or "n + 1," and if it is "n + 1," what is "1"? (For a full discussion of "n + 1," see Chapter 4.)

In speech, we have %AL_{CONS} as a guide to our desired design parameters. In music, what are the limiting parameters? Is Dan Dugan's concept of "fidelity" perhaps a beginning point for further theorizing on this subject? This large array is faithful to the musical concept of a pipe organ, and pipe organs do perform well in massive environments, especially when the music allows and the artists adapt their performance to the massive environment.

Summary

This example of sound-system design has been presented without a computer tape. This is not because such techniques are not applicable to the parts of the sound system, but because the philosophical approach must come first in all departures from what is considered conventional, and then the application of the conventional techniques can be fruitfully applied to the individual portions of the overall system.

COMMENTS AND OBSERVATIONS

Following the format presented here will organize your design approach. Working with the architect and his engineer at the drawing-board stage will reveal if they know what RT_{60} is expected or how many sabins are planned into the room. When they haven't thought about it, both of you had best beware. If you bid someone else's design for the job, include tactful disclaimers of any responsibility for the performance, and install according to plans and specifications. When they do listen to you, make sure that they attend the proof-of-

Fig. 10-28. Sound system in Houston Astrodome.

performance checks and see and hear that you were correct.

It is not difficult to see that most playback systems are a matter of selecting Q to cover the listening area at a ratio of direct-to-reflected sound that is desirable and of calculating the needed power to achieve the desired dynamic range. Playback in large spaces follows the same %AL$_{CONS}$ rules as reinforcement systems.

Failure to achieve a 25-dB s/n ratio reduces the clarity of the system in terms of speech.

The basic physical measurement of the space, either from the drawing board or at the site, is fundamental to every job. Experience indicates that you need at least a half dozen jobs in which you fully use this method before you give it your full confidence and enthusiasm.

AN OVERALL GUIDELINE

The following "flow chart" gives a logical path through the myriad choices of systems for gathering and analyzing the necessary data.

Sound System Design Worksheet

Physical Measurements

In irregularly shaped rooms, record largest dimension in each category.

1. Length of room = _____ ft or m

2. Width of room = _____ ft or m

3. Height of room = _____ ft or m

4. Internal volume = _____ ft³ or m³

5. Boundary surface area = _____ ft² or m² (Use environmental analysis worksheet, Chart 10-1.)

6. Reverberation time = _____ seconds   Measured? _____

   (If material is not evenly distributed, use Fitzroy.)   Calculated? _____

   If calculated, indicate which equation was used.

   Sabine _____   Norris-Eyring _____   Room Constant _____

   $$RT_{60} = \frac{0.049V}{S\bar{a}}$$ $$RT_{60} = \frac{0.049V}{-S\ln(1-\bar{a})}$$ $$RT_{60} = \frac{0.049V}{R}$$

   (Metric constant = 0.161)

7. Average absorption coefficient = _____

   Indicate which equation was used:

   Sabine _____   Norris-Eyring _____   Room Constant _____

   $$\bar{a} = \frac{0.049V}{S \cdot RT_{60}}$$ $$\bar{a} = 1 - e^{-\frac{0.049V}{S \cdot RT_{60}}}$$ $$\bar{a} = \frac{1}{1 + \dfrac{S \cdot RT_{60}}{0.049V}} = \frac{R}{R+S}$$

   (Metric constant = 0.161)

8. D_2 = _____ ft or m   (n + 1) = _____ (If not known, use 1.)

9. Minimum Q that allows 15%AL_{CONS} = _____

   $$\text{Min } Q = \frac{641.81(D_2)^2(RT_{60})^2(n+1)}{15V}$$

   (Metric constant = 200)

   Is the Q value a Realizable one?   Yes _____   Go to 10.

                                             No _____   Go to 11.

10. What angles of coverage are required?   Horiz _____°
                                                   Vert _____°

    Will Q value allow coverage?   Yes _____   Go to 13.

                                          No _____   Go to 11.

    $$Q_{GEOM} = \frac{180}{\arcsin\left[\sin\left(\dfrac{horiz}{2}\right) \times \sin\left(\dfrac{vert}{2}\right)\right]}$$

11. Maximum D_2 an allowable Q value will permit = _____ ft or m
    If answer to 9 and 10 is yes, use value at step 8. Otherwise, calculate new maximum D_2; if new D_2 is not useable, go to step 12.

    $$\text{Max } D_2 \text{ that allows an } AL_{CONS} \text{ of } 15\% = \sqrt{\frac{15VQ}{641.81(RT_{60})^2(n+1)}}$$

    Metric constant = 200

12. Number of Sabins needed to allow the use of the available Q and D_2 = _____ ft² or m²
    (Use Sabine S$\bar{a}$)
    Metric S$\bar{a}$ in m², English S$\bar{a}$ in ft²

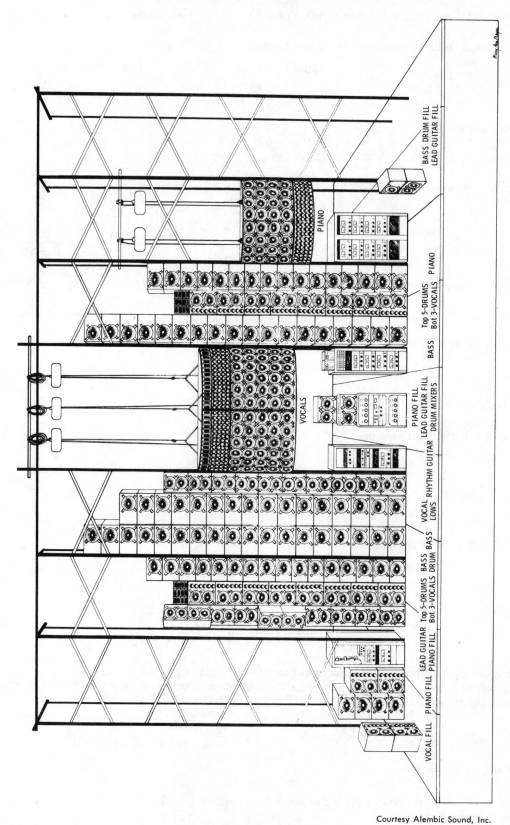

Courtesy Alembic Sound, Inc.

Fig. 10-29. Example of a rock music system.

Chart 10-1. Environmental Analysis

Description of Surface Area and Surface Material	$S =$ Length $\times$ Width of Material $=$ Surface Area	$\times$ $\rightarrow$	a of Material $=$	$=$ $\rightarrow$	Sa Sabins	$=$ $\leftarrow$	Sabins per Object or Unit Length	$\times$ $\leftarrow$	Description of Objects Rated in Sabins and Number of Objects
1		$\times$		$=$		$\leftarrow$		$\times$	1
2		$\times$		$=$		$\leftarrow$		$\times$	2
3		$\times$		$=$		$\leftarrow$		$\times$	3
4		$\times$		$=$		$\leftarrow$		$\times$	4
5		$\times$		$=$		$\leftarrow$		$\times$	5
6		$\times$		$=$		$\leftarrow$		$\times$	6
7		$\times$		$=$		$\leftarrow$		$\times$	7
8		$\times$		$=$		$\leftarrow$		$\times$	8
9		$\times$		$=$		$\leftarrow$		$\times$	9
10		$\times$		$=$		$\leftarrow$		$\times$	10
11		$\times$		$=$		$\leftarrow$		$\times$	11
12		$\times$		$=$		$\leftarrow$		$\times$	12
13		$\times$		$=$		$\leftarrow$		$\times$	13
14		$\times$		$=$		$\leftarrow$		$\times$	14
15		$\times$		$=$		$\leftarrow$		$\times$	15
16		$\times$		$=$		$\leftarrow$		$\times$	16
17		$\times$		$=$		$\leftarrow$		$\times$	17
18		$\times$		$=$		$\leftarrow$		$\times$	18
19		$\times$		$=$		$\leftarrow$		$\times$	19
20		$\times$		$=$		$\leftarrow$		$\times$	20
21		$\times$		$=$		$\leftarrow$		$\times$	21
22		$\times$		$=$		$\leftarrow$		$\times$	22
23		$\times$		$=$		$\leftarrow$		$\times$	23
24		$\times$		$=$		$\leftarrow$		$\times$	24

Total S $=$

Total Sa $=$

$$\bar{a} = \frac{\text{Total Sa}}{\text{Total S}}$$

"a" values used (check one):

Sabine _____

$$a = \frac{0.049V}{S \cdot RT_{60}}$$

Norris-Eyring _____

$$a = 1 - e^{-\frac{0.049V}{S \cdot RT_{60}}}$$

Room Constant _____

$$a = \frac{1}{1 + \dfrac{S \cdot RT_{60}}{0.049V}}$$

or

$$a = \frac{R}{R + S}$$

$$\text{Min Sabine S}\bar{a} \text{ for } 15\% \text{ AL}_{\text{CONS}} = \frac{1.24D_2V}{\sqrt{15VQ}}$$

Use English dimensions.

Select the appropriate $\bar{a}$ conversion equation:

$$\bar{a}_S = \frac{0.049V}{S\bar{a}_S} \quad \bar{a}_S = -\ln(1 - \bar{a}_{NE}) \quad \bar{a}_S = \frac{-\bar{a}_R}{(\bar{a}_R - 1)}$$

$$\text{Min metric Sabine S}\bar{a} \text{ for } 15\% \text{ AL}_{\text{CONS}} = \frac{2.28D_2V}{\sqrt{15VQ}}$$

13. Final $D_2 =$ _____ ft or m $\Delta D_2 =$ _____ dB*
    $D_2 =$ what multiple of D_c? _____ D_c
    *See step 25.

14. $(n + 1) =$ _____
    Does this detrimentally affect the D_c multiple in relation to maximum D_2?

    Yes _____   Go to 13.
    No _____   Go to 15.

15. Is a calculatable M present? $M =$ _____

$$M = \frac{1 - \bar{a}}{1 - a_c}$$

where a_c is the absorption coefficient of the audience area.
(Only when the Q of the sound source is nearly ideal and almost totally covering only the audience should M be calculated.)

16. Critical distance = _____ ft or m
    Indicate which equation was used:

    Sabine _____   Norris-Eyring _____   Room Constant _____

$$*D_c = 0.141 \sqrt{\frac{QS\bar{a}M}{(n + 1)}} \qquad *D_c = 0.141 \sqrt{\frac{Q[-S \ln(1 - \bar{a})]M}{(n + 1)}} \qquad *D_c = 0.141 \sqrt{\frac{QRM}{(n + 1)}}$$

$$*D_c = 0.03121 \sqrt{\frac{QVM}{RT_{60}(n + 1)}}$$
    *See step 25.

17. Ambient noise level = _____ dBA
    Is ambient noise in a room with an $RT_{60} \geqq 1.6$ seconds?

    Yes _____   Go to 19.
    No _____   Go to 18.

18. Signal-to-noise ratio required for 15 % $AL_{CONS} =$ _____ dB

0.25 s = 6 dB	0.75 s = 15 dB	1.5 s = 24 dB
0.5 s = 10 dB	1.0 s = 18 dB	>1.6 s = 25 dB

19. Minimum signal level at EAD = _____ dBA
    (Ambient noise + required s/n = minimum signal level)

20. $D_8 =$ _____ ft or m $\Delta D_8 =$ _____ dB*

21. EAD = _____ ft or m ΔEAD = _____ dB*
    Is EAD $\geqq D_c$?   Yes _____   (Sound system not required for amplification, may be needed to help articulation)
                  No _____
    If no, is EAD $\geqq 2D_8$?   Yes _____ (Single source allowed)
                       No _____ (Single source not allowed)
    *See step 25.

22. $D_1 =$ _____ ft or m $\Delta D_1 =$ _____ dB*
    Is $D_1 \geqq D_c < 45$ ft?   Yes _____   Go to 23.
                    No _____   Explain why not.
    If, no have you considered maximum possible gain, time delay, etc.?

    _____
    _____
    _____

23. $\Delta 4$ ft = _____ dB

24. NOM = _____   10 log NOM = _____ dB*

    * See step 25.

25. At this point in the design, solve for the unknown parameter using the following equations:

    $\Delta D_x \equiv (f)D_x$; -10 log and $-\Delta D_x$ mean change sign.

    $\Delta D_x = 20$ log D_x, where limit is $(D_x > D_c = D_c)$ $(D_c$ method$)$

    * Any quantity marked with an asterisk may be left for solution at step 25.

Hopkins-Stryker Method

$$\Delta D_x = -10 \log \left[\frac{Q}{4\pi(D_x)^2} + A \right]$$

$$D_x = \sqrt{\frac{Q}{4\pi\left(10^{\frac{-\Delta D_x}{10}} - A\right)}}$$

ΔD_x	Step Number
ΔD_1	22
ΔD_8	20
ΔD_2	13
ΔEAD	21
10 log NOM	24

Indicate which "A" equation was used:

Sabine _____	Norris-Eyring _____	Room Constant _____
$A = \dfrac{4(n+1)}{S\bar{a}M}$	$A = \dfrac{4(n+1)}{[-S\ln(1-\bar{a})]M}$	$A = \dfrac{4(n+1)}{RM}$

Min $\Delta D_1 = \Delta D_8 + \Delta D_2 - \Delta EAD + 10$ log NOM + 6 dB − FSM (Check step 22)

Min $\Delta EAD = \Delta D_8 + \Delta D_2 - \Delta D_1 + 10$ log NOM + 6 dB − FSM (Check step 21)

Max $\Delta D_8 = \Delta D_1 + \Delta EAD - \Delta D_2 - 10$ log NOM − 6 dB − FSM (Check steps 20 & 21)

Max $\Delta D_2 = \Delta D_1 + \Delta EAD - \Delta D_8 - 10$ log NOM − 6 dB − FSM (Check step 11)

Max NOM = $10^{\frac{\Delta D_1 + \Delta EAD - \Delta D_8 - \Delta D_2 - 10 \log NOM - 6 dB - FSM}{10}}$ (Check step 24)

Make sure that no calculated D_x value violates the earlier limits by checking the indicated steps before going on with the design.

26. Maximum desired program level at D_2 = _____ dBA

    Does this level provide the required s/n ratio found in step 19?

    Yes _____ Go to 27.

    No _____ Readjust either ambient noise or program level.

27. Loudspeaker 4-foot, 1-watt sensitivity = _____ dB-SPL

28. Loudspeaker efficiency = _____ %

    % eff = $10^{\frac{\text{(4-ft, 1-watt sens)} - (10 \log Q + 107.47)}{10}} \times 100$

29. Electrical power required = _____ watts

$$EPR = 10^{\frac{(\text{Prog level} + 10) + (\Delta D_2 - \Delta 4 \text{ ft*}) - (\text{L sens})}{10}}$$

*$\Delta 4$ ft found in step 23.

This is EPR per driver. Total EPR is EPR times number of drivers.

30. Maximum program level possible from the actual power available = _____ dB-SPL

$$\text{Max prog level poss} = 10 \log \frac{\text{Watts avail}}{10} - (\Delta D_2 - \Delta 4 \text{ ft}) + (\text{L sens})$$

CHAPTER 11

Specifications

It is a simple fact that the majority of sound-system specifications are written by sound contractors. While the ideal would be that a highly qualified consultant would write the specification, supervise the installation, and oversee the proof-of-performance tests, this is seldom done due to the lack of qualified personnel. Since almost every town with a population above 50,000 people has at least one firm in the sound contracting business, it is inevitable that these same firms will assist the customer when he needs advice on what to do about sound and the nearest consultant is hundreds of miles away.

IDEAL APPROACH

The ideal way to obtain a really good sound system and, more important, how to keep it that way is to hire a thoroughly competent consultant, have him prequalify the potential contractors, and after he and the owner select the contractor they would like to use, let the consultant negotiate the contract. Such a consultant (and he should be the model contractors follow as well, if they are to work directly with the customer) will:

1. Perform the design work and issue a performance specification.
2. Prequalify available contractors, determining:
   A. Financial ability to handle the job.
   B. Personnel available, their skills, union affiliations, compliance with federal rules (race, etc.), experience in type of job, etc.
   C. Their test equipment, shop tools.
   D. The official standing with their suppliers.
   E. Their desire to do the job.
3. Supervise the installation by:
   A. Inspecting all electronic racks, both at the contractor's and then at the site.
   B. Aligning the loudspeaker when installed.
   C. Certifying that all specified items have been provided.
4. Equalize the system when installed.
5. Work with the contractor's personnel and the customer's personnel to ensure their understanding of the basic intent of the system and how to maintain the system at the desired level of performance.

WRITING THE SPECIFICATION

The specification should be a document that lists the functions desired, the uniformity of coverage required, and the maximum SPL demanded over what frequency range and at what distortion level. Minimum Q and maximum RT_{60} can be listed. The sound contractor should submit back to the consultant:

1. A single-line block diagram of the proposed system capable of meeting the performance requirements.
2. An equipment list.
3. Personnel available and their qualifications.
4. Measurement data, either from the contractor or the manufacturer he works with, certifying the Q of the loudspeaker.
5. Necessary financial and bonding data.
6. Test equipment available.
7. A statement of their scheduling of work and their ability to devote sufficient time and men to the job if it is awarded to them.

Checking references given by prospective contractors can be of vital importance. One such form is shown in Fig. 11-1.

The architects and engineers associated with the project must be included in this evaluation of prospective contractors. It is not too difficult to gain the full cooperation of the owner toward negotiation when his consultant has the concurrence of the other professionals in the project that a given contractor represents the most qualified choice. This can be accomplished by using a contractor evaluation form such as that shown in Fig. 11-2.

Finally, where any of the professionals involved have had actual on-the-job experience with proposed contractors, it is possible to acquire a performance evaluation as well (Fig. 11-3).

Contractor's Reference Checks

DATE: _____

REFERENCE:

1. Did the contractor meet or exceed all of the major scheduled milestones?

2. Was the contract fixed price or cost-plus negotiated fee?

3. Did the contractor perform within the price quoted?

    A. Was there any evidence of material substitutions or other corner-cutting activities?

4. Were there any instances of delay caused by the lack of coordination between subcontractors or the unavailability of materials at the site when needed?

5. Did the contractor maintain a harmonious labor-management atmosphere?

6. To the best of your knowledge, did the contractor maintain a good working relationship with his subcontractors throughout the construction program?

7. Did the contractor maintain a harmonious community relationship during the program?

8. Are there any items appearing now as substandard in the building which can be attributed to the negligence of the contractor?

9. Was the assigned field superintendent sufficiently knowledgeable to adequately supervise the activities of all subcontractors, or was there some evidence of the subcontractors operating independently on their assigned portions of the program?

10. Did the contractor show a tendency towards overpricing customer-requested changes?

11. What is your overall impression of his ability to perform major construction programs?

Fig. 11-1. An example of how a consultant obtains a report from a contractor's references.

Performance Rating based on (Architect's knowledge) and/or check with (other clients) (other architects). Circle as appropriate.

	Excellent	Good	Fair	Poor
a. Top Management attention to project				
b. Staffing of job to assure home office and field supervision, expediting and coordination of the work of all trades				
c. Ability to meet construction schedules.				
d. Cooperation, speed and reasonableness in pricing and performing changes in the work.				
e. Promptness and completeness in submission of samples and shop drawings.				
f. Provision of materials of quality and quantity as called for in specifications and delivery of same on schedule.				
g. Selection of qualified and reputable material suppliers and subcontractors				
h. History of competitive bidding				
i. Quality of workmanship				
j. Maintenance of up-to-date as-built drawings				
k. Maintenance of up-to-date records on schedule, materials and cost				
l. Cooperation with Owner and Architect				
m. Promptness in payments to material suppliers and subcontractors				
n. Overall performance rating				

Rating based on:
1) Type of construction/facility _____
2) Location of facility _____
3) Dollar Value and Year $_____

Fig. 11-3. A performance-rating form for evaluating the experienced contractor's work.

A SAMPLE SPECIFICATION

Fundamental functional requirements must be listed carefully for the contractor. A sample specification might read as follows:

Contractor Evaluation

Name of Contractor _____ Address _____

Telephone Number _____

Project for which evaluated: _____

	Project Title	Location

I. **General Background**

	Consid-erable	Fair Am't.	None
a. Experience in construction of this type facility			
b. Construction experience in general geographical area of proposed project			
c. Average Value of projects handled	$		
d. Average Annual Volume of Work in Place	$		
e. Current workload (Value of uncompleted work)	$		

	Yes	No
f. Able to undertake this project within *normal* workload		
g. Financial strength (current tangible net worth)	$	

	Excellent	Good	Fair	Poor
h. Credit rating				

	Yes	No
i. Stated interest in bidding this project		
j. Has contractor successfully used Critical Path Method (CPM) of Scheduling		

II. **Project Architect's recommendation** (in order of preference of all Contractors considered, after having completed performance ratings based on personal knowledge, and/or work performed under at least three (3) other clients and architects.

(Attached Performance rating sheets)

No.____ of ____ evaluated.

Signature of Architect or his representative

Fig. 11-2. An example of a form used by a consultant to obtain the architect's evaluation of the contractor.

The basic requirements for this sound system are:

1. To provide sound reinforcement from the pulpit, lectern, altar, and baptismal area to listeners in the auditorium . . . No listener shall experience a s/n ratio of less than 25 dB, or an AL_{CONS} of more than 15%. The EAD shall not exceed 8 feet, at a maximum D_s of 2.5 feet when NOM = 1. At the maximum D_2, the system shall be capable of supplying 90–dB-SPL program level plus 10-dB peaking factor without deformation of the waveform as observed on an oscilloscope connected to the output of the SLM when it is located at the maximum D_2 position.

2. Distribution of sound in the church auditorium from 500 Hz to 5000 Hz shall vary not more than ±3 dB at any location, as viewed on a ⅓-octave real-time audio-frequency analyzer.

3. Microphones shall be permanently installed at the pulpit (1), the lectern (1), the altar (2), and the baptismal area (1). Additionally, two lavaliers should be available as substitute microphones for any of the above. These microphones shall not deviate from the consultant's measuring microphone by more than ±5-dB relative response from 500 Hz to 10,000 Hz (see Fig. 11-4). No two identical models shall vary in response from each other by more than ±1½ dB. Automated floormat switching shall ensure an NOM of unity in every case but the altar area, where an NOM of 2 is accepted. Flush mounting of altar microphones is suggested.

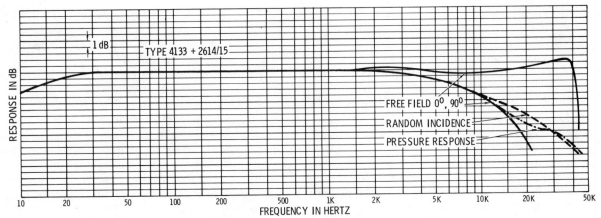

Fig. 11-4. Response of a typical measuring microphone.

4. The foyer system shall be time delayed and electrically isolated from the main system.

5. The nursery area shall be provided with an independent subsystem, electrically isolated from the main system.

6. The contractor shall submit:
   A. A single-line block diagram of his proposed system.
   B. A loudspeaker orientation drawing.
   C. A full equipment list.
   D. A full list of personnel the owner and consultant are to work with.
   E. A computer printout of the system calculations supporting the proposed loudspeaker and system layout.

7. The contractor shall submit a statement from the manufacturer who supplies the equipment he is bidding that he is their authorized outlet fully empowered to support their warranty program.

A specification of this type relies on the prequalification stages to select a basic supplier of reliable equipment. Therefore, it is fairly safe to assume that the contractor:

1. Is a local businessman responsible for the warranty program.

2. Has guaranteed the performance of the system for the warranty period.

3. Has identified his manufacturer affiliation at the prequalification stage.

Therefore, the contractor will be as interested as the owner in supplying well-constructed, reliable equipment.

Again, a specification such as the above requires a close association between the consultant and the contractor. The contractor must realize that the consultant will insist that the performance minimums be met. It also allows the exceptional contractor the freedom to do creative design work around the specification wherein his experience, special proprietary equipment,

or other advantages can be added to the original intent, greatly enhancing the final result.

The specification ensures that clear, intelligible sound will be received by each listener in the auditorium. There have been written weighty tomes that covered literally hundreds of detailed specified items right down to the color, length, and threads of the hardware mounting screws *but which did not mention anywhere that the system had to make a sound.*

TECHNICAL SPECIFICATIONS

Where bidding is insisted upon and you are requested to prepare a specification to be bid, great care needs to be taken to include in the specification as many exclusions of the unqualified as the owner will permit. One such specification is the following:

SOUND REINFORCEMENT SYSTEM
Subject to the general conditions.
1. SCOPE:
   A. The intent of this specification is to provide a complete and satisfactory operating system for the pickup, amplification, distribution, and reproduction of voice and/or other audio program material. The system shall be of modular design to facilitate both expansion and service and shall be completely transistorized. All equipment and installation material required to fulfill the above shall be furnished whether or not specifically enumerated herein or on the drawings. All necessary hookup and installation shall be by a factory approved representative. The installation supervisor shall also instruct the personnel designated by the owner as to the correct operation of the system. A minimum of 3 hours time for this shall be included in the bid.
   B. This specification is based upon equipment as manufactured by _____. Equipment manufactured by other reputable companies shall be acceptable if deemed equal by the en-

gineer. Complete engineering data, diagrams, and acoustic calculations shall be submitted with the bid for substitute system.

C. The contractor shall provide two complete sets of the following data: installation wiring diagrams, complete instruction manuals, schematic drawings, and service instructions.

D. The system shall be guaranteed for a period of one (1) year from the date of acceptance or first beneficial use, whichever is first, against defective materials, design, workmanship, and improper adjustment. Any defective material shall be replaced at no expense to the owner, provided it does not show abuse.

E. The contractor, if requested to do so by the engineer, shall be prepared to show by "proof-of-performance" test that the equipment being furnished "on-the-job" is equal to or better than the equipment specifications listed herein. This proof shall be shown by actual tests and not by printed sales literature. To this end, the contractor shall provide qualified audio technicians and such test equipment as required to perform this function. The following test equipment shall be considered minimum for the above stated purpose. Sound level meter, ⅓- and ⅒-octave-band wave analyzer, sine- and square-wave generator, impedance (CRL) bridge, audio oscilloscope, distortion analyzer, graphic level recorder, calibrated microphone, real-time spectrum analyzer, beat-frequency oscillator, random-noise generator, etc. Instruments as manufactured by General Radio, Tektronix, Hewlett-Packard, and Brüel & Kjaer are considered acceptable for measurements. Nonprofessional test equipment or "home-built kit" type gear shall not be acceptable under these specifications.

F. The system of room equalization used shall be the product of a manufacturer or manufacturers who shall be properly licensed to manufacture this type of equipment and defend the contractor and owner against any patent-infringement suits.

G. The work herein specified shall be performed by fully competent workmen, in a thorough manner. All materials furnished by the contractor shall be new, and all work shall be completed to the satisfaction of the engineer.

H. At the time of submittal, the contractor shall submit a complete and accurate listing of all major items of equipment to be used in assembling the system, including all items of equipment listed under this specification, as well as contractor's block diagrams indicating the proposed interconnection of all equipment to be furnished. A detailed listing of all proposed deviations from specifications shall be included. All modifications of standard equipment necessary to meet specifications shall be explained fully and must be accompanied by schematic diagrams.

I. All equipment, except portable equipment, shall be held firmly in place. This shall include loudspeakers, amplifiers, cables, etc. (The exception to this rigid-mounting clause is, of course, when it is required to use resilient shock mounting to decouple the array from the structure it is being mounted in.) Fastenings and supports shall be adequate to support their loads with a safety factor of at least three (3). All switches, connectors, outlets, etc., shall be clearly, logically, and permanently marked during installation.

J. The contractor must take such precautions as are necessary to guard against electromagnetic and electrostatic hum, to supply adequate ventilation, and to install the equipment so as to provide maximum safety to the person who operates it.

K. Care shall be exercised in wiring so as to avoid damage to the cables and to the equipment. All joints and connections shall be made with rosin-core solder or with mechanical connectors approved by the engineer. All wiring shall be executed in strict adherence to standard broadcast practices.

The contractor shall submit to the engineer a "certificate of completion" to assure that the system has passed all the tests required in subsequent parts of this specification and is in proper operating condition. Final tests shall be made in the presence of the engineer, who shall be notified of the test date a minimum of five (5) days prior to that date.

2. FUNCTIONS AND OBJECTIVES:

A. Provide sound reinforcement on the auditorium floor and bleachers, separately or simultaneously.

B. Provide console inputs for "owner provided" (N.I.C. auxiliary audio sources such as tape recorder, motion-picture projector, phonograph, etc.)

C. Provide for microphone pickup of "live" program material from locations as shown on the drawings.

D. Provide an acoustic gain of _____ dB.

E. Provide even distribution of the reinforced sound throughout the seating area, typically plus or minus 3 dB front to back and side to side for the one-octave band centered at 4000 Hz. Total variation from the worst to the best seats shall not exceed plus or minus 4 dB.

F. Provide uniform frequency response throughout the audience area. Typically, plus or minus 3 dB as measured with ⅓-octave bands of pink noise at positions across the main seating area selected by the engineer.

G. Provide adequate dynamic range at an acoustic distortion level sufficiently low to ensure minimum listening fatigue. The system should be capable of delivering 75-dB average program level with additional 10-dB-SPL peaking margin to any seat in the audience area at an acoustic distortion level below 5% thd.

3. EQUIPMENT:

A. The Main Console: Shall consist of a floor-standing equipment rack housing all controls and switches for the operation of the system with the necessary amplifiers and auxiliary sources of equipment as herein specified. Racks shall be completely enclosed with front and rear doors having hinges, locks, and keys. The cabinet shall be treated with a rust inhibitor and finished with a baked enamel. Rack color shall be that of the major equipment manufacturer whose components shall be used in the rack. Wiring shall be secured with Ty-Rap ties and identified with Brady tags terminated in screw-type terminals, approved plugs, or connections made with rosin-core solder only. Markings on front panels shall be embossed letters or engraved Lamacoid plates.

B. The Mixer-Preamplifier: Shall be all solid-state type, designed to control up to five independent input signals. Gain: 87 dB with _____ microphone preamplifier (five required). Frequency response: ±1 dB, 20 to 20,000 Hz. Power output: +18 dBm at less than 0.5% thd. Monitor output: 6 dB below amplifier output into 600 ohms, source impedance 150/250 ohms with _____ microphone preamplifier balanced. Noise Level: −120-dBm equivalent input noise. Controls: Five mixer, one master, one bass, one treble, one monitor volume, dialog equalizer switch for each input (−6 dB at 100 Hz), articulation equalizer switch for output (+3 dB at 5 kHz), VI meter range switch, test tone, and off-on switch. Mixer-preamplifier: Equipped with three microphone preamplifiers, one phono preamplifier, one bridging input transformer, and VI meter.

C. Mixing and Splitting Networks: 600 ohms in and out, balanced. See drawings for type and quantity.

D. Line Amplifier: Rack-mounting type. Gain: 77 dB. Frequency response: ±1 dB, 30 − 20,000 Hz. Power output: +20 dBm at less than 1.0% thd, 30 to 20,000 Hz; +18 dBm at less than 0.5% thd, 20 − 20,000 Hz. Source impedance: Input No. 1, 150/250 ohms; input No. 2, 600 to 15,000 ohms with transformer. Controls: Two mixers, one power switch.

E. Filters: Wideband, narrowband, high-pass, low-pass. See Section 3B, Equalization, Electronic and Acoustical Tests section of this specification.

F. Power Amplifiers (Three Types Required):

(1) Type: Rack-mounting power amplifier. Gain: 67 dB. Input sensitivity: 0.8 volt for rated output. Power output: 200 watts at less than 1.0% thd, 50 to 12,000 Hz. Frequency response: ±1 dB, 20 to 20,000 Hz. Input impedance: 15,000 ohms. Load impedance: 6.25/8 and 25/32 ohms. Load voltage: 35 and 70 volts. Noise level: Output 85 dB below rated output. Controls: Volume control, continuously variable, composition; power switch; high-pass switch.

(2) Type: As above. Gain: 64 dB. Sensitivity: As above. Power output: 100 watts at less than 1% thd, 50 to 20,000 Hz. Frequency response: ±1 dB 20 to 20,000 Hz. Input impedance: 15,000 ohms. Source impedance: 150 to 600 ohms, with _____ transformer. Load impedance: 4, 8, 16, and 50 ohms. Load voltage: 20, 28, 40, and 70 volts. Noise level: 85 dB below rated output. Controls: Volume control, as above.

(3) Type: As above. Gain: 61 dB. Sensitivity: As above. Power output: 50 watts at less than 1% thd, 45 to 20,000 Hz. Frequency response: As above. Load impedance: 4, 8, 16, and 100 ohms. Load voltages: 14, 20, 28, 70. Noise level: 85 dB below rated output. Controls: As above.

(4) Type: As above. Stage monitor amplifier: The mixer amplifier shall be self-contained and shall employ all solid-state devices. Without accessories, the mixer amplifier shall be capable of mixing two independent input signals originating from either a ceramic phono pickup, high-impedance microphone, or equivalent, and from either a radio tuner, tape machine, or equivalent. Either of the two inputs shall be capable of accepting 600-ohm low-impedance sources. Input connection shall be made in one of two ways: direct connection to terminal strips provided for the separate inputs, or standard phono plugs for the high-impedance input, magnetic phono input, and tuner input. The mixer amplifier shall have separate volume controls on each input and shall have a treble tone control common to both inputs. In addition, each input shall have a socket provided for the use of various types of plug-in accessories, enabling the mixer amplifier to accept signals from low-impedance sources,

magnetic pickups, and bridged low-impedance lines.

The mixer amplifier shall have a frequency response of ±1 dB, 10 to 20,000 Hz, and shall deliver 18 watts at less than 2% thd, 30 to 15,000 Hz, to a 4-8 ohm load. The output of the mixer amplifier shall be of the transformerless type, capable of delivering 25 watts into loads ranging from 4 to 16 ohms.

The mixer amplifier shall have a self-contained power supply operating from 120 volts ac (requiring no more than 42 watts when delivering full power), and shall have self-resetting circuit breakers in both the primary and the transistor supply circuits. Fuse or manual resetting devices are not acceptable. Provide with _____ bridging transformer.

G. Microphones: Type: Moving-coil dynamic, cardioid, with Mylar diaphragm having tangential compliance to protect against shocks and blasts. An internal pop-screen filter shall be provided. Frequency response: Uniform from 40 Hz to 16 kHz. Output level: At least −54 dBm/10 dynes per square centimeter. Output impedance: 150/250 ohms balanced to ground. Front-to-back average discrimination; 20 dB. Hum: No greater than −120 dB. The microphone serial numbers shall be clearly marked on the microphones and on the accompanying factory calibration curves. The factory calibration curves shall be a complete record of the frequency response of each microphone and shall be submitted to the owner upon the completion of the installation. Separate curves shall be provided for each microphone to ensure conformity of performance. Provide shock mounts and stands (two required).

H. Loudspeakers (High- and Low-Frequency Units):

(1) High-Frequency Units: Type: Multicellular with appropriate throats, as required, coupled with compression-type drivers hereinafter specified. The horns shall be constructed to individual metal cells with a special damping-material coating on the external surfaces of each cell. The cells shall be straight with an exponential expansion. Folded or re-entrant horns or horns fabricated of wood or other fibrous materials will not be acceptable. Two different models of multicellular horns shall be furnished: Two (2), two-cell, 20° by 40° horns, and three (3) eight-cell, 35° by 70° horns. All five horns shall be coupled to drivers of the following specifications: They shall utilize an aluminum diaphragm coupled to a voice coil that shall be edge-wound of aluminum ribbon and that shall be 1.75 inches in diameter. The voice-coil gap shall have a flux density of at least 15,000 gauss, produced by an Alnico V magnet having a weight of at least 3.4 pounds. Power rating: 30 watts (based on continuous operation with white noise 500 Hz to 5000 Hz and a dividing network). Frequency response: 500 to 16,000 Hz. Pressure sensitivity: 111.5 dB-SPL with one-watt input measured 4 feet from the mouth of a 2-cell horn or 110.0 dB-SPL with one-watt input measured 4 feet from the mouth of an 8-cell horn (pink-noise source). At 30 feet, the SPLs for full 40-watt input are, respectively, 110.0 dB and 109.0 dB.

(2) Low-Frequency Units: Type: Cone. Pressure sensitivity: 103 dB-SPL at 4 feet from 1 watt measured on axis. Voice coil: Diameter, 3 inches, of edge-wound copper ribbon. Flux density: 14,750 gauss. Magnet: 4.4-pound Alnico V. Free-air resonance: 25 Hz. Continuous power rating: 35 watts. Frequency response: Uniform from 20 to 1000 Hz.

(3) Low-Frequency Speaker Cabinets: The speaker cabinets (4) shall be of the utility type measuring 29½ inches high, 25½ inches wide, and 17¾ inches deep. They shall be of heavy wood construction and finished in gray. They shall be of the bass-reflex type. Cabinets employing folded horns or tuned slots shall not be acceptable under this specification. The cabinet shall contain 6.15 cubic feet, weigh at least 55 pounds, and contain proper acoustical material. The cabinet shall be furnished with a "grilled" opening for housing a 15-inch speaker.

(4) Stage Monitor: The loudspeaker shall be 15⁵⁄₁₆ inches in diameter and of the 2-way duplex type, having a continuous power rating of 35 watts and a peak power rating of 50 watts. The loudspeaker shall be capable of reproducing a frequency range from 20 to 22,000 Hz and shall have a minimum pressure sensitivity of 112.4 dB-SPL at 4 feet from 35 watts, measured on axis. The loudspeaker shall employ a full-section dividing network having a 1600-Hz crossover frequency and a continuously adjustable range of high-frequency attenuation from 0 to −10 dB.

The loudspeaker shall have a nominal impedance of 16 ohms. The low-frequency cone shall have a free-air resonance frequency of 25 Hz; the lf voice coil shall be of edge-wound copper ribbon, having a diameter of 3 inches, and shall operate in a magnetic gap having a flux density of 11,000 gauss, derived from an Alnico V magnet having a weight of 2.25 pounds. The outer edge (rim) of the lf cone shall utilize a high-compliance, mechanically damped, cloth surround which, complemented by the correct apex suspension (spider), shall be capable of reproducing the stated low-frequency response.

The high-frequency diaphragm shall be of aluminum, having elastomer compliance, and shall be properly loaded, acoustically, by a multicellular horn, compression-molded of heavy, high-impact plastic. The frequency distribution pattern of the loudspeaker, owing to the use of this multicellular horn, shall be 90° by 40°. The hf voice coil shall be of edge-wound aluminum ribbon, having a diameter of 1¾ inches and shall operate in a magnetic gap having a flux density of 14,000 gauss, derived from an Alnico V magnet having a weight of 0.531 pound. High-frequency diaphragms having tangential compliances and/or utilizing horns with spherical radiation patterns shall be unacceptable under this specification. Provide suitable enclosure and mounting accessories.

(5) Speaker Line-Matching Transformers: The transformers shall be of high quality for 70 volts line to voice coil. Frequency response: ±1 dB from 30 to 15,000 Hz with a maximum insertion loss of 0.5 dB. Output: 32, 16, and 8 watts.

I. Dual-Channel Biamplifier Control Panel: This control panel shall be an assembly consisting of two ladder attenuator controls, each connected to an individual dividing network and terminal board and mounted on a standard 19-inch rack panel 3½ inches high. Input and output impedances of each control-network assembly shall be 600 ohms. Crossover frequency of each network shall be 800 Hz. The attenuation rate of each network shall be 12 dB/octave, and the insertion loss of each network shall be 0 dB within the bandpass. Each ladder attenuator control shall be a rotary type with 20 steps of 2 dB each, tapered to infinity. Provide termination of unused low-frequency side area circuit.

J. Power Distribution Panel: The panel shall provide six ac outlets in the rear side controlled by a 20-ampere switch (117-120 volts). A pilot light shall be provided. Two additional outlets (unswitched) shall be located on the front of the panel. All outlets shall be of the three-wire type.

K. Jack Panel: The jack panel shall be 1¾ inches high and 19 inches wide. It shall contain 12 pairs of jacks with a designation strip. The jacks shall be the 3-terminal normalled-through type.

L. Audio Cable: Microphone and loudspeaker cable shall be as recommended by the equipment manufacturer; however, in no case shall any cable be used which is smaller than 20 AWG stranded.

EQUALIZATION, ELECTRONIC AND ACOUSTICAL TESTS

1. General Requirements: Provide all required testing apparatus specified herein to complete successfully the equalization and tests. Provide factory trained personnel to perform the tests and adjust the equalizers required. The purpose of the equalization is to adjust the acoustic amplitude response of the sound system to a specified uniformity measured throughout the entire audience area. This adjustment is made to realize maximum acoustic gain and optimum tonal balance from the sound system throughout the audience area and stage-monitored area.

2. Instrumentation: Provide the following minimal standard laboratory test equipment. Any substitutions or additions to the following list must be approved by the engineer. [This is an eclectic list; substitute within reason the test equipment available to you.]

A. General Radio Model 1650B impedance bridge

B. General Radio Model 1309A audio oscillator

C. General Radio Model 1382 random-noise generator

D. General Radio Model 1933 precision sound-level meter

E. General Radio Model 1564A sound analyzer

F. General Radio Model 1921 real-time audio-frequency analyzer with 1921-P2 display, or

G. Hewlett-Packard Model 1201B oscilloscope

H. General Radio Model 1562A sound-level calibrator

I. Master equalizer set with narrow-band, high-pass, and low-pass filters, plus comparator switch and attenuator

J. Polaroid camera Type CR-9

Kits, home-built, and other nonprofessional test equipment shall be unacceptable under this specification.

3. Inspection of Sound System Prior to Equalization: Prior to undertaking equalization of the sound system, perform the following inspections on the sound system, and submit to the engineer the

written results of each inspection for inclusion in the permanent records of the sound system.

A. Measure and record the impedance of each loudspeaker line before connecting it to the output of its respective amplifier. The load impedance shall be equal to or greater than the rated impedance. Record the total impedance.

B. Measure and record the output impedance of each active device operating as a source to any passive device or series of passive devices. Record the dc resistance of any buildout resistor used.

C. Measure and record the input impedance of any active device used to terminate passive devices, and record the total impedance of all such devices. Record the dc resistance of any terminating resistor used.

D. Measure and record the acoustic distribution of the loudspeakers in the sound system throughout the entire seating area. Record the location of all positions in the seating area where any ⅓-octave band, from 250 to 5000 Hz, deviates more than ±3 dB from the desired house curve.

E. Measure and record the phasing of all loudspeakers.

F. Measure and record the polarity of all microphones to be used in the system.

G. Measure and record, with an oscilloscope, the output of each power amplifier. The input source to each amplifier being measured shall be a sine-wave oscillator with less than 0.5% thd adjusted to 10 dB less than full power output of the amplifier. Inspect the output sine wave appearing on the oscilloscope for complete freedom from hum, noise, parasitic oscillation, and rf interference.

H. Measure and record the frequency response of each mixer preamplifier and power amplifier in the system.

4. House-Curve Equalization: Temporarily install the master equalizer set in the appropriate link circuit in the sound system. Use pink noise as a source signal, and place a calibrated measuring microphone in the seating area at twice the critical distance ($2D_c$). (Critical distance is defined as that distance from the sound source at which the direct sound from the source and the reverberant sound are in a ratio of one to one). The acoustic amplitude response that appears on the screen of the real-time spectrum analyzer shall be recorded. Point-to-point measurements, averaging estimates, and other nonreal-time dynamic measurements shall be unacceptable under this specification. After the unequalized acoustic amplitude response is recorded, the master equalizer set shall be used to bring the observed acoustic amplitude with ±3-dB uniformity (or better, if

possible) and to conform to the predetermined high-frequency rolloff dictated by the combination effect of humidity, air absorption, and the random incidence of the measuring microphone. The equalized house curve shall be recorded.

5. Control of Microphone Characteristics and Preferred Feedback Frequencies: Install the required filters in the link circuit ahead of the power-amplifier input; then reconnect the master equalizer set in the link circuit following the microphone mixer amplifier. The sound system gain shall be adjusted until it reaches regeneration (feedback). Determine the frequency of regeneration either by means of Lissajous figures (oscilloscope) or by observing the response of the real-time audio spectrum analyzer, and adjust the appropriate filter until the observed regeneration ceases. This procedure shall be continued until the specified potential acoustic gain (PAG) is achieved. (See "Objectives" for required gain.)

At the conclusion of the tuning of the house curve and the feedback corrections, the electrical amplitude response of the equalizers shall be recorded, first the house-curve filters alone and then the combined house-curve filters and feedback-correction filters. The source shall be a beat-frequency oscillator, and the recording instrument shall be a graphic level recorder or a real-time analyzer with camera. The inverse of these curves shall be compared, first with the unequalized house curve made with the measuring microphone and then with the unequalized house curve made with the sound-system microphone. Records of each comparison shall be made. Measurements made by a point-to-point or averaged estimate shall be unacceptable under this specification.

6. Microphone Proximity Instability: Suppress the tendency of the sound-system microphone to become unstable when approached by a talker. Identify the ⅓-octave band affected by the approach of a person, and provide enough attenuation to ensure stability. Records shall be made of additional attenuation provided.

7. Filter Records: At the conclusion of the equalization, record the calibrated settings of each series filter used.

8. Documentation of Tests, Measurements, and Adjustments Performed:

A. List of personnel and certified test equipment used.

B. Impedance of all loudspeaker lines.

C. Output impedance of all active sources connected to passive devices and the value of any buildout resistor used.

D. The input impedance of all active devices used to terminate passive devices and the value of any termination resistor used.

E. The variation of acoustic distribution throughout the seating area above and below a reference level at each ⅓-octave center frequency from 350 to 5000 Hz.

F. The recorded polarity and phase measurements of the loudspeakers.

G. The list of microphones polarity tested.

H. The recorded inspection results observed for hum, noise, parasitic oscillation, and rf interference from the output of each power amplifier.

I. The unequalized house curve made with the measuring microphone.

J. The equalized house curve made with the measuring microphone.

K. The electrical response of the house-curve filters without the microphone filters.

L. The electrical response of the house-curve filters with the microphone filters.

M. The unequalized house curve made with the sound-system microphone.

N. The proximity frequencies and attenuations.

O. All filter settings.

P. The factors D_c, $\%AL_{CONS}$, D_1, D_s, D_2, D_o, NAG, PAG, EAD, and EPR for the sound system and the room:

D_c = Critical distance. See definition above in this specification.

$$\%AL_{CONS} = \frac{641.81\,(D_2)^2(RT_{60})^2}{VQ}$$

D_o = Distance from the talker to the farthest listener

D_1 = Distance from the microphone to the nearest loudspeaker

D_s = Distance from the microphone to the talker

D_2 = Distance from the loudspeaker to the farthest listener

NAG = Needed acoustical gain

PAG = Potential acoustic gain

EAD = Equivalent acoustical distance

EPR = Electrical power required

Q = Directivity of the loudspeaker

RT_{60} = Reverberation time

V = Volume of room in cubic feet

9. Equalization Filters.

A. No filters shall be accepted that are not constant-K, 600-ohm filters. Any filter whose impedance changes at its resonant frequency will not be accepted. Filters that do not have detented, step-by-step adjustments, fully calibrated, will not be acceptable.

B. Active circuit equalizers of the minimum-phase band-rejection type may be substituted for the constant-K passive type.

This is a well-written detailed specification that will exclude "fly-by-night" operators if adhered to. CAUTION: This specification applies to a specific acoustic environment and is not necessarily applicable to any other acoustic environment.

A PERFORMANCE SPECIFICATION

The following specification from Northern Communications Area at Griffiss Air Force Base illustrates how to insure acceptable performance without having to mention a single proprietary piece of equipment. It is an excellent compromise between the ideal specification and the technical specification described earlier in this chapter. It is well worth studying when a performance-type specification is desired but it will have to go out for bids. Refer to Fig. 11-5.

SOUND REINFORCEMENT SYSTEM

PERFORMANCE SPECIFICATIONS

FOR

ABC CHAPEL

IN

EVERYWHERE AIR FORCE BASE

PROJECT ENGINEER: John Doe

RELEASING ENGINEER: Richard Roe

1. SCOPE

1.1 The purpose of this specification is to provide the operational concepts and the minimum performance specification for the sound reinforcement system to be installed in ABC Chapel at Everywhere AFB.

1.2 The contractor shall engineer the sound system for the chapel in accordance with the operating concept and performance specification as detailed herein.

1.3 The contractor shall furnish all equipment, material, cable, conduit, and supplies required to effect the complete installation of this sound system.

1.4 The contractor shall provide two complete sets of the following data: Installation wiring diagrams, complete instruction manuals, schematic drawings, service instructions, and test documentation listed in Section 5.

1.5 The system shall be guaranteed for a period of one (1) year from the date of acceptance against defective materials, design, workmanship, and improper adjustment. Any defective material shall be replaced at no expense to the Government, provided it does not show abuse.

1.6 The work herein specified shall be performed by fully competent workmen, in a thorough manner. All materials furnished by the contractor shall be new and shall conform to applicable requirements of the Underwriters Laboratories and the National Standards Institute.

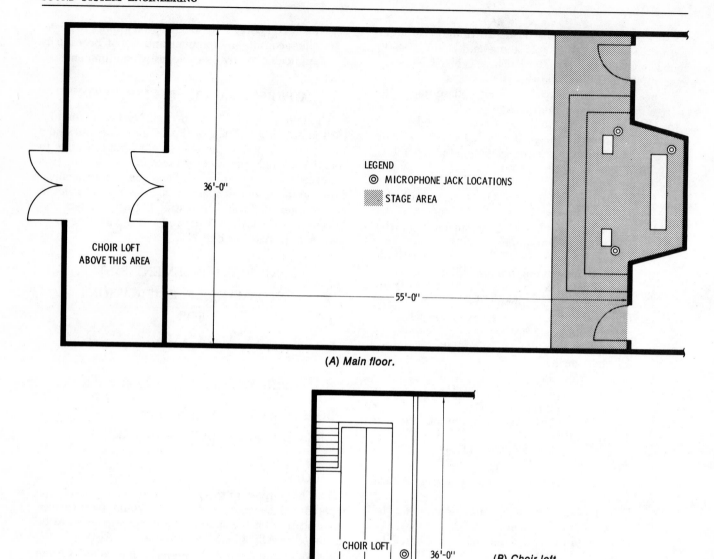

LEGEND
◎ MICROPHONE JACK LOCATIONS
▒ STAGE AREA

36'-0"

55'-0"

CHOIR LOFT
ABOVE THIS AREA

(A) Main floor.

CHOIR LOFT

36'-0"

(B) Choir loft.

11'-5"

Fig. 11-5. Chapel floor plan.

1.7 All equipment, except portable equipment, shall be held firmly in place. This shall include loudspeakers, amplifiers, cables, etc. (The exception to this rigid mounting clause is, of course, when it is required to use resilient shock mounting to decouple the array from the structure it is being mounted in.) Fastenings and supports shall be adequate to support their loads with a safety factor of at least three (3). All switches, connectors, outlets, etc., shall be clearly, logically, and permanently marked during installation.

1.8 The contractor must take such precautions as are necessary to guard against electromagnetic and electrostatic hum, to supply adequate ventilation, and to install the equipment so as to provide maximum safety to the operator.

1.9 Care shall be taken in wiring so as to avoid damage to the cables and to the equipment. All joints and connectors shall be made with rosin-core solder or with mechanical connectors approved by the major equipment manufacturer. All wiring shall be executed in strict adherence to standard broadcast practices.

1.10 Any speakers, horns, wire, conduits, junction boxes, jacks, etc., shall be decoratively baffled, covered, or hidden so that they fit inconspicuously into the decor of the chapel.

1.11 Final tests shall be made in the presence of a representative of the contracting officer, who shall be notified of the test date a minimum of ten (10) days in advance.

2. Operational Concept

2.1 Microphone Inputs. There will be four (4) independent microphone inputs into the system as follows:

A. One microphone shall be located on the altar. This microphone shall be mounted on a desk stand with a slip-on adapter. The microphone cord shall be sufficiently long to allow it to be moved easily to any place on the altar. The jack for this input shall be located in the floor behind the altar.

B. There shall be one microphone located on the pulpit and one on the lectern. These microphones shall be mounted on a flexible mounting (gooseneck) with a slip-on adapter. The cords shall be long enough to allow the chaplain to move freely around the stage area well, hand holding either microphone. The jacks for the microphone cords are to be floor mounted immediately behind the pulpit and lectern.

C. The fourth microphone shall be located in the choir area. The microphone shall have a floor-stand mount with a slip-on adapter. The cord shall be long enough to allow the microphone to be moved to any part of the choir area. The jack for this microphone cord shall be floor mounted in the center front choir area.

2.2 The contractor shall supply two additional microphone floor-stand mounts with slip-on adapters. These stands will be in addition to the one required under paragraph 2.1.C.

2.3 600-Ohm Input. A standard three-circuit female phone jack shall be installed in the equipment cabinet. This jack shall be terminated in 600 ohms. The purpose of this input will be to connect "owner provided" auxiliary audio sources, such as tape recorder, motion-picture projector, phonograph, telephone line, etc.

2.4 The system shall be of modular design to facilitate both expansion and service and shall be completely transistorized.

2.5 The system shall have a monitor output jack for recording or monitoring program material. This output shall have its own level control and shall be arranged so that it will feed into a 600-ohm load at a level of 14 dB with the monitor level control fully on.

2.6 The system shall have a mixer-preamplifier designed to control a minimum of 5 independent input signals. It shall be equipped with four (4) microphone preamplifiers (for inputs of paragraph 2.1) and one (1) line transformer (used to provide isolation between the mixer bus and the high-level input of paragraph 2.3).

2.7 The exact location of the microphone jacks will be determined by the base chaplain and the contractor. However, the general location shall be as specified in paragraph 2.1.

2.8 Fig. 11-5 shows the location of the stage area, altar, pulpit, lectern, and choir area, and the approximate locations where all microphone jacks are to be placed.

2.9 The system shall provide even distribution of the reinforced sound throughout the seating area and choir area, typically ±3 dB front to back and side to side for the one-octave band centered at 4000 Hz. Total variation from the worst to the best seat shall not exceed ±4 dB. However, the choir area may be allowed to drop as low as 6 dB below the seating area.

2.10 A uniform frequency response throughout the audience area shall be provided by the system, typically, ±3 dB as measured with 1/3-octave bands of pink noise at positions across the main seating area selected by the engineer.

2.11 If equalization is necessary, the filters shall be active equalizers of the minimum-phase band-rejection type. Any filter whose impedance changes at its resonant frequency will not be accepted.

2.12 The system shall provide adequate dynamic range at an acoustic distortion level sufficiently low to ensure minimum listening fatigue. The system should be capable of delivering a 75–dB-SPL average program level with an additional 10–dB-SPL peaking margin to any seat in the audience area at an acoustic distortion level below 5% total harmonic distortion (thd). The articulation loss of consonants must not exceed 15% within the seating area.

2.13 All controls and switches for the operation of the system with the necessary amplifiers and auxiliary equipment shall be housed in a floor-standing equipment cabinet that is completely enclosed with front and rear doors having hinges, locks, and keys. Wiring shall be laced and terminated in screw-type terminals, approved plugs, or connections made with rosin-core solder only. Markings on front panels shall be embossed letters or engraved Lamacoid plates.

3. Contractor Submittal

3.1 Contractor sound-reinforcement-system calculations supporting their proposed loudspeaker and system layout. If calculations are furnished by a consultant, name and background of consultant shall also be included.

3.2 The calculations determining the following factors

shall be considered a minimum to satisfy the requirements stated in paragraph 3.1:

D_c = Critical distance (See note below.)

$$\%AL_{CONS} = \frac{641.81(D_2)^2(RT_{60})^2}{VQ}$$

D_o = Distance from the talker to the farthest listener

D_1 = Distance from the microphone to the nearest loudspeaker

D_s = Distance from the microphone to the talker

D_2 = Distance from the loudspeaker to the farthest listener

NAG = Needed acoustical gain

PAG = Potential acoustic gain

EAD = Equivalent acoustical distance

EPR = Electrical power required

Q = Directivity of the loudspeaker

RT_{60} = Reverberation time

V = Volume of room in cubic feet

NOTE: Critical distance is defined as that distance from the sound source at which the direct sound from the source and the reverberant sound are in a ratio of one to one.

3.3   A single-line block diagram of the proposed system.

3.4   Loudspeaker-orientation drawing.

3.5   A full equipment list of engineered system.

3.6   The measurement data, from either the contractor, or the manufacturer he works with, certifying the directivity factor of the loudspeakers.

3.7   Test equipment available.

3.8   The contractor shall submit a statement from the manufacturer who supplies the equipment he is bidding that he is their authorized outlet fully empowered to support their warranty program. The system shall be guaranteed for a period of one (1) year from the date of acceptance or first beneficial use, whichever is first, against defective materials, design, and workmanship, and against improper adjustment. Any defective material shall be replaced at no expense to the U.S. Air Force, provided it does not show abuse.

3.9   A listing of key personnel available during the installation period along with their sound-system qualifications.

4.   System Testing

4.1   The contractor shall have the following test equipment available on-site during the installation and testing.

A.   Sound-level meter
B.   ⅓- and ⅒-octave-band wave analyzer
C.   Sine- and square-wave generator
D.   Impedance bridge
E.   Oscilloscope
F.   Calibrated microphone
G.   Real-time spectrum analyzer
H.   Random-noise generator

4.2   Nonprofessional test equipment or "home-built kit" gear shall not be acceptable under these specifications.

4.2.1   The contractor shall perform all tests necessary to determine the data required in Section 5 and submit it as required under paragraph 1.4.

5. Documentation of Tests, Measurements, and Adjustments Performed.

A.   List of personnel and certified test equipment used.

B.   Impedance of all loudspeaker lines.

C.   Output impedance of all active sources connected to passive devices and the value of any buildout resistor used.

D.   The input impedance of all active devices used to terminate passive devices and the value of any termination resistor used.

E.   The variation of acoustic distribution throughout the seating area relative to a reference level at each ⅓-octave center frequency from 350 to 5000 Hz.

F.   The recorded polarity and phase measurements of the loudspeakers.

G.   The list of the polarity of microphones tested.

H.   The recorded inspection results observed for hum, noise, parasitic oscillation, and rf interference from the output of each power amplifier.

I.   The unequalized house curve made with the measuring microphone.

J.   The equalized house curve made with the measuring microphone.

K.   The electrical response of the house-curve filters without the microphone filters.

L.   The electrical response of the house-curve filters with the microphone filters.

M.   The unequalized house curve made with the sound-system microphone.

N.   The proximity frequencies and attenuations.

O.   All filter settings.

P.   The factors D_c, $\%AL_{CONS}$, D_1, D_s, D_2, D_o, NAG, PAG, EAD and EPR for the sound system and the room. (See definitions in paragraph 3.2.)

PROTECTION CLAUSES

Many times, if you are specifying a high level of performance, you need also to specify the limits at which your specification is no longer valid. The two most important limits it is usually necessary to bring to the attention of the architect, engineer, and owner are:

1.   The maximum allowable ambient noise level (NC curves are most useful here). This is necessary because the ambient noise level will directly affect the required s/n ratio needed for low articulation losses for consonants in speech.

2.   The maximum reverberation time. This value will affect D_c, the maximum acoustic gain possible, the ratio of direct to reverberant sound, etc.

Large arrays weigh many tons. It is simple wisdom to disclaim any responsibility for their structural integrity and insist upon their mounting design being handled by a fully qualified, responsible structural engineer.

In specifying acoustic gain, request the maximum PAG possible, but allowance should be made for a tolerance of up to −4 dB when the contractor doing the job has been thorough in his work and the room parameters have added together unfavorably.

SUMMARY

It can be observed that detailed hardware specifications often result from a lack of basic system-design knowledge on the part of the sound contractor, or the lack of understanding by the owner of what a performance specification can mean to him. Specifications can be as simple as the promise to a minister that you can "deliver sound to the rear pew that sounds the same as our face-to-face conversation at 8 feet."

Symbols and Abbreviations

a	Absorption coefficient; a_S = Sabine, a_N = Norris-Eyring, a_R = room constant	L_{SENST}	Loudspeaker sensitivity
ā	Average absorption coefficient	**M**	A D_c modifier
C$_\angle$	Coverage angle	**n + 1**	Number of loudspeaker groups contributing equal power to the reverberant sound field
dB	Decibel(s)—a ratio expressed on a logarithmic scale	**NAG**	Needed acoustic gain
dBA	A weighted sound-pressure level in decibels	**NG**	Noise generator
dBm	Decibels with a reference of 1 milliwatt	**NOALA**	Noise operated automatic level adjuster
dB-PWL	Power level with a reference of 10^{-12} watt (metric) or 10^{-13} watt (English); indicated as dB-PWL$_{-12}$ or dB-PWL$_{-13}$, respectively	**NOM**	Number of open microphones
		NOMA	Number of open microphone attenuators (an automatic mixer)
dB-SPL	Sound-pressure level in decibels with a reference of 0.00002 N/m²	**OBA**	Octave-band analyzer
		PA	Power amplifier
dBV	Decibels with a reference of 1 volt	**PAG**	Potential acoustic gain
D$_c$	Critical distance	**Pascal**	1 newton/square meter $\cong$ 94 dB-SPL
D$_D$	Direct sound	**Pink**	
D$_f$	Directivity factor, Q or R_θ	**noise**	Equal noise energy per octave
D$_I$	Directivity index	**Q**	Directivity factor or electrical quality factor (used with resonance equation); *see also* R_θ.
D$_L$	Limiting distance		
D$_m$	Measured distance	**R**	Room constant
D$_o$	Distance from talker to farthest listener	**rms**	Root mean square
D$_R$	Reflected sound	**RNG**	Random-noise generator
D$_r$	Reference distance	**RPN**	Reverse Polish notation (Lukasiewicz)
D$_s$	Distance from talker to microphone	**RTA**	Real-time analyzer
D$_x$	Any given distance	**RT$_{60}$**	Reverberation time
D$_1$	Distance between microphone and loudspeaker	**R$_\theta$**	Directivity ratio (also designated Q)
		S	Total boundary surface area
D$_2$	Distance from loudspeaker to farthest listener	**Sā**	Sabins; usually supplied by material manufacturers in Sa$_S$
		Sabin	Unit of absorption
EAD	Equivalent acoustic distance	**SAG**	Sufficient acoustic gain
E$_o$	Open-circuit voltage	**SLM**	Sound level meter
EPR	Electrical power required	**s/n**	Signal-to-noise
FSM	Feedback stability margin	**S$_p$**	Microphone power sensitivity (with a reference of 10 dynes/cm²/1 milliwatt)
GLR	Graphic level recorder		
G$_M$	EIA microphone sensitivity rating	**SPL**	Sound pressure level

$\overline{\text{SPL}}$ Sound-pressure level averaged over a spherical surface area

SPL_D Sound pressure level in decibels for a directional radiator

SPL_S Sound pressure level in decibels for a spherical radiator

S_V Microphone sensitivity with a reference of 1 dyne/cm²/1 volt

thd   Total harmonic distortion

V   Volume of a room

VI   Volume indicator

VU   Volume units

X_c Capacitive reactance

X_L Inductive reactance

White noise   Equal noise energy per hertz

Z   Impedance (magnitude)

$\%\text{AL}_{cons}$ Articulation loss for consonants, expressed in percentage

% Effic   Percentage of loudspeaker efficiency

θ Phase angle

NOTE: Mathematical symbols and terms may be found in Appendix VIII.

Bibliography

Acoustical Materials Association. *The Use of Architectural Materials—Theory and Practice.*

Altec Technical Letters No. 105, 109, 113, 121, 141, 166, 167, 183, AV-3, 192, 194, 201A, 203, 210, 211, 212A, 213, 214, 215, 216, 218.

Ancha, R. F., "Eleven-Day Sound System for 325,000 People," *J. Audio Eng. Soc.,* Vol. 20 (Sept. 1972).

Antman, H. S., "Extension to the Theory of Howlback in Reverberant Rooms," *J. Acoust. Soc. Am.,* Vol. 39 (Feb. 1966).

Ashley, J. R., A. Saponas, and R. C. Matson, "Test Signals for Music Reproduction Systems," *IEEE Spectrum* (July 1971).

Atal, B. S., M. R. Schroeder, G. M. Sessler, and J. E. West. "Evaluation of Acoustic Properties of Enclosures by Means of Digital Computers," *J. Acoust. Soc. Am.,* Vol. 40, No. 2 (1966).

Augustadt, H. W., and W. F. Kannenberg. "Longitudinal Noise in Audio Circuits," *J. Audio Eng. Soc.,* Vol. 16, No. 3 (1968).

Backus, J. *The Acoustical Foundations of Music.* New York: W. W. Norton & Co., Inc., 1969.

Baumzweiger (Bauer). "Graphical Determination of the Random Efficiency of Microphones," *J. Acoust. Soc. Amer.,* Vol. 11 (April 1940), 477-479.

Engineering Staff of Belden Corp. *Electronic Cable Handbook.* Indianapolis: Howard W. Sams & Co., Inc., 1966.

Benson, J. E., and D. F. Craig. "A Feedback-Mode Analyser/ Suppressor Unit for Auditorium Sound-System Stabilisation," *Proceedings of I.R.E.E., Australia* (March 1969).

Beranek, L. L. *Acoustic Measurements.* New York: John Wiley & Sons, Inc., 1949.

Beranek, L. L. *Acoustics.* New York: McGraw-Hill Book Co., 1954.

Beranek, L. L. *Music, Acoustics, and Architecture.* New York: John Wiley & Sons, Inc., 1962.

Beranek, L. L. *Noise Reduction.* New York: McGraw-Hill Book Co., 1960.

Bernstein, J. L. *Audio Systems.* New York: John Wiley & Sons, Inc., 1966.

Boner, C. P., and C. R. Boner. "A Procedure for Controlling Room-Ring Modes and Feedback Modes in Sound Systems with Narrow-Band Filters," *J. Audio Eng. Soc.,* Vol. 13 (Oct. 1965).

Boner, C. P., "Behavior of Sound Reinforcement in Large Halls," *J. Audio Eng. Soc.* (Project Notes), Vol. 19 (Feb. 1971).

Boner, C. P., and C. R. Boner. "Minimizing Feedback in Sound Systems and Room-Ring Modes with Passive Networks," *J. Acoust. Soc. Am.,* Vol. 37 (Jan. 1965).

Bruel, P. V. *Sound Insulation and Room Acoustics.* Chapman & Hall, 1951.

Cable, C. R. "Acoustics and the Active Enclosure," *J. Audio Eng. Soc.,* Vol. 20 (Dec. 1972).

Cable, C. R. *Loudspeaker Q—What Does It Mean?* Audio Engineering Society Convention, May 1974, Preprint No. 956 (J-5).

Catania, C. J. "Sound System Design for St. Mary's Cathedral, San Francisco," *J. Audio Eng. Soc.* (Oct. 1971).

Chory, G. "Measuring a Power Amplifier's True Output Impedance," *Syn-Aud-Con Newsletter,* Vol. 1, No. 3 (1974).

Connor, W. K. "Theoretical and Practical Considerations in the Equalization of Sound Systems," *J. Audio Eng. Soc.,* Vol. 15 (Apr. 1967).

Connor, W. K. "Experimental Investigation of Sound-System-Room Feedback," *J. Audio Eng. Soc,* Vol .21 (Jan. 1973).

Corry, A. "Unauthorized Tap Detector," *Syn-Aud-Con Newsletter,* Vol. 1, No. 3 (1974).

Corry, A. "70 Volt Line Tester During Installation," *Syn-Aud-Con Newsletter,* Vol. 1, No. 3 (1974).

Damiani, A. S. "Prequalifying a Contractor—A Major Construction Decision," *Plant Engineering* (Dec. 1970).

Davis, A. H. *Modern Acoustics.* Macmillan, 1934.

Davis, D. *The Acousta-Voicing Manual, Second Edition.* Altec Corp., 1970.

Davis, D. *Acoustical Tests and Measurements.* Indianapolis: Howard W. Sams & Co., Inc., 1965.

Davis, D. "Analyzing Loudspeaker Locations for Sound Reinforcement Systems," *J. Audio Eng. Soc.,* Vol. 17 (Dec. 1969).

Davis, D. "The Computer in Sound System Design," *Audio* (Aug. 1970).

Davis, D. "Considerations in Acousta Voicing Studio Monitors," *dB* (Dec. 1970).

Davis, D. "Equivalent Acoustic Distance," *J. Aud. Eng. Soc.,* Vol. 21 (Oct. 1973), 646-649.

Davis, D. "Facts and Fallacies on Detailed Sound System Equalization," *Audio* (1969).

Davis, D. "How Much Amplifier Power," *Audio* (June 1971).

Davis, D. "On Standardizing the Measurement of Q," *J. Aud. Eng. Soc.,* Vol. 21 (Nov. 1973) 730-731.

Davis, D. "Pertinent Sound System Practices," *Audiovisual Journal of Arizona* (Sept. 1969).

Davis, D. "Real Time Audio Spectrometry," *Recording Engineer/Producer* (1971).

Davis, D. *A Real Time Regenerative Response Method of Equalizing a Sound System.* Aud. Eng. Soc. Paper (May 1973).

Davis, D. "Sound Systems Equalization," *Progressive Architecture* (Sept. 1969).

Davis, D. "Interpreting Field Measurements of Directivity Factor and Their Relation to the Proposed Standard Method of Measuring the Directivity Factor of Loudspeakers Used in Commercial Sound Work," Aud. Eng. Soc. Preprint 1031 (K-3) Part I, May 1975.

Davis, D. "Experiments in the Enhancement of the Artist's Ability to Control His Interface With the Acoustic Environment in Large Halls," Aud. Eng. Soc. Preprint 1033 (D-2) Part I.

Davis, R. *Technical Specification.* Altec Corp., 1971.

Eshbach, O. W. *Handbook of Engineering Fundamentals,* Second Edition. New York: John Wiley & Sons, Inc., 1952.

Feves, A. *Syn-Aud-Con Newsletter,* Vol. 2, No. 2, 1975.

Fitzroy, D. "Reverberation Formula Which Seems to Be More Accurate With Nonuniform Distribution of Absorption," *J. Acoust. Soc. Am.,* Vol. 31 (July 1959), 893-897.

Fletcher, H. *Speech and Hearing in Communication.* New York: D. Van Nostrand Co. (1953).

Furduev, V. V. "Limiting Amplification of Sound in Closed Rooms," *Soviet Phys.-Acoust.,* Vol. 11 (Jan.-Mar. 1966).

Furduev, V. V. "Stability of Stereophonic Sound Amplification Systems," *Soviet Phys.-Acoust.,* Vol. 13 (Apr.-June 1968).

General Radio Co. *Useful Formulas, Tables, Curves for Random Noise.* Tech. Letter, June 1963.

Haas, H. "The Influence of a Single Echo on the Audibility of Speech," *J. Audio Eng. Soc.,* Vol. 20 (Mar. 1972).

Hall, V. "Area Covered by Ceiling Mounted Loudspeakers and Number Required for Even Distribution," *Syn-Aud-Con Newsletter,* Vol. 1, No. 4 (1974).

Harris, C. M. *Handbook of Noise Control.* New York: McGraw-Hill Book Co., 1957.

Heyser, R. C. "Breakthrough in Speaker Testing," *Audio* (Nov. 1973), 20-30.

Heyser, R. C. "Loudspeaker Characteristics and Time Delay Distortion," *J. Audio Eng. Soc.* (Jan. 1969, April 1969, and Dec. 1971).

Hilliard, J. K. "The Application of Acoustics to Jet and Missile Problems," *Altec Tech Memo* (April 18, 1958).

Hilliard, J. K. "Notes on How Phase and Delay Distortions Affect the Quality of Speech, Music and Sound Effects," *IEEE Transactions on Audio* (March-April 1964).

Hodge, S. "A Bridging Attenuator Box," *Syn-Aud-Con Newsletter,* Vol. 2 (Sept. 1974).

Hunt, F. V. *Electroacoustics.* Cambridge, Mass.: Harvard University Press, 1954.

Indlin, Y. A. and V. V. Furduev. "Regenerative Reverberation Associated with Sound Amplification in Closed Rooms," *Soviet Phys.-Acoust.,* Vol. 14 (Oct.-Dec. 1968).

ITT. *Reference Data for Radio Engineers,* Fifth Edition. Indianapolis: Howard W. Sams & Co., Inc., 1968.

Keast, D. N. *"Measurements in Mechanical Dynamics."* New York: McGraw-Hill Book Co., 1967.

Kendig, P. M., and R. E. Mueser. "Simplified Method for Determining Transducer Directivity Index," *J. Acoust. Soc. Am.,* Vol. 19, No. 4, July 1947, pp 691-694.

Klein, W. "Articulation Loss of Consonants as a Basis for the

Design and Judgement of Sound Reinforcement Systems," *J. Audio Eng. Soc.,* Vol. 19 (Dec. 1971).

Klepper, D. L. "Sound Systems in Reverberant Rooms for Worship," *J. Audio Eng. Soc.,* Vol. 18 (Aug. 1970).

Knudsen, V. O. and C. M. Harris. *Acoustical Designing in Architecture.* New York: John Wiley & Sons, Inc., 1950.

Knudsen, V. O. *Architectural Acoustics.* New York: John Wiley & Sons, Inc., 1932.

Kock, W. E. *Seeing Sound.* New York: Wiley Interscience, 1971.

Kundert, W. R. and A. P. G. Peterson, "Spectrum Analyses of Stationary Noise Signals," *Sound and Vibration* (June 1969).

Lenk, J. D. *Applications Handbook for Electrical Connectors.* Indianapolis: Howard W. Sams & Co., Inc., 1966.

Lessing, L. *A Man of High Fidelity: Edwin Howard Armstrong.* Philadelphia: J. B. Lippincott Co., 1956.

Lethert, E. "Impedance Measuring Device," *Syn-Aud-Con Newsletter,* Vol. 1, No. 2 (1973).

Lindsay, B. R. *Acoustics—Historical and Philosophical Development.* Stroudsburg, Pa.: Dowden, Hutchinson & Ross, Inc., 1973.

Ling Electronics. *Workshop Manual,* 1967.

Mankovsky, V. S. *Acoustics of Studios and Auditoria.* Communication Arts Books, 1971.

Massa, F. *Acoustic Design Charts.* Blakiston Co.

Moir, J. *High Quality Sound Reproduction.* New York: Macmillan, Inc., 1958.

Newman, R. B., and W. J. Cavanaugh. "Design for Hearing," *Progressive Architecture* (May 1959).

Noble, J. J. Altec Corp., Verbal communications.

Norris, R. F. "A Discussion of the True Coefficient of Sound Absorption—A Derivation of the Reverberation Formula." Appendix II, Pages 603-605, Knudsen, *Architectural Acoustics* (see above).

Oliver, B. M., and J. M. Cage. *Electronic Measurements and Instrumentation.* New York: McGraw-Hill Book Co., 1971.

Olson, H. F. *Acoustical Engineering.* New York: D. Van Nostrand Co., 1957.

Olson, H. F. *Music, Physics, and Engineering.* New York: Dover Publications, Inc., 1966.

Olson, H. F. *Solutions of Engineering Problems by Dynamical Analogies.* New York: D. Van Nostrand Co., 1943.

Parkin, P. H., and H. R. Humphreys. *Acoustics Noise and Buildings.* Frederick Praeger, 1958.

Peterson, A. P. G., aind E. E. Gross, Jr. *Handbook of Noise Measurement,* Seventh Edition. General Radio Co.

Peutz, V. M. A. "Articulation Loss of Consonants as a Criterion for Speech Transmission in a Room," *J. Audio Eng. Soc.,* Vol. 19 (Dec. 1971).

Peutz, V. M. A. "Designing Sound Systems for Speech Intelligibility," Audio Engineering Society Convention, May 1974, Preprint No. 956 (J-1).

Read, O., and W. L. Welch. *From Tin Foil to Stereo.* Indianapolis: Howard W. Sams & Co., Inc., 1959.

Reim, R. E. *The World's Most Powerful Sound System.* Altec Reprint (1971).

Rettinger, M. *Practical Electro Acoustics.* New York: Chemical Publishing Co., Inc., 1955.

Rudmose, W. "Equalization of Sound Systems," *Noise Contr.,* Vol. 24 (July 1958).

Sabine, P. E. *Acoustics and Architecture.* New York: McGraw-Hill Book Co., 1932.

Sabine, W. C. *Collected Papers on Acoustics.* Dover Publications, 1964.

Schroeder, M. R. "Computers in Acoustics: Symbiosis of an

Old Science and a New Tool," *J. Acoust. Soc. Am.*, Vol. 45, No. 5 (1969).

Schroeder, M. R. "Improvement of Acoustic-Feedback Stability by Frequency Shifting," *J. Acoust. Soc. Am.*, Vol. 36 (Sept. 1964).

Shankland, R. S. "Acoustics of Greek Theaters," *Physics Today* (Oct. 1973), 30-35.

Sivian, L. J., H. K. Dunn, and S. D. White, "Absolute Amplitudes and Spectra of Certain Musical Instruments and Orchestras." *IRE Transactions on Audio* (May-June 1959), 47-75.

Snow, W. B. "Basic Principles of Stereophonic Sound," *J. Soc. Mot. Pict. and Tele. Eng.*, Vol. 61 (Nov. 1953), 567-589.

Snow, W. B. "Effects of International Interference With Speech Intelligibility," *J. Audio Eng. Soc.*, Vol. 17 (Jan. 1969), 42-48.

Snow, W. B. "Frequency Characteristics of a Sound-Reinforcing System," *J. Audio Eng. Soc.*, Vol. 3 (April 1955).

Sobieralski, A. "Finding a Loudspeaker's Q by the Critical Distance Method," *Syn-Aud-Con Tech Topics*, Vol. 1, No. 4 (1974).

Sprinkle, M. C. *The Gain of Audio Amplifiers.* Page Engineering, Inc., R-1152-0068 (July 1965).

Sprinkle, M. C. "The Ultimate Noise," *dB* (June 1969).

Stanley, C. M. "To Bid or Not to Bid," *Consulting Engineer* (Jan. 1972).

Stephens, R. W. B., and A. E. Bate. *Acoustics and Vibrational Physics.* New York: St. Martin's Press, Inc., 1966.

Story, R. "Converting Tables to Equations Cuts Program Length for Calculator Use," *Electronics,* Vol. 47 (April 18, 1974), 114-115.

Symmes, W. "Simplified Method of Calculating PAG/NAG Formulas Without Use of Logs," *Syn-Aud-Con Newsletter,* Vol. 1, No. 2 (1973).

Terman, F. E. *Radio Engineers' Handbook.* New York: McGraw-Hill Book Co., 1943.

Thompson, S. P. *Calculus Made Easy.* Macmillan & Co., Ltd., 1937.

Townsley, R. R. *Passive Equalizer Design Data.* Blue Ridge Summit, Pa.: Tab Books, 1973.

Tremaine, H. M. *Audio Cyclopedia,* Second Edition. Indianapolis: Howard W. Sams & Co., Inc., 1969.

Von Bekesy, G. "Auditory Backward Inhibition in Concert Halls," *Science,* Vol. 171 (Feb. 1971).

Waterhouse, R. V. "Theory of Howlback in Reverberant Rooms," *J. Acoust. Soc. Am.,* Vol. 37 (May 1965).

Watson, F. R. *Acoustics of Buildings.* New York: John Wiley & Sons, Inc., 1923.

White Electromagnetics, Inc., *A Handbook on Electrical Filters—Synthesis, Design and Applications.* White Electromagnetics, Inc., 1963.

Wiedman, O. E. "Transmission Lines in Studios," *J. Audio Eng. Soc.,* Vol. 18 (April 1970).

Wilson, G. L. "More on Measurement of the Directivity Factor," *J. Aud. Eng. Soc.,* Vol. 22 (April 1974).

Wolff, I., and L. Malter. "Directional Radiation of Sound," *J. Acoust. Soc. Am.,* Oct. 1930, pp 201-241.

Wood, C. E. "Bridging and Mixing Techniques," *J. Aud Eng. Soc.,* Vol. 12 (Jan. 1964).

Young, R. W. "Sabine Reverberation Equation and Sound Power Calculations," *J. Acoust. Soc. Am.,* Vol. 31, No. 7. July 1959, pp 912-921.

GROUNDING PRACTICES BIBLIOGRAPHY

1. Haskett, T. R. "Removing the Mystery from Grounding," *Broadcast Engineering,* Vol. 8 (Feb. 1966).

2. Morrison, R. *Grounding and Shielding Techniques in Instrumentation.* New York: John Wiley & Sons, Inc., 1967.

3. "Recommended Wiring Practices," RCA broadcast equipment catalog.

4. Robinson, T. A. "The Role of Grounding in Eliminating Electronic Interference," *IEEE Spectrum* (July 1965).

5. *"Grounding and Noise Reduction Practices for Instrumentation Systems."* Santa Monica, Cal.: Scientific Data Systems.

6. Tremaine, H. M. *Audio Cyclopedia,* Second Edition. Indianapolis: Howard W. Sams & Co., Inc., 1969.

7. Vogelman, J. H. "A Theoretical Analysis of Grounding," *IEEE Transactions on Aerospace,* Vol. AS-2 (April 1964).

Recommended Wiring Practices

The material on installation practices contained in this appendix is presented through the courtesy of Ling Electronics.

SOLDERING TOOLS AND EQUIPMENT

Soldering Iron

Selection—The selection of the proper size of soldering iron is important, since the areas to be joined are to be heated to or above the flow temperature of the solder. Selection of an iron of insufficient size results in prolonged heating of the connection and causes cold joints. Too large an iron can cause permanent damage to electronic components. Transformer-type solder guns should not be used due to the lack of temperature control and the high possibility of component overheating and damage.

Wattage—The wattage of a soldering iron determines the rate at which heat is generated by the element. Soldering irons with wattage ratings from 20 to 60 watts are recommended for delicate instruments and very small soldering operations. A 35-watt soldering iron is recommended for printed circuit boards. A 35- to 100-watt soldering iron is recommended for general electronic work. Larger soldering irons are for extra large connections, sweating large seams, etc.

Soldering-Iron Tip—Soldering-iron tips are made in various shapes, including pointed, chisel, bent, blunt, and concave, for general or specific use (Fig. III-I). The shape of the tip used should be carefully selected for the item to be soldered. For general-purpose soldering, the pointed or chisel shapes are recommended.

Soldering-iron maintenance—The soldering iron must be properly cared for in order to obtain the best solder joints. The soldering tip should always be checked for full insertion into the heating element and tight attachment to the iron. A good grade of antiseize compound should be used on that part of the tip inserted into the heating element to aid in later removal. This will also ensure good heat transfer between the heating element and the tip.

Only soldering irons with plated tips should be used. These surface-treated tips should be cleaned, while cold, by polishing with emery cloth of approximate No. 320 grit size until the surface is bright. A *file should not be used.*

Re-tin with rosin-core solder of high tin content, such as 60/40 (tin-lead), by applying the solder to the tip as the iron is heating. Rubbing the hot tip on a clean wiping cloth will aid in distributing the solder.

The soldering iron should be maintained in good condition by keeping the tip well tinned and free from residue and pits. Oxidation scale should not be allowed to accumulate between the heating element and the tip. A bright, thin, but continuous tinned surface should be maintained on the working surface of the tip to ensure proper heat transfer and to avoid transfer of impurities to the solder connection.

Keep the tip in good working condition by wiping the hot tinned tip lightly on a wet, fine-textured natural or synthetic sponge.

Insulation Strippers

Recommended—Hand or machine precision cutting-type strippers (Fig. III-2) should be used to remove insulation from wire sizes AWG No. 12 to No. 26. It is very important to use the correct setting for the particular size of wire being stripped.

POINTED   CHISEL   BENT   BLUNT   CONCAVE

Fig. III-1. Types of soldering-iron tips.

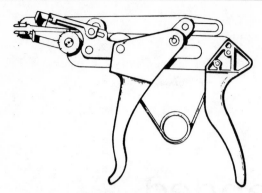

Fig. III-2. Recommended insulation stripper.

Limited Usage—The insulation stripper shown in Fig. III-3 should be used only when the recommended type will not satisfactorily perform the task. This would be especially so when stripping wire larger than AWG No. 16. On some of the very large cables, a knife may be required to remove the insulation satisfactorily.

Regardless of the type of tool being used to remove insulation from wire, great care must be taken to avoid nicking or cutting the wire strands. Such a condition weakens the wire and results in an unreliable connection. (See the section headed "Insulation Removal" for the allowable number of damaged strands.)

Strippers other than the type mentioned may be used provided that the wire is not stretched, cut, nicked, or scraped.

Fig. III-3. Limited-usage stripper.

Thermal Shunts

To prevent damage due to heat while soldering, thermal shunts (heat clamps) should be used between the solder joint and component when precision resistors, diodes, transistors, semiconductors, etc., are soldered. When in doubt, use a shunt.

Thermal shunts should be of such material, size, shape, and design as to permit rapid application and removal with minimum interference to the soldering procedure and to provide rapid heat removal from the area being soldered. They should be held in place by friction, spring tension, or any other suitable means which will prevent damage to the surface and insula-

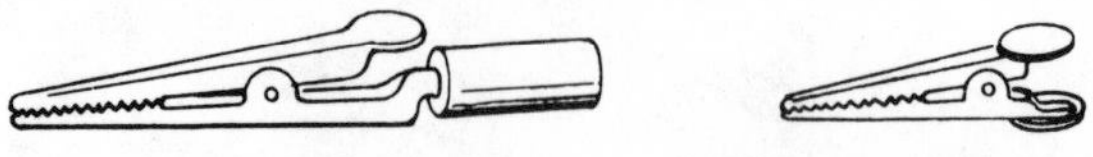

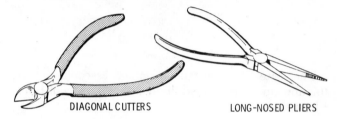

Fig. III-4. Typical thermal shunts.

tion of the wire and to the component being soldered. See Fig. III-4.

Pliers and Bending Tools

Appropriate diagonal-cutting pliers or long-nosed pliers (Fig. III-5) should be used for cutting wire and for attaching, removing, and forming wire ends. Wire-bending tools should have round, smooth bending surfaces and should be used to bend leads without nicking, ringing, or other damage to the lead or component.

Fig. III-5. Pliers and cutters.

Soldering Aid

Suitable soldering aids may be used for cleaning holes in terminals, removing oxides from terminals to be soldered, and for exerting minimum force on soldered connections to test for security.

The wire-brush end of the soldering aid is not to be used to remove flux from soldered connections. Such an action results in dulling the surface of the connection and gives the appearance of a cold joint.

SOLDERING MATERIALS

Solder

Common solder is an alloy of the soft metals tin and lead. Its composition is designated by two numbers, such as 30/70 or 60/40, the first number indicating the percentage of tin and the second the percentage of lead.

Most solder is made with a core that contains flux. All common metals are covered with a nonmetallic film known as an oxide. Unless this film is removed, soldering action cannot take place. The purpose of the flux is to melt at a lower temperature than the solder and flow ahead of it, cleaning and removing the oxides from the materials to be joined.

In professional sound, 60/40 cored solder is commonly used. With the application of minimum heat, this solder makes a good electrical connection with a clean, bright, glossy appearance.

While 60/40 solder melts at approximately 370°F, a somewhat higher temperature is required to complete the joining action. Most soldering-iron temperatures range from 600°F to 1000°F, which is sufficient for all common soldering. Fig. III-6 shows the melting behavior of the various compositions of solder.

Except where otherwise required by the design drawings or specifications, solder should conform to Federal Specifications QQ-S-571, SN 60, or SN 63.

The core should contain no ingredients which would remain in the flux residue and cause corrosion of the base metal or solder or promote electrical leakage if the residue is not removed. Solder with acid fluxes must not be used in electronic assemblies because of the corrosive action of the flux.

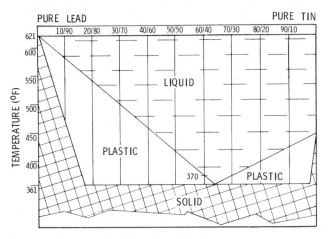

Fig. III-6. Solder flow chart.

Solvent

Solvent used for the removal of grease, oil, dirt, or excess flux may be any noncorrosive, commercially available type which will perform as intended without damage to the equipment. Ethyl alcohol conforming to Federal Specification O-E-760, Grade I, Class A or Class B; the best commercial 99% pure (by volume) isopropyl alcohol; Clorthane-NU; and perchlorethylene are acceptable. Solvent containing carbon tetrachloride should *not* be used due to the fact that it is detrimental to the health of the user.

PREPARATION FOR SOLDERING

The general soldering work area and work benches should be maintained in a clean and orderly condition. All wire and insulation cuttings, solder splatter, and other foreign matter should be removed promptly from the immediate working area. The supplies, tools, and equipment required for the soldering operation should be arranged and adjusted for best performance with the least amount of effort. The soldering-iron cord should allow sufficient room to permit free use of the iron without presenting a safety hazard.

Soldering Iron

A soldering iron of the proper wattage and tip type should be chosen for the soldering operation to be per-

formed. Ensure that the soldering iron selected is clean and in proper operating condition.

Solder

The solder to be used was described in the section headed "Solder." Since this solder is available in various diameters, it is important to choose the diameter applicable to the connection being soldered. For example, use 0.028-inch diameter for small connections; use 0.040-inch diameter for general-purpose soldering.

Choice of the proper diameter of solder to be used will aid in obtaining a satisfactory connection. Using too small a diameter of solder will result in prolonged heating of the connection while the required amount of solder is applied. If the diameter of the solder is too large, an excessive amount will be applied.

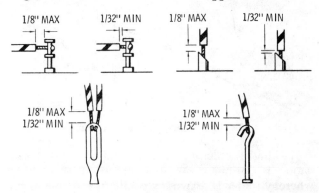

Fig. III-7. Insulation clearance.

Insulation Removal

The removal of insulation from conductors was discussed under "Insulation Strippers." Stranded wire should be twisted in the direction of the lay (natural twist of wire strands) during the stripping operation in order to maintain its original form after stripping.

The insulation should be stripped from the wire so that the insulation gap is a minimum of $\frac{1}{32}$ inch and a maximum of $\frac{1}{8}$ inch from the solder joint. (Fig. III-7).

After stripping, wire strands should be examined to ensure that the wires have not been nicked, cut, scraped, or otherwise damaged. The number of broken or damaged strands should not exceed that shown in Table III-1.

Table III-1. Allowable Number of Broken Strands

Number of Strands in Conductor	Number of Allowable Broken or Cut Strands
1-7	0
8-15	1
16-18	2
19-25	3
26-36	4
37-40	5
41 Up	6

Prior to soldering or lugging, varnish-covered conductors should have the varnish removed with Claude Michaels Super X-Var Stripper No. 622 or equivalent.

Tinning Wires

All portions of stranded wires which come in contact with the area to be soldered should be tinned (Fig. III-8) prior to attachment. The tinning should extend only far enough onto the wire to take full advantage of the area coming in contact with the connector or solder joint. Tinning or solder on the wire strands under the insulation or where flexing may occur is not acceptable, because it will cause stiffness of the wires and result in breakage.

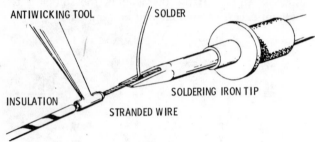

Fig. III-8. Tinning of stranded wire.

Wicking of solder up to the point of insulation termination is permitted. Wicking describes a condition whereby solder is drawn, by capillary action, into the strands of the wire and under the insulation due to excessive heat, solder, and soldering time.

Wires that are prepared for termination in any type of solderless crimped connection should not be pretinned.

Connecting Wires to Terminals

Just prior to attachment to terminals and soldering, the ends of component leads and wires should be bent into the form required by the terminal.

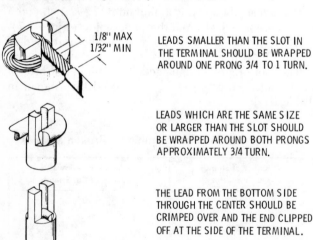

LEADS SMALLER THAN THE SLOT IN THE TERMINAL SHOULD BE WRAPPED AROUND ONE PRONG 3/4 TO 1 TURN.

LEADS WHICH ARE THE SAME SIZE OR LARGER THAN THE SLOT SHOULD BE WRAPPED AROUND BOTH PRONGS APPROXIMATELY 3/4 TURN.

THE LEAD FROM THE BOTTOM SIDE THROUGH THE CENTER SHOULD BE CRIMPED OVER AND THE END CLIPPED OFF AT THE SIDE OF THE TERMINAL.

Fig. III-9. Lead wrapping on bifurcated terminals.

Reduction of the conductor size for any reason should be avoided. Wires containing broken or nicked strands in excess of the numbers shown in Table III-1 should not be used.

Whenever possible, component leads and wires should be wrapped around the terminal or other connecting point so that a connection that is secure both electrically and mechanically is assured. A wrap of 3/4 to 1 turn around the terminal is required for mechanical security. The wire lead should be crimped or squeezed and cut to length after wrapping. See Figs. III-9 through III-13. (Component leads soldered to Tektronix strips do not require a mechanical wrap prior to soldering.)

THE WRAP SHOULD EXTEND THROUGH THE HOLE 3/4 TO 1 TURN.

Fig. III-10. Lead wrapping on lug-type terminals.

SMALL LEADS OR WIRES SHOULD BE WRAPPED THROUGH THE HOLE 3/4 TO 1 TURN.

LARGE WIRE OR LEADS WHICH WOULD DAMAGE THE TERMINAL WHEN CRIMPED SHOULD NOT BE BENT AFTER PASSING THROUGH THE HOLE.

Fig. III-11. Lead wrapping on thin-section terminals.

No wire should be taut. Sufficient slack must be provided to compensate for temperature changes and vibration. A service loop is also necessary to allow removal and reconnection of the wire during normal service. See section titled "Wire Routing."

THE WRAP SHOULD EXTEND AROUND THE TERMINAL 3/4 TO 1 TURN.

Fig. III-12. Lead wrapping on turret terminals.

THE LEAD SHOULD EXTEND AROUND THE TERMINAL 3/4 TO 1 TURN.

Fig. III-13. Lead wrapping on hook terminals.

For solder-cup terminals of connectors, the tinned wire or lead should not be bent or formed. All conductors terminating in a solder cup should bottom in the cup (Fig. III-14). Pretinned wire and terminals should

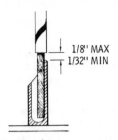

Fig. III-14. Solder-cup terminal.

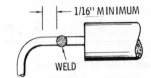

Fig. III-16. Welded lead with proper bend.

be used when soldering to connectors. Additional solder is not usually required then. Care should be taken to ensure that the correct lettered or numbered pin and wire are mated together prior to soldering.

When leads are soldered to a connector, a jig should be used to hold the connector in place. The jig should be positioned so that the terminal cups of the connector are tilted backward slightly to allow flux and gasses to rise to the surface.

Vinyl sleeving or insulation should be placed over all bus wires, component leads, and jumpers which, due to their close proximity to other components, could cause an electrical short. The vinyl sleeving should be of such a length that specified insulation clearance is maintained.

Component Mounting

Whenever possible, components should be mounted so that all values or part numbers may be read and are oriented in the same direction. The components should rest firmly on the mounting board.

Component leads should emerge from the component body a minimum of $\frac{1}{16}$ inch prior to bending. This will assure that a strain has not been placed on delicate portions of the component.

To prevent damage, component leads should be bent with a suitable bending tool. The radius of the bend should be equal to or greater than twice the lead diameter (Fig. III-15).

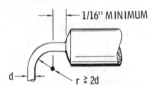

Fig. III-15. Minimum lead bend.

On components, such as tantalum capacitors, that have a welded lead, the lead should be held firmly by a suitable tool on the side of the weld away from the component body during the bending operation. The minimum distance from the weld to the start of the bend should be $\frac{1}{16}$ inch (Fig. III-16).

No component lead should be taut. Sufficient slack must be provided to compensate for temperature changes and vibration. Fig. III-17 illustrates examples

of acceptable and unacceptable mounting of components.

Special tools which crimp a loop into the component lead are available. When such a tool is used, the loop should begin a minimum of $\frac{1}{4}$ inch from the component body or weld joint in the lead, and a loop is required in only one of the leads.

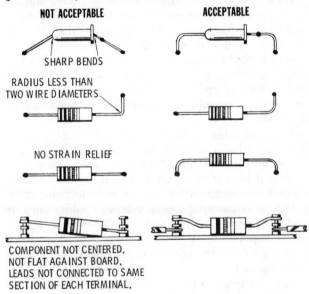

Fig. III-17. Component mounting.

Whenever possible, parts should be centered between their mounting points. A minimum of $\frac{1}{4}$ inch of lead should be maintained between the body of the part and the solder joint.

Component leads and wires should be wrapped to a terminal in such a manner that any tension on the wire will be transmitted to the terminal and not to the solder (Fig. III-18).

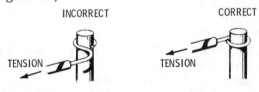

Fig. III-18. Wire wrap.

Whenever possible, component leads should be connected above permanent wiring on terminals to facilitate repair without distributing the wiring. See Fig. III-19.

Fig. III-19. Connection of component leads to terminals.

SOLDERING

Requirements

Solder is not glue or cement. It does not simply stick together the metals to be joined, but forms a new alloy of tin and lead and the metals being soldered. In order for satisfactory solder joints to be formed, the parts to be joined must be clean, and the proper amount of heat must be applied.

Cleanliness is of utmost importance, and the surfaces to be joined must be entirely free from foreign matter and oxide (corrosion) films. Normally, the cleansing action of the flux in cored solder is sufficient; however, it sometimes becomes necessary to remove oxides by a physical means, such as with a special lead-cleaning tool. Handling and touching the leads of components and areas to be soldered should be avoided whenever possible.

The application of heat melts the solder, changes the flux into a liquid so that its cleaning action can take place, and allows the alloying to reach completion. Sufficient heat must be applied to bring the temperature of the base metal up to the melting point of the solder, thus ensuring a proper flow of solder with the edges feathering out to a thin line. Excessive heat damages components and insulation, while insufficient heat causes cold solder connections (which will be discussed later).

In order to learn how to make a good solder joint, it will help to know what happens when molten solder is applied to a properly cleaned and heated joint. The molten solder, even though it is hundreds of degrees cooler than the temperature required to melt either copper or steel, actually dissolves some of the copper or steel. The copper or steel then goes into solution with the solder. Upon solidifying, the copper or steel remains dissolved in the solder, and, at the area of contact between the solder and the metals being joined, a new alloy is formed. This new alloy provides a continuous metallic path from conductor metal to solder to conductor metal.

Solder Application

Apply the flat face of the adequately heated soldering iron directly against the metals to be joined, and at the same time apply the cored solder at the exact point of iron contact. Complete the joint by applying solder to the assembly on the side opposite the soldering-iron tip. Do not remove the iron from the assembly before solder has been drawn to all parts of the joint.

Solder should *not* be applied to the soldering-iron tip and allowed to flow over the joint. Such an action contaminates the joint with impurities from the soldering-iron tip and burns off the flux required for cleaning the metals to be joined.

Sufficient solder should be applied to cover the terminal, but application of excessive solder should be avoided. The contour of the wire should be visible after soldering.

Avoid any movement of the wire or other parts of the joint before the solder has solidified. The wire must be fused directly to the terminal. Otherwise, the result is a "fractured joint." The solder should be allowed to cool normally, while any movement of the wire is restricted.

It is not necessary to fill the eye of closed-type terminals with solder. Use only sufficient solder to attain a good joint. However, when large wires cannot be mechanically secured to thin-section terminals (Fig. III-11), the eye of the terminal must be filled with solder.

After soldering, there should be no evidence of charring, burning, or other damage from the soldering operation. There should be no splattering of flux or solder on adjacent parts.

Solder Connections

A properly soldered connection appears shiny and smooth. The quantity of solder used should be just sufficient to make a good electrical bond and allow the contour of the wire to be visible. The solder will spread evenly, rather than build up, and should flow completely around the base of the terminal and form a small fillet at the junction. The edges of the solder should feather out and not turn under (Fig. III-20).

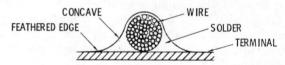

Fig. III-20. Cross section of properly soldered connection.

A "cold" solder connection (Fig. III-21) is not acceptable. This highly resistive joint appears dull and uneven and is caused by (1) not applying enough heat to allow the solder to flow freely, (2) "packing" solder on top of an unclean terminal, or (3) moving the conductor before the solder has cooled and hardened.

Excessive solder is indicated by peaks, domes, or an overflow of solder. When the proper amount of solder is used, the joint should be covered, and the contour of the wire should be visible.

A "rosin joint" has the appearance of a good solder connection; however, when inspected by probing, the wire will move under pressure. This is caused by the

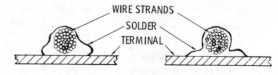

Fig. III-21. Cold solder connections.

presence of flux deposits at the junction of the elements soldered.

A "fractured joint" has a coarse crystalline appearance and separations at the junction of the elements soldered. This is caused by movement of the elements during cooling and solidifying of the solder.

Solder-cup terminals such as those on Cannon connectors should be prefilled with solder prior to insertion of the wire. Minimum and maximum amounts of solder build-up on cup terminals are shown in Fig. III-22. Sufficient heat should be applied to solder-cup terminals to allow any trapped rosin flux to escape to the surface.

Extreme care must be taken when soldering to prevent burning of wire insulation and components with the soldering iron.

After the soldering operation is completed, flux should be removed as described previously in the section on solvents.

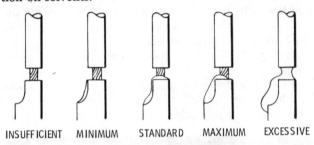

Fig. III-22. Solder in solder-cup terminals.

Soldering connections which must be reworked should first have all excess solder removed from the wires and terminals so that they are neat and clean. The means for removing this solder may be one of the following:

1. The use of a well-tinned soldering-iron tip that is hot enough to melt and draw off the solder
2. Wicking—using stranded wire with a hot soldering-iron tip on the terminal so that the excess solder flows onto and up the stranded wire
3. The use of a suction device which draws off the molten solder from the terminal.

Reworking Solder Connections

After the terminal is clean and ready to be resoldered, instructions contained earlier in this section should be followed for making the new connection.

Inspection of Soldered Connections

The quality of each soldered connection should be 100% visually inspected. Reliable soldered electrical connections should be clean and have a shiny, bright appearance; no porosity; good fillet between conductor and terminal; good adherence of conductor to terminal; and no excess solder.

In all applications except for solder cups, the contour of the wire or lead should be visible after soldering, and the end of the wire or lead should not extend beyond the terminal dimensions (except as specified later for printed circuit boards). In solder-cup applications, the contour of the wire and leads should be visible from the insulation to the point of entry into the cup.

Evidence of any defects, including but not limited to the following, should be cause for rejection of a soldered connection:

1. Charring, burning, wicking or other damage to insulation
2. Splattering of flux or solder on adjacent connections or components
3. Solder points (peaks)
4. Pits, scars, or holes
5. Excessive solder which obscures the connection configuration
6. Excessive wicking
7. Loose leads or wires
8. Cold solder connection
9. Rosin solder connection
10. Disturbed (fractured) solder connection
11. Cut, nicked, or scraped leads or wires
12. Unclean connection (lint, residue, flux, solder splash, dirt, etc.)
13. Insufficient solder

(A) Acceptable solder joint.

(B) Acceptable wrap.   *(C) Unacceptable wrap.*

Fig. III-23. Leads attached to turret terminal.

(A) Acceptable wrap.

(B) Acceptable solder joint.

(C) Unacceptable wrap.

(D) Unacceptable joint.

Fig. III-24. Connection of a lead to a turret terminal.

Examples of acceptable and unacceptable wraps and soldered connections are illustrated in Figs. III-23 through III-31. Fig. III-23A shows even solder flow, the outline of the leads is visible, and the insulation is a good distance from the joint. In Fig. III-23B, the leads

(A) Acceptable wrap and solder joint.

(B) Unacceptable wrap and solder joint.

Fig. III-25. Two leads connected to turret terminal.

are tightly wrapped for mechanical strength, the leads are in full contact with the terminal, and there is good spacing of the insulation. By contrast, in Fig. III-23C, the top lead is too long and is not wrapped tightly enough, the middle lead is poorly wrapped, the bottom lead is too long and has more than one full wrap, and the insulation on all three leads is too close to the terminal.

In Fig. III-24A, the lead is properly wrapped to one full turn and is in full contact with the terminal, and the insulation is a good distance from the terminal. Fig. III-24B shows a joint in which the solder is well sweated, the outline of the wire and wire strands is visible, and the insulation is a good distance from the terminal. Fig. III-24C shows a wrap with more than one full turn; also, the insulation is too close to the terminal, and there are broken wire strands. Fig. III-24D shows cold solder—the solder is not drawn to all parts of the joint because insufficient heat was applied. In addition, there is stray solder where the iron hit the terminal, and there is too much solder on the front of the lead and none on the rear.

In Fig. III-25A, both component leads show good wrap, the solder is well filleted on the top and bottom and between the leads, and the outline of the leads is visible. In Fig. III-25B, the top (stranded) lead is too long and is not properly wrapped, and there is no sol-

(A) Two leads poorly wrapped and soldered.

(B) Single lead poorly wrapped and soldered.

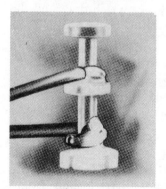

(C) Two leads poorly soldered.

(D) Component lead poorly wrapped and soldered.

Fig. III-26. Improper connections to a turret terminal.

der fillet on top of the lead. The bottom lead is too long, is is not properly wrapped (not in full contact with the terminal), and there is excess solder.

Fig. III-26 shows additional examples of unacceptable connections. In Fig. III-26A, solder has not flowed to the underside of the top component lead, there is no solder on the bottom component lead, the bottom component lead is improperly wrapped, and there is solder splatter on the terminal. In Fig. III-26B, the lead is poorly wrapped (more than one full turn), the insulation extends into the solder, the lead is poorly positioned, and solder has not flowed around the lead. Fig. III-26C shows two stranded leads. The top lead has sufficient solder on the underside but none of the upper surface, and the insulation is in the solder. The bottom lead has a cold solder joint, and the insulation is in the solder. In Fig. III-26D, the lead is improperly positioned and poorly wrapped (more than one full turn). The joint is dirty and is a cold solder joint, and there is excess solder.

Fig. III-27 shows acceptable and unacceptable wraps and solder joints involving hook terminals. In Fig. III-27A, there is maximum contact of the stranded wire with the terminal, and the insulation is a good distance from the joint. In Fig. III-27B, the outline of the stranded wire is visible, the outline of the hook is visible, solder has not wicked up the wire to the insulation, and the insulation is a good distance from the joint. In Fig. III-27C, however, the insulation is too close to the joint, the lead end is too long, and the terminal was

bent during application of the wire to the terminal. In Fig. III-27D, there is excess solder, the hook is completely filled, the outline of the wire and hook are hidden, and solder has wicked up the wire to the insulation.

Fig. III-28A shows an acceptable wrap around a lug terminal. The wrap is a full turn without overlap, and the insulation is a good distance from the joint. Fig. III-28B shows an acceptable solder joint, in which the outline of the wire and strands is visible and the insulation is a good distance from the joint. In Fig. III-28C, the wrap is too long (more than one full turn), and in Fig. III-28D, the mechanical wrap is poor, the insulation is too far from the joint, the joint is dirty, and there is excess solder.

Fig. III-29A is another example of a good wrap with the insulation a good distance from the terminal. In Fig. III-29B, the outline of the stranded wire is visible, there is a good fillet, the insulation is a good distance from the terminal, and solder has not wicked up to the insulation. In Fig. III-29C, the wrap extends too far above the top of the terminal, the insulation is too far

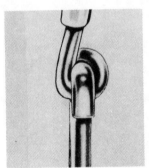

(A) Acceptable wrap.

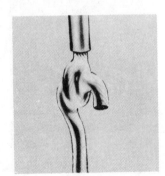

(B) Acceptable solder joint.

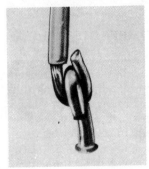

(C) Unacceptable wrap.

(D) Unacceptable joint.

Fig. III-27. Connections to hook terminals.

(A) Acceptable wrap.

(B) Acceptable solder joint.

(C) Unacceptable wrap.

(D) Unacceptable joint.

Fig. III-28. Connections to a lug terminal.

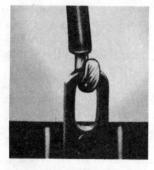

(A) Acceptable wrap.

(B) Acceptable solder joint.

(C) Unacceptable wrap.

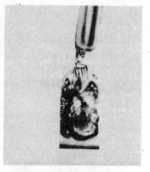

(D) Unacceptable joint.

Fig. III-29. Connections to a terminal.

from the terminal, and the wire is poorly wrapped. In Fig. III-29D, excess solder fills the aperture, the joint is dirty, it is a cold solder joint, and solder has wicked up to the insulation.

Fig. III-30 shows additional examples of solder joints. In Fig. III-30A, note the good wraps, the joint well filleted, and the outline of wires visible through the solder. In Fig. III-30B, note the poor wraps and the

(A) Acceptable solder joint.

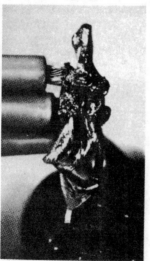

(B) Unacceptable joint.

Fig. III-30. Three wires connected to one terminal.

bottom insulation extending into the solder. Note also that the solder is dirty and that excess solder has run down the terminal.

Fig. III-31A shows another example of a good wrap with good insulation length. Fig. III-31B shows a good wrap with good insulation length and good soldering. In Fig. III-31C, the wrap is too long (more than a full turn), and the insulation is too close to the terminal. Fig. III-31D is another example of a cold solder joint.

(A) Acceptable wrap.

(B) Acceptable solder joint.

(C) Unacceptable wrap.

(D) Unacceptable joint.

Fig. III-31. Additional examples of wraps and solder joints.

SOLDERING OF PRINTED CIRCUIT BOARDS

The mounting of components should generally be as described earlier in the section headed "Component Mounting." Circuit boards with circuitry on each side connected with eyelets or plated-through holes should have solder applied in such a manner as to ensure flow through the hole or eyelet to provide an electrical connection to each side of the board. (Fig. III-32). Useco-type terminals swaged to the circuit board and connected to the circuitry should also be soldered to the circuitry to ensure good electrical contact.

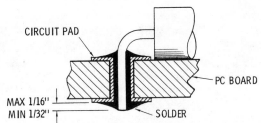

CIRCUIT PAD

PC BOARD

MAX 1/16"
MIN 1/32"

SOLDER

Fig. III-32. Component mounting on printed circuit board.

Resistors of five-watt size and larger mounted parallel to the circuit board should be mounted a minimum of ⅛ inch and a maximum of ¼ inch above the board to prevent damage to the board due to heat dissipation and to allow free air circulation. Wires should not be routed beneath resistors of this size.

Component leads should be cut to a length that will allow the lead to extend a minimum of $\frac{1}{32}$ inch and a maximum of $\frac{1}{16}$ inch beyond the opposite side of the board (Fig. III-32). Component leads that must be bent over after emerging from the circuit board, in order to hold the component in place during soldering, should be bent parallel to and in the direction of the circuitry, and the bent end should not be longer than ⅛ inch (Fig. III-33).

After all soldering operations are complete, flux should be removed as described in the section on solvents.

Components that are not adequately sealed by design must not be subjected to a cleaning bath while on a circuit board. They must be mounted after the cleaning bath and then hand soldered.

When hand soldering to printed circuit boards, use only sufficient heat to cause the solder to flow readily. Excessive heat may delaminate the printed conductor from the board.

Typical satisfactory and unsatisfactory soldered printed circuit board connections are illustrated in Figs. III-34 through III-37. In Fig. II-34A, note the good preforming of the lead and the appearance of a well sweated and filleted joint formed with sufficient solder. Fig. II-34B shows excess solder and solder too far up on the component lead. Fig. III-34C shows a cold solder joint, the lack of a fillet around the component lead, and the possible presence of oxide on the component lead.

Similarly, in Fig. III-35A note the good preforming of the component leads and the fact that the joint is well

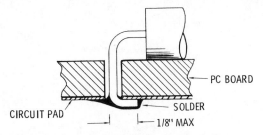

CIRCUIT PAD

PC BOARD

SOLDER

1/8" MAX

Fig. III-33. Component-lead bend on printed circuit board.

sweated and filleted. Note the varying heights of the component leads, as a result of different-sized components. In contrast, Fig. III-35B shows poor preforming of the leads, cold solder, excess solder, and a dirty joint.

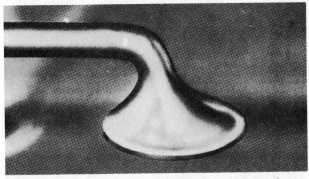

(A) Acceptable.

(B) Unacceptable—excess solder.

(C) Unacceptable—cold solder.

Fig. III-34. Single leads soldered to printed board.

Fig. III-36 shows five lead ends soldered to a printed board. Note the characteristics of the joints, identified by numbers as follows:

1. (Unacceptable) Oxide or rosin exposed on pigtail end.
2. (Acceptable) Outline of pigtail end visible through solder; joint well filleted.
3. (Unacceptable) Pigtail end not straight through eyelet; not covered with solder.
4. (Unacceptable) Pigtail end partly exposed to oxidation.
5. (Unacceptable) Cold solder; dirty joint; no fillet.

Fig. III-37A shows a good crimp of the end of a lead. Fig. 37B shows a crimped lead soldered to the foil in an acceptable manner; note that the outline of the lead is visible and the joint is well filleted. Fig. III-37C shows a poorly crimped, dirty pigtail. Fig. III-37D shows an unacceptable solder joint; note that there is excess solder, but it has not flowed freely, and that the joint is dirty.

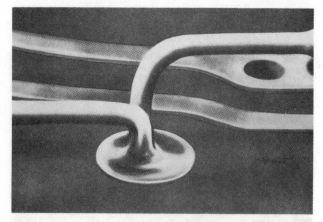

(A) Acceptable.

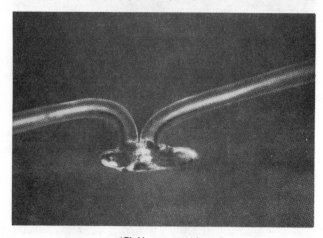

(B) Unacceptable.

Fig. III-35. Two leads soldered to printed board.

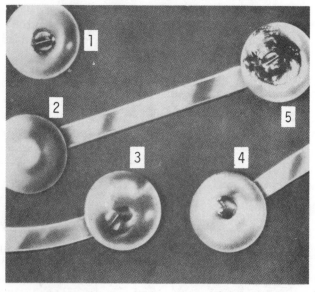

1. Unacceptable.
2. Acceptable.
3. Unacceptable.
4. Unacceptable.
5. Unacceptable.

Fig. III-36. Lead ends soldered to printed board.

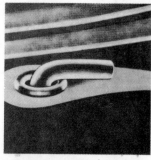

(A) Acceptable crimp.   (B) Acceptable solder.

(C) Unacceptable crimp.   (D) Unacceptable solder.

Fig. III-37. Crimped leads on printed circuit board.

GENERAL ASSEMBLY METHODS

The assembly of hardware is a major activity in the installation of equipment. The screws, bolts, nuts, and washers used are simple mechanical parts selected to fulfill a specific purpose. The common types of hardware used in professional sound are shown in Fig. III-38.

Mechanical Assembly

Acceptable types of hardware assesmblies for the different sizes of hardware to be used are shown in Fig.

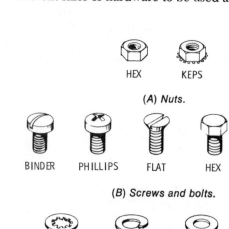

HEX   KEPS

(A) Nuts.

BINDER   PHILLIPS   FLAT   HEX   HEX SOCKET, BUTTON

(B) Screws and bolts.

INTERNAL TOOTH STAR   SPLIT   FLAT   BELLEVILLE

(C) Washers.

Fig. III-38. Types of hardware.

III-39. The hardware is arranged to provide a safe and secure clamping action.

In general, standard vendor shelf items should be assembled with vendor-supplied hardware. When other hardware is specified, discard the vendor-supplied hardware and assemble accordingly.

For hardware up to and including ⅜-inch diameter, internal-tooth lockwashers and Keps nuts should be used. For hardware larger than ⅜-inch diameter, split-ring lockwashers and hex-head nuts should be used.

A flat washer is necessary between the material and the lockwasher or screw head only when oversize or slotted holes are encountered.

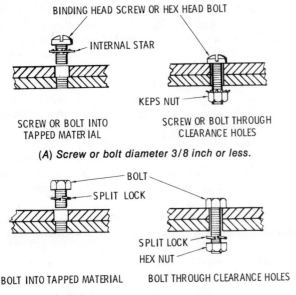

BINDING HEAD SCREW OR HEX HEAD BOLT

INTERNAL STAR

KEPS NUT

SCREW OR BOLT INTO TAPPED MATERIAL

SCREW OR BOLT THROUGH CLEARANCE HOLES

(A) Screw or bolt diameter 3/8 inch or less.

BOLT

SPLIT LOCK

SPLIT LOCK

HEX NUT

BOLT INTO TAPPED MATERIAL

BOLT THROUGH CLEARANCE HOLES

(B) Bolt diameter greater than 3/8 inch.

Fig. III-39. Hardware assemblies.

Self-tapping or sheet-metal screws do not normally require the use of additional hardware. A flat washer may be required when oversize or slotted holes are encountered.

Soft, nonmetallic washers are required when ceramic or other brittle material is to come in contact with a metallic surface. The washer is placed between the ceramic and the metallic surface.

All assembly hardware should be tightened so that it cannot be tightened further without damage to the threads or objects being joined.

A flat-head screw being assembled into tapped material does not require a lockwasher under the head. Glyptal compound should be applied to the screw threads to prevent the screw from loosening. Glyptal compound is a locking compound that dries semihard, and, although it may be broken later, it will prevent an item from loosening as a result of vibration.

After assembly, nuts, bolts, and screws with burrs or abrasions should be replaced. Screws, bolts, or threaded rod cut to size should have the cut end neatly dressed with a file.

Thread Engagement

Screws or bolts entering tapped material should have a thread engagement of at least the diameter of the screw or bolt being used unless specified otherwise (Fig. III-40A). In soft material such as aluminum or brass, the thread engagement should be at least 1½ times the diameter of the screw or bolt being used unless specified otherwise (Fig. III-40B). When hardware is assembled into tapped material, the projection of the screw or bolt through the material should be kept to a minimum.

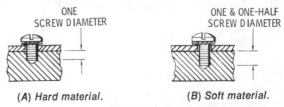

ONE SCREW DIAMETER

ONE & ONE-HALF SCREW DIAMETER

(A) Hard material.

(B) Soft material.

Fig. III-40. Minimum thread engagement.

When hardware is assembled into through-holes, the screw or bolt should extend not less than 1½ threads beyond the face of the nut, but not more than the next standard length required for the 1½ thread minimum (Fig. III-41).

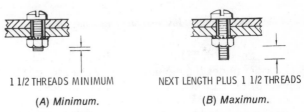

1 1/2 THREADS MINIMUM

NEXT LENGTH PLUS 1 1/2 THREADS

(A) Minimum.

(B) Maximum.

Fig. III-41. Minimum and maximum screw or bolt length.

Chassis and Panel Mounting Into Enclosures

The use of Phillips-head screws and flat washers to mount chassis and panels into enclosures reduces the possibility of scratching the panel by slippage of the screwdriver. A lockwasher is not required. Special filler panels should be mounted with the oval-head Phillips screw, cup washer, and nylon washer supplied with the panel.

Front-Panel Assembly—Hardware Usage

For all permanent attachments of components to front panels of chassis if the mounting hardware would be visible from in front of the unit, black button-head, hexagon-socket machine screws and black flat washers may be used. A lockwasher is not required.

Special Assembly of Electrical Parts

Special electrical parts such as indicator lamps, fuse holders, and variable resistors vary in size and shape and thus require different mounting methods. See Figs. III-42, III-43, and III-44.

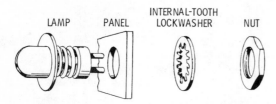

Fig. III-42. Typical installation of lamp assembly.

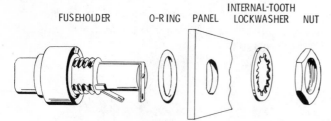

Fig. III-43. Typical installation of fuseholder.

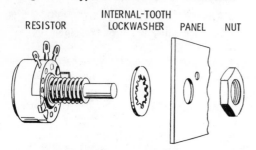

Fig. III-44. Typical installation of variable resistor.

Transistors with TO-3 cases require an internal-tooth lockwasher under the mounting screw head for positive contact of the case with the conducting surface. A thin, even coating of Wakefield Thermal Compound or equivalent should be applied to the transistor mounting surface prior to mounting (Fig. III-45). If a mica washer is used to insulate the transistor from the mounting surface, apply nonconducting thermal compound to the mounting surfaces on each side of the mica washer.

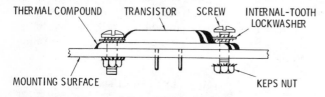

Fig. III-45. Uninsulated mounting of transistor in TO-3 case.

Transistors in TO-5 cases should be mounted so that a minimum distance of ¼ inch is maintained from the transistor body to the solder joint. When such transistors are mounted on printed circuit boards, transistor mounting pads should be used whenever possible.

When mounting SCR's, apply a thin, even coating of Wakefield Thermal Compound or equivalent to the mounting surface and install as in Fig. III-46. The specified number of Belleville washers should be used,

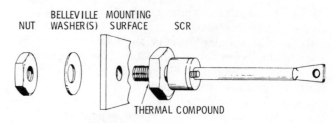

Fig. III-46. Mounting of an SCR.

and all washers are to be mounted in the same direction.

After installation, each SCR or stud-mounted diode should be tightened to the appropriate torque specified by the manufacturer. Glyptal compound may be applied to the junction of the threads and retaining nut to indicate that the device has been torqued to specifications.

Stud-mounted semiconductors do not require the use of thermal compound when mounted without heat sinks. When they are mounted on a heat sink or metalwork intended as a heat sink, apply a thin, even coating of thermal compound to the mounting surface of the semiconductor. If a mica washer is used to insulate the semiconductor from the heat sink, apply thermal compound of the nonconducting type to the mounting surfaces on each side of the mica washer.

Feedthrough-type BNC connectors are normally mounted in such a manner as to isolate them electrically from the mounting surface (Fig. III-47). If it should be required that the connector body be in direct contact with the mounting surface, the fiber washers are eliminated from the arrangement shown.

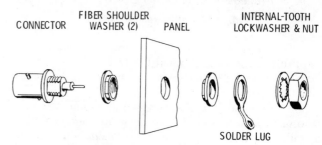

Fig. III-47. Mounting of BNC connector.

Although such a practice is not desirable, it sometimes becomes necessary to attach component leads or wires to other component leads. When this must be done, these leads or wires should be attached a minimum of ¼ inch from the component body. See Fig. III-48.

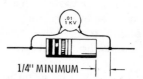

Fig. III-48. Attachment of component to component leads.

Cinch–Jones–type terminal boards provided with two mounting holes on each end may be mounted utilizing only one of the holes on each end.

Hubbel ac connectors should be wired as follows using 3-wire cable: brass terminal—hot wire; copper or plated terminal—common wire; green terminal—ground.

Solderless Lugs and Lugging

One method of attaching hookup wire to components is by using solderless lugs. The smaller sizes are insulated, color-coded, and used on stranded wire sizes AWG No. 22 to No. 10. Noninsulated types are used on wires ranging from AWG No. 8 to No. 2 and 1/0 to 4/0.

The common types of solderless insulated lugs are shown in Fig. III-49. The spade type is normally used only on terminal boards or relays, lights, etc., supplied with U washers. The ring type is used for all other screw-down applications. Push-on lugs are used on relays and switches that have terminals to accept such a lug.

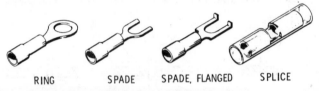

RING   SPADE   SPADE, FLANGED   SPLICE

Fig. III-49. Solderless insulated lugs.

The selection of the proper lug will be governed by the size of the wire and the size of the screw which will be used to attach it.

The color of the lug barrel indicates the size of wire which may be lugged to it reliably. Color codes of insulated lugs are as follows:

AWG No. 22 to No. 18—Red
AWG No. 16 to No. 14—Blue
AWG No. 12 to No. 10—Yellow
AWG No. 12 to No. 10—Yellow Large Bell (White)

The wire for insertion into the lug should be stripped to a length which is 2/3 that of the terminal barrel and then inserted into the barrel up to the insulation. The insulation should butt firmly against the internal shoulder of the barrel (Fig. III-50).

The free end of the wire strands should be no less than flush with the far end of the barrel, but they

should not extend more than 1/16 inch past the far end of the barrel. See Fig. III-50.

The lug, when inserted into the jaws of the lugger, should be placed so that the crimp will be made at the exact top and bottom of the barrel. The lugger should be of the same color and manufacture as the lug.

Wire splicing is not encouraged, but sometimes it becomes necessary. Splice lugs are transparent so that the tip of the wire may be seen and are color-coded for the wire size.

It is sometimes necessary to use insulated lugs on solid wire. After crimping, the wire must be soldered to the lug for added reliability. Minimum heat should be applied to avoid excessive swelling of the lug insulation. Whenever tinned stranded wire is lugged, the wire must be soldered to the lug for added reliability the same as for solid wire.

When crimped with the proper tool, a red lug will have a single raised dot in the die mark on top of the lug; a blue lug will have two raised dots. If crimped red or blue lugs display other than the number of dots specified, this indicates the wrong lugger was used, which is cause for rejection.

Noninsulated lugs for AWG No. 8 and larger wire are crimped with hydraulic or pneumatic luggers. Care must be taken to ensure that the proper die for the lug to be crimped is accurately positioned in the jaws of the lugger.

The lug should be placed in the jaws of the lugger so that the crimp will be made on the exact top or all four sides of the lug, depending on the type of lugger used.

The wire for insertion into the lug should be carefully stripped to a length which will allow the wire strands to be no less than flush with and no more than 1/16 inch past the far end of the barrel. See Fig. III-51. The gap between the noninsulated lug and the wire insulation should be a minimum of 1/16 inch and a maximum of 3/16 inch.

Any fraying of wire insulation at the lug should be neatly and uniformly covered with vinyl sleeving or other suitable material. Electrical tape should not be used. The gap between the insulation and the lug should not be covered.

Noninsulated lugs for AWG No. 22 to No. 10 wire are usually restricted for use with solid wire. When they are crimped with the Amp Type W lugger, the wire does not have to be soldered to the lug. The lug should be placed in the jaws of the lugger so that the

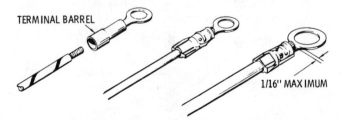

TERMINAL BARREL

1/16" MAXIMUM

Fig. III-50. Wire insertion and proper crimp for insulated lug.

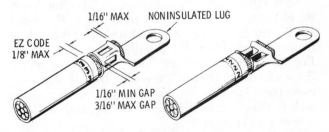

1/16" MAX   NONINSULATED LUG

EZ CODE
1/8" MAX

1/16" MIN GAP
3/16" MAX GAP

Fig. III-51. Noninsulated lug assembly (AWG No. 8 and larger).

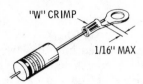

Fig. III-52. Noninsulated lug on resistor lead.

crimp will be made on the exact top of the lug. See Fig. III-52. The end of the wire, after lugging, should be no less than flush with and no more than $\frac{1}{16}$ inch past the far end of the barrel.

Noninsulated push-on lugs are for use with small wire in special cases. The Amp Type F lugger may be used to crimp the lug around the stranded wire and a portion of its insulation. The wire for insertion into this type of lug should be carefully stripped to a length which will allow the wire strands to be no less than flush with and no more than $\frac{1}{16}$ inch past the end of the center section of the lug while the entire rear section of the lug supports the wire insulation. The insulation should not become crimped by the center section. See Fig. III-53. The wire does not have to be soldered to the lug unless solid wire or wire smaller than AWG No. 22 is used.

Fig. III-53. Noninsulated push-on lug assembly.

Compression lugs have a bolt or Allen screw that compresses the wire in the lug. The wire for insertion into these lugs should be carefully stripped the same as for noninsulated lugs. The minimum and maximum lengths of free wire strands through the lug, and the gap between the lug and wire insulation are the same as for noninsulated lugs. Any fraying of wire insulation at the lug should be neatly and uniformly covered with vinyl sleeving or other suitable material. Electrical tape should not be used. The gap between the insulation and the lug should not be covered. Wires should not be tinned prior to insertion into compression lugs. Heating of the lug during equipment operation may cause the solder to flow, resulting in a loose connection.

Electrical Connections With Lugs

Acceptable types of hardware assemblies for securing electrical connections are shown in Figs. III-54 and III-55. For hardware up to and including $\frac{3}{8}$ inch in diameter, internal-tooth lockwashers, flat washers, and Keps nuts should be used. The only purpose of the flat washer is to prevent turning of the lug when the connection is tightened. For hardware large than $\frac{3}{8}$ inch in diameter, split-ring lockwashers and hex-head nuts should be used.

Fig. III-56 shows the proper assembly of a ceramic

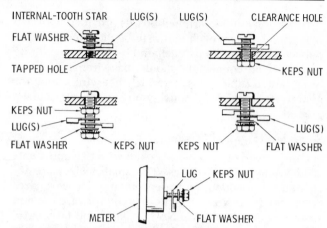

Fig. III-54. Hardware and lug assemblies for bolt or screw diameter of 3/8 inch or less.

insulator used as a tie-point and the connection of lugs to it.

When wires are attached to terminal boards, flanged spade-type lugs should be used. Use hardware supplied with the terminal board and do not add lockwashers.

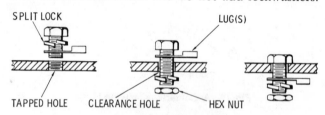

Fig. III-55. Hardware and lug assemblies for bolt or screw diameter greater than 3/8 inch.

When more than one lug must be attached to any one terminal on a terminal board or component, the lugs should be inserted back-to-back. The top lug should be a flanged spade lug; the bottom lug(s) should be the regular spade type. No more than three lugs should be attached to any one terminal, except for separate ground connections.

When attaching wires to components that are supplied with "U" washers and screws, use the supplied hardware and do not add lockwashers. The lugs to be used should be the regular spade type.

Identification of Wire Ends

In general, the ends of wires should be marked or coded to identify the terminal number or point to

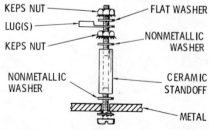

Fig. III-56. Ceramic standoff used as tie point.

which they attach. This does not apply to the ends of wires that are attached by soldering or to wires attached to a common ground or bus bar.

Three methods commonly used for identifying wire ends are:

1. EZ Codes or Brady labels
2. Ty-Rap markers
3. Special cloth tape

EZ Codes—Wires attached with red, blue, yellow, or white insulated lugs may have EZ Codes applied, neatly and uniformly, to the terminal barrel of the lug (Fig. III-57).

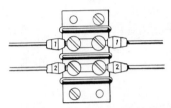

Fig. III-57. Identification of insulated lugs.

Matching connectors (plugs) for chassis should be identified with the connector (jack) number or abbreviated name on the chassis they mate with. The last EZ Code in the identification should be placed on the wire(s) ⅛ inch from the end of the plug.

Wires of No. 8, No. 6, and No. 4 size should have the EZ Code neatly and uniformly applied to the wire insulation not more than ⅛ inch back from the end of the insulation.

Jumpers less than 6 inches in length whose termination is obvious, such as to banks of capacitors or resistors, need not be marked.

Ty-Rap—Wires larger than No. 4 or a group of wires tied together and terminating at one point should have the Ty-Rap marker applied to the end of the wire or around the group of wires no more than ½ inch back from the end of the insulation.

Special Cloth Tape—Special cloth tape, as used in consoles, is to identify individual harnesses with the chassis to which they connect. Generally, this tape is applied in the center of the individual harness after break-out from the main harness.

To the extent possible, all wire markers should be applied in such a way that they may be read in the same direction within the assembly. All temporary markers should be removed after assembly.

CABLING AND WIRING

Wire Routing

The neat appearance of a finished chassis or unit is due, in part, to the forming and positioning of its wire harness. As an aid to improve neatness, the following may be considered when building, installing, and connecting harness, cables, and individual wires.

The harness should be laid in the equipment with lead breakouts visible and the cable not twisted. The harness should be formed to conform to its original shape. The minimum inside radius for hookup wire should be not less than two times the wire outside diameter. For coaxial wire, see the section headed "Coaxial Wire."

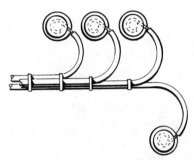

Fig. III-58. Lead dress and service loop.

The correct dressing of a cable leg shows neat lead-breakouts with the conductor wrap a continuation of the lead breakout. See Fig. III-58.

The direction of lead wrap around a terminal should be in the direction of the service loop (Fig. III-59).

Leads should be run by the shortest practical route to avoid excessive lengths of wire and wire crossovers. The ends of all wires (from harness breakout to termination) should have sufficient slack to avoid breakage of wires or solder connections due to strain or vibration. No wire should be taut.

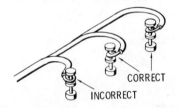

Fig. III-59. Direction of lead wrap.

With small wires (AWG No. 18 and smaller), the amount of slack, or service loop, should provide for reconnecting the wire to the terminal a minimum of two and a maximum of four times. For wires larger than AWG No. 18, the amount of slack should provide for reconnecting the wire to the terminal a minimum of three and a maximum of six times. The amount of slack provided to the terminal points on an assembly or component should be consistent. That is, one wire should not be at its minimum while another is at its maximum. When a panel channel is used to hold wires, the provided service loop may be contained within the panel channel.

Care must be taken to avoid the dressing of wires near heat-producing parts or moving parts. Wires should be dressed at least ½ inch from the body of a heat-producing part.

Care also must be taken in the running of hookup wire to ensure that it is not carried over or bent around any sharp corners or objects which might, in time, cut through the insulation.

Wires in a cable harness or bundle should lie essentially parallel and not entwine other conductors (with the exception of twisted pairs used in filament leads, ac wiring, etc.)

Wires should be properly arranged at breakout points, and those connecting nearest the harness should be brought to the harness side next to the terminals to which they connect. See Fig. III-60.

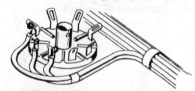

Fig. III-60. Lead breakout from harness.

In the routing of wires, clearance should be provided for all hardware and stenciled or silk-screened markings.

Typical examples of wiring placement and dress are shown in Fig. III-61.

Cable Clamps

Wires and cables should be clamped properly to prevent stress, chafing, vibration, or interference with moving parts. The clamps must be of the proper size to encircle the cable completely and hold it snugly in place without pinching wires.

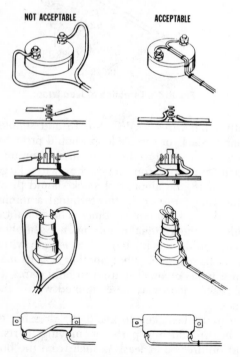

Fig. III-61. Examples of wire dress.

Care should be taken in installing clamps so that wires are not left out of the bundle and pinched by the mating surfaces of the clamp. Plastic Adel clamps require the use of a "D" washer in the hardware buildup to position the ends of the clamp properly.

Wiring of Connectors

Before soldering wires to connectors, slip onto the wires whatever coupling rings, cases, clamps, etc., are necessary. Position the wires into a neat parallel dress and install Ty-Rap. Due to vibration and temperature changes, it is essential that no lead be taut. See Fig. III-62.

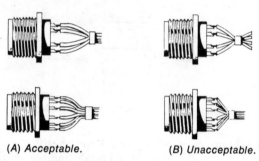

(A) Acceptable.   (B) Unacceptable.

Fig. III-62. Connector wire dress.

Ty-Raps

Ty-Raps are a quick method of bundling large cables or groups of wires for a neat appearance. A tool is used to cinch the Ty-Rap on the wires and cut off the excess nylon strap.

Usage on Cables in Cabinets and Chassis—For securing bundles of wires there are three sizes most often used:

1. TY-23M—for cables less than ½ inch in diameter
2. TY-25M—for cables ½ to 1½ inches in diameter
3. TY-27M—for cables larger than 1½ inches in diameter

For securing wires to cabinet walls, chassis brackets, etc., the two sizes provided with mounting tabs most often are used:

1. TY-35M—No. 10 screw hole for mounting (same size as TY-25M)
2. TY-37M—¼-inch bolt hole for mounting (same size as TY-27M).

The spacing between Ty-Raps on straight cable runs should be such that a minimum number is used to maintain the intended shape of the cable (a in Fig. III-63). Place one Ty-Rap at each wire breakout (b in Fig. III-63). On corners and T joints, place a Ty-Rap on both sides of corners (c in Fig. III-63) and on all three sides of T joints (d in Fig. III-63). An alternate method for securing T joints is the use of one Ty-Rap in an X configuration as shown at e in Fig. III-63. In

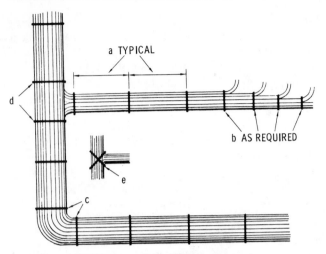

Fig. III-63. Use of Ty-Rap on a harness.

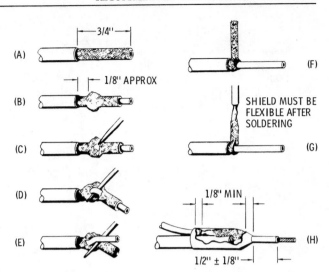

Fig. III-64. Preparation of shield on coaxial wire.

some cases, especially on large cables, it may be necessary to use Ty-Rap one size larger on corners and T joints for added strength.

Usage on Interconnecting Cables—The size of Ty-Rap to be used is determined from the information at the beginning of this section. The spacing of the Ty-Raps is determined by the size of the wire in the bundle: When the bundle contains only small wires (up to and including No. 8), the Ty-Raps should be placed at 6-inch intervals; when the bundle contains larger wires (No. 6 and up), the Ty-Rap should be placed at 12-inch intervals.

Should it become necessary to add a wire to a cable, remove the original Ty-Rap at certain intervals, lay in the added wire, and replace the Ty-Rap.

Care should be taken to assure that the Ty-Rap is not cinched too tightly around the wires. It should be tightened sufficiently to hold the wires in place, but it should not distort or damage the insulation on the wires.

Coaxial Wire

Coaxial wire must be protected against small-radius bends. The minimum inside bend radius of coaxial wire should be not less than six times the outside diameter of the wire.

The amount of unshielded center conductor wire to be exposed at termination points is ½ inch ± ⅛ inch (Fig. III-64).

To prepare a shielded lead for a pigtail shield termination, carefully strip the jacket to expose approximately ¾ inch of shielding as shown at A in Fig. III-64. When a suitable tool such as a "Little Joe" lead extractor is available, skip the next paragraph. If the proper tool is not available for the size of coaxial wire being prepared, complete the preparation according to the instructions beginning in the next paragraph.

Push the shielding back as indicated, and make an opening in the bulged portion. Use care to avoid damage to the shield strands or center-conductor insulation.

Work a nonmetallic probe under the inner conductor, and ease it through the opening in the shield.

With the fingers, gently pull the center conductor and shield taut. Open the end of the shield to allow insertion of the pigtail. Cut the pigtail to the required length, strip ¼ inch of insulation from the end and insert the pigtail into the open end of the shield. Do not allow the pigtail insulation to enter the shield, and use a heat sink on the shield prior to soldering. The shield must be flexible after soldering, and there must be no evidence of burned insulation.

Lay the soldered pigtail and shield back on the cable, and slide the proper size of shrink tubing over the exposed shield and solder joint. The tubing should cover completely and extend a minimum of ⅛ inch beyond any portion of exposed shield or pigtail conductor. After inspection, shrink the tubing with a heat gun, being careful not to damage the wire or adjacent components by overheating.

Wiring Protection

Wires routed across the edge of or through a hole in a metal chassis part must be protected from abrasion by sleeving, grommets, resilient edging, or radiusing of the metal part.

Whenever wiring must be routed against a metal edge and is subject to constant pressure, the metal parts must have a 1/16-inch minimum radius. However, if constant pressure is not present between the wire and the sharp edge, sleeving or an equivalent protection is acceptable.

Where it is necessary to use added protection for a wire or cable, the protective material must be secured in such a way as to assure its intended function. Wiring must also be kept clear of high-temperature sources and moving parts.

Examples of acceptable and unacceptable conditions are shown in Fig. III-65.

WIRE OVER SHARP OBJECT WITH NO PRESSURE, BUT NO PROTECTION ON WIRE

WIRE OVER SHARP OBJECT WITH PRESSURE EXERTED AND SLEEVING ON WIRE FOR PROTECTION

(A) Unacceptable.

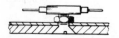 

WIRE OVER SHARP OBJECT WITH NO PRESSURE EXERTED AND WIRE PROTECTED BY SLEEVING

PROTECTION PROVIDED ON SHARP OBJECT RATHER THAN ON WIRE

(B) Acceptable.

 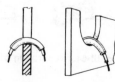

NO PROTECTION ON CHASSIS OR WIRE

SLEEVING OVER WIRE WITH PRESSURE ON CHASSIS

(C) Unacceptable.

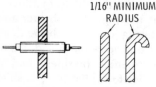 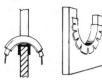

1/16" MINIMUM RADIUS

SLEEVING OVER WIRE WITH NO PRESSURE ON CHASSIS

METAL EDGE ROLLED OR ROUNDED TO PROPER RADIUS

PRESSURE ON WIRE BUT CHASSIS COVERED BY RESILIENT CHANNEL

(D) Acceptable.

Fig. III-65. Examples of wire protection.

Wires Not Terminated

Wires which by design or modification are not terminated should be insulated by inserting approximately ⅝ inch of the wire into a 1-inch piece of shrink-fit tubing of the proper size and shrinking the tubing in place. Unused leads over 2 inches in length should be tied down.

MISCELLANEOUS

Insulating Material

When it becomes necessary to cut insulating material such as Glastic, Micarta, or Bakelite, the cut edges must be sprayed with a coating of a material such as clear Krylon to prevent the entrance of moisture into the insulating material, which would reduce its insulating capabilities.

Ground Connections to Cabinetry

Ground connections to cabinetry should be made by: (1) determining the size and area required for the ground lug, (2) removing the paint and other coatings in this area down to the base metal, (3) applying a thin, even coat of Alcoa No. 2 or equivalent to clean the area, and (4) attaching the ground lug or other means of connection to this prepared area.

Color Code for Fixed Carbon Resistors

Table III-2 shows the standard colors and the method for determining the value of a fixed carbon resistor.

Table III-2. Fixed Carbon Resistor Color Code (Resistance in Ohms)

Color	First Figure	Second Figure	Number of Zeros	Tolerance
Black	0	0	—	—
Brown	1	1	0	—
Red	2	2	00	—
Orange	3	3	000	—
Yellow	4	4	0000	—
Green	5	5	00000	—
Blue	6	6	000000	—
Violet	7	7	0000000	—
Gray	8	8	00000000	—
White	9	9	000000000	—
Gold	—	—	× 0.1	±5%
Silver	—	—	× 0.01	±10%
No Color	—	—	—	±20%

Identification of Mica and Paper Capacitors

Table III-3 shows the standard colors and the method for determining the values of mica and paper capacitors. The first dot, positioned in the upper left-hand corner of the capacitor, is designated dot A and is the MIL identifier. When it is black, the capacitor has a mica dielectric; when dot A is silver, the capacitor has a paper dielectric.

The second dot (B) stands for the first significant figure of the capacitance value, the third dot (C) represents the second significant figure, and the fourth dot (D) indicates the decimal multiplier. The fifth dot (E) refers to the tolerance on the capacitance value, and the sixth dot (F) indicates the characteristic. This states the stability of the capacitance with respect to temperature.

Mica-dielectric capacitors are molded in red phenolic cases. Paper-dielectric capacitors are molded in brown or tan phenolic.

Ceramic Capacitors

The method of identifying ceramic capacitors is shown in Fig. III-66. The color code in Table III-3 should be used with this figure.

Table III-3. Mica (Glass) and Paper Capacitor Color Code (Capacitance in pF)

Dot Color	Significant Figures		Decimal Multiplier	Tolerance	Characteristic
	B	C	D	E	F
Black	0	0	—	±20%	—
Brown	1	1	10	—	B
Red	2	2	100	±2%	C
Orange	3	3	1000	—	D
Yellow	4	4	10,000	—	E
Green	5	5	100,000	—	—
Blue	6	6	1M	—	—
Violet	7	7	10M	—	—
Gray	8	8	100M	—	—
White	9	9	1000M	—	—
Gold	—	—	0.1	±5%	—
Silver	—	—	0.01	±10%	—

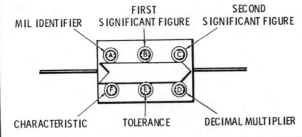

MIL IDENTIFIER — FIRST SIGNIFICANT FIGURE — SECOND SIGNIFICANT FIGURE

CHARACTERISTIC — TOLERANCE — DECIMAL MULTIPLIER

Diode Identification

The color code for a diode is read starting at the cathode end with the prefix 1N. Fig. III-67 shows the color code for a 1N457 diode. The numbers corresponding to each color are the same as those listed in column

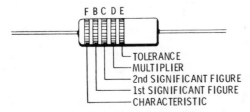

TOLERANCE
MULTIPLIER
2nd SIGNIFICANT FIGURE
1st SIGNIFICANT FIGURE
CHARACTERISTIC

Fig. III-66. Identification of ceramic capacitors.

B of Table III-3. Colored bands, a colored dot, arrows, or other appropriate symbols are used to locate the cathode lead or terminal (Fig. III-68).

YELLOW GREEN VIOLET

Fig. III-67. Diode identification.

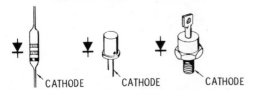

CATHODE CATHODE CATHODE

Fig. III-68. Identification of cathode terminal on diodes.

Transistor Lead Identification

Transistor terminations can be of the pin or flexible-lead style, and their arrangements vary according to type. Fig. III-69 shows some representative examples. However, it is advisable to consult a specification sheet or manual to determine the terminal connections of a specific type of transistor.

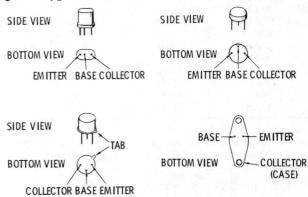

SIDE VIEW | SIDE VIEW
BOTTOM VIEW — EMITTER BASE COLLECTOR | BOTTOM VIEW — EMITTER BASE COLLECTOR
SIDE VIEW — TAB | BASE — EMITTER
BOTTOM VIEW — COLLECTOR BASE EMITTER | BOTTOM VIEW — COLLECTOR (CASE)

Fig. III-69. Identification of transistor leads.

Hole Sizes for Sheet-Metal Screws

Table III-4 lists the recommended hole sizes to be used for the various sizes of sheet-metal screws and thickness of the metal they are being attached to. There are two types of sheet-metal screws most commonly used in professional sound. Type A is a coarse-thread sheet-metal screw with a uniform, sharp gimlet point. It is primarily designed for use in light gauges of sheet

Table III-4. Recommended Hole Sizes for Sheet-Metal Screws (See Text)

			Hex Head, Type B (Z)					
Type A			In Sheet Metal			In Aluminum Alloy		
Screw Dia	Metal Thickness (Inches)	Drill Size No.	Screw Dia	Metal Thickness (Inches)	Drill Size No.	Screw Dia	Metal Thickness (Inches)	Drill Size No.
4	0.015-0.018	44	6	0.024-0.048	37	6	0.030-0.048	37
	0.024-0.030	42		0.060	35		0.060	36
	0.036	40		0.075	33		0.075	35
6	0.015-0.024	39		0.105-0.135	31		0.105	34
	0.030	38		0.164	30		0.125-0.135	33
	0.036	36	8	0.024-0.036	32		0.164	32
8	0.018-0.024	33		0.048	31		0.187-0.250	31
	0.030	32		0.060	30	8	0.030-0.036	32
	0.036	31		0.075	29		0.048	31
	0.048	30		0.105	28		0.060	30
10	0.018-0.030	30		0.125-0.135	27		0.075	29
	0.036	29		0.164	25		0.105	28
	0.048	25	10	0.024-0.048	27		0.125-0.135	27
				0.060	25		0.164	25
				0.075	24		0.187-0.375	24
				0.105	22	10	0.036-0.060	27
				0.125-0.135	20		0.075-0.105	26
				0.164	18		0.125-0.135	23
							0.164	21
							0.187-0.375	19

Table III-5. Tap Drill and Clearance-Hole Drill Sizes

Screw or Bolt Size	Tap Drill Size	Clearance-Hole Drill Size
4-40	43	30
6-32	36	25
8-32	29	16
10-24	25	7
10-32	21	7
1/4-20	7	H
1/4-28	3	H
5/16-18	F	Q
5/16-24	I	Q
3/8-16	5/16	X
3/8-24	Q	X
7/16-14	U	15/32
7/16-20	25/64	15/32
1/2-13	27/64	17/32
1/2-20	29/64	17/32

metal, resin impregnated plywood, asbestos compositions, wood, etc. Type B (Z) is a coarse-thread sheet-metal screw having a blunt point and with thread pitches generally somewhat finer than Type A screws. It is for use in light and heavy gauges of sheet metal, nonferrous castings, plastics, resin impregnated plywood, asbestos compositions, etc.

For satisfactory results, holes must be neither too large nor too small. The size of the hole depends on the kind of material, its hardness, uniformity, etc. In most cases, the hole sizes shown are suitable. If the material is very hard, a size larger drill might be necessary; if the material is very soft, a size smaller drill should be used. Table III-5 lists tap and clearance-hole drill sizes for various screw or bolt sizes. For reference, Tables III-6 and III-7 list various drill sizes, and Table III-8 gives decimal equivalents of fractions.

Table III-6. Decimal Equivalents of Letter Drill Sizes

Letter	Size of Drill in Inches	Letter	Size of Drill in Inches
A	0.234	N	0.302
B	0.238	O	0.316
C	0.242	P	0.323
D	0.246	Q	0.332
E	0.250	R	0.339
F	0.257	S	0.348
G	0.261	T	0.358
H	0.266	U	0.368
I	0.272	V	0.377
J	0.277	W	0.386
K	0.281	X	0.397
L	0.290	Y	0.404
M	0.295	Z	0.413

Table III-7. Decimal Equivalents of Number Drill Sizes

Drill No.	Size of Drill (Inches)	Drill No.	Size of Drill (Inches)	Drill No.	Size of Drill (Inches)	Drill No.	Size of Drill (Inches)
1	0.2280	21	0.1590	41	0.0960	61	0.0390
2	0.2210	22	0.1570	42	0.0935	62	0.0380
3	0.2130	23	0.1540	43	0.0890	63	0.0370
4	0.2090	24	0.1520	44	0.0860	64	0.0360
5	0.2055	25	0.1495	45	0.0820	65	0.0350
6	0.2040	26	0.1470	46	0.0810	66	0.0330
7	0.2010	27	0.1440	47	0.0785	67	0.0320
8	0.1990	28	0.1405	48	0.0760	68	0.0310
9	0.1960	29	0.1360	49	0.0730	69	0.0292
10	0.1935	30	0.1285	50	0.0700	70	0.0280
11	0.1910	31	0.1200	51	0.0670	71	0.0260
12	0.1890	32	0.1160	52	0.0635	72	0.0250
13	0.1850	33	0.1130	53	0.0595	73	0.0240
14	0.1820	34	0.1110	54	0.0550	74	0.0225
15	0.1800	35	0.1100	55	0.0520	75	0.0210
16	0.1770	36	0.1065	56	0.0465	76	0.0200
17	0.1730	37	0.1040	57	0.0430	77	0.0180
18	0.1695	38	0.1015	58	0.0420	78	0.0160
19	0.1660	39	0.0995	59	0.0410	79	0.0145
20	0.1610	40	0.0980	60	0.0400	80	0.0135

Table III-8. Decimal Equivalents of Fractions

Fraction	Decimal	Fraction	Decimal
1/64	0.0156	33/64	0.5156
1/32	0.0312	17/32	0.5312
3/64	0.0468	35/64	0.5468
1/16	0.0625	9/16	0.5625
5/64	0.0781	37/64	0.5781
3/32	0.0937	19/32	0.5937
7/64	0.1093	39/64	0.6093
1/8	0.1250	5/8	0.6250
9/64	0.1406	41/64	0.6406
5/32	0.1562	21/32	0.6562
11/64	0.1718	43/64	0.6718
3/16	0.1875	11/16	0.6875
13/64	0.2031	45/64	0.7031
7/32	0.2187	23/32	0.7187
15/64	0.2343	47/64	0.7343
1/4	0.2500	3/4	0.7500
17/64	0.2656	49/64	0.7656
9/32	0.2812	25/32	0.7812
19/64	0.2968	51/64	0.7968
5/16	0.3125	13/16	0.8125
21/64	0.3281	53/64	0.8281
11/32	0.3437	27/32	0.8437
23/64	0.3593	55/64	0.8593
3/8	0.3750	7/8	0.8750
25/64	0.3906	57/64	0.8906
13/32	0.4062	29/32	0.9062
27/64	0.4218	59/64	0.9218
7/16	0.4375	15/16	0.9375
29/64	0.4531	61/64	0.9531
15/32	0.4687	31/32	0.9687
31/64	0.4843	63/64	0.9843
1/2	0.5000	1	1.0000

Establishing Loudspeaker Directivity Figure of Merit

When competitive directivity control devices (DCDs), are compared, two primary parameters are normally examined. These are: coverage angle, C_L, and directivity factor, Q. The coverage angle is invaluable in determining the uniform distribution of sound energy. The C_L is determined by the points on the horizontal and vertical polar plots at which the dB-SPL is −6 dB with reference to the on-axis SPL. Directivity factor is a vital parameter that allows the calculation of intelligibility indoors and on-axis sensitivities outdoors. It should be possible to compare the effectiveness of DCDs on the basis of their ability to approach the ideal case.

DEFINING THE IDEAL CASE

The well-known Malloy equation calculates theoretical Q possible if all of the sound energy passed only through the C_L and had ± 0 dB variation over the area bounded by the C_L at the surface of a sphere intersecting the angles. The "ideal" loudspeaker, on the other hand, would put all the energy into the area bounded by the C_L but would have a level that changed with increasing angle from 0 dB on axis to −6 dB at each boundary (Fig. IV-1).

THE MALLOY EQUATION

The Malloy equation fits the theoretical case exactly:

$$\text{Theoretical Q} = \frac{180°}{\arcsin\left(\sin\frac{\phi}{2} \cdot \sin\frac{\theta}{2}\right)}$$

where,
ϕ is the vertical angle,
θ is the horizontal angle.

For conical coverage, such as that of a single cone loudspeaker:

$$Q = \frac{2}{1 - \cos\frac{\theta}{2}}$$

where θ is the assigned coverage angle.

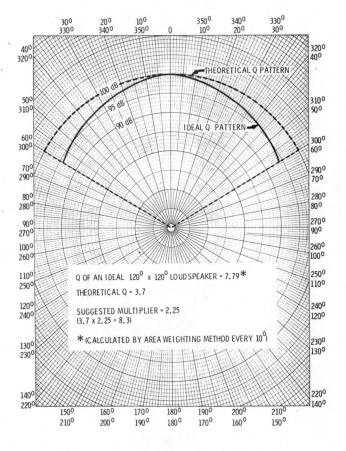

Fig. IV-1. Theoretical and ideal Q patterns.

Inside figure:

Q OF AN IDEAL 120° x 120° LOUDSPEAKER = 7.79*

THEORETICAL Q = 3.7

SUGGESTED MULTIPLIER = 2.25
(3.7 x 2.25 = 8.3)

* (CALCULATED BY AREA WEIGHTING METHOD EVERY 10°)

APPROXIMATING THE IDEAL Q FROM THE THEORETICAL Q

By integrating a number of available cases including a limiting one, it was found that multiplying the theoretical Q by a factor of 2.25 approximates a useful figure for the ideal Q. The actual factor tends to be slightly lower, but the higher value is chosen to avoid numbers in excess of 100% where measurement data is difficult to interpret.
Therefore:

$$\text{Ideal } Q = 2.25 \frac{180}{\arcsin\left(\sin\frac{\phi}{2} \cdot \sin\frac{\theta}{2}\right)}$$

for cases where the levels change relatively smoothly from on-axis to C_L.

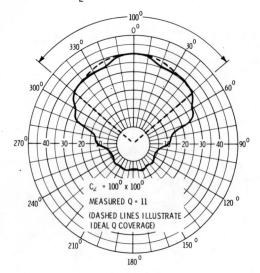

(A) Example 1.

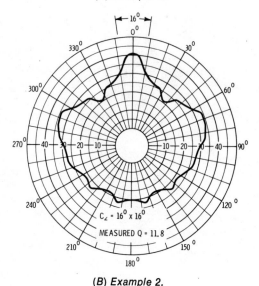

(B) Example 2.

Fig. IV-2. Loudspeaker patterns.

CALCULATING THE DFM AS A PERCENTAGE

We can now construct a percentage equation that expresses the efficiency with which the C_L matches the Q by:

$$\text{DFM} = \frac{\text{Measured Q}}{\text{Ideal Q}} \times 100$$

Example 1: We have a loudspeaker at a given ⅓ octave band that has a C_L of 100° × 100° and a measured Q of 11 (Fig. IV-2A). Therefore:

$$\text{DFM} = \frac{11}{2.25 \dfrac{180}{\arcsin\left(\sin\frac{100}{2} \cdot \sin\frac{100}{2}\right)}} \times 100 = 97.4\%$$

Example 2: In this case the loudspeaker has a very narrow C_L by definition, but at the expense of control of Q, which in this case measures 11.8 (Fig. IV-2B). Therefore:

$$\text{DFM} = \frac{11.8}{2.25 \dfrac{180}{\arcsin\left(\sin\frac{16}{2} \cdot \sin\frac{16}{2}\right)}} \times 100 = 3.2\%$$

SUMMARY

The directivity figure of merit method is a suggested way to compare directivity control devices on an engineering basis. Limiting cases are contrasted here to illustrate the method and to give a feeling for the meaning the percentages have relative to real devices. The constant 2.25 is a choice made by evaluating a series of DCDs and is considered approximate but practical. It is felt that in the majority of cases involving a comparison of DCDs that are competitive and that are assigned similar parameters, the DCD with the highest percentage rating should be selected, so far as acoustical reasons are concerned. Price, size, etc., obviously are not considered in this formula.

APPENDIX V

Priority Systems

Priority provisions are specified for many industrial systems, whether or not the industry itself is engaged in defense activity. In some cases, a number of priority levels must be provided. The following is typical of the priority system requirements of large aircraft plants:

1. Area page—no priority
2. Area boss—capable of taking over from all other microphones in his area
3. General page—capable of taking over from all systems, in all areas, interrupting local paging that may be in progress
4. Big boss—capable of taking entire system from general page originating stations
5. Tone signals—generally required to interrupt any announcement of lower priority.
6. Security officer—top priority over entire system

NOTE: In some instances, the respective priorities of 5 and 6 above may be reversed.

Priority requirements extend downward from the foregoing six-level example to the relatively simple case of only one degree of priority ("overcall") without signal lights, the most common example of which is the suppression of background music while paging. Compressors afford a handy means of obtaining a two-level priority system such as this without the complication of special cables, ganged switches, and/or relays. When

a compressor is used in this type of two-level priority system, the gain of the priority microphone preamplifier is set at a higher level than the gain of the nonpriority microphone preamplifier (or the background-music preamplifier). By this means, the priority signal will cause the compression to increase and, thus, substantially suppress a nonpriority signal which may be transmitted at the same time. If, for example, the compression settings are such that the nonpriority signal produces 10 dB of compression and the priority signal level to the compressor is 20 dB higher than the nonpriority input, the compression will increase to 25 dB on the priority call. The priority signal, therefore, will be reproduced 5 dB louder than the nonpriority signal, which becomes virtually inaudible (15 dB below "normal" level and 20 dB below the priority call).

If a greater difference between the reproduced level of priority and nonpriority signals is required (e.g., 30 dB), the difference in input levels to the compressor is made 30 dB, and the compression for the nonpriority signal is reduced to about 5 dB in order to avoid overloading the compressor when a priority call is made. The nonpriority call then reproduces 20 dB below normal level, and the priority signal is about 10 dB louder than the nonpriority call (or background-music signal). Care must be taken to assure that the system amplifiers(s) is(are) not overloaded by this level increase.

Fig. V-1. Compressor-mixer for paging systems.

Courtesy Shure Brothers Inc.

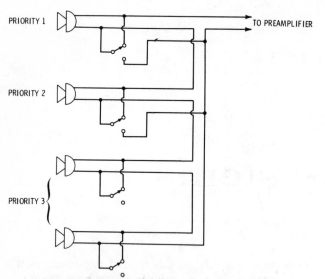

Fig. V-2. Priority system using microphone switches.

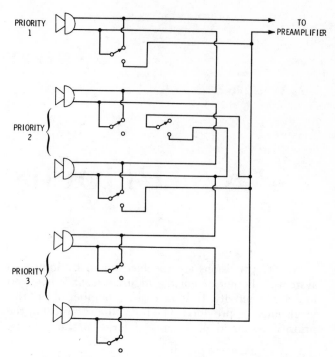

Fig. V-3. More than one microphone on a priority level.

The operating point referred to in the second paragraph leaves a good compression range available for the other purpose of the compressor—that of equalizing variations in voice and music levels. The settings referred to in the third paragraph reduce the range of the compressor by a considerable amount but do not eliminate the range entirely.

Fig. V-1 shows a gated compressor-mixer for use in paging systems.

In larger systems, priority is usually accomplished by microphone switches or by relays controlled by the

microphone push-to-talk switch. In Fig. V-2, all switching is done by the microphone switches. In this type of connection, the microphones are all in series, each being normally shorted out by its own switch. When the switch for No. 2 is actuated, the short is removed from No. 2 and the line to No. 3 is shorted. Thus micro-

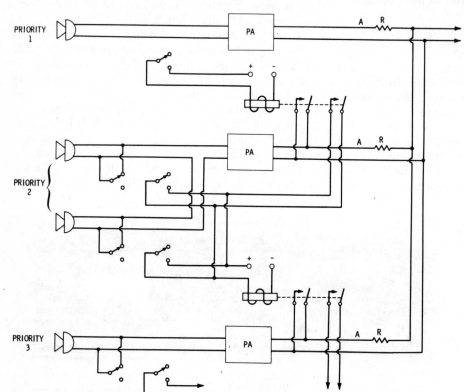

Fig. V-4. Priority system using relays.

phone 2 is given priority over microphone 3. Similarly, microphone 1 has priority over microphones 2 and 3. This system can be extended to many microphones on a given priority level and to any number of priority levels.

Fig. V-3 shows connections for the use of more than one microphone on a given priority level. In this system, three-conductor shielded cable must be used for each priority microphone. It may be preferred to use control wiring and relays in place of the third signal conductor, the relays being allowed to perform their switching in the low-level lines when the system layout makes no other location available. It is safer to keep relays out of the low-level circuits; therefore, it is often preferred to perform switching after the preamplifiers when this is possible. If each preamplifier employs a build-out resistor in series with its output, the relay may be arranged to short out the circuit just ahead of this resistor. Fig. V-4 illustrates circuitry for three levels of priority, controlled by relays.

APPENDIX VI

Directivity of Instruments and Devices

Fig. VI-1 illustrates how polar response charts are made, and Figs VI-2 through VI-11 show such plots for a number of musical instruments.

Loudspeakers can be divided broadly into the following categories:

1. Cone-type radiators
2. Line Radiators (either cones or horns)
3. Horn radiators
   (A) Sectoral or radial
   (B) Multicellular (or, in the case of a single-cell horn, exponential)
   (C) Re-entrant
4. Combinations

Figs. VI-12 through VI-20 illustrate the basic polar responses and Q of each type of device.

Fig. VI-12A shows a single-cone loudspeaker (in an enclosure), and Fig. VI-12B compares the polar responses for a single unit (left half of graph) and for two units in a simple line array (column) (right half of graph).

Fig. VI-13 illustrates a line array (also called a sound column) of single-cone loudspeakers.

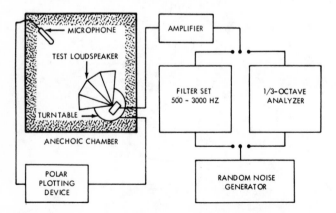

Fig. VI-1. Test setup for measuring polar response.

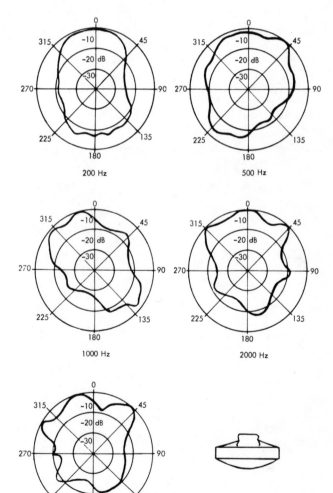

Fig. VI-2. Directional characteristics of a violin for five different frequencies.

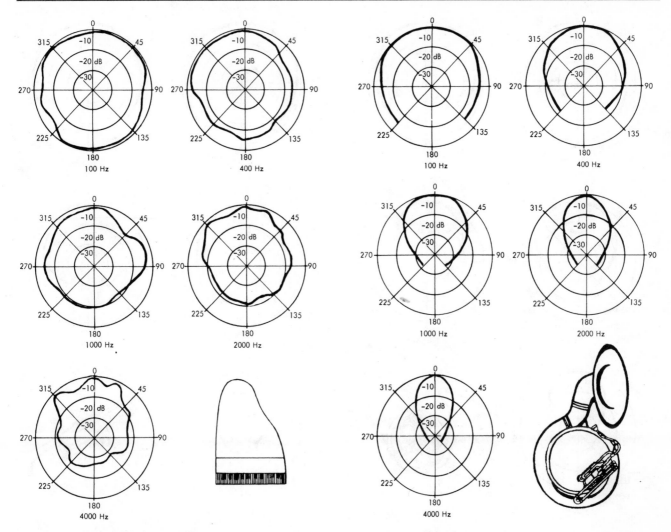

Fig. VI-3. Directional characteristics of grand piano for five different frequencies.

Fig. VI-4. Directional characteristics of tuba for five different frequencies.

Fig. VI-14A shows a typical sectoral (or radial) horn which allows the use of either single or multiple drivers through the use of different throat castings. Fig. VI-14B shows the polar response of a sectoral horn at 1000 Hz. Fig. VI-14C shows Q for a smaller sectoral horn (300 Hz), and Fig. VI-14D shows Q for a larger sectoral horn (300 Hz).

Fig. VI-15 shows examples of multicellular horns. Fig. VI-16 shows polar response patterns for multicell horns, and Fig. VI-17 shows Q curves for the indicated horns.

Fig. VI-18 shows three cone-type loudspeakers and their corresponding Q curves.

Fig. VI-19A shows a 15-inch loudspeaker of a type that is widely used as a studio monitor. Fig. VI-19C shows Q for this loudspeaker in the enclosure of Fig. VI-19B.

Fig. VI-20A illustrates a typical high-quality musical-system loudspeaker. Fig. VI-20B shows curves of Q versus frequency for such a loudspeaker.

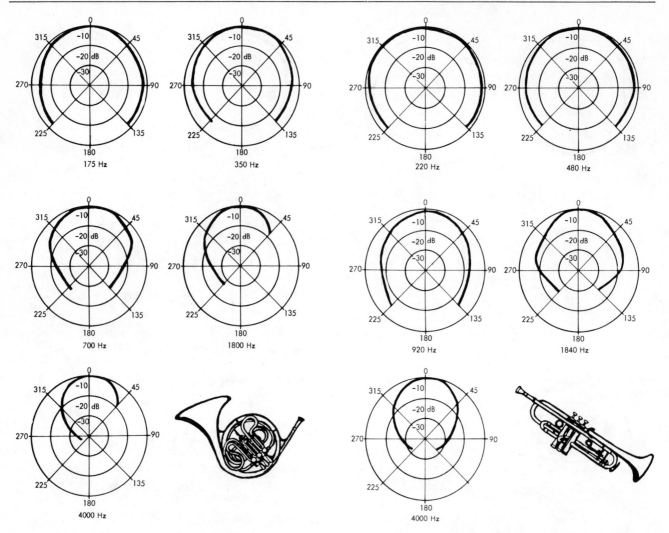

Fig. VI-5. Directional characteristics of French horn for five frequencies. (After Martin)

Fig. VI-6. Directional characteristics of trumpet for five frequencies. (After Martin)

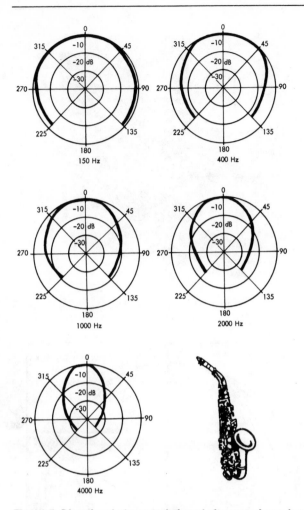

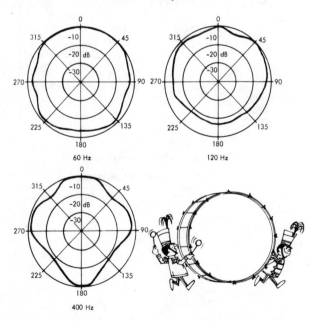

Fig. VI-7. Directional characteristics of alto saxophone for five different frequencies.

Fig. VI-8. Directional characteristics of 26-inch bass drum for three different frequencies.

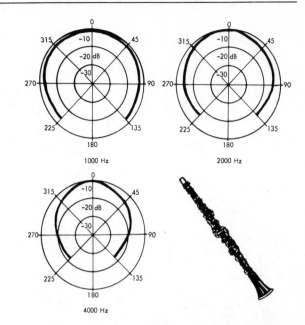

Fig. VI-9. Directional characteristics of clarinet for three different frequencies.

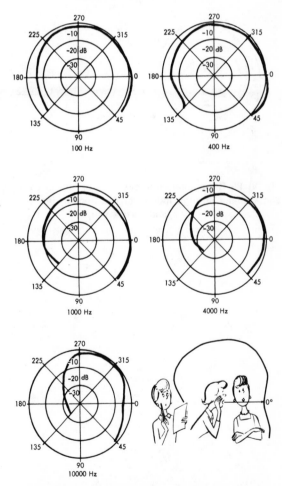

Fig. VI-10. Directional characteristics of human voice in bilaterally symmetrical vertical plane through mouth for five frequencies. (After Dunn and Farnsworth)

251

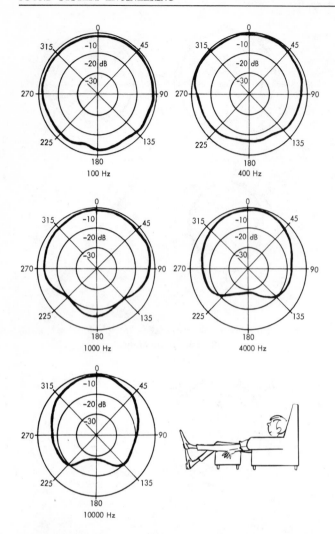

Fig. VI-11. Directional characteristics of human voice in horizontal plane through mouth for five frequencies. (After Dunn and Farnsworth)

(A) Loudspeaker in enclosure.

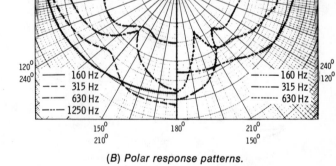

(B) Polar response patterns.

Fig. VI-12. Single-cone loudspeaker.

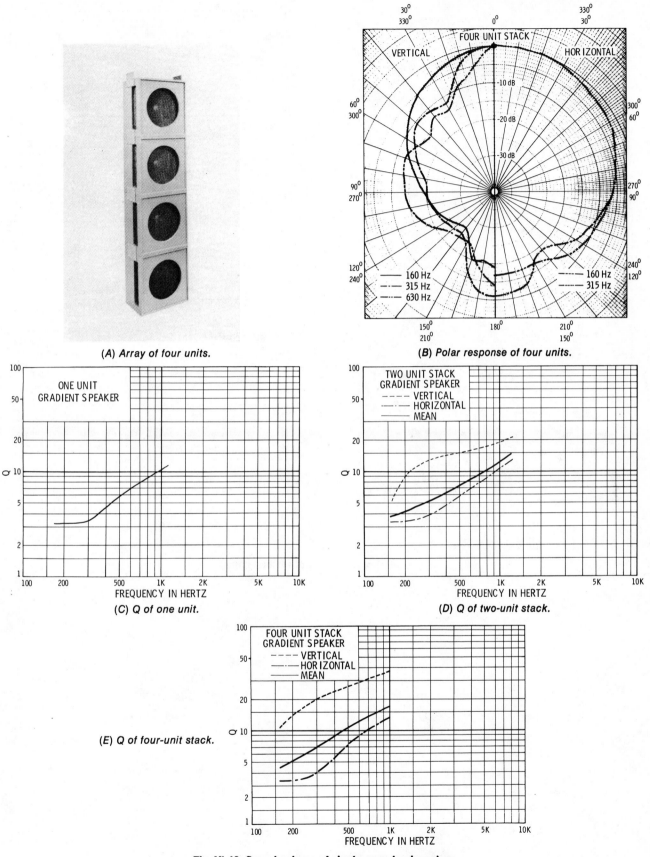

(A) Array of four units.

(B) Polar response of four units.

(C) Q of one unit.

(D) Q of two-unit stack.

(E) Q of four-unit stack.

Fig. VI-13. Sound column of single-cone loudspeakers.

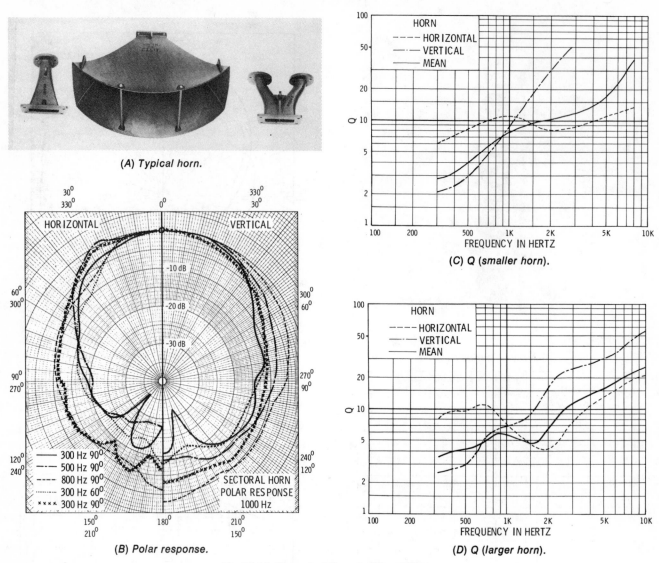

(A) Typical horn.

(B) Polar response.

(C) Q (smaller horn).

(D) Q (larger horn).

Fig. VI-14. Characteristics of sectoral horns.

(A) Eight-cell horn.

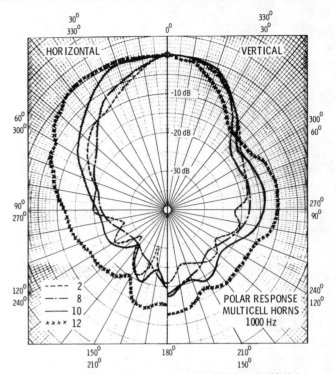

Fig. VI-16. Polar response of multicell horns (1000 Hz).

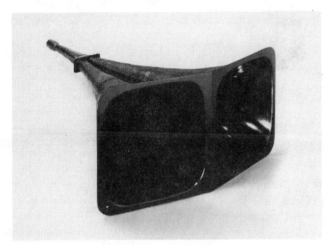

(B) Two-cell horn.

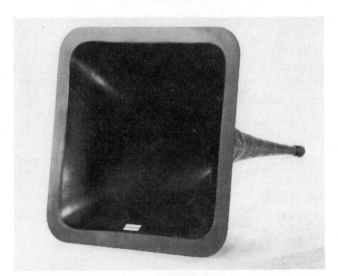

(C) One-cell (exponential) horn.

Courtesy Strom Communications Corp.

Fig. VI-15. Multicellular horns.

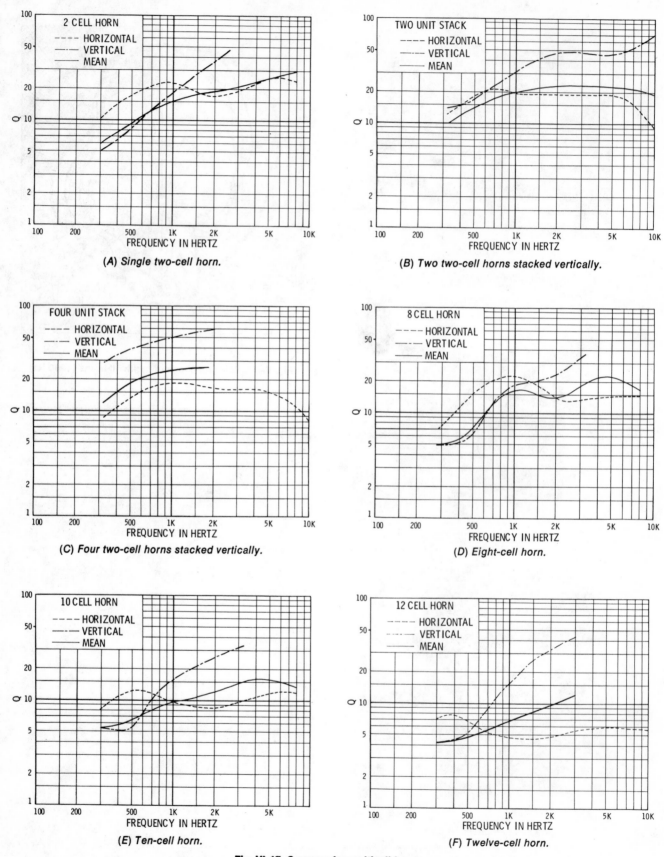

Fig. VI-17. Q curves for multicell horns.

(A) Single two-cell horn.

(B) Two two-cell horns stacked vertically.

(C) Four two-cell horns stacked vertically.

(D) Eight-cell horn.

(E) Ten-cell horn.

(F) Twelve-cell horn.

(A) 8-inch coaxial-type loudspeaker.

(B) 8-inch Western Electric design.

(A) Loudspeaker.

(B) Enclosure.

(C) 4-inch high-quality commercial sound loudspeaker.

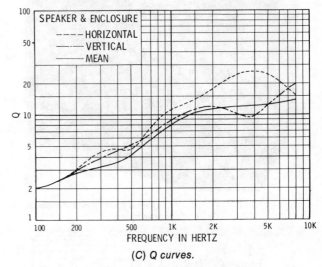

(C) Q curves.

Fig. VI-19. Studio monitor loudspeaker.

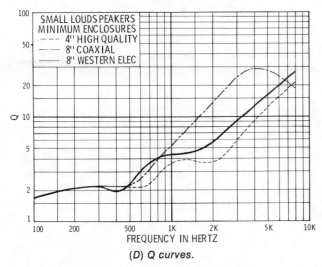

(D) Q curves.

Fig. VI-18. Cone-type loudspeakers.

Courtesy Sunn Musical Equipment Co.

(A) Loudspeaker system.

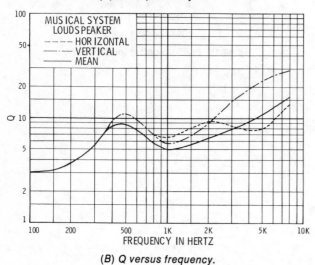

(B) Q versus frequency.

Fig. VI-20. Musical system loudspeaker.

APPENDIX VII

Ventilation of Electronic Components

Heat is the common enemy of all electrical components. Resistors, capacitors, vacuum tubes, transistors, and transformers all have life expectancies inversely related to operating temperature. A reduction in temperature of as little as 10°C may extend the useful life of such components by as much as three times. Examine Fig. VII-1, which relates transformer life to temperature. Note that as the temperature increases above about 100°C, the service life becomes inordinately short. How, then, is temperature rise controlled, and whose responsibility is it?

To answer these questions, let us examine the transformer design. From a knowledge of the temperature limits of organic insulating materials, a minimum "hot-spot" temperature within the transformer of 105°C has been accepted as an industry standard. Since one cannot be exactly sure where the hottest spot will be, each winding is measured by the change-of-resistance method and limited to 95°C on the assumption that the hot-spot gradient will not exceed 10°C. The next question is the ambient temperature; how hot will the surrounding air be? Again the industry has adopted a standard of 40°C, which is roughly equivalent to summer desert temperatures in the shade (see Table VII-1). If the maximum temperature is to be 95°C with a possible ambient of 40°C, the allowable transformer temperature rise will be 95 minus 40, or 55°C.

At this point, the equipment designer who also designs his own transformers has an edge over many of his competitors. The design engineer's knowledge of the immediate environment, including heat from power tubes and the probable end use, makes it possible for the transformer to be tailor-made for the application. In most cases, the transformer will be larger and have a lower temperature rise than the industry standard.

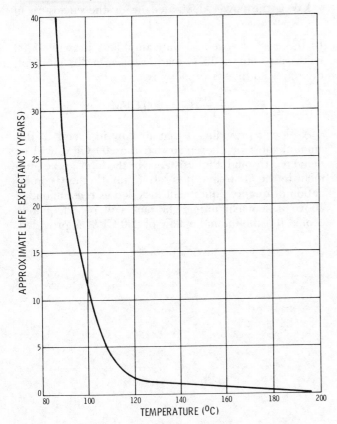

Fig. VII-1. Approximate life expectancy of a transformer having class-A insulation.

Table VII-1. Temperature Conversion Table

Degrees Celsius	Degrees Fahrenheit
0	32
10	50
20	68
30	86
40	104
50	122
60	140
70	158
80	176
90	194
100	212

As a case in point, let us look at an ultraconservative amplifier design. Normal temperature test results with the unit mounted in an open relay rack are as listed in Table VII-2. The test conditions are:

1. Line voltage adjusted to 120 volts, 60 Hz
2. Continuous signal input developing ⅓ rated output into matched load
3. Mounting—Open relay rack
4. Ambient temperature, 25°C

Table VII-2. Sample Temperature Test Results

Location of Thermocouples	Measured Temp °C	Component Maximum °C	Margin °C
Power-Transformer Windings	61	95	34
Power-Transformer Leads at Exit	57	105	48
Output-Transformer Windings	45	95	50
Electrolytic Capacitor	41	85	44
Wiring Near Sockets	47	90	43

Observe the comfortable 34°C transformer temperature margin. If the ambient increases to 40°C, the installation can cause an additional heat rise of 19° before maximum limits are reached. On the other hand, if the areas are air conditioned so that the ambient never exceeds 25°C, the installation can cause a full 34°C temperature rise. Here, then, is the division of responsibility. The manufacturer has provided a device which will operate within the range of normally encountered temperatures and has provided an excess margin to compensate for heat rise due to installation design. The professional sound engineer must ascertain what the highest ambient to be expected might be, what impediments the installation will offer to free air convection cooling, and the effect of other heat-producing apparatus mounted in the same area in raising the ambient air temperature in the immediate vicinity of the equipment in question.

Often, some type of forced ventilation becomes necessary. When the exhaust system blower method is used, even though the major air intake is provided with a filter, the equipment will become dirty due to the passage of unfiltered air through the many air leaks in a typical rack cabinet. A method which overcomes these problems and is recommended where blowers are indicated, consists of pressurizing the cabinet. The blower is mounted at the bottom of the cabinet from front or rear with a replaceable filter on the air intake. It is important that all louvers or other openings in the cabinet be sealed. Perforated panels should be placed between the amplifiers and above the top unit. Because the cabinet is pressurized, only filtered air passes through the leaks, the equipment remains clean, and the air flow is distributed around each amplifier where it is needed.

If you have a known temperature margin above the expected ambient, you can calculate roughly the size of blower required from the following equation:

$$T = \frac{1764}{CFM} \, kW$$

where,

T is the permissible temperature rise in degrees Celsius,

CFM is the volume of air moved in cubic feet per minute,

kW is the power dissipated inside the enclosure in kilowatts.

In the case of seven 80-watt amplifiers drawing 1700 watts, assuming a 15°C margin above a 40° ambient, the required blower capacity is:

$$\frac{1764}{15} \, 1.7 = 200 \, CFM$$

A blower providing a *free* air flow in excess of this amount must be chosen so that the 200 CFM will be delivered through the resistance of the filter and equipment in the airstream. It is safe to say that any combination of quality equipment installed as recommended above in a maximum-height rack will be adequately cooled if a minimum air flow of 200 CFM is provided.

Useful Equations in Sound-Engineering Work

The advent of very small, very powerful calculators has made it convenient for sound engineers to use directly an original equation rather than a nomograph developed from the equation. Greater accuracy to several more places is one reward of this approach. More important, perhaps, is the familiarity with the equations themselves, as many new and more usable combinations of them tend to suggest themselves.

OHM'S LAW

1. $E = IR$, $\quad E = \sqrt{WR}$, $\quad E = \dfrac{W}{I}$

    where,
    E is the emf in volts,
    I is the current in amperes,
    R is the resistance in ohms,
    W is the power in watts.

2. $W = \dfrac{E^2}{R}$, $\quad W = I^2R$, $\quad W = EI$

3. $I = \dfrac{E}{R}$, $\quad I = \dfrac{W}{E}$, $\quad I = \sqrt{\dfrac{W}{R}}$

4. $R = \dfrac{E}{I}$, $\quad R = \dfrac{E^2}{W}$, $\quad R = \dfrac{W}{I^2}$

5. $R_T = \dfrac{R_1R_2}{R_1 + R_2}$ $\qquad$ (See Fig. VIII-1.)

6. $R_2 = \dfrac{R_1R_T}{R_1 - R_T}$ $\qquad$ (See Fig. VIII-1.)

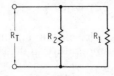

Fig. VIII-1. Resistors in parallel.

7. N resistors in parallel:

    $$R_T = \cfrac{1}{\dfrac{1}{R_1} + \dfrac{1}{R_2} + \dfrac{1}{R_3} \cdots + \dfrac{1}{R_N}}$$

8. N resistors in series:

    $$R_T = R_1 + R_2 + R_3 \ldots + R_N$$

9. N capacitors in series:

    $$C_T = \cfrac{1}{\dfrac{1}{C_1} + \dfrac{1}{C_2} + \dfrac{1}{C_3} \cdots + \dfrac{1}{C_N}}$$

10. N capacitors in parallel:

    $$C_T = C_1 + C_2 + C_3 \ldots + C_N$$

11. N inductors in series:

    $$L_T = L_1 + L_2 + L_3 \ldots + L_N$$

12. N inductors in parallel:

    $$L_T = \cfrac{1}{\dfrac{1}{L_1} + \dfrac{1}{L_2} + \dfrac{1}{L_3} + \cdots \dfrac{1}{L_N}}$$

13. $Z = R + jX$ $\qquad$ (Cartesian form)
    where,
    Z is the magnitude of the impedance in ohms,
    j is an operator signifing a 90° phase shift,
    X is the net reactance, equal to $(X_L - X_C)$,
    where X_L is the inductive reactance and X_C is the capacitive reactance,
    R is the ac resistance.

14. $Z = \sqrt{R^2 + (X_L - X_C)^2}$ $\qquad$ (Polar form)

15. Impedance phase angle $= \arctan \dfrac{(X_L - X_C)}{R}$

16. Power factor $= \cos$ (phase angle) $= \dfrac{R}{Z} = PF$

17. $Z = \dfrac{R}{PF}$, $\quad R = Z \times PF$

18. $X_C = \dfrac{1}{2\pi fC}$

where,

  X_C is the capacitive reactance in ohms,
  f is the frequency in hertz,
  C is the capacitance in farads.

19. $X_L = 2\pi fL$

where,

  X_L is the inductive reactance in ohms,
  L is the inductance in henrys.

20. $C = \dfrac{1}{2\pi fX_C}$, $\quad f = \dfrac{1}{2\pi CX_C}$

21. $L = \dfrac{X_L}{2\pi f}$, $\quad f = \dfrac{X_L}{2\pi L}$

DECIBEL EQUATIONS

22. Power ratio in dB $= 10 \log_{10} \dfrac{P_1}{P_2}$

23. Voltage ratio in dB $= 20 \log_{10} \dfrac{E_1}{E_2}$

24. Power ratio $= 10^{\frac{dB}{10}}$

25. Voltage ratio $= 10^{\frac{dB}{20}} = K$

26. $10^{\frac{dB}{10}} = e^{\ln 10 \times \frac{dB}{10}}$

27. $10^{\frac{dB}{20}} = e^{\ln 10 \times \frac{dB}{20}}$

28. Power ratios in dB expressed as a percentage:

$$\% = 100 \times 10^{\pm\frac{dB}{10}}$$

29. Voltage ratios in dB expressed as a percentage:

$$\% = 100 \times 10^{\pm\frac{dB}{20}}$$

30. Power ratios in percentage expressed as dB:

$$dB = 10 \log \left(\dfrac{\%}{100}\right)$$

31. Voltage ratios in percentage expressed as dB:

$$dB = 20 \log \left(\dfrac{\%}{100}\right)$$

32. Power change in dB equal to a given percentage:

$$dB = 10 \log \left(\dfrac{100 \pm \%}{100}\right)$$

33. Voltage change in dB equal to a given percentage:

$$dB = 20 \log \left(\dfrac{100 \pm \%}{100}\right)$$

34. $dBm = 10 \log \dfrac{P}{0.001}$

35. $P = 0.001 \times 10^{\frac{dBm}{10}}$

36. $dB\text{-}SPL = 20 \log \dfrac{SPL_1}{0.0002}$

or

$dB\text{-}SPL = 20 \log \dfrac{SPL_2}{0.00002}$

where,

  SPL_1 is the sound pressure level relative to 0.0002 dyne/cm²,
  SPL_2 is the sound pressure level relative to 0.00002 newton/m².

37. $SPL_1 = 0.0002 \times 10^{\frac{dB\text{-}SPL}{20}}$,

$SPL_2 = 0.00002 \times 10^{\frac{dB\text{-}SPL}{20}}$

38. $dB\text{-}PWL = 10 \log \left(\dfrac{\text{Acoustic power}}{10^{-12} \text{ watt}}\right)$

39. Acoustic power $= 10^{-12} \times 10^{\frac{dB\text{-}PWL}{10}}$

40. Adding decibels:

$$\text{Total dB} = 10 \log \left(10^{\frac{dB\text{-}SPL_1}{10}} + 10^{\frac{dB\text{-}SPL_2}{10}} \ldots + 10^{\frac{dB\text{-}SPL_N}{10}}\right)$$

41. Subtracting decibels:

$$\text{Total dB} = 10 \log \left(10^{\frac{dB\text{-}SPL_1}{10}} - 10^{\frac{dB\text{-}SPL_2}{10}}\right)$$

TIME-DELAY EQUATIONS

42. $V = 49 \sqrt{459.4 + {}^\circ F}$

where,

  V is the velocity of sound in feet per second,
  °F is the temperature in degrees Fahrenheit.

43. ${}^\circ F = \left(\dfrac{(V)^2}{(49)^2}\right) - 459.4$

44. $V = 20.06 \sqrt{273 + {}^\circ C}$

where,

  V is the velocity of sound in meters per second,
  °C is the temperature in degrees Celsius.

45. ${}^\circ C = \left(\dfrac{(V)^2}{(20.06)^2}\right) - 273$

46. Distance $\left(\dfrac{x\ ms}{ft}\right)$ = Time in ms

47. Time in ms $\left(\dfrac{x\ ft}{ms}\right)$ = Distance in ft

48. $D = VT$, $V = \dfrac{D}{T}$, $T = \dfrac{D}{V}$

   where,
   D is the distance in feet or meters,
   V is the velocity in feet per second or meters per second,
   T is the time in seconds.

REVERBERATION-TIME EQUATIONS

Sabine

49. $RT_{60} = \dfrac{0.049\ V}{S\bar{a}}$

   where,
   RT_{60} is the reverberation time in seconds (time required for interrupted steady-state signal to decay 60 dB),
   V is the internal volume of the room in cubic feet,
   S is the internal boundary surface area in square feet,
   $\bar{a}$ is the average absorption coefficient.

   $\bar{a} = \dfrac{s_1 a_1 + s_2 a_2 \ldots + s_n a_n}{S}$

   where,
   s_1, s_2, etc., are the individual surface areas,
   a_1, a_2, etc., are the individual absorption coefficients.

50. $V = \dfrac{RT_{60}(S\bar{a})}{0.049}$

51. $S = \dfrac{0.049\ V}{RT_{60}(\bar{a})}$

52. $\bar{a} = \dfrac{0.049\ V}{S(RT_{60})}$

If the dimensions in these equations are in meters, change the constant from 0.049 to 0.161.

Norris-Eyring

53. $RT_{60} = \dfrac{0.049\ V}{-S \ln(1 - \bar{a})}$

54. $V = \dfrac{-S \ln(1 - \bar{a}) RT_{60}}{0.049}$

55. $S = \dfrac{0.049\ V}{-RT_{60} \ln(1 - \bar{a})}$

56. $\bar{a} = 1 - e^{-\left(\frac{0.049\ V}{S\ RT_{60}}\right)}$

   (This form gives true absorption figures from 0.0 for no absorption to 1.0 for total absorption.)
If the dimensions are in meters, change the constant from 0.049 to 0.161.

Fitzroy

57. $RT_{60} = \dfrac{0.049\ V}{S^2}\left(\dfrac{2(xy)}{-\ln(1 - a_{xy})}\right.$
   $\left. + \dfrac{2(xz)}{-\ln(1 - a_{xz})} + \dfrac{2yz}{-\ln(1 - a_{yz})}\right)$

   where,
   x is the length in feet,
   y is the width in feet,
   z is the height in feet.

If the dimensions are in meters, change the constant from 0.049 to 0.161.

Hopkins-Stryker

58. $RT_{60} = \dfrac{0.049V}{R}$, $R = \dfrac{0.049V}{RT_{60}}$, $V = \dfrac{RT_{60}R}{0.049}$

59. $\bar{a} = \dfrac{R}{R + S}$, $R = \dfrac{S\bar{a}}{1 - \bar{a}}$

   $S = \left(\dfrac{R}{\bar{a}}\right) - R = \dfrac{R(1 - \bar{a})}{\bar{a}}$

60. $S\bar{a} = R(1 - \bar{a})$
   (When same $\bar{a}$ is used for both expressions)

ARTICULATION-LOSS EQUATIONS

61. Max D_2 for AL_{CONS} of 15% =
   $$\sqrt{\dfrac{15\ VQM}{641.81(RT_{60})^2(n + 1)}}$$

62. Max RT_{60} for AL_{CONS} of 15% =
   $$\sqrt{\dfrac{15\ VQM}{641.81(D_2)^2(n + 1)}}$$

63. Min V for AL_{CONS} of 15% =
   $$\dfrac{641.81(D_2)^2(RT_{60})^2(n + 1)}{15\ QM}$$

64. Min Q for AL_{CONS} of 15% =
   $$\dfrac{641.81(D_2)^2(RT_{60})^2(n + 1)}{15\ VM}$$

65. $\%\ AL_{CONS} = \dfrac{641.81(D_2)^2(RT_{60})^2(n + 1)}{VQM}$

In equations 61 through 65,
   D_2 is the distance in feet from the sound-system loudspeaker to the most distant listener,
   Q is the directivity factor (axial),
   $(n + 1)$ is the total number of loudspeaker groups contributing to the reverberant field. ("1" represents that group that also contributes direct sound to the measuring point.)
   M is the critical-distance modifier; $M = (1 - \bar{a})/(1 - \bar{a}_c)$.

If the dimensions are in meters, change the constant to 200. The equations are not valid when $D_2 > 3.16\ D_c$.

66. Min Sabine $\bar{a}$ for 15% $AL_{CONS} = \dfrac{1.24\, D_2 V}{S\sqrt{15\, VQ}}$

67. Min Norris-Eyring $\bar{a}$ for 15% $AL_{CONS} =$

$$1 - e^{-\frac{1.24\, D_2 V}{S\sqrt{15\, VQ}}}$$

68. Min Sabine $S\bar{a}$ for 15% $AL_{CONS} = \dfrac{1.24\, D_2 V}{\sqrt{15\, VQ}}$

69. Min Norris-Eyring $S\bar{a}$ for 15% $AL_{CONS} =$

$$S\left(1 - e^{-\frac{1.24\, D_2 V}{S\sqrt{15\, VQ}}}\right)$$

HOPKINS-STRYKER AND CRITICAL-DISTANCE EQUATIONS

70. Relative attenuation in dB:

$$\Delta D_x = 10 \log \left(\frac{Q}{4\pi(D_x)^2} + \frac{4}{R}\right)$$

where,
ΔD_x is the relative attenuation in dB,
D_x is the attenuation distance,
R is the room constant,
Q is the directivity factor.

71. $D_x = \sqrt{\dfrac{Q}{4\pi\left(10^{\frac{\Delta D_x}{10}} - \frac{4}{R}\right)}}$

For calculators not equipped for negative numbers, equations 72 and 73 may be used.

72. $\Delta D_x = 10 \log \left(\dfrac{1}{\dfrac{Q}{4\pi(D_x)^2} + \dfrac{4}{R}}\right)$

73. $D_x = \sqrt{\dfrac{Q}{4\pi\left(\dfrac{1}{10^{\frac{\Delta D_x}{10}}} - \dfrac{4}{R}\right)}}$

74. Critical distance:

$$D_c = 0.141 \sqrt{\frac{QRM}{n+1}}$$

$$\text{or}\quad D_c = 0.03121 \sqrt{\frac{QVM}{RT_{60}(n+1)}}$$

75. $Q = \dfrac{(D_c)^2(n+1)}{0.019881\, RM}$

76. $R = \dfrac{(D_c)^2(n+1)}{0.019881\, QM}$

77. $n + 1 = \dfrac{0.019881\, QRM}{D_c^2}$

78. $S = \dfrac{(n+1)D_c^2(1-\bar{a})}{0.019881\, Q\bar{a}M}$

79. $\bar{a} = \dfrac{\dfrac{D_c^2(n+1)}{0.019881\, Q}}{\left(\dfrac{D_c^2(n+1)}{0.019881\, Q}\right) + S}$

80. $Q\text{ mult} = \dfrac{1 - \bar{a}}{1 - a_c}$

where,
$\bar{a}$ is the average absorption coefficient,
a_c is the absorption in the area covered by the loudspeaker.

81. Peutz Equation (when $D_x > D_c$):

$$\Delta D_x = -10 \log \left(\frac{Q}{4\pi(D_x)^2} + \frac{4}{R}\right)$$
$$+ \left(\frac{0.734\sqrt{V}}{h(RT_{60})}\right)\left(\log \frac{D_x > D_c}{D_c}\right)$$

where h is the height of the ceiling in feet.

82. $\text{dB-SPL} = \text{dB-PWL}_{-12} - 10 \log \left(\dfrac{4\pi D_x^2}{Q}\right) + 10$
(For D_x in feet)

83. $\text{dB-SPL} = \text{dB-PWL}_{-12} - 10 \log \left(\dfrac{4\pi D_x^2}{Q}\right)$
(For D_x in meters)

84. $\text{dB-PWL}_{-12} = \text{dB-SPL} + 10 \log \left(\dfrac{4\pi D_x^2}{Q}\right) - 10$
(For D_x in feet)

85. $\text{dB-SPL} =$

$$\text{dB-PWL}_{-12} + 10 \log \left(\frac{Q}{4\pi D_x^2} + \frac{4}{R}\right) + 10.5$$

(For D_x in feet)

86. $\text{dB-PWL}_{-12} =$

$$\text{dB-SPL} - 10 \log \left(\frac{Q}{4\pi D_x^2} + \frac{4}{R}\right) - 10.5$$

(For D_x in feet)

87. Decay rate:

$$D = \frac{60}{T}$$

where,
D is the decay rate in dB/second,
T is the time in seconds,
60 is 60 dB of decay.

88. $\text{dB-PWL}_{-12} =$

$$\text{dB-}\overline{\text{SPL}} + 10 \log V + 10 \log D - 47.3$$

where dB-$\overline{\text{SPL}}$ is the average reverberant-field sound level.

89. $\text{dB-}\overline{\text{SPL}} =$

$$\text{dB-PWL}_{-12} - 10 \log V - 10 \log D + 47.8$$

DIRECTIVITY EQUATIONS

Geometric Q

The angles in these equations are defined as follows: α, both angles equal; θ, horizontal angle; ϕ, vertical angle (Fig. VIII-2).

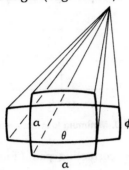

Fig. VIII-2. Angles for directivity equations.

90. For angles from 180° to 0°:

$$Q = \frac{180}{\arcsin\left[\left(\sin\frac{\theta}{2}\right)\left(\sin\frac{\phi}{2}\right)\right]}$$

91. For angles from 180° to 360° one angle = 180°; the other angle = some value between 180° and 360°.

$$Q = \frac{360°}{\text{angle}}$$

92. $\text{Area} = \dfrac{\arcsin\left[\left(\sin\frac{\theta}{2}\right)\left(\sin\frac{\phi}{2}\right)\right]}{180}$

$$Q = \frac{180}{\arcsin\left[\sin^2\left(\frac{\alpha}{2}\right)\right]}$$

$$\alpha = 2\arcsin\sqrt{\sin\frac{180}{Q}}$$

93. $\phi = 2\arcsin\left[\dfrac{\sin^2\left(\frac{\alpha}{2}\right)}{\sin\left(\frac{\theta}{2}\right)}\right]$

94. $\theta = 2\arcsin\left[\dfrac{\sin^2\left(\frac{\alpha}{2}\right)}{\sin\left(\frac{\phi}{2}\right)}\right]$

Axial Q

95. Relative SPL times area weighting = SPL_W.

$$10\log\left(\text{SPL}_{W1} + \text{SPL}_{W2} + \text{SPL}_{W3}\right.$$
$$\left. \ldots + \text{SPL}_{Wn}\right) = \text{dB-}\overline{\text{SPL}}$$

96. $Q = 10^{\frac{\text{dB-SPL on axis} - \text{dB-}\overline{\text{SPL}}}{10}}$

97. Directivity index:

$$D_I = 10\log Q$$

98. $Q = 10^{\frac{D_I}{10}}$

Relative Q

99. $\text{Rel } Q = 10^{\frac{\text{dB-SPL at off-axis point} - \text{dB-}\overline{\text{SPL}}}{10}}$

Apparent Q

100. $\text{Appar } Q = \dfrac{\text{Axial } Q \times Q\text{ Mult}}{Q\text{ Divisors}}$

101. Zonal area $= \cos\theta_1 - \cos\theta_2$

MICROPHONE SENSITIVITY EQUATIONS

102. $20\log E_o - (\text{dB-SPL}) + 74 = S_V$

where,
S_V is the open-circuit voltage response in dB re: 1 volt/1 microbar,
E_o is the open-circuit voltage,
dB-SPL is the acoustic level of the test signal.

103. $E_o = 10^{\frac{S_V + \text{dB-SPL} - 74}{20}}$

104. $\text{dB-SPL} = 20\log E_o - S_V + 74$

105. $S_P = S_V - 10\log Z + 44$

where S_P is the open-circuit power response in dBm/10 microbars.

106. $S_V = S_P + 10\log Z - 44$

107. $Z = 10^{\frac{S_V - S_P + 44}{10}}$

108. $G_M = S_V - 10\log R_{MR} - 50$

where,
G_M is the EIA sensitivity,
R_{MR} is a nominal Z according to rules of EIA standard.

109. $S_V = G_M + 10\log R_{MR} + 50$

110. $R_{MR} = 10^{\frac{S_V - G_M - 50}{10}}$

111. Thermal noise re: 1 volt:

$$\text{TN/1 volt} = -198\,\text{dB} + 10\log \text{BW} + 10\log Z$$

where,
BW is the bandwidth in hertz (−3 dB points)

112. Equivalent input noise:

$$\text{EIN} = -174\,\text{dBm} + 10\log \text{BW}$$

113. $\text{EIN} = -198\,\text{dB} + 10\log \text{BW}$
$$+ 10\log 600 - 6 - 20\log (0.775)$$

IMPEDANCE EQUATIONS

114. Build-out resistor, R_b:

$$R_b = R_D - R_S$$

where,
 R_D is the impedance desired,
 R_S is the the source impedance.

115. Termination Resistor:

$$R_T = \frac{R_L R_D}{R_L - R_D}$$

where R_L is the measured load impedance.

116. R_b insertion loss in dB:

$$Loss = 20 \log \left[\frac{\dfrac{R_D}{R_S + R_b + R_D}}{\dfrac{R_D}{R_S + R_D}} \right]$$

117. R_T insertion loss in dB:

$$Loss = 20 \log \left[\frac{\dfrac{R_D}{R_S + R_D}}{\dfrac{R_L}{R_L + R_S}} \right]$$

118. Constant-current impedance measurement:

$$Z = Ref\ Z \times 10^{\frac{\pm dB}{20}}$$

119. $\pm dB\ diff = 20 \log \dfrac{Z}{Ref\ Z}$

120. $VU = 20 \log \dfrac{E}{0.775} + 10 \log \dfrac{600}{Z}$

121. $Z_X = (\sqrt{Z_H} - \sqrt{Z_L})^2$
  where,
   Z_X is the impedance across the amplifier taps,
   Z_H is the higher impedance tap,
   Z_L is the lower impedance tap.

122. $Z_I = \dfrac{5000}{(Pwr\ to\ spkr)\,10^{\frac{Insertion\ loss\ dB}{10}}}$

where Z_I is the impedance of the line.

123. Number of loudspeakers safe to attach to line:

$$Number\ of\ loudspeakers = \frac{Z_I}{Amp\ Z}$$

$$= \frac{Total\ Amplifier\ Power}{(Pwr\ to\ spkr)\,10^{\frac{Insertion\ loss\ dB}{10}}}$$

124. Minimum loss matching pad (Fig. VIII-3):

$$R_1 = Z_S \sqrt{1 - \frac{Z_L}{Z_S}}$$

$$R_3 = \frac{Z_L}{\sqrt{1 - \dfrac{Z_L}{Z_S}}}$$

$$Loss\ in\ dB = 10 \log \left(\sqrt{\frac{Z_S}{Z_L}} + \sqrt{\frac{Z_S}{Z_L} - 1} \right)^2$$

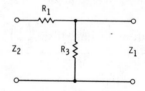

Fig. VIII-3. Minimum loss matching pad.

125. Impedance correcting pad (Fig. VIII-4) when $Z_2 > Z_1$:

$$R_1 = \frac{Z_1}{\sqrt{\dfrac{Z_1 + Z_2}{Z_2 - Z_1}} + 1}$$

$$R_3 = Z_1 \sqrt{\frac{Z_1 + Z_2}{Z_2 - Z_1}}$$

$$Insertion\ loss\ in\ dB = 20 \log \frac{\dfrac{Z_1 R_3}{Z_1 + R_3} + R_1}{\dfrac{Z_1 R_3}{Z_1 + R_3}}$$

$$Mismatch\ loss = 10 \log \frac{(Z_1 + Z_2)^2}{4 Z_1 Z_2}$$

Fig. VIII-4. Impedance correcting pad.

126. Impedance correcting pad (Fig. VIII-4) when $Z_1 > Z_2$:

$$R_1 = Z_1 \sqrt{\frac{Z_1 - Z_2}{Z_1 + Z_2}}$$

$$R_3 = Z_1 \left(1 + \sqrt{\frac{Z_1 + Z_2}{Z_1 - Z_2}} \right)$$

$$Insertion\ loss\ in\ dB = 20 \log \frac{Z_1 + R_1}{Z_1}$$

$$Mismatch\ loss = 10 \log \frac{(Z_1 + Z_2)^2}{4 Z_1 Z_2}$$

127. The following formulas apply to the pad circuits shown in Fig. VIII-5:

$$K = 10^{\frac{dB}{20}}$$

$$R_1 = R_0 (K - 1)$$

$$R_2 = R_0 \frac{1}{K - 1}$$

$$R_3 = R_0 \frac{K - 1}{K + 1}$$

$$R_4 = R_0 \frac{K + 1}{K - 1}$$

$$dB = 20 \log_{10} K$$

$$R_5 = R_0 \frac{K - 1}{K}$$

$$R_6 = R_0 \frac{K}{K - 1}$$

$$R_7 = \frac{R_0}{2} \frac{K^2 - 1}{K}$$

$$R_8 = 2 R_0 \frac{K}{K^2 - 1}$$

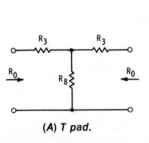

(A) T pad.

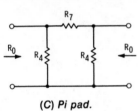

(C) Pi pad.

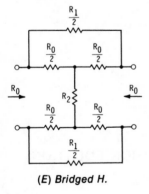

(E) Bridged H.

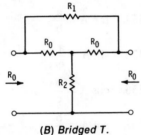

(B) Bridged T.

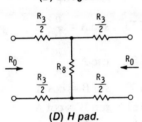

(D) H pad.

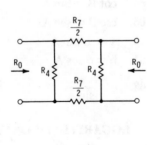

(F) O pad.

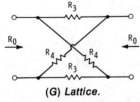

(G) Lattice.

Fig. VIII-5. Pad circuits.

ACOUSTIC GAIN EQUATIONS

128. $NAG = \Delta D_0 - \Delta EAD + 6 \, FSM + 10 \log NOM$

where,

ΔD_0 is the distance from the talker to the listener converted into relative loss in dB,

ΔEAD is the desired equivalent acoustic distance in dB,

FSM is the feedback stability margin in dB,

NOM is the number of open microphones,

NAG is the needed acoustic gain in dB.

129. $PAG = \Delta D_0 + \Delta D_1 - \Delta D_8 - \Delta D_2$

where,

ΔD_1 is the distance between the loudspeaker and the microphone in relative dB,

ΔD_8 is the distance between the talker and the microphone in relative dB,

ΔD_2 is the distance between the loudspeaker and the listener in relative dB.

130. $\Delta D_1 + \Delta EAD - \Delta D_8 - \Delta D_2$
$$- 10 \log NOM - 6 = 0$$

131. $Max \, D_8 = \dfrac{D_1 \times EAD}{2D_2 \sqrt{NOM}}$

132. $Min \, D_1 = \dfrac{2D_8 \times D_2 \times \sqrt{NOM}}{EAD}$

133. $Max \, D_2 = \dfrac{D_1 \times EAD}{2D_8 \sqrt{NOM}}$

134. $Min \, EAD = \dfrac{2D_8 \times D_2 \times \sqrt{NOM}}{D_1}$

135. $Max \, NOM = \left(\dfrac{D_1 \times EAD}{D_8 \times 2D_2} \right)^2$

LOUDSPEAKER EFFICIENCY

136. $\% \, Eff = 10^{\frac{4', \, 1 \, watt \, sens - (10 \log Q + 107.47)}{10}} \times 100$

$$Q = 10^{\frac{4', \, 1\text{-watt} \, sens - 10 \log \frac{\% \, Eff}{100} - 107.47}{10}}$$

CALCULATING THD

137. $THD =$
$$\sqrt{\left(\frac{10,000}{10^{\frac{dB}{10}}} \right)_1 + \left(\frac{10,000}{10^{\frac{dB}{10}}} \right)_2 \cdots + \left(\frac{10,000}{10^{\frac{dB}{10}}} \right)_n}$$

RECTANGULAR-TO-POLAR CONVERSION

138. Vector length $= \sqrt{x^2 + y^2}$

139. Angle $= \arctan \dfrac{y}{x}$

$$= \arctan \dfrac{-y}{x}$$

$$= \arctan \frac{y}{-x} + 180°$$

$$= \arctan \frac{-y}{-x} - 180°$$

POLAR-TO-RECTANGULAR CONVERSION

140. $\sin \text{angle} \times \text{vector} = y$

141. $\cos \text{angle} \times \text{vector} = x$

HYPERBOLIC-FUNCTION EQUATIONS

In these equations, x is in radians.

142. $\sinh x = \dfrac{e^x - e^{-x}}{2}$

143. $\text{arcsinh } x = \ln [x + (x^2 + 1)^{\frac{1}{2}}]$

144. $\cosh x = \dfrac{e^x + e^{-x}}{2}$

145. $\text{arccosh } x = \ln [x + (x^2 - 1)^{\frac{1}{2}}]$

146. $\tanh x = \dfrac{e^x - e^{-x}}{e^x + e^{-x}}$

147. $\text{arctanh } x = \frac{1}{2} \ln \left(\dfrac{1 + x}{1 - x}\right)$

PERCENTAGE EQUATIONS

148.   Percentage profit on the selling price:

$$\% \text{ POSP} = 100 \left(1 - \frac{CP}{SP}\right)$$

149.   Percentage markup on the cost price:

$$\% \text{ MOCP} = 100 \left(\frac{SP}{CP} - 1\right)$$

150.   Markup ratio:

$$MR = \frac{SP}{CP}$$

151.   Cost price for a desired percentage profit on selling price:

$$CP = SP - \frac{\%}{100} SP$$

152.   Markup ratio for given profit on selling price:

$$MR = 100 \left(\frac{1}{100 - \% \text{ POSP}}\right)$$

153.   Selling price for desired profit on selling price:

$$SP = \left(\frac{100}{100 - \% \text{ POSP}}\right) CP$$

TRIGONOMETRIC EQUATIONS

For these equations, refer to Fig. VIII-6.

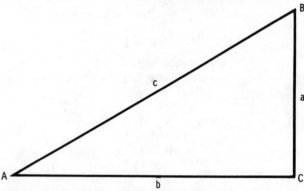

Fig. VIII-6. Parts of a triangle for trigonometric relationships.

154. $\tan A = \dfrac{a}{b}$

155. $\sin A = \dfrac{a}{c}$

156. $\cos A = \dfrac{b}{c}$

157. $\cot A = \dfrac{b}{a}$

158. $\sec A = \dfrac{c}{b}$

159. $\csc A = \dfrac{c}{a}$

160. $\sin B = \cos A$

161. $\tan B = \cot A$

162. $\sec B = \csc A$

163. $\cos B = \sin A$

164. $\cot B = \tan A$

165. $\csc B = \sec A$

166. $a = b \tan A$

167. $b = c \cos A$

168. $c = \dfrac{a}{\sin A}$

LOGARITHM CONVERSION EQUATIONS

169. $N = b^L$

$\ln N = L \times \ln b$

$\dfrac{\ln N}{\ln b} = L$

170. $x \log y = z$

$x = \dfrac{z}{\log y}$

171. $\log x = \dfrac{\ln x}{\ln 10}$

172. $x = e^{\ln 10 \times \log x}$

173. $\ln x = \dfrac{\log x}{\log e}$

174. $x = 10^{\log e \times \ln x}$

175. $\operatorname{colog} N = \log \dfrac{1}{N}$

176. $\operatorname{colog} N = \log 1 - \log N$

$\log 1 = 0 \quad \therefore \log \dfrac{1}{N} = -\log N$

MISCELLANEOUS ROOM EQUATIONS

177. $\text{Mean free path} = \dfrac{4V}{S}$

178. $\bar{a}_{\text{N.E.}} = 1 - e^{-\bar{a}_{\text{sab}}}$

179. $\bar{a}_{\text{sab}} = -\ln(1 - \bar{a}_{\text{N.E.}})$

180. $\dfrac{\text{Direct sound}}{\text{Reflected sound}} = 10 \log\left(\dfrac{QR}{16\pi D_x^2}\right)$

181. When $D_2 > 3.16\, D_c$, then $\%AL_{\text{CONS}} = 9\, RT_{60}$.

182. Total number of room modes (N) up to a given frequency (f_c):

$$N = 4\, V \left(\dfrac{f_c}{C}\right)^3$$

where C is the velocity of sound in feet per second.

Limit: $f_c > \dfrac{4\, C}{V^{1/3}}$

183. Modes per hertz at a given frequency:

$$\dfrac{\text{Modes}}{\text{Hz}} = \dfrac{12\, V\, f_c^2}{C^3}$$

FILTER BANDWIDTH EQUATIONS

184. True ISO center frequencies:

For octave: $10^{0.3} \times 10^{0.3} \ldots \times 10^{0.3}$

For $\frac{1}{3}$ octave: $10^{0.1} \times 10^{0.1} \ldots \times 10^{0.1}$

185. Bandwidth:

Lower limit $= 0.5^{0.5\ (\text{Octave fraction})} \times f_c$

Upper limit $= 2^{0.5\ (\text{Octave fraction})} \times f_c$

where f_c is the center frequency.

186. Spectrum level correction $= 10 \log (\text{Upper limit} - \text{Lower limit})$

187. Octave band from $\frac{1}{3}$ octave band correction:

$$L_{\text{Oct Band}} = 10 \log \dfrac{\text{Oct BW}}{\frac{1}{3}\, \text{Oct BW}}$$

DISTRIBUTED LOUDSPEAKER EQUATION

188. $N_s = \dfrac{3\,(\text{Ceiling area})}{2\pi \left[(\text{Ceiling height} - 4)\tan \dfrac{\text{angle}}{2} \right]^2}$

where,

N_s is the number of speakers required for the desired overlap,

Ceiling area is in square feet,

Ceiling height is in feet.

CRITICAL DISTANCE EQUATION

189. $D_c = \text{Ref dist} \times 10^{\frac{\text{Ref dist dB-SPL} - \text{Reverb dB-SPL}}{20}}$

MATHEMATICAL SYMBOLS

$\times$ or $\cdot$	Multiplied by
$\div$ or $:$	Divided by
$+$	Positive; plus; add
$-$	Negative; minus; subtract
$\pm$	Positive or negative; plus or minus
$\mp$	Negative or positive; minus or plus
$=$ or $::$	Equals
$\equiv$	Identity
$\cong$	Is approximately equal to
$\neq$	Does not equal
$>$	Is greater than
$\gg$	Is much greater than
$<$	Is less than
$\ll$	Is much less than
$\geqq$	Greater than or equal to
$\leqq$	Less than or equal to
$\therefore$	Therefore
$\angle$	Angle
Δ	Increment or decrement (As used in this text, Δ indicates a conversion to decibel equivalent.)
$\perp$	Perpendicular to
$\parallel$	Parallel to
$\lvert n \rvert$	Absolute value of n
$\doteq$	Equals in the limit
$f(x)$	Function of x

MATHEMATICAL CONSTANTS

π	$=$	3.1415962654
2π	$=$	6.283185307
$(2\pi)^2$	$=$	39.47841760
4π	$=$	12.56637061
π^2	$=$	9.869604401
$\dfrac{\pi}{2}$	$=$	1.570796327
$\dfrac{1}{\pi}$	$=$	0.318309886
$\dfrac{1}{2\pi}$	$=$	0.159154943

$$\frac{1}{\pi^2} = 0.101321184$$

$$\frac{1}{\sqrt{\pi}} = 0.564189584$$

$$\sqrt{\pi} = 1.772453851$$

$$\sqrt{2} = 1.414213562$$

$$\sqrt{3} = 1.732050808$$

$$\frac{1}{\sqrt{2}} = 0.707106781$$

$$\frac{1}{\sqrt{3}} = 0.577350269$$

$$\log \pi = 0.497149873$$

$$\log \frac{\pi}{2} = 0.196119877$$

$$\log \pi^2 = 0.994299745$$

$$\log \sqrt{\pi} = 0.248574936$$

$$e = 2.718281828$$

ALGEBRA

Exponents and Radicals

$$a^x a^y = a^{(x+y)}$$

$$(ab)^x = a^x b^x$$

$$\sqrt[x]{\frac{a}{b}} = \frac{\sqrt[x]{a}}{\sqrt[x]{b}}$$

$$(a^x)^y = a^{xy}$$

$$\sqrt[x]{ab} = \sqrt[x]{a}\ \sqrt[x]{b}$$

$$a^{\frac{1}{x}} = \sqrt[x]{a}$$

$$\frac{a^x}{a^y} = a^{(x-y)}$$

$$\left(\frac{a}{b}\right)^x = \frac{a^x}{b^x}$$

$$a^{-x} = \frac{1}{a^x}$$

$$\sqrt[x]{\sqrt[y]{a}} = \sqrt[xy]{a}$$

$$a^{\frac{x}{y}} = \sqrt[y]{a^x}$$

$$a^0 = 1$$

Transposition of Terms

If

$$A = \frac{B}{C}$$

then

$$B = AC$$

$$C = \frac{B}{A}$$

If

$$\frac{A}{B} = \frac{C}{D}$$

then

$$A = \frac{BC}{D}$$

$$B = \frac{AD}{C}$$

$$C = \frac{AD}{B}$$

$$D = \frac{BC}{A}$$

If

$$A = \frac{1}{D\sqrt{BC}}$$

then

$$A^2 = \frac{1}{D^2 BC}$$

$$B = \frac{1}{A^2 D^2 C}$$

$$C = \frac{1}{A^2 D^2 B}$$

$$D = \frac{1}{A\sqrt{BC}}$$

If

$$A = \sqrt{B^2 + C^2}$$

then

$$A^2 = B^2 + C^2$$

$$B = \sqrt{A^2 - C^2}$$

$$C = \sqrt{A^2 - B^2}$$

Solution of a Quadratic

Quadratic equations in the form

$$ax^2 + bx + c = 0$$

may be solved by the following:

$$x = \frac{-b \pm \sqrt{b^2 - 4ac}}{2a}$$

Definitions of Terms

The definitions in this appendix are reproduced, with permission, from IEEE Standard No. 151, *Standard Definitions of Terms for Audio and Electroacoustics*

Definitions of Terms for
AUDIO AND ELECTROACOUSTICS

Amplification

An increase in signal magnitude from one point to another, or the process causing this increase.

Amplification, Current

Either

(1) an increase in signal current magnitude in transmission from one point to another, or the process thereof, or

(2) of a transducer, the scalar ratio of the signal output current to the signal input current.

Note: The ratio in (2) is sometimes expressed in decibels by multiplying its common logarithm by 20. This leads to ambiguity if the currents being considered flow into unequal impedances, in which case the numerical result should be qualified by the statement, "dB current amplification." See "Decibel," IEEE No. 145 (48 IRE 2, 11, 15. S1).

Amplification, Voltage

Either

(1) an increase in signal voltage magnitude in transmission from one point to another, or the process thereof, or

(2) of a transducer, the scalar ratio of the signal output voltage to the signal input voltage.

Note: The ratio in (2) is sometimes expressed in decibels by multiplying its common logarithm by 20. This leads to ambiguity if the voltages being considered are across unequal impedances, in which case the numerical result should be qualified by the statement "dB voltage amplification." See "Decibel," IEEE No. 145 (48 IRE 2, 11, 15. S1).

Amplifier

A device which enables an input signal to control power from a source independent of the signal and thus be capable of delivering an output which bears some relationship to, and is generally greater than, the input signal.

Amplifier, Balanced

An amplifier in which there are two identical signal branches connected so as to operate in phase opposition and with input and output connections each balanced to ground.

Amplifier, Bridging

An amplifier with an input impedance sufficiently high so that its input may be bridged across a circuit without substantially affecting the signal level of the circuit across which it is bridged.

Amplifier, Clipper

An amplifier designed to limit the instantaneous value of its output to a predetermined maximum.

Amplifier, Distribution

A power amplifier designed to energize a speech or music distribution system and having sufficiently low output impedance so that changes in load do not appreciably affect the output voltage.

Amplifier, Isolation

An amplifier employed to minimize the effects of a following circuit on the preceding circuit.

Amplifier, Line

An amplifier which supplies a transmission line or system with a signal at a stipulated level.

Amplifier, Monitoring

A power amplifier used primarily for evaluation and supervision of a program.

Amplifier, Peak Limiting

See Peak Limiter.

Amplifier, Power

An amplifier which drives a utilization device such as a loudspeaker.

Amplifier, Program

See Amplifier, Line.

Amplitude Distortion

See Distortion, Harmonic and Distortion, Intermodulation.

Amplitude-Frequency Distortion

See Distortion, Amplitude-Frequency.

Amplitude-Frequency Response

The variation of gain, loss, amplification, or attenuation as a function of frequency.

Note: This response is usually measured in the region of operation in which the transfer characteristic of the system or transducer is essentially linear.

Amplitude Range

The ratio, usually expressed in decibels, of the upper and lower limits of program amplitudes which contain all significant energy contributions.

Attack Time

The interval required, after a sudden increase in input signal amplitude to a system or transducer, to attain a stated percentage (usually 63 percent) of the ultimate change in amplification or attenuation due to this increase.

Attenuation

A decrease in signal magnitude from one point to another, or the process causing this decrease.

Attentuation, Current

Either

(1) a decrease in signal current magnitude, in transmission from one point to another, or the process thereof, or

(2) of a transducer, the scalar ratio of the signal input current to the signal output current.

Note: The ratio in (2) is sometimes expressed in decibels by multiplying its common logarithm by 20. This leads to ambiguity if the currents being considered flow into unequal impedances, in which case the numerical result should be qualified by the statement, "dB current attenuation." See "Decibel," IEEE No. 145 (48 IRE 2, 11, 15. S1).

Attenuation, Voltage

Either

(1) a decrease in signal voltage magnitude in transmission from one point to another, or the process thereof, or

(2) of a transducer, the scalar ratio of the signal input voltage to the signal output voltage.

Note: The ratio in (2) is sometimes expressed in decibels by multiplying its common logarithm by 20. This leads to ambiguity if the voltages being considered are across unequal impedances, in which case the numerical result should be qualified by the statement, "dB voltage attenuation." See "Decibel," IEEE No. 145, (48 IRE 2, 11, 15. S1).

Attenuator

An adjustable passive network which reduces the power level of a signal without introducing appreciable distortion.

Audio Frequency

Any frequency corresponding to a normally audible sound wave.

Note: Audio frequencies range roughly from 15 to 20,000 cycles per second.

Audio-Frequency Noise

See Noise, Audio-Frequency.

Audio-Frequency Oscillator

(Audio Oscillator)

A nonrotating device for producing an audio-frequency sinusoidal electric wave, whose frequency is determined by the characteristics of the device.

Audio-Frequency Response

See Amplitude-Frequency Response.

Audio-Frequency Spectrum

(Audio Spectrum)

The continuous range of frequencies extending from the lowest to the highest audio frequency.

Automatic Gain Control (AGC)

A process or means by which gain is automatically adjusted as a function of input or other parameter.

Automatic Volume Control (AVC)

A process or means by which a substantially constant output volume is automatically maintained in a system or transducer.

Available Power

The maximum power obtainable from a given source by suitable adjustment of the load.

Note: For a source that is equivalent to a constant sinusoidal electromotive force in series with an impedance independent of amplitude, the available power is the mean square value of the electromotive force divided by four times the resistive part of the impedance of the source.

Babble

The aggregate crosstalk from a large number of interfering channels.

Balanced

In communication practice, the term usually signifies

(1) electrically alike and symmetrical with respect to a common reference point, usually ground, or

(2) arranged to provide conjugacy between certain sets of terminals.

Note: The term balanced may also be employed to signify a proper relationship between two or more entities, such as stereophonic channels.

Balanced Amplifier

See Amplifier, Balanced.

Band-Elimination Filter

See Filter, Band-Elimination.

Band-Pass Filter

See Filter, Band-Pass.

Bass Boost

An accentuation of the lower audio frequencies in the amplitude-frequency response of a system or transducer.

Bridging

The shunting of one signal circuit by one or more circuits usually for the purpose of deriving one or more circuit branches.

Note: A bridging circuit often has an input impedance of such a high value that it does not substantially affect the circuit bridged.

Bridging Amplifier

See Amplifier, Bridging.

Bridging Gain

The ratio of the signal power a transducer delivers to its load (Z_B) to the signal power dissipated in the main circuit load (Z_M) across which the input of the transducer is bridged.

Note: Bridging gain is usually expressed in decibels.

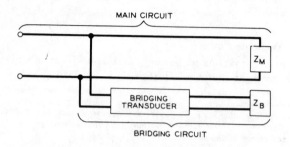

Bridging Loss

(1) The ratio of the signal power dissipated in the main circuit load (Z_M) across which the input of a transducer is bridged, to the signal power the transducer delivers to its load (Z_B).

(2) The ratio of the signal power delivered to that part of the system following the bridging point before the connection of the bridging element, to the signal power delivered to the same part after the connection of the bridging element.

Note 1: Bridging loss is usually expressed in decibels.

Note 2: In (2), bridging loss may be considered as a special case of insertion loss.

Clipper Amplifier

See Amplifier, Clipper.

Compandor

A combination of a compressor at one point in a communication path for reducing the amplitude range of signals, followed by an expander at another point for a complementary increase in amplitude range.

Note: The purpose of a compandor is to improve the ratio of the signal to the interference entering the path between the compressor and the expander.

Compressor

A transducer which, for a given input amplitude range, produces a smaller output range.

Conjugate Branches

Of a network, any two branches such that an electromotive force inserted in one branch produces no current in the other branch.

Conjugate Impedances

See Impedances, Conjugate.

Crosstalk

Undesired energy appearing in one signal path as a result of coupling from other signal paths.

Note: Path implies wires or other localized or constrained transmission systems.

Cue Circuit

A one-way communication circuit used to convey program control information.

Cutoff Frequency

The frequency that is identified with the transition between a pass band and an adjacent attenuation band of a system or transducer.

dBm

A unit for expression of power level in decibels with reference to a power of one milliwatt (0.001 watt).

Decade

The interval between any two quantities having the ratio of 10:1.

De-Emphasis

In a system, a process which has an amplitude-frequency characteristic complementary to that used for pre-emphasis.

Delay Distortion

See Distortion, Delay.

Delay, Envelope

The slope of the phase-versus-frequency characteristic, $\dfrac{d\phi}{d\omega}$ of a system or transducer.

Delay, Phase

The ratio of the total phase shift (radians) experienced by a sinusoidal signal in transmission through a system or transducer, to the frequency (radians/second) of the signal.

Note: The unit of phase delay is the second.

Distortion

Of a signal, an undesired change in waveform.

Distortion, Amplitude

See Distortion, Harmonic; and Distortion, Intermodulation.

Distortion, Amplitude-Frequency

Distortion due to an undesired amplitude-frequency characteristic.

Distortion, Envelope Delay

Of a system or transducer, the difference between

the envelope delay at one frequency and the envelope delay at a reference frequency.

Distortion Frequency

See Distortion, Amplitude-Frequency.

Distortion, Harmonic

Nonlinear distortion of a system or transducer characterized by the appearance in the output of harmonics other than fundamental component when the input wave is sinusoidal.

Note: Subharmonic distortion may also occur.

Distortion, Intermodulation

Nonlinear distortion of a system or transducer characterized by the appearance in the output of frequencies equal to the sums and differences of integral multiples of the two or more component frequencies present in the input wave.

Note: Harmonic components also present in the output are usually not included as part of the intermodulation distortion. When harmonics are included, a statement to that effect should be made.

Distortion, Nonlinear

Distortion caused by a deviation from a linear relationship between specified measures of the input and output of a system or transducer.

Note: The specified characteristics may be, for example, the modulation of an input carrier and the resultant detected signal.

Distortion, Percent Harmonic

A measure of the harmonic distortion in a system or transducer, numerically equal to 100 times the ratio of the square root of the sum of the squares of the root-mean-square voltages (or currents) of each of the individual harmonic frequencies, to the root-mean-square voltage (or current) of the fundamental.

Note: It is practical to measure the ratio of the root-mean-square amplitude of the residual harmonic voltages (or currents), after the elimination of the fundamental, to the root-mean-square amplitude of the fundamental and harmonic voltages (or currents) combined. This measurement will indicate percent harmonic distortion with an error of less than 5 percent if the magnitude of the distortion does not exceed 30 percent.

Distortion, Phase Delay

Of a system or transducer, the difference between the phase delay at one frequency and the phase delay at a reference frequncy.

Distortion, Phase-Frequency

See Distortion, Phase Delay.

Distribution Amplifier

See Amplifier, Distribution.

Dividing Network
(Crossover Network)

A frequency selective network which divides the spectrum into two or more frequency bands for distribution to different loads.

Dynamic Range

The difference, in decibels, between the overload level and the minimum acceptable signal level in a system or transducer.

Note: The minimum acceptable signal level of a system or transducer is ordinarily fixed by one or more of the following: noise level, low-level distortion, or interference.

Echo

A wave which has been reflected or otherwise returned with sufficient magnitude and delay to be perceived in some manner as a wave distinct from that directly transmitted.

Envelope Delay Distortion

See Distortion, Envelope Delay.

Equalizer

A device designed to compensate for an undesired amplitude-frequency or phase-frequency characteristic, or both, of a system or transducer.

Expander

A transducer which, for a given input amplitude range produces a larger output range.

Filter
(Wave Filter)

A transducer for separating waves on the basis of their frequency.

Note: A filter introduces relatively small insertion loss to waves in one or more frequency bands and relatively large insertion loss to waves of other frequencies.

Filter, Band-Elimination

A filter which has a single attenuation band, neither of the cutoff frequencies being zero or infinite.

Filter, Band-Pass

A filter which has a single transmission band, neither of the cutoff frequencies being zero or infinite.

Filter, High-Pass

A filter having a single transmission band extending from some cutoff frequency, not zero, up to infinite frequency.

Filter, Low-Pass

A filter having a single transmission band extending from zero to some cutoff frequency, not infinite.

Filter, Sound Effects

A filter used to adjust the frequency response of a system for the purpose of achieving special aural effects.

Frequency Distortion

See Distortion, Amplitude-Frequency.

Frequency Response

See Amplitude-Frequency Response.

Gain

(Transmission Gain)

The increase in signal power in transmission from one point to another.

Note: Gain is usually expressed in decibels.

Gain Control

A device for adjusting the gain of a system or transducer.

Harmonic Distortion

See Distortion, Harmonic.

High-Pass Filter

See Filter, High-Pass.

Hiss

Audio-frequency noise having subjective characteristics analogous to prolonged sibilant sounds.

Hum

(Power Supply Hum)

Interference from a power system characterized by the presence of undesired energy at power supply frequency or harmonics thereof.

Hybrid Coil

A single transformer having effectively three windings, which is designed to be connected to four branches of a circuit so as to render these branches conjugate in pairs.

Hybrid Set

Two or more transformers interconnected to form a network having four pairs of accessible terminals to which may be connected four impedances so that the branches containing them may be made conjugate in pairs when the impedances have the proper values but not otherwise.

Ideal Transducer

See Transducer, Ideal.

Ideal Transformer

See Transformer, Ideal.

Image Impedances

See Impedances, Image.

Impedance, Input

The impedance presented by the transducer to the source.

Note: Input impedance is sometimes incorrectly used to designate source impedance.

Impedance, Iterative

That impedance which, when connected to one pair of terminals of a transducer produces an identical impedance at the other pair of terminals.

Note 1: It follows that the iterative impedance of a transducer is the same as the impedance at the input terminals when an infinite number of identical transducers are formed into an iterative or recurrent structure.

Note 2: The iterative impedances of a four-terminal transducer are, in general, not equal to each other, but for any symmetrical transducer the iterative impedances are equal and are the same as the image impedances. The iterative impedance of a uniform line is the same as its characteristic impedance.

Impedance, Load

The impedance presented by the load.

Impedance, Output

Of a device, the impedance presented by the device to the load.

Note: Output impedance is sometimes incorrectly used to designate load impedance.

Impedance, Source

The impedance presented by a source of energy to the input terminals of a device.

Impedances, Conjugate

Impedances having resistance components which are equal, and reactance components which are equal in magnitude but opposite in sign.

Impedances, Image

The impedances which will simultaneously terminate all inputs and outputs of a transducer in such a way that at each of its inputs and outputs the impedance in both directions will be equal.

Note: The image impedances of a four-terminal transducer are, in general, not equal to each other, but for any symmetrical transducer the image impedances are equal and are the same as the iterative impedances.

Input Impedance

See Impedance, Input.

Insertion Gain

The ratio of the power delivered to that part of a transmission system following a transducer, to the power delivered to that same part of the system before the insertion of the transducer.

Note 1: The "insertion of a transducer" includes bridging of an impedance across the transmission system.

Note 2: Insertion gain is usually expressed in decibels.

Insertion Loss

The ratio of the power delivered to that part of a transmission system which will follow a transducer, to the power delivered to that same part of the system after the insertion of the transducer.

Note 1: The "insertion of a transducer" includes bridging of an impedance across the transmission system.

Note 2: Insertion loss is usually expressed in decibels.

Intermodulation Distortion

See Distortion, Intermodulation.

Isolation Amplifier

See Amplifier, Isolation.

Isolation Transformer

See Transformer, Isolation.

Iterative Impedance

See Impedance, Iterative.

Level (in audio)

The magnitude of a quantity considered in relation to a reference value.

Note 1: Most frequently, level is proportional to the logarithm of the ratio of the quantity to a specific reference value, expressed in decibels.

Note 2: Level sometimes is stated in units in which the quantity itself is measured (for example, volts, ohms, etc.), but this usage is deprecated.

Line Amplifier

See Amplifier, Line.

Line Transformer

See Transformer, Line.

Load

(1) A device which receives power.

(2) The power delivered to such a device.

Load Impedance

See Impedance, Load.

Loss

(Transmission Loss)

The decrease in signal power in transmission from one point to another.

Note: Loss is usually expressed in decibels.

Low-Pass Filter

See Filter, Low-Pass.

Microphonics

The noise caused by mechanical shock or vibration of elements in a system.

Mixer (in audio techniques)

A device having two or more inputs, usually adjustable, and a common output, which operates to combine linearly in a desired proportion the separate input signals to produce an output signal.

Motorboating

An undesired oscillation in an amplifying system or transducer, usually of a pulse type, occurring at a subaudio or low audio frequency.

Network

A combination of elements.

Noise, Audio-Frequency

Any unwanted disturbance in the audio-frequency range.

Noise Level

(1) The noise power density spectrum in the frequency range of interest,

(2) the average noise power in the frequency range of interest, or

(3) the indication on a specified instrument.

Note 1: In (3), the characteristics of the instrument are determined by the type of noise to be measured and the application of the results thereof.

Note 2: Noise level is usually expressed in decibels relative to a reference value.

Octave

In communication, the interval between two frequencies having a ratio of 2:1.

Output Power

The power delivered by a system or transducer to its load.

Overload Level

Of a system or component, is that level above which operation ceases to be satisfactory as a result of signal distortion, overheating, or damage.

Pad

A nonadjustable passive network which reduces the power level of a signal without introducing appreciable distortion.

Note: A pad may also provide impedance matching.

Passive Transducer

See Transducer, Passive.

Peak Limiter

A device which automatically limits the magnitude

of its output signal to approximate a preset maximum value by reducing its amplification when the instantaneous signal magnitude exceeds a preset value.

Note: Normal usage refers to a device whose amplification is quickly reduced when the instantaneous magnitude of the signal exceeds a predetermined value, and is slowly restored when the signal becomes less than that value.

Peak Limiting Amplifier

See Peak Limiter.

Percent Harmonic Distortion

See Distortion, Percent Harmonic

Phase Distortion

See Distortion, Phase Delay.

Phase-Frequency Distortion

See Distortion, Phase Delay.

Power Amplifier

See Amplifier, Power.

Power Gain

The ratio of the signal power that a transducer delivers to its load to the signal power absorbed by its input circuit.

Note 1: Power gain is usually expressed in decibels.

Note 2: If the output signal power is at a frequency other than the input signal power, the gain is a conversion gain.

Power Level

The magnitude of power averaged over a specified interval of time.

Note: Power level may be expressed in units in which the power itself is measured or in decibels indicating the ratio to a reference power. This ratio is usually expressed either in decibels referred to one milliwatt, abbreviated dBm, or in decibels referred to one watt, abbreviated dBW.

Power Loss

The ratio of the signal power absorbed by the input circuit of a transducer to the signal power delivered to its load.

Note: Power loss is usually expressed in decibels.

Preamplifier

An amplifier connected to a low-level signal source to present suitable input and output impedances and provide gain so that the signal may be further processed without appreciable degradation in the signal-to-noise ratio.

Note: A preamplifier may include provision for equalization and/or mixing.

Pre-Emphasis

In a system, a process which increases the magnitude of some frequency components with respect to the magnitude of others in order to reduce the effects of noise introduced in subsequent parts of the system.

Program

A sequence of signals transmitted for entertainment or information.

Program Amplifier

See Amplifier, Line.

Program Level

The magnitude of program in an audio system expressed in vu.

Push-Pull Amplifier Circuit

See Amplifier, Balanced.

Recovery Time

The time interval required, after a sudden decrease in input signal amplitude to a system or transducer, to attain a stated percentage (usually 63 percent) of the ultimate change in amplification or attenuation due to this decrease.

Reference Volume

The volume which gives a reading of O vu on a standard volume indicator.

Remote Line

A program transmission line between a remote-pickup point and the studio or transmitter site.

Roll-Off

A gradually increasing loss or attenuation with increase or decrease of frequency beyond the substantially flat portion of the amplitude-frequency response characteristic of a system or transducer.

Signal

(1) A visual, aural, or other indication used to convey information;

(2) The information to be conveyed over a communication system;

(3) A wave, in a communication system, which conveys information.

Signal Level

The magnitude of a signal, especially when considered in relation to an arbitrary reference magnitude.

Note: Signal level may be expressed in the units in which the quantity itself is measured (for example, volts or watts) or in units expressing a logarithmic function of the ratio of the two magnitudes.

Singing

An undesired self-sustained oscillation in a system or transducer.

Note: Very-low-frequency oscillation is sometimes called "motorboating," which is defined elsewhere in this Standard.

Singing Margin

(Gain Margin)

The ratio of the singing point to the operating gain of a system or transducer.

Note: Singing margin is usually expressed in decibels.

Singing Point

The minimum value of gain of a system or transducer that will cause singing to start.

Single-Ended Amplifier

An amplifier in which each stage normally employs only one active element (tube, transistor, etc.), or, if more than one active element is used, in which they are connected in parallel so that operation is asymmetric with respect to ground.

Single-Edged Push-Pull Amplifier Circuit

An amplifier circuit having two transmission paths designed to operate in a complementary manner and connected so as to provide a single unbalanced output without the use of an output transformer.

Sound-Effects Filter

See Filter, Sound-Effects.

Source

That which supplies signal power to a transducer.

Source Impedance

See Impedance, Source.

Standard Volume Indicator

A standardized instrument having specified electrical and dynamic characteristics and read in a prescribed manner, for indicating the volume of a complex electric wave such as that corresponding to speech or music.

Note: The instrument and its use are described in IEEE No. 152 (53 IRE 3 S2 and ASA C16.5).

Subharmonic

A sinusoidal quantity having a frequency which is an integral submultiple of the fundamental frequency of a periodic quantity from which it is derived.

Note: For example, a wave the frequency of which is half the fundamental frequency of another wave is called the second subharmonic of that wave.

Thump

A low-frequency transient disturbance in a system or transducer characterized audibly by the onomatopoeic connotation of the word.

Transducer

A device capable of being actuated by signals from one or more systems or media and of supplying related signals to one or more other systems or media.

Note: The signals in the input and output may be of the same or different types (e.g., electric, acoustic, or mechanical).

Transducer, Active

A transducer whose output signal is dependent on power that is controlled by one or more actuating signals.

Transducer, Ideal

A hypothetical linear passive transducer that transfers the available power of the source to the load.

Transducer, Passive

A transducer that has no source of power other than the input signal(s), and whose output signal-power cannot exceed that of the input.

Transducer Gain

The ratio of the power the transducer delivers to its load, to the available power of the source.

Note: Transducer gain is usually expressed in decibels.

Transducer Loss

The ratio of the available power of the source, to the power the transducer delivers to its load.

Note: Transducer loss is usually expressed in decibels.

Transformer, Ideal

A hypothetical transformer that neither stores nor dissipates enegry and has unity coefficient of coupling.

Note: An ideal transformer has self inductances of finite ratio and its self and mutual impedances are pure inductances of infinite magnitude.

Transformer, Isolation

A transformer inserted in a system to separate one section of the system from undesired influences of other sections.

Note: Isolation transformers are commonly used to isolate system grounds and prevent the transmission of undesired currents.

Transformer, Line

A transformer connecting a transmission line to terminal equipment used for such purposes as isolation, line balance, impedance matching, or additional circuit connections.

Transformer Loss (in communication)

The ratio of the signal power an ideal transformer would deliver to a load, to the power delivered to the same load by the actual transformer, both transformers having the same impedance ratio.

Note: Transformer loss is usually expressed in decibels.

Transition Loss

At a junction between a source and a load, the ratio of the available power to the power delivered to the load.

Note: Transition loss is usually expressed in decibels.

Treble Boost

An accentuation of the higher audio frequencies in the amplitude-frequency response of a system or transducer.

Unbalanced

Not balanced.

Note: Frequently, unbalanced signifies a circuit one side of which is grounded.

Volume

In an electric circuit, the magnitude of a complex audio-frequency wave as measured on a standard volume indicator.

Note 1: Volume is expressed in vu.

Note 2: The term volume is used loosely to signify either the intensity of a sound or the magnitude of an audio-frequency wave.

Volume Control

See Gain Control.

Volume Indicator

See Standard Volume Indicator.

Volume Limiter (Deprecated)

See Peak Limiter.

vu

The unit of volume in which the standard volume indicator is calibrated.

Note: A change of one vu is the same as a change of one decibel for a sine wave, but vu should not be used to express results of measurements of complex waves made with devices having characteristics differing from those of the standard volume indicator.

APPENDIX X

Test Questions

TEST 1

1. A. Write $\sqrt[4.5]{10}$ in exponential form.

    B. Write $10^{2.5}$ in arithmetic form.

    C. Convert $\frac{x}{y} = Z^w$ to logarithmic form.

    D. Convert $30 \log 6 = 23.34454$ to a ratio equal to a power of a base.

    E. Write $\frac{1}{10,000}$ in exponential form.

    F. Express $10^{\left(\frac{\log a}{b} + \frac{\log c}{d}\right)}$ in conventional form.

2. You find that a $\frac{2}{1}$ ratio = 9 dB; therefore $x \log \frac{2}{1} = 9$. What is the multiplier that should be used in this case?

3. You have a sound source that has $Q = 2$ and that delivers 110 dB-SPL at 10 feet. What is its dB-PWL$_{-12}$?

4. In the question above, how many acoustic watts are being developed?

5. Find $\log_2 15$.

6. You have a loudspeaker in a high ambient noise level and read a program-level signal of 95 dB-SPL. Turning the loudspeaker off, you find that the ambient noise level is 89 dB-SPL. How many dB-SPL was your loudspeaker really putting out?

7. You put a VI meter across a circuit and read +12 VU. Later you are told you were across a 125-ohm line. What was the true level?

8. You measure the output from a loudspeaker outdoors and find it is 80 dB-SPL. You know its sensitivity to be 111.5 dB-SPL at 4 feet with 1 watt. How far are you from the loudspeaker?

9. In the question above, what is the EIA rating of the loudspeaker?

10. How would you determine that the output impedance of a test oscillator is as labeled?

11. You measure two harmonics. One is at -38 dB and the other at -41 dB. What is the thd percentage?

12. You aim a signal of 100 dB-SPL at a surface that has an absorption coefficient of a = 0.85. What dB-SPL would you expect the first reflection to have?

13. From a polar chart you read:

0° = 100 dB	60° = 91 dB
10° = 99 dB	70° = 88 dB
20° = 98 dB	80° = 85 dB
30° = 96 dB	90° = 86 dB
40° = 95 dB	100° = 88 dB
50° = 94 dB	

    What is the coverage angle? If the dB-$\overline{\text{SPL}}$ = 88.7 dB, what is the Q for this unit at this frequency?

14. What is the average length of a reflection path in a room with a volume of 600,000 cubic feet and a surface area of 60,000 square feet?

15. Match the following formulas with the appropriate applications:

    A. Sabine   1. For use in small "dead" rooms with good diffusion.

    B. Norris-Eyring   2. For use in rooms with the majority of absorption on a single surface.

    C. Fitzroy   3. Best general-use formula in rooms above 1.6-second with reasonable diffusion characteristics.

16. In a reverberant gymnasium, you measure a room constant (R) of 3500 using your test loudspeaker. You then measure at 2000 Hz with a new loudspeaker. You are considering a dB-SPL of 100 at 8 feet and a dB-SPL of 87 at a distance greater than $2D_c$. What is the critical distance, and what is the Q of this loudspeaker at 2000 Hz?

17. Which of the following statements does not match the others?

    A. The voltage was raised 3 dB.

    B. The dB-SPL was raised from 86 dB-SPL to 89 dB-SPL.

C. The electrical power was doubled.
D. The electrical power level went from 32 dBm to 35 dBm.
E. The voltage was doubled.

18. Match the following:

A. dB   1. Complex waveforms
B. dBm   2. A ratio
C. dB-SPL   3. Microphone sensitivity reference
D. dB-PWL   4. 0.001 watt
E. dBV   5. 10^{-12} watt
F. VU   6. 0.00002 newton/meter^2

19. Match the following laws, devices, and formulas to their originators.

A. Weber-Fechner   1. The invention of the compression driver
B. Ohm   2. $RT_{60} = \dfrac{0.049V}{S\bar{a}}$
C. Norris-Eyring   3. Time-delay analysis
D. Fletcher-Munson   4. %AL$_{CONS}$ formulated
   5. Next stimulus proportional to last stimulus.
E. Wente and Thuras   6. FSM defined and demonstrated
F. Haas, Fay-Hall, Henry, et al   7. Voltage equals current times resistance
G. Sabine
H. William Snow   8. $RT_{60} = \dfrac{0.049V}{-S\ln(1-\bar{a})}$
I. Peutz & Klein   9. Sensitivity of human ear at various frequencies

20. An acoustic signal is at 96 dB-SPL. How much will the level rise if a second acoustic signal is introduced at 93 dB-SPL?

21. The sound system is linear. The input voltage is raised from 0.25 volt to 0.50 volt. How much is each of the following raised?
A. Output power in dBm
B. SPL in dB-SPL
C. Input voltage in dB
D. System gain in dB
E. Acoustic power in dB-PWL

22. In the above question, by what ratio did the output power increase? The input voltage? The system gain?

23. At what distance is a dB-SPL approximately equal to a dB-PWL?

24. A level of 60 dB-SPL is measured from a loudspeaker outdoors. The loudspeaker has a sensitivity rating of 100 dB-SPL at 4 feet with 1 watt. How far from the loudspeaker is the measurement taken, if 1-watt input is assumed?

25. In the question above, if the sensitivity of the loudspeaker had been 88 dB-SPL at 4 feet with 1 watt, how many watts would be needed to make a reading of 60 dB-SPL at 400 feet?

26. A harmonic is 35 dB below the fundamental. What is the percent distortion?

27. If you have a room that absorbs 75% of the sound power and you aim a 100 dB-SPL signal at one of its surfaces, what value in dB-SPL will the reflection have?

28. If you get back a reflection that is 14 dB lower than the sending signal, what is the absorption coefficient of the reflecting surface? Assume a single reflection from the surface in question.

29. Refer to Fig. X-1.

A. What is the total volume in cubic feet?
B. What is the total surface area in square feet?
C. What is the average absorption coefficient ($\bar{a}$)?
D. What is the Norris-Eyring RT_{60} in seconds?
E. What is the Norris-Eyring RT_{60} in seconds with 1000 people present?

TEST 2

1. You need a time delay of 20 milliseconds between two sound sources. The room temperature is 80°F. What difference in path length between the sources and the listener should you provide?

2. You measure a time delay of 105 milliseconds between a front loudspeaker and an under-balcony array. You have determined that a delay device is required. What time delay do you need to provide for the rear loudspeaker?

3. You need to find the change in level between 4 feet and 95 feet in a large church in order to calculate the EPR. The loudspeaker has Q = 12. The volume of the room is 500,000 cubic feet, the surface area is 42,500 square feet, and the reverberation time is measured at 3.8 seconds. What will the level change be? (Use Norris-Eyring equation for room data.)

4. You are in a room for which the AL$_{CONS}$ formula says you need Q = 20. The D_2 distance is 100 feet. The room volume is 600,000 cubic feet, and the surface area is 50,000 square feet. You would like to use a loudspeaker with Q = 5. How many sabins should you add to the room? (Use Sabine equation for room parameters.)

5. In an ambient noise field of 46 dBA with a professional talker who provides a 2-foot reading on the SLM of 85 dBA, what maximum EAD could you choose?

6. You wish to achieve a 110 dB-SPL program level at 100 feet from an array. You will have available a number of large theater bin-type arrays. If the room constant (R) is 12,000 ft^2 and the arrays have a Q of 10, how many will you need if their 4-foot, 1-watt sensitivity is 112 dB-SPL and their power rating is 200 watts each? (Assume Q remains 10.)

7. In the question above, if the 4-foot, 1-watt sensitivity had been 89 dB-SPL, what power and how many units would you have needed (assume 50 watts per unit)?

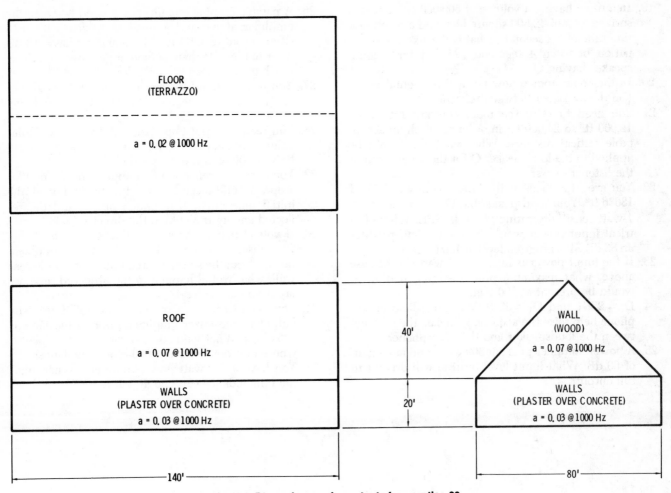

Fig. X-1. Dimensions and constants for question 29.

8. You have a microphone that measures 1.5 millivolts open circuit with an acoustic test signal of 10 dynes/cm². The impedance rating is 150 ohms. If the maximum program level expected from the performer is 90 dB-SPL, what maximum input level in dBm should the system be capable of handling at the first stage of the microphone amplifier?

9. If, in the case above, the microphone-level amplifier had a maximum output of +4 dBm, what gain would you want the amplifier to have?

10. In the question above, over a bandpass of 50 to 15,000 Hz, what would the theoretical signal-to-noise ratio be for this performer?

11. How many loudspeakers would you require in order to have center-to-center overlap in a room 100 × 75 feet with an 18-foot ceiling? (Loudspeaker has 60° dispersion angle.)

12. Find the values of the necessary build-out and termination resistors for the circuit in Fig. X-2, and calculate their losses.

13. What is the impedance between the 8- and 4-ohm taps on an amplifier?

14. You need a 12-dB pad in the 600-ohm link between two amplifiers because of excessive gain overlap. What values provide the desired attenuation? (Make an unbalanced T pad.)

15. You have "biamped" an old theater system with its 24-ohm drivers. Two of them are fed in parallel from the high-frequency amplifier (800 Hz and up). What value of capacitor should you use?

16. You are designing a 70-volt line for use with a 100-watt amplifier. You want to apply 10 watts to each loudspeaker. The transformers available have an insertion loss of 1.5 dB. How many loudspeakers can you safely attach to the amplifier?

17. What length of daily exposure to a level of 105 to 110 dB-SPL does OSHA allow?

18. With a given array of 2 speakers, how would you change the Q (A) to be larger? (B) to be smaller?

Fig. X-2. Diagram for question 12.

19. In a room having a volume of 500,000 cubic feet, a surface area of 42,500 square feet, and a reverberation time of 3.2 seconds, what is the acoustic attenuation between 4 feet and 125 feet for a loudspeaker having $Q = 5$.

20. In the room above, how far will the sound travel (on the average) between reflections?

21. You need to raise the room constant (R) from 12,000 ft² to 24,000 ft² in order to reach an acceptable critical distance. What multiplier could be applied to the loudspeaker Q for the same result at the listener's ears?

22. You are in a space with a room constant (R) of 13636 ft². Your loudspeaker has $Q = 5$ and a 4-foot, 1-watt sensitivity rating of 99 dB-SPL. What electrical input power would be required to produce an 85 dB-SPL program level at 100 feet?

23. If the input power is raised to 50 watts in the case above, what maximum program level in dB-SPL would be present at 100 feet?

24. $D_c = 25$ ft, and $D_1 = 35$ ft. Will a cardioid microphone help raise the acoustic gain, i.e., the gain between the loudspeaker and the microphone?

25. A power amplifier puts out 300 watts and has a gain of 60 dB. What input level in dBm will drive it to full output?

26. A passive graphic equalizer is needed between the amplifier above and a mixer amplifier with +18 dBm output capability. The equalizer has a 16-dB insertion loss. Is there sufficient gain overlap? How much gain overlap is available?

27. You have a sound system in feedback with all microphones disconnected. What is the most likely cause?

28. You read an input impedance of 1560 ohms. What value of resistor should be placed where in order to have a 600-ohm input impedance?

29. You observe a reflection that appears on the oscilloscope 23 milliseconds after the beginning of the initial tone burst. How much farther did the reflected energy travel than the direct signal?

30. If you suspected the rear wall as the cause of this 23-millisecond delay and you move the microphone farther from the sound source but closer to the rear wall, what would happen to the observed time delay if you are correct?

31. You need to insert a pi-network cutoff filter. The output of the mixer amplifier prior to the filter is 130 ohms. What value of resistor should be placed where in order to have a 600-ohm impedance?

32. You have a 100-watt power amplifier. What minimum impedance can you attach to its 70-volt line?

Answers to Test Questions

TEST 1

1. A. $10^{0.2222\cdots}$ or $10^{\frac{1}{4.5}}$

   B. $100 \times \sqrt{10}$ or $316.23\ldots$

   C. $\log_z \frac{x}{y} = w$

   D. $\frac{6}{1} = 10^{\frac{23.34454\cdots}{30}}$

   E. 10^{-4}

   F. $\sqrt[b]{a} \times \sqrt[d]{c}$

2. $\frac{2}{1} = 10^{\frac{9}{x}}$; therefore, $\log 2 = \log 10 \times \frac{9}{x}$

   $x = \frac{\log 10}{\log 2} \times 9$

   or, $x = \frac{9}{\log 2} = 29.90$

3. $\text{dB-PWL}_{-12} = \text{dB-SPL} + 10 \log \left(\frac{4\pi D_x^2}{Q} \right) - 10$

   (D_x in feet)

   $110 + 10 \log \left(\frac{4\pi 10^2}{2} \right) - 10 = 127.98$

4. $\text{dB-PWL}_{-12} = 10 \log \frac{\text{Acoustic power}}{10^{-12} \text{ watt}}$

   $\frac{\text{Acoustic power}}{10^{-12}} = 10^{\frac{\text{dB-PWL}_{-12}}{10}}$

   $\text{Acoustic power} = 10^{\frac{\text{dB-PWL}_{-12}}{10}} \times 10^{-12}$

   $10^{\frac{127.98}{10}} \times 10^{-12} = 6.28 \text{ watts}$

5. $\log_2 15 = x$; $15 = 2^x$; $\ln 15 = \ln 2 \times x$

   $\frac{\ln 15}{\ln 2} = x = 3.906\ldots$

6. $10 \log \left(10^{\frac{LS + N}{10}} - 10^{\frac{N}{10}} \right) = LS$

   $10 \log \left(10^{\frac{95}{10}} - 10^{\frac{89}{10}} \right) = 93.74 \text{ dB-SPL}$

7. $VU = 20 \log \frac{E}{0.775} + 10 \log \frac{600}{Z}$

   $VU = 12 + 10 \log \frac{600}{125}$

   $= 12 + 6.81 = 18.81$

   Therefore the true level is 18.81 VU.

8. $20 \log \frac{x}{4} = 111.5 - 80$

   $\frac{x}{4} = 10^{\frac{111.5 - 80}{20}}$

   $x = 4 \times 10^{\frac{111.5-80}{20}} = 150.33 \text{ feet}$

9. $111.5 + 20 \log \frac{4}{30} + 10 \log \frac{0.001}{1} = 64 \text{ dB-SPL}$

   $20 \log \frac{4}{30}$ changes 4 feet to 30 feet, and $10 \log \frac{0.001}{1}$ changes from 1 watt to 0.001 watt.

10. Refer to Fig. XI-1. Measure an arbitrary "open-circuit" level. Place a load resistor equal to the rated impedance across the output of the oscillator. If $R_S = R_Z$, the voltmeter will show a 6-dB drop.

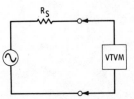

(A) Open-circuit reading.

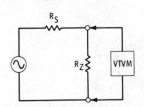

(B) Load resistor connected.

Fig. XI-1. Output-impedance test.

11. $10 \log \left(10^{\frac{-38}{10}} + 10^{\frac{-41}{10}}\right) = -36.24$

$100 \left(10^{-\frac{36.24}{20}}\right) = 1.54\%$

Combine the decibel values first. Note that the multiplier is 20 because a tunable voltmeter is used to measure distortion.

12. Power is being absorbed; therefore,

$10 \log \dfrac{100 \pm \%}{100} = \text{dB change}$

$10 \log \dfrac{100 - 85}{100} = -8.24 \text{ dB}$

$100 - 8.24 = 92 \text{ dB-SPL}$

13. $100°$ (-6-dB points)

$100 - 88.7 = 11.3 \text{ dB}$; therefore,

$Q = 10^{\frac{11.3}{10}} = 13.49$

14. $\dfrac{4V}{S} = \text{Mean free path}$

$4 \left(\dfrac{600,000}{60,000}\right) = 40 \text{ feet}$

15. A. (3.) The Sabine equation is normally proposed for use in rooms above 1.6 seconds with reasonable diffusion characteristics. It is the best general-use equation.

B. (1.) The Norris-Eyring equation is normally proposed as the equation to use in small "dead" rooms with good diffusion, especially when ā values are being calculated.

C. (2.) The Fitzroy equation is for use in rooms with the majority of absorption on only one or two surfaces.

16. $D_c = \text{Ref dist} \times 10^{\frac{\text{Ref dB-SPL} - \text{Reverb dB-SPL}}{20}}$

$D_c = 8 \times 10^{\frac{100 - 87}{20}} = 35.73 \text{ feet}$

$Q = \dfrac{(D_c)^2}{0.019881R} = \dfrac{(35.73)^2}{0.019881 \times 3500} = 18.35$

17. E.

18. A. 2
B. 4
C. 6
D. 5
E. 3
F. 1

19. A. 5
B. 7
C. 8
D. 9
E. 1
F. 3
G. 2

H. 6
I. 4

20. $10 \log \left(10^{\frac{96}{10}} + 10^{\frac{93}{10}}\right) = 97.76 \text{ dB-SPL}$

$97.76 - 96 = 1.76 \text{ dB-SPL}$

21. A. Output power in dBm: +6 dB
B. SPL in dB-SPL: +6 dB
C. Input voltage in dB: +6 dB
D. System gain in dB: Electrical, unchanged; acoustic, +6 dB
E. Acoustic power in dB-PWL: +6 dB

22. Output power increase: 4 to 1
Input voltage increase: 2 to 1
System gain increase: Electrical, no change; acoustic, 4 to 1

23. For 10^{-13} W, 0.283 foot; for 10^{-12} W, 0.283 meter

24. $100 \text{ dB} - 60 \text{ dB} = 40 \text{ dB}$; $20 \log \dfrac{x}{4} = 40 \text{ dB}$

$10^{\frac{40}{20}} = \dfrac{x}{4}$

$x = 4 \times 10^{\frac{40}{20}} = 400 \text{ feet}$

25. $100 \text{ dB} - 88 \text{ dB} = 12 \text{ dB}$

$10^{\frac{12}{10}} = 15.85 \text{ watts}$

26. $100 \times 10^{-\frac{35}{20}} = 1.78\%$

27. Assume 100 watts into the surface, and therefore 25 watts reflected. The loss is:

$\dfrac{100}{25} = 4$; $10 \log 4 = 6 \text{ dB}$

$100 \text{ dB-SPL} - 6 \text{ dB} = 94 \text{ dB-SPL}$

28. $100 \times 10^{\frac{dB}{10}} = \%$; $100 \times 10^{\frac{-14}{10}} = 4\%$

$100 - 4 = 96\%$ absorbed; $a = 0.96$

29. A. Volume:

$20 \times 80 \times 140 \qquad = 224,000 \text{ ft}^3$

$\tfrac{1}{2} \times 80 \times 40 \times 140 = 224,000 \text{ ft}^3$

Total volume $\qquad = 448,000 \text{ ft}^3$

B. Surface area:

Floor (80×140) $\qquad = 11,200 \text{ ft}^2$

Roof $2(56.57 \times 140)$ $\qquad = 15,839 \text{ ft}^2$

Lower side walls $2(140 \times 20)$ $\quad = 5,600 \text{ ft}^2$

Lower end walls $2(20 \times 80)$ $\quad = 3,200 \text{ ft}^2$

Upper end walls $2(\tfrac{1}{2} \times 80 \times 40) = 3,200 \text{ ft}^2$

Total $\qquad\qquad 39,039 \text{ ft}^2$

C. Average absorption coefficient ($\bar{a}$):

Floor $11,200 \times 0.02$ $= 224$

Roof $15,839 \times 0.07$ $= 1109$ ·

Side and lower end walls $8800 \times 0.03 = 264$

Upper end walls 3200×0.07 $= \underline{224}$

1821

$$\bar{a} = \frac{1821}{39,039} = 0.047$$

D. Norris-Eyring RT$_{60}$:

$$RT_{60} = \frac{0.049V}{-S \ln(1-\bar{a})} = \frac{0.049 \times 448,000}{-39039 \ln(1-0.047)}$$
$$= 11.68$$

E. Norris-Eyring RT$_{60}$ (1000 people):

Allow 4.5 sabins per person; $1000 \times 4.5 = 4500$

$4500 + 1821 = 6321$

$$\frac{6321}{39039} = 0.162$$

$$RT_{60} = \frac{0.049 \times 448,000}{-39039 \ln(1-0.162)} = 3.18$$

TEST 2

1. $V = 49 \sqrt{459.4 + {}^\circ F}$

$V = 49 \sqrt{459.4 + 80} = 1138$ ft/s

20 ms $\times 1.138 = 22.76$ ft difference

2. $105 + 20 = 125$ ms

The extra 20 milliseconds provides the precedence effect that causes the listener to think the sound source is at the front.

3. $\bar{a} = 1 - e^{-\frac{0.049V}{S(RT_{60})}} = 0.141$

$R = -S \ln(1 - \bar{a}) = 6459$ ft^2

$-10 \log \left(\frac{12}{4\pi 16} + \frac{4}{6459} \right) = 12.20$ dB

$-10 \log \left(\frac{12}{4\pi 9025} + \frac{4}{6459} \right) = 31.40$ dB

$31.40 - 12.2 = 19.20$ dB

4. $S\bar{a} = \frac{1.24 \, D_2 V}{\sqrt{15VQ}} = 5545$ for $Q = 20$;

$S\bar{a} = 11,090$ for $Q = 5$

Needed sabins $= 11,090 - 5545 = 5545$ ft^2

5. $2 \times 10^{\frac{14}{20}} = 10$ feet

6. 4 ft $= +13$dB, and 100 ft $= +33.84$ dB, a difference of 20.84 dB

$$10^{\frac{(110+10)+20.84-112}{10}} = 765 \text{ watts}$$

$$\frac{765 \text{ watts}}{200 \text{ watts}} = 3.83, \text{ so 4 units are required.}$$

7. $10^{\frac{120+20.84-89}{10}} = 152,756$ watts

$$\frac{152,756 \text{ watts}}{50 \text{ watts}} = 3055.13; \text{ 3056 units would be required.}$$

8. $(20 \log 0.0015) - 94 + 74 = -76.48$ dB with reference to 1 volt at 1 dyne/cm^2

$-76.48 - 10 \log 150 + 44 = -54.24$ dBm/10 dynes/cm^2

-54.24 dBm $+ 6$ dB $= -48.24$ dBm

9. $+4 - (-48.24) = 52.24$ dB

10. -174 dBm for 1 Hz (theoretical thermal noise threshold)

-174 dBm $+ 10 \log (15,000 - 50) = -132.25$ dBm or,

-198 dB/1 volt $+ 10 \log (15,000 - 50)$

$+ 10 \log 600 - 6 - 20 \log \frac{0.775}{1} = -132.25$ dBm

$(-44.24) - (-132.25) = 88.01$ dB s/n

11. Number of speakers for center-to-center overlap $=$

$$\frac{3(\text{Ceiling area in sq ft})}{2\pi \left[(\text{Ceiling ht} - 4) \tan \frac{\text{angle}}{2} \right]^2}$$

$$= \frac{3(100 \times 75)}{2\pi \left[(18 - 4) \tan \frac{60}{2} \right]^2} = 54.81$$

Approximately 55 speakers are required.

12. Value of buildout resistor:

$600 - 160 = 440 \, \Omega$

Value of termination resistor:

$$\frac{600 \times 2400}{2400 - 600} = 800 \, \Omega$$

Loss due to buildout resistor:

$$20 \log \frac{\frac{600}{160 + 440 + 600}}{\frac{600}{160 + 600}} = -3.97 \text{ dB}$$

Loss due to termination resistor:

$$20 \log \frac{\frac{600}{600 + 600}}{\frac{2400}{2400 + 600}} = -4.08 \text{ dB}$$

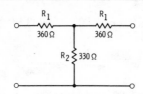

Fig. XI-2. T pad for 12-dB loss.

13. $Z_x = (\sqrt{Z_H} - \sqrt{Z_L})^2$
$= (\sqrt{8} - \sqrt{4})^2 = 0.686$ ohms

14. Refer to Fig. XI-2.

$K = 10^{\frac{dB}{20}} = 10^{\frac{12}{20}} = 3.98$

$R_1 = Z\left(\frac{K-1}{K+1}\right) = 600\frac{2.98}{4.98} = 359\ \Omega$

$R_2 = 2Z\left(\frac{K}{K^2-1}\right) = 1200\frac{3.98}{14.84} = 321\ \Omega$

The nearest EIA standard values are shown in Fig. XI-2.

15. $C = \frac{10^6}{2\pi fZ} = \frac{10^6}{2\pi(400)12} = 33.16\ \mu F$

The capacitor value is calculated for a frequency one octave below the regular crossover point to avoid adding 6 dB/octave to the regular crossover slope.

16. $Z_I = \dfrac{5000}{(P_{spkr})\left(10^{\frac{\text{Insertion loss dB}}{10}}\right)}$

$= \dfrac{5000}{10\left(10^{\frac{1.5}{10}}\right)} = 354\ \Omega$

$\frac{354}{50} = 7.08;$ 7 units may be connected.

17. ½ hour

18. A. Stack
    B. Stack and splay

19. $\bar{a} = 1 - e^{-\frac{0.049V}{S(RT_{60})}} = 0.165$
$R = -S\ln(1-\bar{a}) = 7664$
$D_c = 0.141\sqrt{QR} = 27.6\ \text{ft}$
$\Delta 4\ \text{ft} = 12\ \text{dB};\quad \Delta 27.6\ \text{ft} = 28.82\ \text{dB};$
$28.82 - 12 = 16.8\ \text{dB}$
$\Delta D_x = 10\log\left(\frac{Q}{4\pi(D_x)^2} + \frac{4}{R}\right)$

For 4 feet, $\Delta D_x = 15.9$ dB; for 125 feet, $\Delta D_x = 32.6$ dB. $32.6 - 15.9 = 16.7$ dB

20. Mean free path $= \frac{4V}{S}$, $\frac{4(500,000)}{42,500} = 47$ feet

21. $\frac{24,000}{12,000} = 2;$ Q must double.

22. $D_c = 0.141\sqrt{QR} = 36.82\ \text{ft}$

$20\log\frac{36.82}{4} = 19.28\ \text{dB}$

$\Delta D_x = 10\log\left(\frac{Q}{4\pi(D_x)^2} + \frac{4}{R}\right)$

For 4 feet, $\Delta D_x = 15.99$ dB; for 100 feet, $\Delta D_x = 34.77$ dB.

$34.77 - 15.99 = 18.72$ dB

$(85 + 10) + 18.72 = 113.72$ dB-SPL required at 4 feet

$113.72 - 99 = 14.72$ dB difference

$10^{\frac{14.72}{10}} = 29.65$ watts

or,

$114.29 - 99 = 15.28$ dB

$10^{\frac{15.29}{10}} = 33.73$ watts

23. Since 29.65 watts produces an 85 dB-SPL program level at 100 feet, then

$85\ \text{dB-SPL} + 10\log\frac{50}{29.65} = 87.27\ \text{dB-SPL},$

or,

$85\ \text{dB-SPL} + 10\log\frac{50}{33.73} = 86.71\ \text{dB-SPL}$

24. No. Being beyond D_c, it no longer receives directional information from the sound source.

25. $10\log\frac{300}{0.001} = 54.77\ \text{dBm};\ 54.77\ \text{dBm} - 60\ \text{dB} = -5.23\ \text{dBm}$

26. $+18\ \text{dBm} - (-5.23\ \text{dBm}) = 23.23\ \text{dB}.$ Since you need to overcome a 16-dB insertion loss and you have 23.23 dB of gain overlap, you do have enough gain.

27. Cross talk between a high-level circuit and a low-level circuit.

28. $R_2 = \frac{R_1R_T}{R_1 - R_T} = \frac{1560 \times 600}{1560 - 600} = 975$ ohms in parallel with the 1560 ohms.

29. $\frac{1130\ \text{ft}}{1\ \text{s}} \times \frac{1\ \text{s}}{1000\ \text{ms}} = 1.13\ \text{ft/ms}$

$23\ \text{ms} \times \frac{1.13\ \text{ft}}{\text{ms}} = 26\ \text{ft}$

30. While the arrival time of the direct sound would increase, the time between its arrival and the reflection would decrease.

31. $600 - 130 = 470$ ohms, which should be placed in series with the 130-ohm output.

32. $Z = \frac{E^2}{W} = \frac{5000}{100} = 50$ ohms

Index